Polysemy

Trends in Linguistics
Studies and Monographs 142

Editors

Walter Bisang
(main editor for this volume)
Hans Henrich Hock
Werner Winter

Mouton de Gruyter
Berlin · New York

Polysemy

Flexible Patterns of Meaning
in Mind and Language

Edited by

Brigitte Nerlich
Zazie Todd
Vimala Herman
David D. Clarke

Mouton de Gruyter
Berlin · New York 2003

Mouton de Gruyter (formerly Mouton, The Hague)
is a Division of Walter de Gruyter GmbH & Co. KG, Berlin.

⊗ Printed on acid-free paper which falls within the guidelines
of the ANSI to ensure permanence and durability.

ISBN 3-11-017616-5

Bibliographic information published by Die Deutsche Bibliothek

Die Deutsche Bibliothek lists this publication in the Deutsche Nationalbibliografie;
detailed bibliographic data is available in the Internet at <http://dnb.ddb.de>.

This book is dedicated to the memory of Andreas Blank (1961–2001), our friend and colleague, who died far too young.

Acknowledgements

This book was written with the generous support of the Leverhulme Trust.

The book has been long in the making. The editors want to express their gratitude to all contributors for their patience and forbearance, to Birgit Sievert for her help and encouragement, and to Simon Cave and Sue Lightfoot for helping the book over its last formatting and indexing hurdles.

Contents

List of contributors

Jean Aitchison, Professor of Language and Communication, University of Oxford, UK.

Andreas Blank, Professor of Romance Linguistics, University of Marburg, Germany.

David D. Clarke, Professor of Psychology, University of Nottingham, UK.

Dr. **Ann Dowker**, Department of Experimental Psychology, University of Oxford, UK.

Dr. **Vyvyan Evans**, Department of Linguistics and English Language, University of Sussex, UK.

Gilles Fauconnier, Professor, Department of Cognitive Science, UC San Diego.

Rachel Giora, Professor, Department of Linguistics, Tel Aviv University, Israel.

Inbal Gur, Department of Linguistics, Tel Aviv University, Israel.

Dr. **Vimala Herman**, English Studies, University of Nottingham, UK.

Dr. **Adam Kilgarriff**, Lexicography MasterClass Ltd. and Information Technology Research Institute, University of Brighton, UK.

Adrienne Lehrer, Professor of Linguistics, Emerita, Department of Linguistics, University of Arizona, USA.

Dr. **Diana Lewis**, Faculty of English Language and Literature, University of Oxford, UK.

Dr. **Brigitte Nerlich**, Institute for the Study of Genetics, Biorisks and Society, University of Nottingham, UK.

Jarno Raukko, Department of English, University of Helsinki, Finland.

Ken-ichi Seto, Professor, Faculty of Literature and Human Sciences, Osaka City University, Japan.

Dr. **John R. Taylor**, Linguistics Section, University of Otago, New Zealand.

Dr. **Zazie Todd**, School of Psychology, University of Leeds, UK.

Mark Turner, Professor, Department of English and Doctoral Program in Neuroscience and Cognitive Science, The University of Maryland, USA.

Dr. **Andrea Tyler**, Department of Linguistics, Georgetown University, USA.

Beatrice Warren, Professor, Department of English, University of Lund, Sweden.

Yorick Wilks, Professor, Department of Computer Science, University of Sheffield, UK.

Setting the scene

Polysemy and flexibility: introduction and overview

Brigitte Nerlich and David D. Clarke

This chapter has three parts. In the first part we provide a brief overview of the varied fortunes of polysemy research since it was made popular by Michel Bréal in 1897 (Bréal 1924 [1897]: Chapter 15; for more details see Nerlich, this volume), we summarize what has been done so far, what has proven problematic in this type of research, and which gaps are still left to be filled. We also link the recent upsurge of interest into polysemy with a renewed interest into the cognitive bases of figurative language (metaphor and metonymy). In the second part we explore various theories of polysemy, proposing ourselves a graded theory of polysemy as flexible meaning, which underlies discursive polysemy, lexicalized synchronic polysemy and diachronic processes of polysemization, and we contrast this view with other monosemous views of meaning. Throughout this introduction, we combine the analysis of central issues with references to the topics discussed in the articles that follow. In the last part of the introduction we shall provide an overview of the chapters that follow and indicate the ways in which they contribute to the overall theme of the book. In all the chapters a case will be made for a theory of polysemy as flexible meaning.

1. Polysemy: problems and solutions

Fifty years ago the linguist and semanticist Stephen Ullmann wrote that polysemy, the fact that some words have a network of multiple but related meanings, is "the pivot of semantic analysis" (Ullmann 1957 [1951]: 117). He was referring to traditional synchronic and diachronic lexical semantics as it had developed after Bréal. Fifty years after Ullmann and a century after Bréal polysemy has become central to modern cognitive semantics of the synchronic and diachronic type as well as to computational semantics and AI (see Brugman 1997). It has become clear that the study of polysemy is of fundamental importance for any semantic study of language and cognition. Polysemy can therefore be regarded as providing a privileged access to the network of interrelated theories of language, meaning and cognition proposed throughout the 20th and into the 21st centuries and as pointing out directions for future research into language and cognition.

And yet, ever since Michel Bréal introduced the term *polysémie* into linguistics, polysemy has caused problems in linguistic research. Some have argued that it actually doesn't exist and is only an artefact of linguistic analysis (see Victorri 1997; Kleiber 1999). It is certainly true that speakers are rarely aware of the multiplicity of meanings unless prompted by the production or comprehension of jokes or puns.

In lexical semantics, where the existence of polysemy is accepted, it has always been difficult to distinguish polysemy from homonymy (see Heger 1963) – the existence of different but unrelated meanings for a single word form – and thus to construct lexical entries coherently. To give a relatively clear-cut example, the homonyms (river) *bank* and (financial) *bank* would be accommodated in two entries, the meanings of the polysemous word *nose* ('facial organ', 'sense of smell' and 'attribute of a wine') would be accommodated in one. But not all cases are so clear-cut.

Another problem arising from polysemy and homonymy is lexical ambiguity, and the precise relationship between polysemy, homonymy, ambiguity and vagueness is still an unresolved issue in lexical semantics. Some solutions are proposed in Andreas Blank's contribution to this volume (see also Geeraerts 1993; Tuggy 1993).

Most importantly, however, polysemy has proven almost intractable within structural, especially feature-based and componential, theories of language (Lyons 1977: 550–579; Wunderli 1995; for a critique see Deane 1988: 325), especially those that are based on the axiom of language as an autonomous system, cut off from cognition, emotion and bodily influences. In their efforts to come to grips with polysemy, structural linguists fought to maintain the theorem of "one form, one meaning" and transformational linguists focused on invariant features to define meaning, leaving out issues of contextual and co-textual modulation. From being an inspirational subject to historical lexical semanticists, as envisaged by Bréal and his followers, polysemy turned into an obstacle to linguistic theory.

This all changed with the advent of cognitive linguistics in the 1980s, when the obstacle became an opportunity, an opportunity to link language back up with mind, meaning and society, a link already made by Bréal (see Nerlich, this volume). This change in perspective was facilitated by the emergence of new theories in anthropology and psychology, most importantly new theories of how humans establish categories on the basis of prototypes and family resemblances. In cognitive linguistics, the word itself with its network of polysemous senses came to be regarded as a category in which the senses of the word (i.e. the members of the category) are related to each other by means of general cognitive principles such as metaphor, metonymy, generalization, specialization, and image-schema transformations.

Unlike traditional research into polysemy inside historical and lexical semantics, these analyses go both "beyond" words and "below" words, studying polysemy at the level of morphological as well as syntactical constructions, and even viewing polysemy as a systemic phenomenon (see Cuyckens and Zawada 2002; Lehrer, this volume).

Despite their inherently controversial nature, multiple (word) meanings have been accounted for in dictionaries for at least two centuries. Polysemy has also been the basis for research into semantic change, which can be regarded as a result of the polysemous accretion and variation of meanings clustering around a word form over time (see Nerlich and Clarke 1992; Geeraerts 1997; Aitchison and Lewis, this volume; Blank, this volume). Using the older insights into metaphor and metonymy as mechanisms of sense extension, polysemy has become the focus of attention for modern cognitive linguists and cognitive semanticists studying metaphors, metonymies and conceptual blending (Fauconnier and Turner; Tyler and Evans; Seto, this volume), prototypes, semantic fields, semantic frames, and semantic networks (Wilks 1977; Brugman 1981; Jongen 1985; Norvig and Lakoff 1987; Deane 1988; Schneider 1988; Schulze 1988, 1994; Lehrer 1990, this volume; Sweetser 1990; Fillmore and Atkins 1992; Taylor 1992; Dölling 1993; Cuyckens 1994; Sinha and Kuteva 1994; Cruse 1995; Geeraerts 1997; Raukko 1999, this volume; Cuyckens and Zawada 2002). In these contemporary fields of research polysemy is no longer regarded as a problem, but rather as an inherent feature of language, language use and cognition.

For the last two decades polysemy has also been at the centre of attention of computational linguistics (see Wilks, this volume), where problems of word senses and word sense disambiguation are vividly discussed (see Kilgarriff, this volume; see also Ostler and Atkins 1991; Pustejovsky 1991, 1995; Asher and Lascarides 1995; Kilgarriff and Gazdar 1995; Viegas and Raskin 1998; Ravin and Leacock 2000).

Psycholinguists and students of AI have also studied polysemy, ambiguity and sense disambiguation for over three decades and have developed various models of semantic networks, first inside the framework of feature semantics, then prototype and frame semantics (see Williams 1992; Rueckl 1995). Polysemy can in fact be regarded as the hub around which all the multiple but related synchronic and diachronic theories of language and cognition turn.

Developmental psychologists and linguists interested in language acquisition have also begun to study polysemy (see Mason, Kniseley and Kendall 1979; Durkin, Crowther and Shire 1986; Johnson 1997, 2001; Nerlich, Todd and Clarke 1998; Israel, to appear). One contribution to this volume will explore the acquisition of the different meanings of the polysemous verb *get* from 4 to 10 years, and it will also investigate whether developmental psychology can shed light on recent developments in cognitive linguistics and *vice versa* (Nerlich, Todd and Clarke, this volume; see also Raukko, this volume, for a parallel investigation of the "adult polysemy" of *get*).

There are still many questions to be answered in this field of research. Here are just a few of them: do children learn the various subsenses of a word in fixed collocational patterns and only later relate them to one core meaning? Or do they first have a very vague global meaning for one word and then tease out the subsenses? Do they learn the most frequently used subsenses first? How do children start to enjoy and understand jokes and puns based on the exploitation of polysemy/ambiguity? Why does this seem to happen only after the age of 7? And why is this difficult for autistic children? As conceptual metaphorical mappings are not primarily matters of language, but part of our conceptual systems which allow us to use sensory–motor concepts in the service of abstract reason, it is assumed by many cognitive linguists that children acquire conceptual metaphorical mappings automatically and unconsciously via their everyday functioning in the world (see Lakoff and Johnson 1999: Chapter 4). All this needs to be studied empirically.

Could it be that children put together knowledge elements into networks that follow the same pathways as the accretion of polysemous meanings by a word form over time? Do children's spontaneous creations of multiple meanings match the patterns of adult polysemy, that is, follow metaphorical and metonymical pathways? And if not, how are children's networks of polysemous meanings adjusted to the adult ones? Another question one should try to answer is: do children readily understand polysemous words? What kind of polysemous words do they understand best? Does it depend on the grammatical category? Does it depend on the frequency/familiarity or salience (see Hughes 1989; Giora 1997)? Does it depend on the type of figurative mapping underlying the multiple meanings of a word? Are metonymical extensions more readily understood than metaphorical ones or *vice versa*? Does it depend on the degree of prototypicality? Or does it depend on a particular combination of all these factors? In this book only a few of these questions can be addressed (see Dowker, this volume; Nerlich, Todd and Clarke, this volume), but they have at least to be stated.

Furthermore, it has become clear that polysemy cannot be studied inside linguistics and psychology alone. It can only be understood if we also look at human culture, as Brown and Witkowski have already stressed:

> Polysemy is ubiquitous in language and its investigation has considerable potential for illuminating human cognition. In addition, the *regular patterns of lexical change* ... indicate that the lexicon is amenable to systematic investigation as are other components of language. Most importantly, the study of *these regular lexical patterns* can contribute significantly to knowledge of the processes and capacities which underlie human language and culture. (Brown and Witkowski 1983: 83, italics added)

Throughout the book we shall attempt to link linguistic, cognitive, and cultural approaches to the study of polysemy, and also to link these to diachronic and synchronic approaches (Fauconnier and Turner; Dowker; Aitchison; Blank, this volume).

In recent years, research in cognitive semantics has shown that the lexicalized meanings of polysemous words can be explained in terms of basic conceptual and cultural metaphors, that polysemy is motivated partially by our metaphorical and metonymical structuring of experience, especially of our bodily experience (Lakoff and Johnson 1980; Bartsch 1984, 2002; Dirven 1985; Gibbs 1994: 40–41; see Seto, this volume). Words do not accumulate meanings at random, but follow certain cognitive pathways or patterns that are natural to human cognition and that structure our acquisition of experience, knowledge and language. So, to understand the emergence and structure of polysemy, we have to understand the nature of metaphor and metonymy, an insight familiar to those studying semantic change a century ago (see Nerlich and Clarke 1997; Blank, this volume; Nerlich, this volume).

More recently, it has become clear that rather than being a system for representing concepts, language is a system of prompts for conceptual integration. In this view linguistic expressions prompt for meanings rather than represent meanings. Polysemy is a dynamic byproduct of this operation of conceptual integration, it is not a static property of the words themselves. Polysemy is therefore ubiquitous but also barely noticeable in most cases.

We only become aware of its existence when the emergent meaning in a blend, for example, seems remarkably distant from the domain of the input from which the words came. When we notice this distance, we call it by one of many names used in traditional semantics: extension, bleaching, analogy, metaphor, and displacement (see Fauconnier and Turner, this volume; Aitchison and Lewis, this volume). The problem of "graded polysemy" will be explored further in the next section. Some of the problems that this view throws up for computational approaches to polysemy are explored in Kilgarriff's contribution to this volume.

2.   Polysemy: theories and hypotheses

In the context of this book, we adopt as a working hypothesis the view that almost every word is more or less polysemous, with senses linked to a prototype by a set of relational semantic principles which incorporate a greater or lesser amount of flexibility. We follow the now common practice in polysemy research and regard polysemy as a graded phenomenon (see Cowie 1982; Lipka 1990; Gibbs 1994; Cruse 1995), ranging between what some call *contrastive* polysemy and *complementary* polysemy (Weinreich 1966; Pustejovsky 1995), where contrastive polysemy deals with homonyms such as *match* (a small stick with a tip which ignites when scraped on a rough surface) and *match* (contest in a game or sport), whereas complementary polysemy deals with interrelated semantic aspects of a word, such as, in the case of *record*, for example, the physical object and the music. Cases, such as *smart* as in "a smart person" or "a smart dress", and *fair* as in "a fair trial" and "fair hair" lie somewhere in between. Other polysemy researchers, such as Cruse, have tried to deal with this semantic gradedness by invoking the notion of sense-nodules or regions of higher semantic density within the extreme variability of senses (Cruse 2000). The concept of gradedness also applies to the difference between literal and metaphorical meaning, as recent research seems to confirm (see Gibbs 1994; Giora, this volume).

Take the following examples:

(1)   *He gave me a book.*
(2)   *He gave me a strange look.*
(3)   *He gave me a hearing test.*
(4)   *He gave me hell.*

In (1) *give* refers to a process in which ownership of an object changes from person A to person B as the result of an action on the part of person A. "Possession" is what prototype theorists would call the most prototypical meaning of *give*. In the other cases this prototypical meaning of "possession" is mapped onto various other human experiences. In (2) *give* refers to another kind of action, in which no change of ownership is involved and the "object" is of an abstract kind. In (3) *give* is synonymous with 'administer', and in (4) the "object transferred" is of an entirely abstract, metaphorical, nature and the expression in which *give* is used has become idiomatic (see Lee 1986: 1–2).

The way in which we understand the various meanings of the word *give* depends on accommodation in context (which includes knowledge about idioms, where accommodation is reduced to "zero" and understanding has become automatic). As Langacker has pointed out:

> It must be emphasized that syntagmatic combination involves more than the simple addition of components. A composite structure is an integrated system formed by coordinating its components in a specific, often elaborate manner. In fact, it often has properties that go beyond what one might expect from its components alone ... . [O]ne component may need to be adjusted in certain details when integrated to form a composite structure; I refer to this as accommodation. (Langacker 1987: 76–77).

In the interpretation of polysemous words (in fact almost any word) there is therefore always a process of accommodation (and assimilation) involved, between what is given semantically, syntactically, and what we infer from the surrounding pragmatic context of discourse – leading to what Fauconnier and Turner call "conceptual integration". As Wittgenstein said in his *Philosophical Grammar*: "Well, 'Understanding' is not the name of a single process accompanying reading or hearing, but of more or less interrelated processes against a background, or in a context" (Wittgenstein 1974, §35: 74).

Wittgenstein, the "father" of the well-known concept of "family resemblances", so central to prototype theory, also stressed the gradedness of the multiple senses of a word in this passage from his *Philosophical Grammar*:

> What a concept-word indicates is certainly a kinship between objects, but this kinship need not be the sharing of a common property or a constituent. It may connect the objects like the links of a chain, so that one is linked to another by *intermediary links*. Two neighbouring members may have common

features and be similar to each other, while distant ones belong to the same family without any longer having anything in common. Indeed even if a feature is common to all members of the family it need not be that feature that defines the concept.

The relations between the members of a concept may be set up by the sharing of features which show up in the family of the concept, crossing and overlapping in very complicated ways.

Thus there is probably no simple characteristic which is common to all the things we call games. But it can't be said either that "game" just has several independent meanings (rather like the word "bank"). What we call "games" are procedures interrelated in various ways with many different transitions between one and another. (Wittgenstein 1974, §35: 75; emphasis added)

This polysemous gradedness is not just a synchronic, but also a diachronic phenomenon, as conversational implicatures generating *ad hoc* ambiguities and polysemies can become conventionalized or grammaticalized over time (see Traugott 1994), and as the distant senses of a polysemous word can at any time change status and generate new homonyms, that is, the semantic link in the network of senses can become obscured. What was motivated once becomes arbitrary. Polysemy always teeters on the edge of the semantic–pragmatic interface and of the synchronic–diachronic interface – between order and disorder.

This means that there is not so much a dichotomy between polysemy and homonymy, but rather a synchronic and diachronic gradient based on complex networks of meaning relations, of which the most basic ones are radial networks surrounding one prototype, and family resemblances, based on several linked prototypes or subnetworks. One can try to distinguish between various types of polysemy along this gradient (see Norrick 1981; Cruse 1995; Blank, this volume), but this will always be fraught with difficulties, as Geeraerts has pointed out (Geeraerts 1993, 1994; see also Nunberg 1979, 1992).

Geeraerts has written a number of important articles on cognitive semantics, polysemy, prototype theory, and semantic change. In his plea for an analysis of semantic change and polysemy in the framework of prototype theory, Geeraerts tries to answer two questions:

(i)   Why should diachronic structures reflect synchronic structures? And
(ii)   Why should the human brain have a prototypical conceptual organization at all? (Geeraerts 1985: 140)

Geeraerts gives three reasons, all of which are linked to the functions of the human mind, namely: storing information or accumulating world knowledge and using it for cognitive purposes.

(i)   *Informational density.* Categories should be as informative as possible, which is achieved by prototypical clustering of subconcepts.

(ii)   *Structural stability.* The categorical system can only work efficiently if it does not change drastically, but at the same time it should not be too rigid.

(iii)   *Flexible adaptability.* Concepts should be able to adapt to changing conditions in the world and to changing expressive needs on the part of the users of the concepts; they should also be able to integrate marginal or new members, without losing their stability and holistic quality.

If it is true that the structure of categories, including semantic categories, should be as dense as possible and as flexible as possible so as to be *conceptually efficient*, then one should expect in natural languages a tendency towards the *maximization* of lexical polysemy. This tendency is evidently at work in languages as any glance at a dictionary can demonstrate, especially an English one.

However, there seems to be a certain point when the network of senses becomes "saturated" and "strained" and begins to "shed" certain meanings (see also Nerlich, Todd and Clarke, this volume). Either senses become so distant that they are perceived as unrelated, such as French *voler* 'to fly' and *voler* 'to steal' (the words become "homonyms"), or the word becomes part and parcel of a free-standing semantic conglomerate. In the case of the highly polysemous verb *get*, for example, standing expressions, such as *Get a life* have developed, as well as phrasal verbs, such as to *get into* something, *get over* something, *get out of* something. These phrasal verbs can again become polysemous themselves, developing their own networks of metaphorical and metonymical senses based on the primary locative ones, and so on. There is therefore an ongoing cycle of emergent polysemy, conventionalized or lexicalized polysemy, and dead polysemy or homonymy.

As Jarno Raukko has pointed out in his contribution to this volume, it is important "to see polysemy as patterns of flexibility in (lexical) meaning in much the same way as it is accepted that situational (utterance or discourse level) meaning is nonfixed, inexact and negotiable."

This view is opposed to the so-called unitary, isomorphic or monosemous view of meaning (on this issue see Bierwisch 1983; Ruhl 1989; Groefsema 1995; Geeraerts 1997; Blank, this volume). What is ideal for certain artificial languages, that is, an unambiguous one-to-one correspondence between a word and its meaning, is far from ideal for ordinary language. In ordinary language we do not match words and meanings one by one, instead we have learned to match (flexible and adaptable) patterns of meanings surrounding a polysemous word (based on natural conceptual patterns) with certain con-textual patterns in which the word is embedded – *we match patterns*. People seem to be able to disambiguate polysemous words instantly and auto-matically by recognizing and adjusting certain correlations between the adaptable and changeable network of senses and the context of discourse in which a word is used habitually; but they can also leave multiple meanings "hanging in the air" if that serves their communicational purpose.

We hypothesize that the relation between words, meanings and context naturally assigns appropriate meanings in the mind of the hearer/child whether the word is polysemous or not. It is not the case that polysemy is a different and harder "semantic nut" to crack for the hearer; rather, monosemous words (e.g. *aspidistra*) have failed to exploit the full power of this mechanism. If this hypothesis is true, the acquisition of polysemous words should not be more difficult, but instead rather easier for children than the acquisition of monosemous words.

Recent research by Pustejovsky is also based on the axiom that there is no direct correspondence between words and meanings and that polysemy is widespread. His theory of how we interpret polysemous words in context has become a high-point of 1990s polysemy research and therefore needs to be summarized briefly (see also Warren, this volume). Following Weinreich's lead, Pustejovksy distinguishes between words which exhibit contrastive polysemy, such as *match* (in sports) and *match* (in the match box) and words which exhibit complementary polysemy, such as *paper*, as in making some-thing out of paper, reading a paper, writing a paper, giving a paper, and so on. He proposes to treat these two types of polysemous words in two different ways.

In the case of contrastive polysemy the meanings correspond to so many different words. In the case of complementary polysemy one word has complementary meanings, what he calls a lexical conceptual paradigm. Pustejovsky claims that a word is structured semantically by being embedded in four fields: the argument structure, the event structure, qualia roles and the structure of lexical inheritance. According to Pustejovsky, nominals have qualia structures which determine their meaning just as argument structures determine verb meaning. He proposes the following qualia roles: constitutive (constituent matter/parts), formal (size, shape, position etc.), telic (purpose) and agentive (ontogeny). When a verb is combined with a noun its argument structure must fit the qualia roles of that noun.

This may lead to the highlighting of particular roles. Take *book* as an example. When highlighting the domain or qualia role of a physical object (constitutive) we can say "I destroyed the book"; when highlighting its telic role we can say "I read the book"; and so on. This highlighting is also exploited in well-known jokes such as this: "I spent two months in the south of France finishing my novel. I am a very slow reader", which plays with two qualia roles, the telic role (a novel "for reading") and the agentive role ("writing" a novel).

As this joke shows, speakers and hearers do not just "disambiguate" polysemous words, they also have the option of *exploiting* polysemy and ambiguity for conversational profit, and this despite the fact that keeping multiple meanings in mind has some cognitive cost (Nerlich and Chamizo Domínguez 1999; Giora, this volume). In ordinary language we often "ambiguate" purposefully so as to negotiate conversational turns and increase our conversational prestige. Exploiting polysemy in this way leads to social bonding (through shared laughter, for example), but it might also increase the semantic, cognitive, and maybe even neuropsychological bonds between meanings and concepts. We want to stress that (lexical) polysemy is not just a phenomenon of the dictionary or of rather sterile disambiguation tasks in psycholinguistics. Polysemy is an ordinary language and ordinary life phenomenon (see Nerlich and Clarke 2001).

However, the exploitation of polysemy for communicative and even commercial purposes (as in advertising) has a price in terms of cognitive processing. Experimental studies of the understanding of polysemous words have shown that processing polysemous words results in the continued activation of inappropriate senses for quite some time after the word has been encountered (Williams 1992; see also Gibbs 1994: 41). Other studies have shown that interlocutors make use of what is available to them, regardless of contextual information or speaker's intent (see Giora, this volume). They access the most salient (frequent, conventionalized) meaning first, which is sometimes neither the literal meaning nor the intended meaning (Giora 1997, 1999). Keeping several semantic options open has therefore cognitive costs, but it may also have communicational benefits, as salient meanings that have not been deactivated may easily be reused by the discourse participants for special purposes. This may then lead to strengthening of the semantic bonds between the senses of a word. Becoming salient in conversation, they will become more accessible and therefore more frequently used and usable. However, the communicational costs of using polysemous words are also obvious. There is always a danger of being misunderstood or of falling into semantic traps: as when the topic of the long overdue renovation of the staff toilets is discussed at a departmental meeting and someone says: "Any movement on this issue would be welcome"...

Any theory of polysemy has to achieve a very precarious balancing act between the maximization of polysemy, where the words themselves carry most of the polysemous workload and speakers just have to choose correctly in context, and a minimization of polysemy which leaves most of the work to the pragmatic component, that is to the interpretational work done by the speakers. One way out of this dilemma is proposed by Anna Wierzbicka (1996) who distinguishes between semantic primes (undefinable words), words that can be defined or paraphrased reductively using these primes and are therefore not polysemous, and words which need several paraphrases and can therefore be regarded as polysemous.

Maximalist descriptions of polysemy differ from minimalist ones in their psycho-communicational consequences. If most of the relevant meaning is coded, it will be recoverable from memory and need not be constructed on the spot. The consequence is reliable functioning of the communication but lack of flexibility. If little of the relevant meaning is coded, the interpreter's memory will not be overburdened, but his reasoning capacity will be occupied in the situation concerned. The message will not become available independently of the communication situation and will be less stereotyped. As a consequence there will be less reliable functioning but more flexibility and creativity (see Posner 1996: 236; on ways out of the minimalist/maximalist dilemma, see Warren, this volume; Tyler and Evans, this volume; Taylor, this volume; Janssen, to appear).

Related to the minimalist/maximalist difference in approaches to polysemy is the abstractivist/cognitivist difference (see Behrens 1999). According to the abstractivist view advocated for example by Caramazza and Grober (1976), each polysemous word has an abstract overall (literal) sense and the extended senses of the word can be derived contextually. This view has been contested in more recent work in lexical semantics which suggests that the meaning of many polysemous words can be explained in terms of basic metaphors, metonymies, cognitive models and frames that motivate the sense extensions (see Gibbs 1994).

As Fritz has recently pointed out, the maximalist and the minimalist approach have their advantages and disadvantages, but the maximalist one is better suited for both synchronic and diachronic semantics:

> Semantic minimalism, advocated both by structuralists ... and, more recently, by Griceans ..., is basically a healthy principle in that it forces researchers to differentiate between what a word means and what is conversationally implicated in a certain context. But it also fosters the tendency to explain as implicatures what must be seen as established uses of expressions. The latter tendency is definitely harmful for historical semantics. Authors working in a cognitive-semantics framework accept polysemy as a fundamental semantic fact and explain the unity of meaning not by a minimalist reduction to basic meanings, but by positing an internal structure within a set of uses. This approach permits treating semantic developments as developments of sets of uses and their internal structures. (Fritz 1998b: 185; see also Fritz 1998a)

A decade or so before Fritz, Lieberman had already pointed out that:

> We know that the word *table* has a fuzzy floating set of references; but we also know that there is some precise limit to the range of references. The trouble comes in attempting to capture formally the precision and the fuzziness. We can use the word *table* to refer to all manners of things that have some property of tableness in a particular setting. The degree to which we all ascribe the property of tableness to something in any setting will vary. And the quality of tableness will change for each of us. What seems to be a table at some time in some place may not be a table to us at another time in another place.
>
> Language is inherently ambiguous and uncertain. That is the problem and the power of the system. ... We *must* always creatively interpret an utterance: the new interpretation always has the potential of achieving a new insight. (Lieberman 1984: 82)

Although there is a danger that this might be taken the wrong (namely modular) way, one could say that it is the function of sentential context to mediate between semantics and pragmatics and, in a sense, between maximalist and minimalist polysemy:

The rules of syntax have a functional purpose: they limit some of the semantic referents of a word. In the sentence *It's important to bank your money*, the syntax of English limits the semantic referents of the word *bank* to the range of concepts relevant to its functioning as a verb. (Lieberman 1984: 85–86)

A tiny bit of syntagmatic bonding is sometimes sufficient to define the sense of an expression successfully. Take for example *rock quarry* and *rock band* (see Osgood 1980: 226). Where such syntagmatic or collocational information is insufficient, as in *rock idol* or *hard rock* (to give two very simplified examples), our world knowledge, our knowledge of context, and our knowledge of conceptual metaphors and metonymies, cognitive models, and frames comes into its own.

Polysemy is a phenomenon that exposes the multiple relations and connections between syntax, semantics and pragmatics, and between language, cognition and social interaction. It can only be studied if we try not to isolate one from another.

3.   Contributions to the volume

This introduction will be followed by two contributions which set the scene for the following articles, a theoretical one by Taylor and a historiographical one by Nerlich, both exploring the puzzles that polysemy has posed to linguists and philosophers of language over time and is still posing to linguists now. The articles by Fauconnier/Turner, Tyler/Evans, Raukko, and Seto explore the wider theoretical and methodological debates connected with issues of polysemy, blending and flexible meaning, and the status of metonymy inside a cognitive theory of polysemy. Fauconnier/Turner and Tyler/Evans focus on polysemy as part of an exploration of human conceptualization by studying examples of blending and the various uses of *over* in (American) English. Raukko's contribution provides detailed comparative analyses of the English word *get* and the Finnish word *pitää*. It establishes a direct link to the chapters by Warren and Lehrer, where polysemous English word forms and polysemous constructions are investigated in detail. All three articles widen the field of polysemy research from the lexicon to morphology and syntactic constructions and make new contributions to methodology. The articles by Aitchison/Lewis and Blank study various levels of polysemy and bleaching from the synchronic as well as diachronic point of view, not only in English, but also in the Romance languages. As Blank focuses on polysemy in the lexicon and in discourse, his article is followed by Giora/Gur's contribution, which discusses irony and polysemy from a psycholinguistic and discursive point of view. The developmental dimension of polysemy (and metaphor) is explored by Dowker, who provides an empirical analysis of children's use of figurative language from a cross-cultural perspective, and by Nerlich/Todd/Clarke, who examine the acquisition of *get* by English children between age 4 and 10. This chapter links back to the empirical investigation of adult uses of *get* by Raukko, with which it shares the experimental approach. In the final part of the book Kilgarriff and Wilks debate whether or not there are word senses and how to disentangle them by computational means.

Following this introduction, **John Taylor** explores the controversies associated with the concept of polysemy, but does not intend to solve them. Instead of refining the concept he examines the cognitive models that are used to frame the conceptualizations of polysemy. He draws attention to three mutually supporting cognitive models: the semiotic model of language, the building block metaphor of syntagmatic combination, and the demarcation of lexicon and syntax.

In her chapter **Brigitte Nerlich** traces the history of the concept of "polysemy" from Antiquity to the first half of the 20th century. Bréal's treatment of polysemy is the pivot around which the article itself turns, as it was Bréal who invented the term "polysemy" a century ago and laid the first theoretical foundations for a study of polysemy as a linguistic, historical and cognitive phenomenon.

In their article "Polysemy and conceptual blending" **Gilles Fauconnier** and **Mark Turner** put polysemy research into the broader context of research in cognitive linguistics and literary theory. They look at some aspects of polysemy which derive from the power of meaning potential. More specifically, they focus on aspects linked to the operation of conceptual blending, a major cognitive resource for creativity in many of its manifestations. They argue that polysemy is pervasive in language and appears in many forms. It is not just an accident of history or of synchrony, but rather an essential manifestation of the flexibility, adaptability, and richness in meaning potential that lie at the very heart of what a language is and what it is for. Fauconnier/Turner review a number of classical cases of polysemy associated with conceptual blending in order to give an idea of the overall importance of blending in polysemy phenomena.

The paper by **Andrea Tyler** and **Vyvyan Evans** (reprinted here with the permission of *Language*) explores lexical polysemy through an in-depth examination of the English preposition *over*. Working within a cognitive linguistic framework, it illustrates the non-arbitrary quality of the mental lexicon and the highly creative nature of the human conceptual system. The analysis takes the following as basic: (i) human conceptualization is the product of embodied experience, i.e. that the kinds of bodies and neural architecture humans have, in conjunction with the nature of the spatio-physical world humans inhabit, determines human conceptual structure; and (ii) semantic structure derives from and reflects conceptual structure. As humans interact with the world, they perceive recurring spatial configurations which become represented in memory as abstract, imagistic conceptualizations. The authors posit that each preposition is represented by a primary meaning, which they term a protoscene. The protoscene, in turn, interacts with a highly constrained set of cognitive principles to derive a set of additional distinct senses, forming a motivated semantic network. Tyler and Evans conclude that previous accounts have failed to adequately develop criteria to distinguish between coding in formal linguistic expression, and the nature of conceptualization which integrates linguistic prompts in a way that is maximally coherent with and contingent upon sentential context and real-world knowledge. To rectify this, they put forward a methodology for identifying the protoscene and for distinguishing among distinct senses.

Like Seto in the following chapter, **Jarno Raukko** disputes some traditional assumptions underlying polysemy research and puts forward a new experimental approach focusing on flexibility. His chapter is therefore entitled: "Polysemy as flexible meaning: experiments with English *get* and Finnish *pitää*". Raukko claims that it is common to view polysemy as a collection or network of several (interrelated) meanings that is fairly stable, fairly unproblematic to segment and establish, and fairly much agreed upon by different speakers. Yet, as he shows in his chapter, there are also opponents who wish to reduce polysemy to patterns of contextual specifications or claim that polysemy is irrelevant to the study of communication. One way of building a bridge between these camps is to see polysemy as patterns of flexibility in (lexical) meaning in much the same way as it is accepted that situational (utterance or discourse level) meaning is nonfixed, imprecise, and negotiable. The view about polysemy as flexible meaning does not imply that word-specific descriptions of semantic variation would be unnecessary, but it seeks to leave room for dynamicity and open-endedness in categorization as well as for intersubjective disagreements in views about the structure of the polysemy of a given word. The article demonstrates some advantages of this view with an analysis of results from polysemy experiments with nonlinguist informants.

Blending research and research into metaphor as sources for polysemous sense extensions are well represented in cognitive linguistics. More recently we have seen a rising concern with metaphor's ugly sister, namely metonymy. Recently published work on metonymy in the framework of cognitive linguistics has shown that metonymy is not only as pervasive as metaphor but also no less important in the daily use of language. However, in his chapter "Metonymic polysemy and its place in meaning extension" **Ken-ichi Seto** claims that the theory of metonymy presented in the mainstream cognitive camp is flawed for a number of reasons. He argues specifically (i) that there has been no satisfactory definition of metonymy yet, this being due to confusions about the difference between entities and categories; (ii) that the ultimate reason why those confusions so often occur resides in the (inevitable) spatial representation of categorical relations; and (iii) that Langacker's network model, which is supposed to deal with polysemy, does not quite work because metonymy has no proper place in the model. Having criticized the prevailing trend in polysemy and metonymy research, Seto then proposes a new way of looking at polysemy: the cognitive triangle whose vertices are metaphor, metonymy, and synecdoche.

The empirical exploration of polysemy in all types of linguistic phenomena is continued in the chapter contributed by one of the earliest and best known researchers in the field of polysemy, namely **Adrienne Lehrer**, working within the framework of lexical field theory. In her chapter, "Polysemy in derivational affixes", she pursues research into a domain of polysemy which has often been overlooked. Whereas polysemy has been well investigated in lexemes, much less research has been done on bound forms, especially on derivational affixes. It has been established that the range of meanings expressed by affixes (and function words) is limited, but in this chapter Lehrer further explores the kinds of polysemy that can be found in derivations, comparing them with the full range found in lexemes.

The chapter by **Beatrice Warren**, entitled "The role of links and/or qualia in modifier–head constructions", adopts one of the novel approaches to polysemy developed by Pustejovsky and puts it to the empirical test. Like the previous chapters by Fauconnier/Turner and Raukko, Warren argues that polysemy is evidence of lexical creativity. But she asks: is this creativity rule-governed as is believed to be the case with syntactic creativity? That is, are there some finite means allowing infinite production of new senses? Her position is that certain aspects of sense-formation are regular and predictable. Building on work by Pustejovsky and herself, Warren traces the origin of a certain kind of polysemy in adjectives, denominal verbs, compounds and metonymies to a common cognitive basis.

With **Jean Aitchison** and **Diane Lewis**'s chapter "Polysemy and bleaching" we leave the detailed analysis of synchronic polysemies and their underlying structures behind to enter the realm of diachronic polysemy and grammatical-ization. We examine the reasons why words become polysemous and what patterns of polysemy are established over time. Aitchison/Lewis argue that words which describe appalling events, such as *disaster* or *catastrophe*, tend to "bleach" (fade in meaning). Yet their older unbleached meanings (such as 'a major catastrophic event') are often retained alongside their new, bleached meanings (such as 'a minor mishap', 'a failure'). Aitchison/Lewis study many examples taken from the *British National Corpus*, a database of modern written and spoken language, such as:

(5)   *At least 62 people were killed and 3,000 missing last night after an underwater earthquake sent 50 ft tidal waves crashing into the coast of Nicaragua. More than 227 people were injured in the* disaster.

(6)   *All other efforts to lose the fat from the offending areas proved to be a* disaster. *If I lost weight below 54 kg my bust disappeared, yet nothing went from my legs or posterior!*

This chapter explores some of the resulting polysemy. It asks two main questions: first, how do hearers successfully interpret such fast-moving, polysemous words? Second, what general processes can be identified in the development of such polysemy? The diachronic theme explored in Aitchison/Lewis's chapter is continued in Blank's chapter.

In his chapter "Polysemy in the lexicon and in discourse" **Andreas Blank** agrees initially with Bréal who claimed that polysemy could be regarded as the "synchronic side" of lexical semantic change. He argues that if we conceive of semantic change as being based on associations between concepts or concepts and linguistic signs, we can describe polysemy as the continuation of these associative relations in synchrony. Blank warns us, however, not to commit an easy fallacy: there is no complete isomorphism between diachronic processes and synchronic states. His first aim is to explain the specific differences between diachrony and synchrony and to provide a typology of the semantic relations that underlie polysemy, i.e. "types of polysemy", such as "metaphoric polysemy", "metonymic polysemy", and so on (relations which are also explored by Dowker, and Seto, this volume). He then addresses another problem that concerns semantics: the distinction between contextual variation ("vagueness"), polysemy, and homonymy ("ambiguity"). Here again, the conception of semantic relations reveals its explanatory power, as it serves as the main criterion used to distinguish between the three topics. Blank also takes into account complex lexical developments, such as initial polysemy that turns into homonymy and initial homonymy that is reinterpreted as polysemy. However, the article not only deals with diachronic processes and synchronic structures on which polysemy is based, but also reveals the underlying discursive bases of polysemy, something often neglected in polysemy research, especially of the diachronic form. Blank therefore had to modify Bréal's view of polysemy as the direct lexicalized consequence of semantic innovation. This is only one type in a set of possibilities.

The chapter by **Rachel Giora** and **Inbal Gur**, "Irony in conversation: salience, role, and context effects", again challenges many presuppositions underlying traditional polysemy research. Polysemy as flexible meaning is directly studied in its discursive context, not from a historical point of view, as in Blank's chapter, but from a psycholinguistics one. This chapter focuses on one aspect of polysemy, namely irony, and it also contributes to the debate about the flexible nature of literal and figurative meaning. Giora/ Gur report that previous research has demonstrated that familiar and less familiar ironies are initially accessed literally. However, while familiar ironies availed their ironic meaning in parallel with the literal meaning, less familiar ironies facilitated ironically related concepts later. These findings support the "graded salience hypothesis", and are inconsistent with the view that context affects comprehension significantly. According to the graded salience hypothesis, salient meanings should always be activated, even when they are incompatible with the context. A meaning of a word or an expression is salient if it is coded, i.e. retrievable from the mental lexicon. Factors contributing to degrees of salience are conventionality, frequency, familiarity, and prior context. Investigating irony reception in a spontaneous environment, the authors show that more often than not, irony is responded to by resonating with its salient literal interpretation. In friendly conversations, listeners very often react to the literal meaning of the ironic utterance while at the same time making it clear that they have also understood the implicated meaning.

After having analysed some of the main synchronic, diachronic and discursive patterns of polysemy, we now come to patterns of polysemy which emerge in and perhaps even structure the acquisition of certain lexical items. Linking back to the articles by Seto, Blank, and Giora/Gur we put polysemy back into the context of the study of figurative language, especially metaphor and metonymy, but from a specifically psychological perspective. **Ann Dowker** stresses in her chapter "Young children's and adults' use of figurative language: how important are cultural and linguistic influences?" that there have been numerous studies of the development and of the use and comprehension of metaphors and other forms of figurative language. At least some types of figurative language appear to develop very early: well before school age. Figurative language seems to be a cross-cultural universal, but the precise forms that it takes vary with language and culture. However, a recent study by the author showed marked cross-cultural differences in the extent to which 4- to 6-year-old children used figurative language in their invented rhymes and chants. One possible reason for cross-cultural variations in figurative language may involve differences in the nature and extent of polysemy in different languages. This chapter discusses (i) the broad course of development of figurative language in early and middle childhood; (ii) cross-cultural similarities and differences in its development and use; and (iii) the extent to which cross-cultural variations in the development of figurative language may reflect cross-linguistic variations concerning polysemy.

The developmental theme is continued in the chapter "Emerging patterns and evolving polysemies: the acquisition of *get* between four and ten years", in which **Brigitte Nerlich**, **Zazie Todd** and **David D. Clarke** study the acquisition of the different meanings of the polysemous verb *get* by children aged between 4 and 10 years. This chapter therefore complements Raukko's chapter devoted to the flexible use of *get* by adults. Fifty-nine children took part in an experiment that involved production and ranking tasks. The production task showed that 4-year-olds only produced the main senses of 'have', 'fetch' and 'obtain'; by 10 years a much wider array of meanings was produced; and at all ages syntactic frames were embedded in everyday experiences. The ranking task involved selecting the best example of *get* from 'obtain', 'fetch', 'go', 'become', and 'understand'. Four-year-olds' knowledge was structured around 'obtain' as the most prototypical meaning, and 10-year-olds' responses were best explained by a prototype model of semantic representation. It seems that in between, that is with the 7-year-olds, knowledge of meaning was not yet organized into a prototypical scene. A theoretical approach to the development of word meaning based on (synchronic and diachronic) theories of polysemy and embodiment is proposed.

With the last two chapters by Kilgarriff and Wilks we enter the computational field of polysemy research and link it to issues in lexicography. However, these papers not only address computational issues, but deal with very fundamental theoretical, methodological and even philosophical issues of polysemy research, such as: what are word senses and how can we distinguish between them? In the provocatively titled chapter "I don't believe in word senses" **Adam Kilgarriff** argues that we often have strong intuitions about words having multiple meanings, and that lexicography aims to capture them, systematically and consistently. But how can lexicographers do this? Can they find help in the literature dealing with the philosophy of language? No, the philosophy literature does not provide a taxonomy of the processes underpinning these intuitions, nor does it analyse the relations between the word sense distinctions a dictionary makes and the primary data of naturally-occurring language. This is a gap that this chapter aims to fill. Kilgarriff shows that various attempts, such as Cottrell's connectionist approach (1989), to provide the concept "word sense" with secure foundations have been unsuccessful. He goes on to consider the lexicographers' understanding of what they are doing when they make decisions about a word's senses, and develops an alternative conception of the word sense, in which it corresponds to a cluster of citations for a word. Citations are clustered together where they exhibit similar patterning and meaning. The various possible relations between a word's meaning potential and its dictionary senses are catalogued and illustrated with corpus evidence, thus linking back to the method used by Aitchison/Lewis.

In "Senses and texts" **Yorick Wilks** addresses the question of whether it is possible to sense-tag systematically, and on a large scale, and how we should assess progress so far. That is to say, how to attach each occurrence of a word in a text to one and only one sense in a dictionary – a particular dictionary of course, and that is part of the problem. The paper does not propose a solution to the question, although the author has reported empirical findings elsewhere, and intends to continue and refine that work. The point of this paper is to examine two well-known contributions critically: the first (see Kilgarriff, this volume) is widely taken to show that the task, as defined, cannot be carried out systematically by humans whereas the second claims strikingly good results at doing exactly that. This means that the aim of this chapter is to attack two claims, both of which are widely believed, though not at once: that sense-tagging of corpora cannot be done, and that it has been solved.

All the chapters in this book either propose novel approaches to polysemy, or stringent criticisms of older approaches, or else are built on older approaches to investigate novel problems. They all combine theoretical analysis with empirical research and provide the reader with a multitude of examples and a wealth of theoretical reflections. We hope that the field of polysemy research will be enriched by them and that readers will come away with a deeper knowledge, not only of polysemy, but of the functioning of language in mind and in discourse, in synchrony and diachrony, in use and in acquisition.

References

Asher, Nicholas and Alex Lascarides
   1995   Lexical disambiguation in a discourse context. *Journal of Semantics* 12(1): 69–108.
Bartsch, Renate
   1984   The structure of word meanings: polysemy, metaphor, and metonymy. In: Fred Landman and Frank Veltman (eds.), *Varieties of Formal Semantics*, 27–54. Dordrecht: Foris.
   2002   Generating polysemy: metaphor and metonymy. In: René Dirven and Ralf Pörings (eds.), *Metaphor and Metonymy in Comparison and Contrast*, 49–74. Cognitive Linguistics Research 2. Berlin and New York: Mouton de Gruyter.
Behrens, Leila
   1999   Aspects of polysemy. In: David A. Cruse, Franz Hundsnurscher, Michael Job and Peter Rolf Lutzeier (eds.), *Lexikologie – Lexicology* (HSK) Vol. 1. Berlin: Walter de Gruyter.
Bierwisch, Manfred
   1983   Semantische und konzeptionelle Repräsentation lexikalischer Einheiten. In: Rudolf Ruzicka and Wolfgang Motsch (eds.), *Untersuchungen zur Semantik*, 61–99. Berlin: Akademie-Verlag.
Bréal, Michel
   1924 [1897] *Essai de sémantique (Science des significations)*. Reprint of the 4th Edition. Paris: Gérard Monfort.
Brown, Cecil H. and Stanley R. Witkowski
   1983   Polysemy, lexical change, and cultural importance. *Man* 18: 72–89.
Brugman, Claudia
   1981   Story of *over*. M.A. thesis. University of California, Berkeley.
   1997   Polysemy. In: Jef Verschueren, Jan-Ola Östman, Jan Blommaert and

Chris Bulcaen (eds.), *Handbook of Pragmatics.* Amsterdam and Philadelphia: John Benjamins. Printed 1999.

Caramazza, Alfonso and Ellen Grober

1976   Polysemy and the structure of the subjective lexicon. In: Clea Rameh (ed.), *Semantics: Theory and Application*, 181–206. Washington, DC: Georgetown University Press.

Cottrell, Garrison W.

1989   *A Connectionist Approach to Word Sense Disambiguation.* London: Pitman.

Cowie, H. P.

1982   Polysemy and the structure of lexical fields. *Nottingham Linguistic Circular* 11(2): 51–65.

Cruse, David A.

1995   Polysemy and related phenomena from a cognitive linguistic point of view. In: Patrick Saint-Dizier and Evelyne Viegas (eds.), *Computational Lexical Semantics*, 33–49. Cambridge: Cambridge University Press.

2000   *Meaning in Language.* Oxford: Oxford University Press.

Cuyckens, Hubert

1994   Family resemblance in the Dutch spatial preposition *op*. In: Schwarz (1994), 179–196.

Cuyckens, Hubert and Britta Zawada (eds.)

2002   *Polysemy in Cognitive Linguistics.* Amsterdam and Philadelphia: John Benjamins.

Deane, Paul D.

1988   Polysemy and cognition. *Lingua* 75: 325–361.

Dirven, René

1985   Metaphor as a basic means for extending the lexicon. In: Wolfgang Paprotté and René Dirven (eds.), *The Ubiquity of Metaphor*, 85–119. Amsterdam: John Benjamins.

Dölling, Johannes

1993   Polyemy and sort coercion in semantic representations. In: Peter Bosch and Peter Gerstl (eds.), *Discourse and Lexical Meaning*, 61–78. Arbeitspapiere des SFB 340, Bericht Nr 30.

Durkin, Kevin, R. D. Crowther and B. Shire

1986   Children's processing of polysemous vocabulary in school. In: Kevin Durkin (ed.), *Language Development in the School Years*. London: Croom Helm.

Fillmore, Charles and B. T. Sue Atkins

1992   Towards a frame-based lexicon: the semantics of *risk* and its neighbors. In: Adrienne Lehrer and Eva F. Kittay (eds.), *Frames, Fields and Contrasts*, 75–102. Hillsdale, NJ: Lawrence Erlbaum Associates.

Fritz, Gerd
    1998a   *Historische Semantik.* Stuttgart and Weimar: Metzler.
    1998b   Review of Geeraerts (1997). *Lexicology* 4(1): 183–192.
Geeraerts, Dirk
    1985   Cognitive restrictions on the structure of semantic change. In: Jacek
            Fisiak (ed.), *Historical Semantics. Historical Word-Formation*, 126–
            153. Berlin, New York, Amsterdam: Mouton de Gruyter.
    1993   Vagueness's puzzles, polysemy's vagaries. *Cognitive Linguistics* 4(3):
            223–272.
    1994   Polysemy. In: R. E. Asher and J. M. Y. Simpson (eds.), *Encyclopedia
            of Language and Linguistics*, 3227–3228. Oxford: Pergamon.
    1997   *Diachronic Prototype Semantics. A contribution to historical lexicology.*
            Oxford: Clarenden.
Gibbs, Raymond W., Jr.
    1994   *The Poetics of Mind: Figurative Thought, Language, and Understanding.*
            Cambridge: Cambridge University Press.
Giora, Rachel
    1997   Understanding figurative and literal language: the graded salience
            hypothesis. *Cognitive Linguistics* 7(1): 183–206.
    1999   On the priority of salient meanings: studies of literal and figurative
            language. *Journal of Pragmatics* 31: 919–929.
Groefsema, Marjolein
    1995   *Can, may, must* and *should* – a relevance theoretic account. *Journal
            of Linguistics* 31(1): 53–79.
Heger, Klaus
    1963   Homographie, Homonymie und Polysemie. *Zeitschrift für Romanische
            Philologie* 79: 471–491.
Hughes, Alva T.
    1989   *Polysemy and Frequency in Word Knowledge Acquisition.* Dissertation
            Abstracts International, 1989 Mar, v49 (n9-B): 4046–4047.
Hüllen, Werner and Rainer Schulze (eds.)
    1988.   *Understanding the Lexicon: Meaning, Sense and World Knowledge
            in Lexical Semantics.* Tübingen: Niemeyer.
Israel, Michael
    (to appear) Systematic idiomaticity in the acquisition of English *get* construc-
            tions. In: Arie Vergagen and Jeroen van de Weijer (eds.), *Agreement
            in Form: Conventions on Different Linguistic Levels.*
Janssen, Theo A. J. M.
    (to appear) Monosemy versus polysemy. In: Hubert Cuyckens, René Dirven and
            John Taylor (eds.), *Cognitive Linguistic Approaches to Lexical Semantics.*
            Cognitive Linguistics Research Series. Berlin: Mouton de Gruyter.
Johnson, Christopher Ronald
    1997   Learnability in the acquisition of multiple senses: SOURCE recon-

sidered. *Proceedings of the 22nd Annual Meeting of the Berkeley Linguistics Society*, 469–480. Berkeley: Berkeley Linguistics Society.

2001 Metaphor vs. conflation in the acquisition of polysemy: the case of *see*. In: Masako K. Hiraga, Chris Sinha, and Sherman Wilcox (eds.), *Cultural, Typological and Psychological Perspectives in Cognitive Linguistics*, 155–170. Amsterdam and Philadelphia: John Benjamins.

Jongen, René (ed.)
1985 *La polysémie*. Louvain-La-Neuve: Cabay.

Kilgarriff, Adam and Gerald Gazdar
1995 Polysemous relations. In: Frank R. Palmer (ed.), *Grammar and Meaning: Essays in Honour of Sir John Lyons*, 1–25. Cambridge: Cambridge University Press.

Kleiber, Georges
1999 *Problèmes de sémantique: La polysémie en question*. Villeneuve d'Ascq: Septentrion.

Lakoff George and Mark Johnson
1980 *Metaphors We Live By*. Chicago: University of Chicago Press.
1999 *Philosophy in the Flesh: The Embodied Mind and its Challenge to Western Thought*. New York: Basic Books.

Langacker, Ronald W.
1987 *Foundations of Cognitive Grammar, Volume 1: Theoretical Prerequisites*. Stanford, CA: Stanford University Press.

Lee, David
1986 *Language, Children and Society: An Introduction to Linguistics and Language Development*. Brighton, UK: The Harvester Press.

Lehrer, Adrienne
1990 Polysemy, conventionality, and the structure of the lexicon. *Cognitive Linguistics* 1(2): 207–246.

Lieberman, Philip
1984 *The Biology and Evolution of Language*. Cambridge, MA: Harvard University Press.

Lipka, Leonhard
1990 *An Outline of English Lexicology: Lexical Structure, Word Semantics, and Word-Formation*. Tübingen: Max Niemeyer.

Lyons, John
1977 *Semantics*, Volume II. Cambridge: Cambridge University Press.

Mason, J. M., E. Kniseley and J. Kendall
1979 Effects of polysemous words on sentence comprehension. *Reading Research Quarterly* 15(1): 49–65.

Nerlich, Brigitte and Pedro J. Chamizo Domínguez
1999 Cómo hacer cosas con palabras polisémicas: El uso de la ambigüedad en el lenguaje ordinario. *Contrastes. Revista Interdisciplinar de Filosofía* IV: 77–96.

Nerlich, Brigitte and David D. Clarke
1992   Semantic change: case studies based on traditional and cognitive semantics. *Journal of Literary Semantics* 21: 204–225.
1997   Polysemy: patterns in meaning and patterns in history. *Historiographia Linguistica* 24(3): 359–385.
2001   Ambiguities we live by. Towards a pragmatics of polysemy. *Journal of Pragmatics* 33: 1–20.
Nerlich, Brigitte, Zazie Todd and David D. Clarke
1998   The function of polysemous jokes and riddles in lexical development. *Cahiers de Psychologie Cognitive/Current Psychology of Cognition* 17(2): 343–366.
Norrick, Neal R.
1981   *Semiotic Principles in Semantic Theory.* Amsterdam: John Benjamins.
Norvig, Peter and George Lakoff
1987   Taking: a study in lexical network theory. *Proceedings of the 13th Annual Meeting of the Berkeley Linguistics Society*, 185–206. Berkeley: Berkeley Linguistics Society.
Nunberg, Geoffrey
1979   The non-uniqueness of semantic solutions: polysemy. *Linguistics and Philosophy* 3: 143–184.
1992   Systematic polysemy in lexicology and lexicography. In: Hannu Tommola et al. (eds.), *Euralex '92 Proceedings II*, 387–396. Tampere, Finland.
        (http://www.parc.xerox.com/istl/members/nunberg/Euralex.html)
Osgood, Charles E.
1980   The cognitive dynamics of synesthesia and metaphor. In: Richard P. Honeck and Robert R. Hoffman (eds.), *Cognitive and Figurative Language*, 203–238. Hillsdale, NJ: Lawrence Erlbaum Associates.
Ostler, Nicholas and B. T. Sue Atkins
1991   Predictable meaning shift: some linguistic properties of lexical implication rules. In: James Pustejovsky and Susan Bergler (eds.), *Lexical Semantics and Knowledge Representation*: ACL SIGLEX Workshop, 87–100. Berkeley, California.
Posner, Roland
1996   Pragmatics. In: Roland Posner, Karl Robering and Thomas A. Sebeok (eds.), *Semiotik/Semiotics. Ein Handbuch zu den zeichentheoretischen Grundlagen von Natur undKultur/A Handbook on the Sign-Theoretic Foundations of Nature and Culture*. Volume 1, 219–246. Berlin and New York: Walter de Gruyter.
Pustejovsky, James
1991   The generative lexicon. *Computational Linguistics* 17(4): 409–441.
1995   *The Generative Lexicon.* Cambridge, MA and London, England: The MIT Press.

Raukko, Jarno
1999   An 'intersubjective' method for cognitive-semantic research on polysemy: the case of *get*. In: Masaka Hiraga, Chris Sinha and Sherman Wilcox (eds.), *Cultural, Psychological, and Typological Issues in Cognitive Linguistics*, 87–105. Current Issues in Linguistic Theory, 152. Amsterdam and Philadelphia: John Benjamins.

Ravin, Yael and Claudia Leacock (eds.)
2000   *Polysemy and Ambiguity: Linguistic and Computational Approaches.* Oxford: Oxford University Press.

Rueckl, Jay G.
1995   Ambiguity and connectionist networks – still settling into a solution. *Journal of Experimental Psychology: Learning, Memory and Cognition* 21(2): 501–508.

Ruhl, Charles
1989   *On Monosemy.* New York: SUNY.

Schneider, Edgar
1988   On polysemy in English, considering *consider*. In: Hüllen and Schulze (1988), 157–169.

Schulze, Rainer
1988   A short story of *down*. In: Hüllen and Schulze (1988), 395–414.
1994   Image schemata and the semantics of *off*. In: Schwarz (1994), 197–214.

Schwarz, Monika (ed.)
1994   *Kognitive Semantik/Cognitive Semantics. Ergebnisse, Probleme, Pespektiven.* Tübingen: Gunter Narr Verlag.

Sinha, Chris and Tania Kuteva
1994   Spatial and non-spatial uses of prepositions: conceptual integrity across semantic domains. In: Schwarz (1994), 215–238.

Sweetser, Eve
1990   *From Etymology to Pragmatics: Metaphorical and Cultural Aspects of Semantic Structure.* Cambridge: Cambridge University Press.

Taylor, John R.
1992   How many meanings does a word have? *Stellenbosch Papers in Linguistics* 25: 133–168.

Traugott, Elizabeth Closs
1994   Grammaticalization and lexicalization. In: R. E. Asher and J. M. Y. Simpson (eds.), *The Encyclopedia of Language and Linguistics*, Volume 3, 1481–1486. Pergamon Press. Reprinted (1999) in: Keith Brown and Jim Miller (eds.), *Concise Encyclopedia of Grammatical Categories,* Oxford: Elsevier Science.

Tuggy, David
1993   Ambiguity, polysemy, and vagueness. *Cognitive Linguistics* 4(3): 273–290.

Ullmann, Stephen
  1951   *The Principles of Semantics*. Oxford: Basil Blackwell; Glasgow:
              Jackson, Sons and Co.
Victorri, Bernard
  1997   La polysémie: un artefact de la linguistique? *Revue de Sémantique
              et Pragmatique* 2: 41–62.
Viegas, Evelyne and Victor Raskin
  1998   *Computational Semantic Lexicon Acquisition – Methodology and
              Guidelines*. Technical Report MCCS-98-315, CRL, NMSU.
Weinreich, Uriel
  1966   Explorations in semantic theory. In: Thomas A. Sebeok (ed.), *Current
              Trends in Linguistics* III, 395–477. The Hague: Mouton.
Wierzbicka, Anna
  1996   *Semantics: Primes and Universals*. Oxford: Oxford University Press.
Wilks, Yorick
  1977   Frames for machine translation. *New Scientist* 76(108): 802–803.
Williams, John N.
  1992   Processing polysemous words in context: evidence for interrelated
              meanings. *Journal of Psycholinguistic Research* 21(3): 193–218.
Wittgenstein, Ludwig
  1974   *Philosophical Grammar*, edited by Rush Rhees; translated by Anthony
              Kenny. Oxford: Basil Blackwell.
Wunderli, Peter
  1995   Strukturelle Semantik, Polysemie und Architektur der Sprache. Zu
              einigen Problemen der Bedeutungsanalyse. In: Ulrich Hoinkes (ed.),
              *Panorama der Lexikalischen Semantik. Thematische Festschrift aus
              Anlaß des 60. Geburtstags von Horst Geckeler*, 791–806. Tübingen:
              Narr.

Cognitive models of polysemy

John R. Taylor

1. Introduction

One of the firmest results to have come out of the Cognitive Linguistics enterprise over the past couple of decades has been the realization that word meanings need to be understood against broader knowledge configurations, variously studied as "frames", "scenes", "domains", and "idealized cognitive models" (Lakoff 1987; Langacker 1987; Croft 1993). Consider, as an illustration, the word *bachelor*, and the fact that it would be odd to speak of the Pope as a bachelor, even though the Pope clearly instantiates each of the four defining features of bachelorhood, namely, "human", "male", "adult", and "unmarried" (Fillmore 1982; Lakoff 1987; Taylor 1995). The problem arises not because the definition of *bachelor* in terms of these four features is wrong in any material sense. Rather, it is because the concept "bachelor" needs to be understood against an idealized cognitive model of bachelorhood, and, more generally, of marriage practices. The model prescribes, for both men and women, a "marriageable age", a stage in life at which a person is expected to marry. *Bachelor* is used to designate males who have reached the marriageable age but fail to marry, because they do not yet want the "commitments" of marriage. The model is "idealized" in the sense that it offers a simplified view of society and overlooks the many individuals and groups who do not meet its background assumptions. For example, the model makes no provision for celibate clergy. Given the presuppositions of the cognitive model, it is quite legitimate to define a bachelor, quite simply, as a man who hasn't married. The application of the word becomes problematic with respect to the Pope, because the Pope lies outside the idealized situation covered by the model.

In this article, I examine some of the cognitive models against which we understand the concept of polysemy. Such an exercise may be useful, for a number of reasons. First, it may wean us away from the idea that polysemy is a well-defined natural category – a "brute fact" (Searle 1969: 50) about language, as it were, which, like brute facts of the material and biological world, exists independently of our conceptualization of it, and whose essence can be discovered by the application of the appropriate analytical tools. The exercise may also suggest that at least some of the problems which we encounter in the study of polysemy may be traceable to the cognitive models that frame our conceptualization of the phenomenon. These models encapsulate idealizations of language, which might not always be applicable to the linguistic data at hand. Just as the celibate clergy are not covered by the cognitive model of bachelorhood, so certain linguistic data may not fully conform with the cognitive models which frame our understanding of polysemy.

Polysemy is commonly defined as the association of two or more related meanings with a single phonological form (Taylor 1995: 99; Cuyckens and Zawada 2001: ix). The definition looks straightforward enough, and unlikely, of itself, to arouse controversy. Nevertheless, problems are likely to be encountered when we try to apply the definition to any particular set of data (Taylor, to appear). Note, first of all, that the definition presupposes that we have procedures in place for reliably identifying, characterizing, and enumerating the meanings of linguistic units. In case we have reasons for supposing that a given linguistic form is associated with more than one meaning, we need to be able to assess whether and in what way the meanings are related. To appreciate that these are very real issues in polysemy research we need look no further than the now sizable literature on the lexical item *over* (Brugman 1981; Lakoff 1987; Vandeloise 1990; Deane 1993; Dewell 1994; Kreitzer 1997; Queller 2001; Tyler and Evans 2001; amongst others). Recurring (and to this day, unresolved) issues have involved determining just how many different meanings this lexical item has, how the meanings are to be characterized, and the manner in which they are related. The definition of polysemy also presupposes that we can be confident that the different (though related) meanings are indeed associated with a single linguistic form. Do we want to recognize the preposition *over* (as in *the lamp over the table*) as the "same" linguistic form as the particle *over* (as in *fall over*), predicative *over* (*The party's over*), adverbial *over* (*Do it over again*), the prefixed morpheme in *overeat* and *overjoyed*, or even the noun *over* (as in cricket) (see Tyler and Evans, this volume). The question also arises, what are the linguistic forms which are candidates for a semantic analysis? Are they word-sized units, such as *over*, multi-word expressions, such as *over here*, constructional idioms, such as [V NP over again], or even fully specified phrases, of the kind *It ain't over till the fat lady sings*?

In this article, I draw attention to three mutually supporting cognitive models of language and their relevance to our understanding of polysemy. These are the semiotic model of language, the building block metaphor of syntagmatic combination, and the demarcation of lexicon and syntax. The models conspire to accord special significance to word-sized units. It is words that are listed in the lexicon, and words are the building blocks which the syntax combines. Words themselves are viewed as stable associations of fixed, determinate "chunks" of semantic information with equally fixed and determinate chunks of phonological material. According to the building block metaphor, then, complex expressions are a compositional function of their fixed and stable parts, at both the phonological and the semantic levels; conversely, complex expressions can be exhaustively broken down into their constituents. The need to postulate sometimes quite extensive polysemy arises from the fact that a chunk of phonological material rarely contributes exactly the same semantic chunk to the various expressions in which it occurs. In order for compositionality to go through, it becomes necessary to associate the phonological chunk with a range of distinct meanings, only one of which is selected on any particular occasion of its use.

The flip-side of sense selection in the compositional process is sense selection on the part of the hearer. Given that a phonological form may be associated with different meanings, and that only one of these is involved in the compositional process, how does a hearer select just that sense that is involved? Suppose that word w is associated with n different meanings. Any expression containing w will be in principle n-ways ambiguous. Since most words may be supposed to be polysemous to some degree, the number of possible readings of an expression will increase exponentially as the length of the expression increases. Thus, an expression containing two words, w_1 and w_2, which are associated with n_1 and n_2 meanings, respectively, will in principle have $n_1 \times n_2$ possible readings.

While disambiguation is indeed a major issue in natural language processing (Ravin and Leacock 2000: 24–5), for most language users, most of the time, sense selection in the comprehension process is actually not a problem at all. Most people, most of the time, are simply unaware of the extent of the ambiguity generated by polysemy. This rather paradoxical situation should give us pause for thought. At issue is not the definition of polysemy as multiple meanings attaching to a single phonological form. Neither should we rush to denounce the cognitive models presupposed by the definition and which lead us to postulate extensive polysemy and the ensuing ambiguities. Rather, it could be the case that the models are applicable only to highly idealized data. Polysemy presents itself as a problematic concept in those cases where the language data do not fit the idealized models.

In the following sections, I discuss the models in more detail, drawing attention to some discrepancies between certain kinds of data and the ideal situation presupposed by the models.

2. The semiotic model

According to the semiotic model, a language is a set of linguistic signs (prototypically: words), each of which associates a phonological structure with a semantic structure. The model was the foundation for Saussure's (1964 [1915]) theory, where the basic unit of language was the "linguistic sign", whose essence resided in the association of a "concept", or signified, with an "acoustic image", or signifier. As Saussure was careful to point out, neither the concept nor the acoustic image were to be identified with the specific details, whether conceptual or phonetic, of an actual utterance. Both sides of the linguistic sign are mental entities which serve to categorize specific instances that occur in an act of speech. The semiotic model, in its mentalistic form proposed by Saussure, has been endorsed by many linguists, including Sapir (1921), Chomsky (1988), Pinker (1994), as well as Lakoff (1987) and Langacker (1987). Thus, the basic unit in Langacker's theory is the "symbolic unit", which associates a phonological representation with a semantic representation.

The semiotic model invites us to imagine an ideal semiotic system, in which each signifier is paired off with a unique signified (Taylor 2003). The ideal is captured by the well-known slogan "one form, one meaning". Degrees of increasing deviation from the one form, one meaning situation can, however, be identified:

(i)   Both pronunciation and conceptual content are liable to vary according to context of use. This kind of variation need not of itself be problematic for the semiotic ideal. As noted, both poles of the linguistic sign, the "concept" and the "acoustic image", are taken to be mental entities, representations which are schematic for the specific semantic and phonological values manifest in an act of speech. Depending on speech tempo, degree of stress, and perhaps other factors, *upper* may be articulated as [ʌpə], with a bilabial stop, or [ʌɸə], with a bilabial fricative. These different pronunciations can still be regarded as instances of the schematic phonological form /ʌpə/. Likewise, whether *eat* is used of eating a steak or eating an ice cream – two very different activities, if we focus on their microstructure – we may still regard the two activities as instances of a more schematically characterized semantic unit [EAT].

(ii)   As the degree of phonological and semantic variation increases, it becomes increasingly difficult to bring the variants under a single schematic representation. While eating a steak and eating an ice cream arguably instantiate the same schematic process (having to do with the ingestion of solid food), we may be less confident about bringing these and other uses of *eat* (as when we say that the acid eats away the metal, or that inflation eats up my savings) under a single schematic representation. In such a situation, we may be inclined to associate *eat* with more than one semantic value; that is to say, we regard the item as polysemous. A comparable situation may obtain with respect to variation in an item's phonological form. This phenomenon is sometimes discussed under the heading of "alternation" (though "polyphony" might be a better label, one, moreover, which brings out the parallels between variation at the semantic pole and variation at the phonological pole). Thus, the indefinite article can appear as [ə], [ən], [æ], [æn], or [ɛɪ]; the morpheme {serene} has a different phonological shape in the adjective *serene* and the noun *serenity*, to cite just two examples.

(iii) The semantic values associated with a phonological form may be so dissimilar that they are not perceived to be related at all, as with *ball* "spherical object" or "social event"; this constitutes homonymy. Alternatively, a semantic unit is associated with two or more unrelated phonological forms, such as [səʊfə] and [kaʊtʃ]; this constitutes synonymy. These extreme deviations from the semiotic ideal are perhaps best regarded as cases of two or more different linguistic units happening to share the same phonological form, or, alternatively, the same conceptual content.

   The three degrees of deviation from the semiotic ideal constitute a continuum, with borderline cases often difficult to classify as, say, polysemy vs. context-conditioned variation, or, alternatively, as polysemy vs. homonymy.

Leaving aside such demarcation issues, we should expect that deviations from the semiotic ideal as characterized under (ii) and (iii) will tend to undermine the communicative efficiency of a language. Through the association of more than one signified with a signifier, polysemy (and homonymy) will generate ambiguity, which, if not properly resolved, may lead to communication failure. To be sure, the "cost" of polysemy may be offset by other factors, whose role may actually enhance the semiotic potential of a language. The number of established phonological forms in a language is going to be smaller by far than the number of conceptual categories that a person may wish to designate. Moreover, in view of the changing environment and changing concerns of language users, conceptual categories, and what count as members of these categories, are liable to undergo modification over time. The possibility that new meanings can accrue to existing word forms renders a polysemy-tolerant language more viable than a rigidly isomorphous system, in which each signifier is associated with a unique semantic representation, and *vice versa* (Geeraerts 1985). It is worth noting that while Langacker, on the opening page of his *Foundations of Cognitive Grammar* (Langacker 1987: 11), is able to endorse the Saussurean conception of the linguistic sign, he is also able to maintain (Langacker 1988: 50) that polysemy constitutes the normal, expected state of affairs in lexical semantics. Indeed, scholars working in the Cognitive Linguistics tradition have often been censured for promoting a "rampant polysemy" (Cuyckens and Zawada 2001: xv), that is, a readiness to associate linguistic forms with an ever-increasing number of distinct senses.

Other linguists have tried to remain true to the semiotic ideal, seeking to minimize the role of polysemy in natural languages (often, though, at the expense of having to postulate additional processes, or levels of representation, in order to account for the range of meaning variation encountered in actual usage). Thus, for Coseriu (1977), polysemes are a matter of usage norms, distinct from the unitary values that constitute the language system. For Kirsner (1993), words are "invariant signals of invariant meaning" (p. 85); polysemy effects arise through the use which speakers make of these linguistic signs. Wunderlich (1993) claims that polysemy, so called, is merely an effect of "conceptual" elaboration of unitary (i.e. non-polysemous) "semantic" representations. Van der Leek (2000) takes a similar line, arguing that words designate "Platonic" (that is, highly general and abstract) concepts, which participate in, but do not uniquely determine, context-specific construals. Concerning phonological representations, it will be recalled that one of the drivers of early generative phonology (Chomsky and Halle 1968) was the desire to associate each morpheme of a language with a single, unique "underlying form", from which all the surface alternants could be derived by rule.

Since variation is not limited to the semantic pole, the possibility arises that deviations from the one meaning ideal may be accompanied by deviations from the one form ideal. Langacker (1987: 398) reports that in his speech, *route* is associated with two distinct phonological shapes, [raʊt] and [ruːt], both pronunciations being possible for the noun, but only the latter for the verb. Orthography suggests that we are here dealing with a single linguistic unit (though the matter is indeed moot). Sometimes, however, orthography is also subject to variation. (Variation at the orthographic level might be referred to as "polygraphy".) Speakers of British-based varieties of English often distinguish, in writing, between "program" and "programme", and between "disk" and "disc". To be sure, the written variants may not be differentiated in pronunciation; they are, however, likely to be differentiated semantically, "program" and "disk" being reserved for computer-related uses. It is again a moot point whether we are here dealing with a single linguistic sign, unified at the phonological pole, or with two different signs differentiated both semantically and orthographically (Love, to appear).

3. The building block metaphor

The semiotic model provides us with a set of linguistic signs, each of which associates a meaning with a phonological form. According to the building block metaphor, complex expressions are formed by assembling these smaller units; conversely, complex expressions can be exhaustively segmented into their component parts. The metaphor requires that each constituent building block have a fixed and determinate semantic and phonological content which it contributes to the whole. Hence, the meaning of a complex expression will be a function of the meanings of its constituent parts, just as the phonological form of a complex expression will result from the alignment of the phonological forms of its constituents.

The metaphor is pervasive in our deliberations on language and its structure; indeed, as Langacker (1991: 186) observes, the metaphor may be unavoidable "for expository purposes", as when we introduce beginning linguistics students to the concept of the morpheme. Yet, paradoxically, it is in the realm of morphology where the metaphor fails most conspicuously. Take the word *butcher*. *Butcher*, like *writer*, appears to contain the agentive suffix *-er*. The semantics fit, as well. Both *butcher* and *writer* characterize a person in terms of what they do. Yet there is no base verb *(to) butch* to which the *-er* morpheme attaches. *Butcher* cannot be exhaustively analysed into its constituent building blocks, even though the word would appear to be morphologically complex.

When it comes to analysing phrasal expressions, problems of segmentation are less likely to arise. (But consider the case of opaque idioms, such as *kick the bucket*,[1] as well as some examples to be discussed in the next section.) Applying the building block metaphor to complex expressions, however, is likely to result in an explosion of polysemes. Take, as an example, the adjective *old*, and its use in expressions such as *old man*, *old friend*, and *old student (of mine)*. In these expressions, *old* does not modify the associated noun in exactly the same way. An "old man" is a man who is advanced in years; an "old friend" is a person who has been a friend (to someone) for a long time (but who need not be advanced in years); an "old student (of mine)" is a person who used to be a student of mine but who no longer is my student. In order for the meanings of these Adj-N combinations to be built up compositionally, we need to postulate three distinct senses of *old*, only one of which is selected for the compositional process. On the other hand, if *old* is indeed polysemous in this way, *old friend* ought to be three-ways ambiguous, with the readings "aged friend", "friend of long standing", and "former friend". This prediction seems not to be entirely correct. If I refer to someone as "an old friend", only the second of these readings is likely to be appropriate.

The example illustrates the fact that a word of a given semantic type may force a specific reading of a word with which it combines. Thus, *old friend* is likely to be interpreted differently from *old man* because of the semantic structure of *friend* (Taylor 1992). The matter was addressed by Pustejovsky (1991), in his study of the ways in which words can mutually "coerce" their readings. *Begin a novel* forces a particular reading of *novel*, namely, "novel-as-text". Contemporaneously, this reading of *novel* triggers an enriched interpretation of *begin*, namely, "begin to read" (see Warren, this volume). We can imagine other mutually coercing interpretations, as when talking of a writer, a typesetter, a translator, a bookbinder, or a book-devouring insect "beginning a novel". Given these coercion effects, we might hesitate to claim that *novel*, or indeed *begin*, is polysemous. We might also begin to question the assumption that word meanings are fixed and determinate entities. For example, how might we characterize the concept that gets coerced into the specific readings "novel-as-text" and "novel-as-object"?

A more general failing of the building block metaphor is that it ignores the possibility that the whole may be organized in ways which go beyond, or which are even at variance with, the properties which are contributed by the parts. Take Langacker's example of a football under the table (Langacker 1987: 279–280). The (literal) interpretation of *football under the table* goes well beyond the compositionally derived meaning of the expression. For example, we would probably picture the football as lying on the floor within an area circumscribed by the table's legs. It is not only that the specifics of this scene are not encoded in the expression; the football, if we consider the matter carefully, is not actually "under" the table at all – the football, that is, is not located at a place that is lower than the place occupied by the table. For the football to be "under" the table, it would have to be under the floor on which the table is standing! Conceptualization of the global scene has forced an elaboration and readjustment of the compositionally derived meaning (Taylor 2002). The matter is equally evident with respect to phonological structure. Typically, *did you* would have the pronunciation [ˈdɪ.dʒʊ], rather than the "compositional" pronunciation [dɪd.juː]. It is not just that the boundary segments of the building blocks [dɪd] and [juː] have mutually influenced each other. Rather, the complex expression has been organized in terms of syllable and foot structure. The component syllables of [ˈdɪ.dʒʊ] do not match up with the units contributed by the component structures; moreover, the two syllables have been structured in terms of a strong–weak relation within a trochaic foot.

The interplay of word meanings (that is, the semantic units which words, in their status as building blocks, contribute to the whole) and the meanings of larger expressions in which the words occur, has come to the fore in studies of constructions. Consider Goldberg's (1995: 29) often-cited example of a person "sneezing the napkin off the table". *Sneeze* does not plausibly belong in the class of caused-motion verbs (*put, push, throw*, etc.). The caused-motion sense of *sneeze* – "cause (a thing) to go (to a place) by sneezing on it" – is contributed by the syntactic construction [V NP PP] in which it occurs. The primacy of the construction over its parts is supported by the fact that in different instantiations of the construction the meanings of the parts are mapped in different ways onto the meanings of the complex expressions (Mandelblit and Fauconnier 2000). Thus, in *sneeze the napkin off the table*, the verb designates the causing activity, whereas in *trot the horse into the stable*, the verb designates the caused activity. Appeal to constructions, then, may again lessen the need to postulate extensive polysemy at the level of words. On the other hand, polysemy is liable to re-emerge at the level of constructions. As argued by Goldberg (1995), the caused-motion construction itself has a number of distinct variants, each of which severely restricts the range of items which are eligible to occur in it.

4. The lexicon and the syntax

Language description is typically couched in terms of a lexicon (which lists the words and their fixed and conventionalized phonological and semantic properties) and a syntax (which lists the rules for the combination of words). Thus, when we study a foreign language, the essential tools are the dictionary and the grammar book. Recent interest in idioms, however, has put in question the validity of this modular view (Jackendoff 1997; Taylor 2002). At issue are not just semantically opaque idioms of the kind *kick the bucket*, which clearly have to be learned as such and which cannot be assembled in the syntax, but the vast inventory of collocations, fixed expressions, formulaic expressions, and constructional idioms.

Consider, for example, Queller's (2001) recent discussion of one use (or, rather, set of uses) of *over*, concerning the expression *all over*. In *water all over the floor*, *over* appears to have the covering sense exemplified in *the tablecloth over the table*, while *all* appears to have its standard quantifying sense. The compositional sense of *water all over the floor*, therefore, would be that there is water covering all of the floor. The problem with this account is that "total coverage" does not capture the distinctive semantic value of *all over*. We should not say of a table cloth, for example, that it is "all over the table", even though the cloth might be completely covering the table (or, at least, the table top). The relevant sense of *all over*, according to Queller, is not so much "total coverage", as "chaotic dispersal". It is for this reason that one might say that there are blood stains all over the table cloth, but not that there are red squares all over the cloth (the red squares being inherent to the design of the table cloth, whereas the blood stains are not). *All over* turns out to be an idiomatic expression, which needs to be separately listed as such in a speaker's mental grammar. Although we can identify its parts (at least, on the phonological level), and perhaps see their relevance to the composite meaning, the expression is not a compositional function of its parts. There could be little point, therefore, in enquiring which of the various senses of *over* is instantiated in *all over*.

Not all uses of *all over* exemplify the chaotic dispersal sense. Consider the expression *He had guilt written all over his face*, in contrast to the oddness of *?He had satisfaction written all over this face*. At issue here is the uncontrolled, or involuntary display of an emotion which interferes with a person's desire to present a front of composure. We might want to say that *all over*, in its status as an idiomatic phrase, is polysemous. But this may not be the appropriate solution. Note that the "uncontrolled display" sense of *all over* is associated with a specific syntactic frame, namely, [NP have EMOTION written all over NP's face]. We are dealing here with a phrasal idiom, some of whose components are lexically specified, the other "slots" in the idiom being able to be filled by any items meeting the idiom's semantic specifications. Again, it could be fruitless to enquire which of its various senses *over*, or indeed *all over*, is contributing to the idiom. Similar remarks apply to lexically fully specified expressions involving *all over*, as when we tell a student that his essay is "all over the place", or say of an experiment that the results are "all over the map".

A comparable situation in the phonological domain is discussed by Bybee and Scheibman (1999). *Don't* may be subject to phonological reduction, even emerging, in *I don't know*, as [ɾə]. Although exemplifying very general processes of reduction which are operative in English, the highly reduced form of *don't* tends to be restricted to the fixed expression *I don't know*, particularly when the expression is used, not to convey the subject referent's ignorance of something (the "compositional" meaning of *don't know*), but to soften a speaker's assertion, or to convey the speaker's polite disagreement. Bybee (2001) emphasizes that the conventionalized pronunciation of *I don't know* (along with its specialized meaning) cannot be regarded as a compositional function of the properties of its parts. It is the whole expression *I don't know*, in both its phonological and semantic aspects, which needs to be listed in a person's mental grammar.

5.   Beyond the models

Although I have focused on some of their problematic aspects, there is a sense in which each of the three models surveyed above is true (or at least, not obviously false). It is entirely legitimate to regard a language as a semiotic system, that is, as a means for associating meanings (or conceptualizations) with phonological (and graphological) forms, the task of the linguist being to identify and to describe the conventionalized associations of form and meaning which the language makes available to its speakers. The building block metaphor also captures an important ingredient of language. It is uncontroversial that speakers do construct new expressions by assembling their smaller parts in new and creative ways, and that hearers, on the whole, are able to interpret these in the sense intended by the speakers. It is equally evident that the creation and interpretation of new utterances is based on knowledge of general patterns of syntagmatic combination which operate over smaller-sized units. To this extent, also, the lexicon–syntax split is fully justified.

Taken together, the cognitive models entail the following idealization of a language:

(i)   A language can be analysed into a lexicon and a syntax. The lexicon lists the words, while the syntax contains general rules for the combination of words.

(ii)   Each word associates a fixed and determinate semantic structure with a fixed and determinate phonological structure.

(iii)   The semantic and phonological properties of a complex expression, as assembled by the syntax, is a compositional function of the semantic and phonological properties of the component words.

Given the above idealizations, polysemy can be straightforwardly and unproblematically defined in terms of a deviation from idealization (ii). Polysemy, namely, consists in the association of a single word form with two or more semantic representations. The need to postulate polysemy follows from idealization (iii). In order to be able to derive the compositional meanings of the complex expressions in which it occurs, it may be necessary for a word to be associated with a range of different meanings, only one of which is selected for a particular expression.

As the discussion in this chapter will have demonstrated, the above idealizations may not be directly applicable to actual language data. The following factors, in particular, distort the ideal situation:

(i)   Complex expressions may indeed be segmented into smaller units. The smaller units are observed to recur in different expressions, and they may well be associated with fairly stable phonological and semantic values. However, these units need not correspond to words, as traditionally defined. The units may comprise multi-word units of various sizes: typical collocations, fixed turns of phrase, formulas, clichés, and all manner of idioms. In the limiting case, the expression itself has unit status.

(ii)   Speakers of a language certainly extract patterns which sanction the combination of smaller units. However, these patterns need not be restricted to the very general phrase structure rules of traditional syntax. They may comprise rather low-level generalizations, which are able to sanction only a small number of instances, or they may have the status of constructional schemas, whose slots can be filled only by items meeting the semantic specifications of the construction. Sometimes, one or more of the slots may be lexically specified, that is, the construction involves the occurrence of particular words. Indeed, knowledge of a word may involve knowledge of the constructions in which it can occur. In the limiting case, the construction may be lexically fully specified.

(iii)   Speakers draw on the resources of their language in order to give expression to particular conceptualizations. Mostly, the available resources allow only a partial and imperfect representation of the desired semantic content. Consequently, the intended meaning of an expression may go beyond, or may even be at variance with, the meaning that is contributed by the parts, in association with the relevant constructional schemas.

Given the extent and the ubiquity of these deviations from the idealizations, it is not surprising that polysemy (understood as the association of related meanings to a single linguistic form) should be such a problematic concept, and one which has engendered so much discussion and controversy. It was not my intention, in this article, to attempt to resolve these controversies. The above discussion may, however, be useful, to the extent that it may throw some light on why the seemingly so straightforward notion of polysemy is so problematic. It also suggests that it may be useful to approach the problematic aspects of polysemy, not so much by a refinement of the concept itself, but by addressing the cognitive models which frame our understanding of it.[2]

Notes

1. The point here is that, although *kick the bucket* can be segmented into words, and can even be regarded as a perfectly regular verb phrase, the (idiomatic) meaning of the expression cannot be distributed over the meanings of its parts.
2. Given my somewhat critical account of the cognitive models discussed in this chapter, it may be asked whether there are other models of language which enable us more accurately to conceptualize the object of our study. Here are two suggestions, which I offer without further discussion, but which I think may be worthy of further investigation:
   (i) The corpus model. Instead of partitioning the facts of a language into a lexicon and a syntax (a dictionary and a grammar book), it may be worth exploring the metaphor of a language as a giant corpus, and to construe knowledge of a language in terms of a mental corpus, comprising memory traces of previously encountered utterances. Words, with their phonological and semantic properties, would then emerge as the summed activation of already encountered instances.
   (ii) The cut-and-paste model. Instead of studying the production of complex expressions in terms of the assembly of smaller units in accordance with the rules of syntax, it may be more appropriate to view language production as a process of sticking together various bits and pieces retrieved from the mental corpus.
   Interestingly, neither model has a place for polysemy, as traditionally understood.

References

Brugman, Claudia
    1981   Story of *over*. M.A. thesis. University of California, Berkeley.
Bybee, Joan
    2001   *Phonology and Language Use*. Cambridge: Cambridge University Press.
Bybee, Joan and Joanne Scheibman
    1999   The effect of usage on degrees of constituency: the reduction of *don't* in English. *Linguistics* 37: 575–596.
Chomsky, Noam
    1988   *Language and Problems of Knowledge*. Cambridge, MA: Massachusetts Institute of Technology Press.
Chomsky, Noam and Morris Halle
    1968   *The Sound Pattern of English*. New York: Harper and Row.

Coseriu, Eugenio
1977   L'Etude fonctionnelle du vocabulaire: précis de lexématique. *Cahiers de léxicologie* 29: 5–23.
Croft, William
1993   The role of domains in the interpretation of metaphors and metonymies. *Cognitive Linguistics* 4: 335–370.
Cuyckens, Hubert and B. Zawada (eds.)
2001   *Polysemy in Cognitive Linguistics*. Amsterdam: Benjamins.
Deane, Paul
1993   Multimodal spatial representations: on the semantic unity of "over" and other polysemous prepositions. Duisburg: Linguistic Agency, University of Duisburg.
Dewell, Robert B.
1994   *Over* again: image-schematic transformations in semantic analysis. *Cognitive Linguistics* 5, 351–380.
Fillmore, Charles
1982   Frame semantics. In: Linguistic Society of Korea (ed.), *Linguistics in the Morning Calm*, 111–138. Seoul: Hanshin.
Foolen, Ad and Frederike van der Leek (eds.)
2000   *Constructions in Cognitive Grammar*. Amsterdam: Benjamins.
Geeraerts, Dirk
1985   Cognitive restrictions on the structure of semantic change. In: Jacek Fisiak (ed.), *Historical Semantics*, 127–153. Berlin: Mouton de Gruyter.
Goldberg, Adèle
1995   *Constructions: A Construction Grammar Approach to Argument Structure*. Chicago, IL: University of Chicago Press.
Jackendoff, Ray
1997   *The Architecture of the Language Faculty*. Cambridge, MA: Massachusetts Institute of Technology Press.
Kirsner, Robert S.
1993   From meaning to message in two theories: cognitive and Saussurean views of the Modern Dutch demonstratives. In: Richard Geiger and Brygida Rudzka-Ostyn (eds.), *Conceptualizations and Mental Processing in Language*, 81–114. Berlin: Mouton de Gruyter.
Kreitzer, Anatol
1997   Multiple levels of schematization: a study in the conceptualization of space. *Cognitive Linguistics* 8: 291–325.
Langacker, Ronald
1987   *Foundations of Cognitive Grammar*, Volume 1. Stanford, CA: Stanford University Press.
1988   A view of linguistic semantics. In: Brygida Rudzka-Ostyn (ed.), *Topics in Cognitive Linguistics*, 49–90. Amsterdam: Benjamins.

46   *John R. Taylor*

1991   *Foundations of Cognitive Grammar*, Volume 2. Stanford, CA: Stanford
              University Press.
Lakoff, George
1987   *Women, Fire, and Dangerous Things: What Categories Reveal about
              the Mind*. Chicago, IL: University of Chicago Press.
Love, Nigel
(to appear)   Rethinking the fundamental assumption of linguistics. In: Hayley G.
              Davis and Talbot J. Taylor (eds.), *Rethinking Linguistics*. Richmond:
              Curzon Press.
Mandelblit, Nili and Gilles Fauconnier
2000   How I got myself arrested: underspecificity in grammatical blends
              as a source for constructional ambiguity. In: Foolen and van der Leek
              (2000), 167–189.
Pinker, Steven
1994   *The Language Instinct*. New York: William Morrow.
Pustejovsky, James
1991   The generative lexicon. *Computational Linguistics* 17: 409–441.
Queller, Kurt
2001   A usage-based approach to modeling and teaching the phrasal lexicon.
              In: Martin Pütz, Suzanne Niemeier and René Dirven (eds.), *Applied
              Cognitive Linguistics*, Volume 2, 55–83. Berlin: Mouton de Gruyter.
Ravin, Yael and Claudia Leacock (eds.)
2000   *Polysemy: Theoretical and Computational Approaches*. Oxford:
              Oxford University Press.
Sapir, Edward
1921   *Language*. New York: Harcourt, Brace and World.
de Saussure, Ferdinand
1964 [1915] *Cours de linguistique générale*. Paris: Payot.
Searle, John R.
1969   *Speech Acts: An Essay in the Philosophy of Language*. Cambridge:
              Cambridge University Press.
Taylor, John R.
1992   Old problems: adjectives in Cognitive Grammar. *Cognitive Linguistics*
              3: 1–46.
1995   *Linguistic Categorization*. Oxford: Oxford University Press.
2002   *Cognitive Grammar: An Introduction*. Oxford: Oxford University
              Press.
2003   Near synonyms as coextensive categories: "high" and "tall" revisited.
              Language Sciences 25: 263–284.
(to appear)   Polysemy's paradoxes. *Language Sciences*.
Tyler, Andrea and Vyvyan Evans
2001   Reconsidering prepositional polysemy networks: the case of *over*.
              Language 77: 724–765. (Reprinted in this volume.)

Vandeloise, Claude
 1990   Representation, prototypes, and centrality. In: Savas Tsohatzidis (ed.),
             Meanings and Prototypes, 403–437. London: Routledge.
Van der Leek, Frederike
 2000   Caused-motion and the "bottom-up" role of grammar. In: Foolen and
             van der Leek (2000), 301–331.
Wunderlich, Dieter
 1993   On German *um*: semantic and conceptual aspects. *Linguistics* 31:
             111–133.

Polysemy: past and present

Brigitte Nerlich

1. Introduction

It is fairly well known that research into polysemy began with the work of the French semanticist Michel Bréal in the late 19th century.[1] It is less well known that the "multiplicity of meaning", with or without the label "polysemy", was quite well researched by students of literature and by lexicographers well before Bréal. It should come as no surprise that the major pathways of polysemous sense extension, namely metaphor, metonymy and synecdoche have also been on the philosophical and linguistic agenda for a long time.

To fully understand the import of the concept of polysemy for contemporary semantic thought, it is useful to reconstruct some of the contexts in which it appeared for the first time. We hope that such a reconstruction may lead to a new evaluation of contemporary concepts and theories. However, one should not expect this work to be definitive, because the field will undoubtedly change under the pressure of new historical discoveries: the historical survey modifying the present status of polysemy research, this latter in turn influencing the future of the former (see Eco 1996: 744).

The first part of this survey will trace the development of various research traditions analysing the pathways of polysemous sense extension before the term "polysemy" was introduced into general linguistics by Bréal in 1887. This means, effectively, looking at research done in the wide field of rhetoric, in the philosophy of metaphor, in etymology and in lexicography, where it was essential to find elegant and plausible ways to write lexical entries for words with multiple meanings. The second part of this survey will be devoted to Bréal's more revolutionary treatment of polysemy and the research leading up to it. In the last part we shall give a brief and necessarily incomplete survey of post-Bréalian research into polysemy.[2]

2.   Metaphor, metonymy, and synecdoche as pathways of polysemous sense extension

Metaphor has had three relatively unrelated waves of fame in the 20th century: the first brought about by Ivor A. Richards, Kenneth Burke, and Max Black in their reflections on metaphor published between 1936 and 1962 (Richards 1936; Burke 1962; Black 1962); the second triggered by Roman Jakobson's papers "Two aspects of language and two types of aphasic disturbances" and "The metaphoric and metonymic poles", published in the 1950s (Jakobson 1983 [1956b], 1956a);[3] the third, more recent one, was unleashed by the George Lakoff and Mark Johnson book *Metaphors We Live By* in the 1980s (Lakoff and Johnson 1980; see also Lakoff and Turner 1989; Lakoff and Johnson 1999). *Metaphors We Live By* has become a standard text for those interested in what has now become a new paradigm in linguistics, namely cognitive semantics. One of the basic claims of this new research paradigm is that "a lexical item is typically polysemic – comprising a family of interrelated senses, forming a network centred on a prototypical value. Although the precise array of senses conventionally associated with the expression is not fully predictable, neither is it arbitrary – as the network evolves from the prototype, each extension is MOTIVATED in some cognitively natural fashion, and often in accordance with a general pattern or principle" (Langacker 1988: 392). Some of the most important patterns or principles are metaphor, metonymy and synecdoche.

Although well aware that modern reflections on metaphor have their roots in Aristotle, and in Greek and Latin rhetoric, and that they have parallels in early 20th-century developments, such as the work done by Burke or Black (see Turner 1999), only a small number of cognitive linguists seem to appreciate just how much research into metaphor, as well as metonymy and synecdoche, was done during the 19th and early 20th centuries in the fields of rhetoric, lexical semantics and philosophy (see Smith 1982; Jäkel 1999; Nerlich 1998; Nerlich and Clarke 1997, 1999, 2000a, 2000b, 2001). These figures of speech were gradually discovered as not only having an aesthetic, but also an essentially cognitive function.

The foundations for this fundamentally new research into metaphor and other core figures of speech were laid in the 17th and 18th centuries with the work of Giambattista Vico, John Locke, Johann Gottfried Leibniz and Johann Heinrich Lambert amongst the philosophers, and César Chesneau Du Marsais amongst the grammarians.

Like many of his philosophical colleagues, Locke had still been sceptical about the value of metaphors, as they seemed to obscure the direct link between words and ideas, but at the same time he saw that metaphors were unavoidable and deeply rooted in our language and thought. He gave the following examples for the metaphorical grounding of mental concepts:

> It may also lead us a little towards the Original of all our Notions and Knowledge, if we remark, how great a Dependence our Words have on common sensible Ideas; and how those, which are made use of to stand for Actions and Notions quite removed from sense, have their rise from thence, and from obvious sensible Ideas are transferred to more abstruse Significations ... v.g. to Imagine, Apprehend, Comprehend, Adhere, Conceive, Instill, Disgust, Disturbance, Tranquility, andc. are all Words taken from the Operations of sensible Things, and applied to certain modes of Thinking. (Locke 1975 [1689]: III, i: 5)

Locke's most quoted example was perhaps that the Latin word for "mind", that is, *spiritus*, had its origin in the word for "breath".[4]

Leibniz, who took up this example, approached the problem not only from a philosophical angle, but also from a decidedly etymological one and came to the conclusion that language was in fact permeated by metaphors, a view that became immediately popular. The German linguist Johann Christoph Adelung, for example, pointed out almost a century after Locke, in his 1798 entry on "metaphor" for his grammatical critical dictionary: "In point of fact most of our words are metaphors. The word *spirit* when designating a spiritual rational entity is a metaphor, as it actually means breath" (Adelung 1798: 192).[5]

In his *Nouveaux essais sur l'entendement humain* published in 1765 (Leibniz 1981), a reply to Locke's *Essay on human understanding* (1975 [1689]), Leibniz also stressed the importance of tropes, especially of metaphor, metonymy and synecdoche for the changes in meanings that one can observe everywhere (see also Leibniz 1882, 1956).

A contemporary of Leibniz, the French philosopher and etymologist Anne Robert Jacques Turgot, continued the reflection on how figures of speech can bring about changes in the meanings of words. But he also pointed out, in a thoroughly modern way, that for these figures to work and these changes to occur, more than just "rhetoric" is needed. The use and uptake of figures of speech depends on our ways of conceptualizing the world, of seeing the world in certain ways.[6] What one would nowadays call "polysemization" is for him the result of the way in which the principal idea of a word spills over onto the secondary idea. Then the word is used in its new extension for other ideas, based solely on the secondary meaning without regard for the primitive one – as when we say *un cheval ferré d'argent* (a horse "ironed" with silver). New metaphors are coined with this new meaning in mind, and then one on top if the other, until we reach a point when a meaning emerges which is completely opposed to the original meaning of the word (Turgot 1756: 105b).

Du Marsais, like Turgot a contributor to Diderot's *Encyclopédie*, developed a rhetoric of ordinary language use in which he studied the multiplication of meanings as well as the forgetting of the original meaning, two processes that go hand in hand. As early as 1730 he claimed that catachresis, or the use of a word in a context that differs from its proper application, was fundamental to the extension and multiplication of meanings, and he rejected the widespread view that catachresis was nothing but the "incorrect" (mis- or ab-) use of a word (see Nerlich 2000). He illustrates this point of view with the same example that Turgot used some time later.

> ... it is the ordinary costume to nail iron horseshoes under the feet of horses, something we call "ferrer un cheval": ... if it so happens that instead of iron we use silver we say that "les chevaux sont ferré d'argent" instead of inventing an entirely new word which nobody would understand. ... And so "ferrer" signifies by extension shoeing a horse with silver instead of iron. (Du Marsais 1977 [1730]: 45)

Another contemporary German philosopher, Lambert (1764), was even more keenly aware than Leibniz and Turgot of the ubiquity of metaphors and their importance for language and thought. And like them he was interested in the process of polysemization.

> It has however been known for a long time that we compare the visible with the invisible, the world of the body with the world of the spirit, sensations with thoughts, and that we use the same words for either. Hence words necessarily acquire a double and sometimes a multiple meaning. Having light in the room and a light in one's thoughts are examples for this way of speaking. (Lambert 1764: Aleth. I., §45)

Metaphors are central to Lambert's "semantic tectonics" (see Ungeheuer 1980). One quote from Lambert's *Neues Organon* (1764) has to suffice here:

... all the words of a language could be divided into three classes, the first of which doesn't need any definition, as one points to the thing itself in its totality, and as one can make an immediate connection between word, concept, and thing. Another class uses the words of the first class in a metaphorical way and uses a *tertium comparationis* instead of a definition. The third class comprises those words which have to be defined, and this insofar as one uses the words of the first two classes to do so. The words of the third class thus defined can again be used for definitions. It is obvious that the words of the third class can also be used metaphorically and that most of them are used in this way already. (Lambert 1764: II, ii: 45)

Lambert tried to provide a solution to a problem that still haunts modern linguists, namely the question: where does meaning come from? For Lambert, it arises from ostensive definitions,[7] on which metaphors then build the semantic structure of language. Modern cognitive semanticists would rather stress the importance of perception, "preconceptual structures" and image schemata, as such a foundation. They have discovered the human body as the main source of "meaning".

Embodiment has become one of the most central tenets of cognitive semantics. Meaning is seen as grounded in the nature of our bodies and in our interaction with the physical, social and cultural environment we live in. This means that concepts are grounded in our bodily experience and then elaborated by structures of imagination, such as metaphor and metonymy. This unity of the inner and outer, the corporal and the mental, had already been stressed by Johann Wolfgang von Goethe. According to him we always spiritualize the corporal and anthropomorphize the mental, and this mainly through metaphor. The philosopher of metaphor, Alfred Biese, quotes from Goethe's poem *Procemion* (Goethe 1816):

> So weit das Ohr, so weit das Auge reicht,
> Du findest nur Bekanntes, das Ihm gleicht,
> Und Deines Geistes Feuerflug
> Hat schon am Gleichnis, hat am Bild genug.
> (Quoted in Biese 1893: 120)

> [As far as ear can reach, or eyesight dim,
> Thou findest but the known resembling Him;
> How high so'er thy fiery spirit hovers,
> Its simile and type it straight discovers.]
> (http://www.everypoet.com/archive/poetry/Goethe/goethe_procemion.htm)

Goethe very much agreed with the 18th-century Neapolitan philosopher Vico, who was one of the most eminent thinkers in the field of "metaphor". Unlike Kant, who only reluctantly accorded imagination and language an important place in his philosophy (but who corresponded with Lambert about this problem), Vico had given language and *imagination*, not reason, a central status in his conception of the mind. "In all languages," he wrote in his *Scienza Nuova*, "the greater part of expressions referring to inanimate objects are taken by transfer from the human body and its parts, from human senses and human passions ... Ignorant man makes himself into the yardstick of the universe" (quoted in Ullmann 1962: 214; see Vico 1948 [1725]).

According to Danesi (1990), Vico saw the relevance of imagination in the fact that it allows us to understand reality – and more.

> For when we wish to give utterance to our understanding of spiritual things, we must seek aid from our imagination to explain them, and like painters, form human images of them. (Vico quoted in Danesi 1990: 228)

A last example of the sustained reflection on metaphor and other figures of speech in the 18th century has to be the famous passage from Du Marsais's book *Des Tropes*. In this passage, which prefigures much of modern semantics, Du Marsais makes it quite clear that the use of figures is as necessary to language as breathing to life. For him there is nothing so natural, ordinary and common as the use of figures of speech in daily discourse – even that of fishwives (Du Marsais 1977 [1730]).[8] As Lakoff and Turner say in their book *More Than Cool Reason*:

> Metaphor is a tool so ordinary that we use it unconsciously and automatically, with so little effort that we hardly notice it. ... metaphor is an integral part of our ordinary everyday thought and language. ... [It] allows us to understand ourselves and our world in ways that no other modes of thought can. (Lakoff and Turner 1989: xi)

In the 19th century the exploration of metaphor and other figures of speech began to be an albeit small part of the new science of historical linguistics, which detached it somewhat from the anthropological and philosophical explorations of the previous centuries. Metaphor, metonymy, generalization and specialization became part and parcel of the instruments used in historical semantics used to study and classify types of semantic change and of meaning extension. This early form of semantics was influenced by rhetoric, association psychology, and aesthetics (see Nerlich 1992).

Aristotle had distinguished between various forms of mental association: by simultaneity, succession, similarity, and contrast (*De memoria*, 2). In 1739 the Scottish philosopher David Hume had tried to establish laws that govern the mental world and which would be analogous to the law of gravity so spectacularly discovered by Newton. He postulated that these laws were laws of association: by *similarity*, by *contiguity* in space or time, and by *cause and effect*. This was the beginning of a long-standing research programme in association psychology, which was only challenged after the advent of Gestalt psychology at the beginning of the 20th century. In 1829 James Mill summarized the by then well-established laws of association as (i) contiguity in time; (ii) contiguity in space; (iii) the relations of cause and effect, of means and end, of part and whole; (iv) contrast or similarity; (v) equal or different forces directed at an object; (vi) objects which by accident are called by similarly sounding names. He then reduced these six laws to two: the law of Simultaneity and the law of Resemblance or Affinity (see Ritter 1972: 550).

Linguists working with the "laws" of rhetoric, such as metaphor and metonymy, could easily see the affinity between these laws of rhetoric and the more scientific "laws of association". They therefore developed a semantics based on a theory of meaning where meanings were equated with mental representations and the associations between mental representations, and where changes in meaning were equated with changes in associations. The first to formulate this new research programme for historical semantics was Christian Karl Reisig, a classicist, who gave lectures on the syntax, etymology and semantics of Latin in about 1829, and stated that:

> The basis for the development of ideas in words is the association of thoughts in the group of representations. ... However, certain associations of ideas are preferred in human representation, and rhetoric has given them certain names, which however are to some extent also appropriate for semasiology, namely *synecdoche, metonymy*, and *metaphor*. Insofar as these so-called figures aim at something aesthetic, they certainly belong to rhetoric, even when individuals make use of them; but insofar as a usage based on these figures of speech has been established in a particular language, and this is particular to the nation, these figures should be dealt with here. (Reisig 1890 [1839]: 2; emphasis added)

Quite independently of these advances in historical linguistics and its new branch "semantics" (or as Reisig called it "semasiology"), the reflection on figures of speech also continued to be part of an ongoing philosophical examination of the relationship between language, thought and imagination, triggered in part by Kant's neglect of language and in part by Kant's analysis of aesthetic judgements (e.g. Herder, Goethe, Jean Paul, Gerber, Vischer, Nietzsche, Biese, Mauthner) (see Schumacher 1997; Nerlich and Clarke 2001).

The analysis of metaphor also continued to be part of an ongoing study of tropes and figures of speech in the more applied fields of rhetoric, poetics and stylistics (e.g. Fontanier, Gross, Kleinpaul, Brinkmann, Wackernagel), an approach which was only partially integrated into the linguistic current of thought on metaphor and which was rejected as mere classificationism by most of the philosophers of metaphor.

By the mid-19th century the linguistic and the philosophical approaches to metaphor began to intermesh in the works of certain scholars (such as Gerber, Wegener, Biese, Mauthner, Stählin, and Cassirer), who looked back for inspiration to earlier philosophico-linguistic studies of metaphor by Vico and Lambert for example. They all recognized the crucial role of metaphor in language and in the structuring of thought and set the stage for such 20th-century developments as Karl Bühler's declaration that metaphor is funda-mental to all concept formation (Bühler 1990 [1934]).

Continuing the 18th-century tradition of stressing the ubiquity of meta-phor in human thought and language, the linguist and philosopher Gustav Gerber (1884) pointed out that there is no real difference between "literal" language and "figurative" language, only between what Hermann Paul (1920 [1886]) later called usual and occasional or established and creative uses of language. For Gerber all language is figurative or pictorial from its inception. Those meanings which have acquired a certain stability through usage can be called "literal" as opposed to those meanings whose special status is highlighted through the use of tropes and figures of speech, which we then can call "figurative". However, both types of meaning are only understood insofar as those who know the language establish connections between the "literal" or the "figurative" meaning and other words in a language (Gerber 1871–1874, II, 1: 21, quoted by Knobloch 1988: 257). He also stressed that the meaning of words and sentences can only be understood in the context of their use and that the meaning of words is therefore never fixed but always flexible and adaptable (Gerber 1884: 104). The meaning of words and sen-tences always has to be "figured out" in text and context.

Based on work by Vico, Lambert, Goethe and Gerber, Alfred Biese then elaborated, at the end of the 19th century, a philosophy of metaphor, which, well before Mark Johnson (1987), proposed a close link between "the body and the mind" as the basis for metaphor. He wrote: "metaphor is therefore not a poetic trope, but an original form of intuition for thought". For Biese, metaphor is the most essential inner schema of the human mind" (Biese 1893: VI). Biese was one of the most outspoken advocates of a philosophy of the metaphoric according to which metaphor was neither just a "figure of speech", nor just a poetic fiction or decoration, but was regarded as underlying the structure and evolution of human thought and language.

A more empirical study of what Eve Sweetser calls the "Mind-as-Body Metaphor" can be found in Hans Kurath's 1921 Chicago dissertation on the semantic sources of the words for the emotions in Sanskrit, Greek, Latin, and the Germanic languages:

> Kurath (1921) notes that Indo-European words for the emotions are very frequently derived from words referring to physical actions or sensations accompanying the relevant emotions, or to the bodily organs affected by those physical reactions. (Sweetser 1990: 28)

Although the link between the historical development of emotion words and the psychosomatic nature of the emotions is not as fundamental as Kurath thinks, we can see here a first insight into the metaphorical nature of expressions such as "my anger boiled over" which have so frequently been studied in modern literature on emotions and metaphors (see Koevesces 2000).

While philosophers such as Biese explored the all-pervasive influence of metaphor on language and thought, linguists continued to study the processes and results of metaphorization in language, and psychologists began to explore what Gilles Fauconnier has recently called "backstage cognition", that is, "how language works in concert with 'behind the scenes' understandings and cognitive processes" (Fauconnier 1998: 277).

In the following we shall first investigate how philosophers and linguists analysed the results of the use of figurative language, namely the increase in the spectrum of meanings of a word, what Bréal called "polysemy", then how Bréal revolutionized this study.

3. Polysemy research before Bréal

The modern term *polysemy* was popularized by Bréal in 1887 (Bréal 1991 [1887]). Most modern linguists dealing with the topic of polysemy refer to this crucial date, but they rarely look further back into the past (but see Nerlich and Clarke 1997).

The roots of the *concept* of "polysemy" lie in Greek philosophy, that is, the debate surrounding the problem of the naturalness or arbitrariness of signs as debated in Plato's (429–347 B.C.) *Cratylus*. In his account of Plato's contribution to linguistics, Fred Householder points out that

> Democritus [460/457–mid-4th century B.C.] (as quoted in Proclus' commentary on the *Cratylus* 16) offered four arguments (with four specially coined names) in favour of arbitrariness: (a) "homonymy" or "polysemy", i.e., the same sequence of phonemes may be associated with two or more unrelated meanings; (b) "polyonymy" or "isorrophy", i.e., the existence of synonyms; (c) "metonymy", i.e., the fact that words and meanings change; (d) "nonymy", i.e. the non-existence of single words for simple or familiar ideas. (Householder 1995: 93)

Polysemy meant primarily what was later to be called "homonymy", referring to the multiple, but *unrelated* meanings of a word. Bréal still subsumed homonymy under the heading of polysemy.

The term *polyonymy* was also used by the Stoics studying how one and the same object can receive many different names, how it can become "many-named" or *polyonymous*.

During the Middle Ages the interpretation of the Holy Scriptures came up against the problem of polysemy, a polysemy that was acknowledged, but one that had to be tamed (by the theory of the "four senses"). One of those who marvelled at the polysemous profundity of the Scriptures was Gilbert of Stanford, who compared them with

> a rapid river that flows by producing new senses which, as it waves and whirls, come one after the other in such a way that no single one annuls the other; instead they accumulate and increasingly enrich this immense treasure of divine wisdom; everyone, according to one's own intellectual ability, can glean something from this inexhaustible storage of senses. (Eco 1996: 739)

The first to use the term *polysemous* in a relatively modern sense was Dante, who wrote about the polysemous character of the poem: "Istius operis non est simplex sensus, immo dici potest polysemum, hoc est plurium sensum" (This work doesn't have one simple meaning, on the contrary, I say that it can be polysemous, that is can have many meanings) (quoted in *OED* 1989, Vol. XII: polysemous, p. 75, col. 1). As Eco points out:

> When presenting his poem to Cangrande della Scala, Dante makes immediately clear that it has to be read as a *"polisemos"* ("polysemic") message. One of the most celebrated examples of what Dante means by polysemy is given in his analysis of some verses of Psalm 113, *In exit Israel de Aegypto*. Following the mediaeval theory [of the four senses, BN], Dante says concerning the first verse of the Psalm: If we look at the letter it means the exodus of the sons of Israel from Egypt at the time of Moses; if we look at the allegory, it means our redemption through Christ; if we look at the moral sense it means the conversion of the soul from the misery of sin to the state of grace; if we look at the mystical sense it means the departure of the sanctified spirit from the servitude of this corruption to the freedom of the eternal glory. (Eco 1996: 741)

The difference between the old reading of the bible and Dante's is that Dante is actually "taking a way of reading the bible as an example of how to read his own mundane poem!" (Eco 1996: 741.) The debate about the literal or figurative, the single or multiple meaning of the bible continued throughout the 16th and 17th centuries and is still with us today (see McFague 1983).

Thinking about meaning, language and its relation to the real and spiritual world advanced enormously during the Renaissance (see Waswo 1987), but real mundane research into the multiplicity of meaning only began in the 18th century, with the study of neologisms, synonyms and the figures of speech. The emancipation of semantics or the study of meaning from religious thought was followed by the emancipation of semantics from etymology or the quest for the true original meaning of a word.

In the early 19th century the literary scholar August Wilhelm Schlegel spoke about the difficulties encountered when dealing with "les termes *polysémantiques*" in dictionaries (Schlegel 1832: 42) and the etymologist August Friedrich Pott pointed out in 1861:

> that even without the creation of new words a language can be enriched through the new conceptual use of old words (Polysemantics [*Polysemantie*]) alone, at least on its internal level, that is, semantically, linguistic structures can gain an extraordinary depth and focus. (Pott 1861: 5)

Historical linguists and lexicographers became increasingly interested in the multiplicity of meaning from the point of view of etymology, historical lexicography or historical semantics. As we have seen, figures of speech, such as metaphor, metonymy and synecdoche provided lexicographers with instant ways of charting the development of the multiple meanings of words. However, lexicographers were no longer merely looking for the true, original, first and etymological meaning of words, but came to examine how words were used to make sense by those who used them in actual texts; they looked at the various "readings" of a word (a theme taken up again in Schlieben-Lange 1997). They were interested in finding the connections between the meanings of polysemous words, in finding patterns in the evolution of meaning and in putting order into the meanings of lexical entries – again a problem that is still with us, especially in computational linguistics and natural language processing.

4.   Bréal's study of polysemy

Bringing this emancipation of semantics from etymology to a head, Bréal felt compelled to create the term *polysémie* at the end of the 19th century because he wanted to establish semantics as a new branch of *general* linguistics, independent of etymology and lexicography. This is the reason why this term and Bréal's research into polysemy were the starting point for a whole new tradition of studies into polysemy. From looking at polysemy in disembodied lexical entries, Bréal turned to polysemy as a phenomenon of language use, language acquisition, language change and even neurolinguistics *avant la lettre*.

Bréal knew that, diachronically, polysemy stems from the fact that the new meanings or values that words acquire in use (through extension, restriction, metaphor, etc.) do not automatically eliminate the old ones – polysemy is therefore the result of semantic innovation. The new and the old meanings exist in parallel (Bréal 1924 [1897]: 143–144; English translation 1964 [1900]: 139–140) (see Blank, this volume, and Blank 1997).

And yet, synchronically, or in language use, polysemy does not really exist (it is rather an artefact of lexicographers) – sense selection in the comprehension process is actually not a problem at all. In the context of discourse a word always has one meaning – except, one should point out, in jokes and puns (see Taylor, this volume). (Sense selection is, however, a problem for computers – see Kilgarriff, this volume; Wilks, this volume.) The most important factor that brings about the multiplication of meanings diachronically and that helps us to "reduce" the multiplicity of meanings synchronically is the context of discourse, a fact already mentioned by Leibniz. We understand polysemous words because the words are always used in the context of a discourse and a situation, which eliminate all the adjoining meanings in favour of only the one in question (Bréal 1991 [1887]: 156–157).

However, in the constant dialectical give and take between synchrony and diachrony, and between meaning and understanding, or what Traugott and Blank call in Gricean terms conversational and conventional implicature (Traugott 1988; Blank 1997: 366–369), incremental changes in the meaning of words occur, insofar as hearers, having understood a word in a certain context in a slightly divergent way, become themselves speakers and might use a word in the newly understood way in yet another context, which again brings about a different type of understanding, and so on. In the long run these slight variations in use and uptake might lead to major semantic changes (see Turgot 1756).

More sudden shifts in meaning are brought about by the use of metaphor and metonymy. Aristotle in *The Rhetoric* had already remarked that "strange words simply puzzle us; ordinary words convey only what we know already; it is from metaphor that we can best get hold of something fresh" (Smith 1982: 128). There are also shifts in meaning which have a more social than poetic root, as when the word *operation*, studied by Bréal, means something different according to the social context in which it is used (by a mathematician, a general, a surgeon, and so on). Analysing the multiplication of meanings based on the speakers' and hearers' social and cognitive needs and activities was central to Bréal's semantics.

Bréal was fascinated by the fact that when talking to each other we neither get confused by the multiplicity of meanings that a word can have, some of which are listed in dictionaries of usage, nor are we bothered with the etymological ancestry of a word, traced by historical dictionaries.

Both the dictionary of usage and the historical dictionary classify the meanings of polysemous words, which have been produced over time by a nation. This is a *social* (abstract and decontextualized) classification, whereas the classification of meanings in the head of a speaker and hearer is in each case an *individual* (concrete and contextual) classification. Bréal has in mind an "isosynchronic competence", a half-conscious type of user knowledge, which only works inside concrete situations (see Desmet and Swiggers 1995: 283). Modern polysemy research still debates whether it should predominantly deal with the former type of polysemy or with the latter, and how to reconcile the one with the other.

Bréal observed that most of the time it is the latest, most modern meaning of the word, yesterday's or today's meaning, with which we first become familiar (Bréal 1991 [1884]: 149) – something recently rediscovered in England:

> In 1985, the department of English at the University of Birmingham ran a computer analysis of words as they are actually used in English and came up with some surprising results. The primary dictionary meaning of words was often far adrift from the sense in which they were actually used. *Keep*, for instance, is usually defined as to retain, but in fact the word is much more often employed in the sense of continuing, as in "keep cool" and "keep smiling". *See* is only rarely required in the sense of utilizing one's eyes, but much more often used to express the idea of knowing, as in "I see what you mean". *Give*, even more interestingly, is most often used, to quote the researcher, as "mere verbal padding", as in "give it a look" or "give a report".
> (Bryson 1990: 143)

Language understanding and language acquisition follow the opposite route of language change. In both cases, the last, not the first or primitive meaning of a word is the basic meaning. In modern parlance one would say that the most salient, not the most "literal" meaning is the one that we acquire first and also use and understand first (see Giora 1997).

Bréal therefore wondered at how children acquire word meanings. He thought that: "In order to recognize how meanings are arranged in our heads, the surest way is to see how they got in there in the first place" (Bréal 1991 [1884]: 149).

> The child who hears a word first pronounced retains it with the meaning with which he has heard it used, and he associates it in his thought with the object itself to which it was applied, and to no other. We could say that for him all names are at first proper names. If a little later he hears the same word applied to other similar objects, then he learns to generalize the meaning. ...
> Let us assume that the same word returns in another context, with another meaning [*valeur*]. If the two meanings are not too far apart, the child senses that it is the same word; he perceives the connexion between the two meanings and, taking stock of the distance travelled, he extends his initial concept. ... If on the other hand, the two meanings are too distant, he does not try to connect

them, and he takes account of the new meaning as if dealing with a separate word. (Bréal 1991 [1884]: 149)

Bréal was acutely aware of the fact that the semantic, cognitive, and developmental side of language studies was not yet on a par with the advances made in the study of phonetics, of the more physiological side of language. In his article "How words are classified in our mind" (Bréal 1991 [1884]), Bréal appeals to the future to supply us with insights into the cognitive aspects of human language and writes:

When we compare intelligence to a file cabinet in which ideas are arranged in order, or to a photographic plate on which images are deposited, or to an instrument whose various strings vibrate in turn, it is clear that these are merely analogies. In fact, the true nature of intellectual phenomena is unknown to us. We perceive the effects, but the cause remains hidden. We are obliged to transpose facts of a higher order into the language of the five senses. To be precise, we should speak neither of ideas nor of words, for there are no such things: there are only states, the habits of our brain and the movements of our vocal apparatus. But if we spoke in this way no one would understand us. Thus it is better to speak in an approximate way, while waiting for the establishment of the science of human intelligence which one of our former colleagues, one of the great figures of the Institute, Claude Bernard, liked to call the science of the twentieth century. (Bréal 1991 [1884]: 151)

With Bréal semantics as a linguistic discipline made a first step into this future, a future in which we are still participating and to which we are still contributing beyond the end of the 20th century, the century of psycholinguistics, artificial intelligence, brain scanning and neuropsychology.

5.   Polysemy research from Bréal to the present

As we have seen, Bréal had provided the conditions for new trends in polysemy research, in general linguistics, in sociolinguistics, in psycholinguistics, and in the study of language acquisition. By the beginning of the 20th century a shift was noticeable from accommodating polysemy in *historical* semantics towards observing and explaining polysemy in *synchronic* semantics, as the study of *la langue* as well as the study of lexical fields. The turn from the 19th to the 20th century also saw a steady influx of new types of psychology which started to compete with association psychology. There were the act psychology of Franz Brentano, the physiological and "cultural" psychology of Wilhelm Wundt, and the psychology of the unconscious of Eduard Hartmann, Carl Gustav Jung and Sigmund Freud, Gestalt psychology, and *Denk*-psychology as developed by Oswald Külpe and Karl Bühler. As in the days of association psychology, all these psychologies had an influence on how linguists studied word meaning, polysemy, vagueness, and semantic change.

Linguists, such as Karl Otto Erdmann and Hans Sperber, began to distinguish between the fundamental semantic value of a word and its emotionally charged secondary meanings (Erdmann 1910 [1900]). According to Sperber (1923), semantic change is driven by emotions. For Sperber semantic change can only be studied as a change in an emotionally "charged" *field* of words.

The Swedish scholar Gustaf Stern tried to integrate all psychological and linguistic approaches to meaning in his 1931 book on semantic change. As Michael K. Smith pointed out in his review of *Metaphors We Live By*, "Stern's masterful book has an excellent discussion of metaphor which includes a much broader taxonomy and numerous examples of each type. In many places Stern is theoretically close to the authors and even applies the term "gestalt" to the relationship between words and concepts" (Smith 1982: 131–132). Stern also developed an elaborate taxonomy of types of polysemy, as summarized in Nerlich and Clarke (1997).

Despite these advances in a psychologically-inspired semantics, little was known about the actual psychological processes underlying the creation and understanding of metaphor, a major field of research in modern theories of blending and conceptual integration. The linguist Philipp Wegener had pointed the way towards the study of these processes. He stated as early as 1885 that sentence understanding in general and metaphor understanding in particular are based on a filtering and blending process. The predicate (the new) is seen through the lens or filter of the exposition (the given, which is either the co-text of the utterance or the situational context), and the exposition is filtered through the predicate. When a word is used in the co-text of a sentence the collocation with other words filters out those mental representations which are congruent in this sentence. The others drop below the level of consciousness (see Wegener 1991 [1885]: 50).

But a new psychology of language was needed to lead to real advances in this area. This new psychology gradually emerged at the beginning of the 20th century. The old association psychology, with its notions of contiguity and similarity inherited from Hume and which had structured most of 19th-century metaphor research up to and including Wilhelm Wundt, was replaced by a psychology of consciousness and thinking, developed mostly in Würzburg, and by a new Gestalt psychology developed mainly in Berlin. Insights from both traditions were merged in empirical research into the understanding of metaphors, especially in the works of Bühler and Wilhelm Stählin (1913), who both explored metaphor as a process of conceptual integration or *Sphärenmischung*.

These advances in the psychology of metaphor and polysemy were accompanied by advances in the sociology of polysemy. The polysemy of words was explained by looking at how different social groups use one and the same word for different purposes. An example (already found in Bréal) for the social differentiation underlying some types of polysemy was the word *operation*, as used by a mathematician, a general or a surgeon, for example (Meillet 1921 [1905]: 193). The end-point and *summa* of this tradition of studying polysemy from a linguistic, conceptual, psychological and sociological point of view was the work of the semanticist Stephen Ullmann (1951).

There followed a period of polysemous latency, so to speak, after the advent of transformational generative grammar with its focus on syntax and later feature semantics. However, polysemy was not completely forgotten, as illustrated by the research undertaken by Hans Blumenberg (1960), Uriel Weinreich (1962, 1996), Harald Weinrich (1967), James McCawley (1968), Jurij Apresjan (1974), Charles Fillmore (1975), Andrew Ortony (1975), and Alfonso Caramazza and Ellen Grober (1976).

At the same time a new wave of polysemy research, under the heading of *poly-isotopie* and *polyphonie*, developed in France in the framework of general rhetoric and text analysis. This type of polysemy research harks back to Dante's first use of the word "polysemous" as indicating the multiple readings of a poetic text. It was directly influenced by the rediscovery of work on the multiplicity of meanings, polyphony, and heteroglossia by the Russian philosopher of language Mikhael Bakhtin (see Todorov 1977).

In the Anglo-American world, polysemy was rediscovered with the advent of cognitive semantics in the 1980s (see Brugmann 1981; Lakoff 1987; Langacker 1987; Geeraerts 1997). Cognitive linguists not only rediscovered metaphor and metonymy as pathways and patterns which structure polysemous sense extensions, they also began to reconnect synchronic and diachronic research into meaning.

Synchronic polysemy and historical change of meaning really supply the same data in many ways. No historical shift of meaning can take place without an intervening stage of polysemy ... But if an intervening stage of polysemy was involved, then all the historical data, as evidence of past polysemy relations, is an interesting source of information about the reflection of cognitive structures in language. Even more crucially, the historical order in which senses are added to polysemous words tells us something about the directional relationship between senses; it affects our understanding of cognitive structure to know that spatial vocabulary universally acquires temporal meanings rather than the reverse. (Sweetser 1990: 9)

More recently polysemy has become central to a wide variety of researchers in computational and "generative" semantics, especially in the works of Adam Kilgarriff and James Pustejovsky.

In Germany, polysemy is explored nowadays in a new approach that tries to integrate advances in cognitive semantics with the older tradition of structural semantics, as well as with Gestalt theory and frame theory (see Blank 1997; Koch 1998). These researchers try to steer a fine line between two other approaches to polysemy proposed in Germany: the type of research done in the framework of Manfred Bierwisch's "two-level-semantics" based on generative linguistics (which makes a distinction between a layer of meaning defined by grammar, and a level of interpretation based upon conceptual knowledge) (see Bierwisch 1983; Bierwisch and Schreuder 1992; Sweetser 1986; Schepping 1994; Schwarze and Schepping 1995; Schwarze 1995; Pause, Botz and Egg 1995), and the "simplest systematics" approach recently proposed by Brigitte Schlieben-Lange (1997) and based on the one hand on Gricean principles, on the other on a type of linguistics elaborated by Eugenio Coseriu (see Koch 1998: 126). Bierwisch's approach has been compared to the Langackerian approach favoured by cognitive linguists working in the Lakoff/Johnson tradition by John Taylor in several articles (see Taylor 1994, 1995, 2000).

In France and Belgium, polysemy is studied by Georges Kleiber (1990, 1999), Dirk Geeraerts (1992, 1997), by the cognitively and hermeneutically inspired François Rastier at the CNRS (Rastier 1987), as well as by the semiotically inspired Pierre Cadiot (1992, 1993) at the University Paris VII, by Catherine Fuchs and Bernard Victorri (see Fuchs 1991, 1996; Victorri and Fuchs 1996; Fuchs and Goffic 2002) at the CNRS and many others. Research into the multiplicity of meaning has certainly come a long way since the first efforts at systematizing the study of "la polysémie" were made by Bréal at the end of the 19th century.

Notes

1. Bréal created the term in 1887 (Bréal 1991 [1887]: 156–157) in his review of two seminal books: Arsène Darmesteter's book *La Vie des mots* (1887) and the second edition of Hermann Paul's book *Prinzipien der Sprachgeschichte* (1886 [1880]). He used it again in his famous *Essai de sémantique* in 1897, and from 1900 onwards, when the *Essai* was translated into English, the term *polysemy* made its way into mainstream linguistics.
2. Some parts of this chapter are based on previously published papers, such as Nerlich and Clarke (1997, 2000a, 2001) and Nerlich (1998).
3. Jakobson's work launched two famous schools of thought, integrating research on metaphor with structuralism, hermeneutics and speech act theory via the work of Claude-Levi Strauss and Paul Ricoeur.
4. In his seminal article on the inescapable metaphoricity of language, H. Walter Schmitz quotes the Dutch philosopher Johann Clauberg (1622–1665) as the first to use this example (see Schmitz 1985). Those interested in Locke's views of metaphor and truth should read Oosthuizen Mouton (to appear).
5. All translations are mine, BN.
6. This type of argument can be found again in modern proponents of "cognitive rhetoric", such as Dan Sperber (1975) and Mark Turner (1991).
7. "Explaining the meaning of a word by ostension, by pointing to something to which the word applies, has been variously thought to constitute (i) a form of explanation which provides language with a foundation, (ii) an explanation which, in presupposing a general grasp of language, is only secondary, and (iii) a procedure which does not qualify as a definition or explanation at all. While ostension may serve to point the learner in the right general direction, there is certainly a question as to how much eventual understanding may owe to any such procedure, and how much it requires exposure to word usage over a period of time." (http://www.xrefer.com/entry/553071)
8. This view echoes Lorenzo Valla's 15th-century saying that "housewives sometimes have a better sense of the meaning of words than the greatest philosophers" (quoted in Waswo 1987: 95).

References

Adelung, Johann Christoph
1798   *Metapher. Grammatisch-kritisches Wörterbuch der Hochdeutschen Mundart.* Dritter Theil, von M-Scr. 2. Vermehrte und verbesserte Ausgabe. Leipzig: Breitkopf und Härtel.
Apresjan, Jurij D.
1974   Regular polysemy. *Linguistics* 142: 5–32.
Bierwisch, Manfred
1983   Semantische und konzeptionelle Repräsentation lexikalischer Einheiten. In: Rudolf Ruzicka and Wolfgang Motsch (eds.), *Untersuchungen zur Semantik*, 61–99. Berlin: Akademie-Verlag.
Bierwisch, Manfred and Robert Schreuder
1992   From concepts to lexical items. *Cognition* 4: 23–60.
Biese, Alfred
1893   *Die Philosophie des Metaphorischen. In Grundlinien dargestellt.* Hamburg and Leipzig: Leopold Voss.
Black, Max
1962   *Models and Metaphors: Studies in Language and Philosophy.* Second printing. Ithaca, New York: Cornell University Press, 1963.
Blank, Andreas
1997   *Prinzipien des lexikalischen Bedeutungswandels am Beispiel der romanischen Sprachen.* (Beiheft der Zeitschrift für romanische Philologie, Volume 285.) Tübingen: Max Niemeyer.
Blumenberg, Hans
1960   Paradigmen zu einer Metaphorologie. *Archiv für Begriffsgeschichte* 6: 7–142.
Bréal, Michel
1924 [1897] *Essai de sémantique (Science des significations).* Reprint of the 4th edition. Paris: Gérard Monfort. First edition 1897.
1964   *Semantics: Studies in the Science of Meaning.* New York: Dover Publications. Translation of *Essai de sémantique* – unabridged and unaltered republication of the work first published by Henry Holt and Company in 1900.
1991 [1884] How words are organized in the mind (1884). In: Bréal, *The Beginnings of Semantics. Essays, lectures and reviews*, edited and translated by George Wolf, 145–151. Oxford: Duckworth.
1991 [1887] The history of words (1887). In: Bréal, *The Beginnings of Semantics. Essays, lectures and reviews*, edited and translated by George Wolf, 152–175. Oxford: Duckworth.
Brugman, Claudia
1981   Story of *over.* M.A. thesis, University of California, Berkeley.

Bryson, Bill
1990   *Mother Tongue: The English Language.* London and New York: Penguin Books.
Bühler, Karl
1990 [1934] *Theory of Language: The Representational Function of Language.* Amsterdam and Philadelphia: John Benjamins. English translation by Donald Fraser Goodwin, edited with an introduction by Achim Eschbach.
Burke, Kenneth
1962   *A Grammar of Motives and a Rhetoric of Motives.* Cleveland: The World Publishing Company.
Cadiot, Pierre
1992   Extensions et glissements polysémiques ... d'une langue à l'autre. In: Michèle Lorgnet (ed.), *Atth della Fiera Internazionale della Traduzione 1*, Riccione, (décembre 1990), ateneo, Forli: 31–57.
1993   Représentations d'objets et sémantique lexicale: qu'est ce qu'une *boîte? Journal of French Language Studies* 4: 1–23.
Caramazza, Alfonso and Ellen Grober
1976   Polysemy and the structure of the subjective lexicon. In: Clea Rameh (ed.), *Semantics: Theory and Application*, 181–206. Washington, DC: Georgetown University Press.
Danesi, Marcel
1990   Thinking is seeing: visual metaphors and the nature of thought. *Semiotica* 80(3/4): 221–237.
Darmesteter, Arsène
1887   *La vie des mots étudiée dans leurs significations.* Paris: Delagrave.
Desmet, Piet and Pierre Swiggers
1995   *De la grammaire comparée à la sémantique.* Textes de Michel Bréal publiés entre 1864 et 1898. Introduction, commentaires et bibliographie par Piet Desmet et Pierre Swiggers. Leuven and Paris: Peeters.
Dirven, René and Johan Vanparys (eds.)
1995   *Current Approaches to the Lexicon.* Frankfurt: Peter Lang.
Du Marsais, César Chesneau
1977 [1730] *Traité des Tropes ou des différents sens dans lesquels on peut prendre un même mot dans une même langue.* Postface de Claude Mouchard, suivi de Jean Paulhan, *Traité des Figures ou La Rhétorique décryptée.* Paris: Le Nouveau Commerce.
Eco, Umberto
1996   History and historiography of semiotics. In: Roland Posner, Kurt Robering and Thomas A. Sebeok (eds.), *Semiotik/Semiotics: Ein Handbuch zu den zeichentheoretichen Grundlagen von Natur und Kultur/A Handbook on the sign-theoretic foundations of nature and culture.* Volume 1, 730–746. Berlin and New York: Walter de Gruyter.

Erdmann, Karl Otto
1910 [1900] *Die Bedeutung des Wortes: Aufsätze aus dem Grenzgebiet der Sprach-psychologie und Logik.* 2. Aufl. Leipzig: Eduard Avenarius. First ed. Leipzig: Haessel; 3rd ed. 1922; 4th ed. 1925.

Fauconnier, Gilles
1998   Mental spaces and conceptual integration. In: Michael Tomasello (ed.), *The New Psychology of Language: Cognitive And Functional Approaches To Language Structure,* 251–280. Mahwah, NJ and London: Lawrence Erlbaum.

Fillmore, Charles J.
1975   An alternative to checklist theories of meaning. *Proceedings of the Annual Meetings of the Berkeley Linguistics Society (BLS)* 1: 123–131.

Fuchs, Catherine
1991   Polysémie, interprétation et typicalité: l'exemple de *pouvoir.* In: Danièle Dubois (ed.), *Sémantique et Cognition: Catégories, Prototypes, Typicalité,* 161–170. Paris: Editions du CNRS (Coll. Sciences du Langage).
1996   L'interprétation des polysèmes grammaticaux en contexte. In: Georges Kleiber and Martin Riegel (eds.), *Les Formes du Sens: Etudes de linguistique française, médiévale et générale offertes à Robert Martin,* 127–133. Louvain: Duculot (Coll. Champs linguistiques).

Fuchs, Catherine and Pierre Le Goffic
2002   La polysémie de *comme.* In: Olivier Soutet (ed.), *La Polysémie.* Paris: Presses de l'Université Paris IV. (Actes du Colloque international "La Polysémie", Paris, novembre 2000).

Geeraerts, Dirk
1992   Polysemy and prototypicality (Review article on Kleiber 1990). *Cognitive Linguistics* 3(2): 219–231.
1997   *Diachronic Prototype Semantics: A Contribution to Historical Lexicology.* Oxford: Clarendon.

Gerber, Gustav
1871–1874 *Die Sprache als Kunst.* 2 Bde. (Bd. 2 in zwei Teilen). Bromberg: Heyfleder. Second ed. 1885; reprint Hildesheim: Olms 1961.
1884   *Die Sprache und das Erkennen.* Berlin: Gaertner.

Giora, Rachel
1997   Understanding figurative and literal language: the graded salience hypothesis. *Cognitive Linguistics* 7(1): 183–206.

Householder, Fred W.
1995   Plato and his predecessors. In: E. F. K. Koerner and Ronald E. Asher (eds.), *Concise History of the Language Sciences,* 9–93. Oxford: Pergamon.

Jäkel, Olaf
1999   Kant, Blumenberg, Weinrich: some forgotten contributions to the
            cognitive theory of metaphor. In: Raymond Gibbs Jr. and Gerdard J.
            Steen (eds.), *Metaphor in Cognitive Linguistics*. Amsterdam and
            Philadelphia: John Benjamins.
Jakobson, Roman
1956a   The metaphoric and metonymic poles. In: Roman Jakobson and
            Morris Halle (eds.), *Fundamentals of Language*, 76–82. Gravenhage:
            Mouton and Co.
1956b   Two aspects of language and two types of aphasic disturbances. In:
            Krystyna Pomorska and Stephen Rudy (eds.), *Language in Literature*,
            95–120. Cambridge, MA; London, England: The Belknap Press of
            Harvard University Press 1983.
Johnson, Mark
1987   *The Body in the Mind: The Bodily Basis of Meaning, Imagination
            and Reason*. Chicago: Chicago University Press.
Kleiber, Georges
1990   *La sémantique du prototype*. Paris: Presses Universitaires de France.
1999   *Problèmes de sémantique: La Polysémie en questions*. Paris: Presses
            Universitaires du Septentrion.
Knobloch, Clemens
1988   *Geschichte der psychologischen Sprachauffassung in Deutschland
            von 1850 bis 1920*. Tübingen: Niemeyer.
Koch, Peter
1998   Saussures *mouton* und Hjelmslevs *træ*: zwei Schulbeispiele zwischen
            Semstructur und Polysemie. In: Edeltraud Werner, Ricarda Liver,
            Yvonne Stork, and Martina Nicklaus (eds.), *Et multum et multa.
            Festschrift für Peter Wunderli zum 60. Geburtstag*, 113–136.
            Tübingen: Gunter Narr.
Koevecses, Zoltan
2000   *Metaphor and Emotion: Language, Culture and Body in Human
            Feeling*. Cambridge: Cambridge University Press.
Lakoff, George
1987   *Women, Fire and Dangerous Things*. Chicago: University of Chicago
            Press.
Lakoff, George and Mark Johnson
1980   *Metaphors We Live By*. Chicago: University of Chicago Press.
1999   *Philosophy in the Flesh: The Cognitive Unconscious and the Embodied
            Mind: How the Embodied Mind Creates Philosophy*. New York: Basic
            Books.
Lakoff, George and Mark Turner
1989   *More Than Cool Reason*. Chicago: University of Chicago Press.

Lambert, Johann Heinrich
  1764   *Philosophische Schriften.* Hrsg. v. Hans-Werner Arndt. Bd. I/II: *Neues*
            Organon oder Gedanken über die Erforschung und Bezeichnung des
            Wahren und dessen Unterscheidung vom Irrthum und Schein. Repro-
            graphischer Nachdruck der Ausgabe. Leipzig: bey Johann Wendler
            1764. Hildesheim: Georg Olms, 1965.
Langacker, Ronald W.
  1987   *Foundations of Cognitive Grammar*, Vol. 1: *Theoretical Prerequisites.*
            Stanford, CA: Stanford University Press.
  1988   Review of George Lakoff: *Women, Fire, and Dangerous Things*,
            Chicago: Chicago University Press. *Language* 64(2): 384–395.
Leibniz, Gottfried Wilhelm
  1981   *Nouveaux essais sur l'entendement humain.* English: *New essays on*
            human understanding. Translated and edited by Peter Remnant and
            Jonathan Bennett. Cambridge: Cambridge University Press.
  1882   *Die philosophischen Schriften von Gottfried Wilhelm Leibniz*, Volume
            V. Edited by C. I. Gerhardt. Berlin: Weidmann.
  1956   *Philosophical Papers And Letters.* A Selection translated and edited,
            with an introduction by Leroy E. Loemker. Volume I. Chicago: The
            University of Chicago Press.
Locke, John
  1975 [1689] *Essay on Human Understanding*, edited by Peter H. Nidditch. Oxford:
            Oxford University Press. First ed. 1689; 5th ed. 1706.
McCawley, James D.
  1968   The role of semantics in grammar. In: Emmon Bach and Robert T.
            Harms (eds.), *Universals in Linguistic Theory.* New York: Holt,
            Rinehart and Winston, Inc.
McFague, Sallie
  1983   *Metaphorical Theology: Models of God in Religious Language.*
            London: SCM Press Ltd.
Meillet, Antoine
  1921 [1905] *Linguistique historique et linguistique générale.* [Vol. I.] Paris:
            Champion.
Nerlich, Brigitte
  1992   *Semantic Theories in Europe 1830–1930.* Amsterdam and Philadelphia:
            John Benjamins.
  1998   La métaphore et la métonymie: aux sources rhétoriques des théories
            sémantiques modernes. *Sémiotiques* 14: 143–170.
  2000   La sémantique et la polysémie: de la conceptualisation à la
            désignation de domaines et concepts linguistiques nouveaux. In
            Gabriel Bergougnioux (ed.), *Bréal et le sens de la Sémantique*, 183–
            194. Orléans: University of Orléans Press.

Nerlich, Brigitte and David D. Clarke
1997   Polysemy: patterns in meaning and patterns in history. *Historiographia Linguistica* 24(3): 359–385.
1999   Synecdoche as a communicative strategy. In: Andreas Blank and Peter Koch (eds.), *Historical Semantics and Cognition*, 197–213. Berlin and New York: Mouton de Gruyter.
2000a   Blending the past and the present. Reflections on conceptual and linguistic integration. *LOGOS. Journal of General Linguistics and Language Theory* 1: 3–18. Reprinted with some changes in René Dirven and Ralf Pörings (eds.), *Metaphor and Metonymy in Comparison and Contrast*, 555–594. Berlin and New York: Mouton de Gruyter.
2000b   Semantic fields and frames. Historical explorations of the interface between language, action and cognition. *Journal of Pragmatic* 32(2): 125–150.
2001   Mind, meaning, and metaphor: the philosophy and psychology of metaphor in nineteenth-century Germany. *History of the Human Sciences* 14(2): 39–61.
OED
1989   *Oxford English Dictionary*. 2nd edition. Oxford: Clarenden.
Oosthuizen Mouton, Nicholas T.
(to appear) Metaphor and truth in the seventeenth century. In: Armin Burkhardt and Brigitte Nerlich (eds.), *Reflections on Tropical Truth: Studies on the Epistemology of Metaphor*. Berlin and New York: Mouton de Gruyter.
Ortony, Andrew
1975   On putting apples into bottles: a problem of polysemy. *Cognitive Psychology* 7: 167–180.
Paul, Hermann
1920 [1886] *Prinzipien der Sprachgeschichte*. Wiederabdruck der 9. Auflage. (*Konzepte der Sprach- und Literaturwissenschaft 6.*) Tübingen: Niemeyer. Second edition 1886.
Pause, Peter E., Achim Botz and Markus Egg
1995   Partir c'est quitter un peu: a two-level approach to polysemy. In: Urs Egli et al. (eds.), *Lexical Knowledge in the Organization of Language*, 245–283. (Current Issues in Linguistic Theory 114.) Amsterdam: Benjamins.
Pott, August Friedrich
1861   *Etymologische Forschungen auf dem Gebiete der Indo-Germanischen Sprachen, unter Berücksichtigung ihrer Hauptformen, Sanskrit; Zend-Persisch; Griechisch-Lateinisch; Littauisch-Slawisch; Germanisch und Keltisch*. 2nd ed. *Zweiten Theiles erste Abtheilung: Wurzeln; Einleitung*. Lemgo-Detmold: Meyersche Hofbuchhandlung.

Rastier François
    1987   *Sémantique interprétative*. Paris: Presses Universitaires de France.
Reisig, Christian Karl
    1890 [1839] *Vorlesungen über lateinische Sprachwissenschaft*. Mit den Anmerkungen
        von Friedrich Haase. Unter Benutzung der hinterlassenen Manuskripte
        neu bearbeitet von Hermann Hagen. Zweiter Bd. 1890. *Lateinische
        Semasiologie oder Bedeutungslehre*. Neu bearbeitet von Ferdinand
        Heerdegen. Berlin: Calvary.
Richards, Ivor Armstrong
    1936   *The Philosophy of Rhetoric*. Second printing 1950. New York: Oxford
        University Press.
Ritter, Joachim (ed.)
    1972   *Historisches Wörterbuch der Philosophie*; herausgegeben von
        Joachim Ritter; unter Mitwirkung von mehr als 700 Fachgelehrten;
        in Verbindung mit Gunther Bien ... [et al.]. Basel: Schwabe 1971–
        <1998>. From Volume 4 edited by Karlfried Grunder.
Schepping, Marie-Thérèse
    1994   Un cas de polysémie dans le domaine verbal: *arriver*. In: Hiltraud
        Dupuy-Engelhardt (ed.), *Actes d'EUROSEM 94*. Colloque du 20 au
        23 septembre 1994, Reims.
Schlegel, August Wilhelm von
    1832   *Réflexions sur l'étude des langues asiatiques adressées à Sir James
        Mackintosh, suivies d'une lettre à M. Horace Hayman Wilson*. Bonn:
        Weber; Paris: Maze.
Schlieben-Lange, Brigitte
    1997   Überrlegungen zu einer einfachen Systematik der Zuweisung von
        (polysemen) Lesarten. In: Ulrich. Hoinkes and Wolfgang Dietrich
        (eds.), *Kaleidoskop der Lexikalischen Semantik*, 239–247. Tübingen:
        Narr.
Schmitz, H. Walter
    1985   Die durchgängige Tropisierung der Sprache. Über einen Aspekt von
        "Zeichen im Wandel". In: Klaus D. Dutz and Peter Schmitter (eds.),
        *Historiographia Semioticae: Studien zur Rekonstruktion der Theorie
        und Geschichte der Semiotik*, 241–270. Münster: MAkS Publikationen.
Schumacher, René
    1997   *"Metapher". Erfassen und Verstehen frischer Metaphern*. (Basler
        Studien zur deutschen Sprache und Literatur 75.) Tübingen und Basel:
        A. Francke.
Schwarze, Christoph
    1995   Polysemie im Sprachvergleich. In: Walter Dahmen et al. (eds.),
        Konvergenz und Divergenz in den romanischen Sprachen, 204–219.
        Romanistisches Kolloquium VIII. Tübingen: Gunter Narr Verlag.

Schwarze, Christoph and Marie-Therèse Schepping
  1995   Polysemy in a two-level-semantics. In: Urs Egli et al. (eds.). *Lexical Knowledge in the Organization of Language*, 283–300. Amsterdam: Benjamins.
Smith, Michael K.
  1982   Metaphor and mind. Review of George Lakoff and Mark Johnson, *Metaphors We Live By*, Chicago: University of Chicago Press 1980. *American Speech* 57: 128–133.
Sperber, Hans
  1923   *Einführung in die Bedeutungslehre*. Bonn–Leipzig: Schroeder.
Stählin, Wilhelm
  1913   Zur Psychologie und Statistik der Metaphern. Eine methodologische Untersuchung. *Archiv für die gesamte Psychologie* 31: 297–425.
Stern, Gustaf
  1931   *Meaning and Change of Meaning: with Special Reference to the English Language*. Göteborg: Elanders Boktryckeri Aktiebolag. (Reprinted, Bloomington and London: Indiana University Press, 1968.)
Sweetser, Eve E.
  1986   Polysemy vs. abstraction: mutually exclusive or complementary? *Berkeley Linguistics Society*, Vol. 12, Berkeley, 528–563.
  1990   *From Etymology to Pragmatics: Metaphorical and Cultural Aspects of Semantic Structure*. Cambridge: Cambridge University Press.
Taylor, John R.
  1994   The two-level approach to meaning. *Linguistische Berichte* 149: 3–26.
  1995   Models of word meaning in comparison: the two-level model (Manfred Bierwisch) and the network model (Ronald Langacker). In: Dirven and Vanparys (1995), 3–26.
  2000   Approaches to word meaning: the network model (Langacker) and the two-level model (Bierwisch) in comparison. In: Bert Peeters (ed.), *The Lexicon-Encyclopedia Interface*, 115–141 (Current Research in the Semantics/Pragmatics Interface, Vol. 5). Amsterdam: Elsevier.
Todorov, Tzvetan
  1977   *Théories du Symbole*. Paris: Editions du Seuil.
Traugott, Elizabeth Closs
  1988   Pragmatic strengthening and grammaticalization. In: *Proceedings of the Annual Meeting of the Berkeley Linguistics Society* 14: 406–416.
Turgot, Anne Robert Jacques, baron de l'Aulne
  1756   Etymologie. In: *Encyclopédie, ou Dictionnaire Raisonné des Sciences, des Arts et des Métiers*. Tome Sixième. Nouvelle impression en facsimilé de la première édition 1751–1780, 98a–111b. Stuttgart–Bad Cannstatt: Friedrich Fromann Verlag (Günther Holzboog) 1967.

Turner, Mark
    1999   Contribution to cogling list, 30 January 1999 on "history of cognitive
                linguistics". X-UIDL: 284bda4409504c43ad4da2924844ab36
Ullmann, Stephen
    1951   *The Principles of Semantics*. Oxford: Basil Blackwell; Glasgow:
                Jackson, Sons and Co.
    1962   *Semantics*. Oxford: Blackwell.
Ungeheuer, Gerold
    1980   Lamberts semantische Tektonik des Wortschatzes als universales
                Prinzip. In: Gunter Brettschneider and Christian Lehmann (eds.),
                *Wege der Universalienforschung. Sprachwissenschaftliche Beiträge
                zum 60. Geburtstag von Hansjakob Seiler*, 87–93. Tübingen: Gunter
                Narr.
Vico, Giambattista
    1948 [1725] *The New Science of Giambattista Vico* (Revised edition; T. G. Bergin
                and M. H. Fisch, editors and translators). Ithaca, NY: Cornell
                University Press, 1948.
Victorri, Bernard and Catherine Fuchs
    1996   *La Polysémie: Construction Dynamique Du Sens*. Paris: Hermès.
Waswo, Richard
    1987   *Language and Meaning in the Renaissance*. Princeton: Princeton
                University Press.
Wegener, Philipp
    1991 [1885] *Untersuchungen über die Grundfragen des Sprachlebens*. Halle a.d.S.:
                Niemeyer. New edition by E. F. K. Koerner with an introduction by
                Clemens Knobloch. Amsterdam and Philadelphia: Benjamins 1991.
Weinreich, Uriel
    1962   Lexicographic definition in descriptive semantics. In: Fred W.
                Householder and Sol Saporta (eds.), *Problems of Lexicography*, 25–
                43. Bloomington, IN: Indiana University Press. Reprinted in:
                Weinreich (1980), 295–314.
    1966   Explorations in semantic theory. In: Thomas A. Sebeok (ed.), *Current
                Trends in Linguistics*, Volume 3, 395–477. The Hague: Mouton.
    1980   *On Semantics*. Edited by William Labov and Beatrice S. Weinreich.
                Philadelphia: University of Pennsylvania Press.
Weinrich, Harald
    1967   Semantik der Metapher. *Folia Linguistica* 1: 3–17.

Cognitive approaches

Polysemy and conceptual blending*

Gilles Fauconnier and Mark Turner

1. Introduction

Science is an eternal battle against common sense. How can it be the earth that moves, when we so clearly see the sun travelling majestically across the sky? Since when do feathers fall as fast as stones? Where did imaginary numbers ever come from?

In thinking about meaning, common sense is no less of an obstacle. What could be more obvious than the platitude that words have meanings, that "dog" means dog and "house" means house? This reasonable and simple view serves us well in everyday life and is widely shared. And yet there is considerable evidence that it is deeply wrong – not just wrong because it is oversimplified and in need of refinement, but more deeply wrong and misleading in the very notion of "meaning" that it takes for granted.

The clash between our common-sense, self-evident view of meaning contained in words and the infinitely more complex and remarkable reality of meaning construction has certainly not escaped the notice of thinkers through the ages. But it is only recently that we have started to come to grips directly with the dynamics of on-line meaning construction and the wealth and variety of cognitive capacities that we bring to bear on the most ordinary, mundane situations.

It has been useful, in approaching such issues, to forget notions like "meaning of an expression", "semantic representation", "truth-function", and the like, and to think instead of the "meaning potential" of a language form. Meaning potential is the essentially unlimited number of ways in which an expression can prompt dynamic cognitive processes, which include conceptual connections, mappings, blends, and simulations. Such processes are inherently creative, and we recognize them as such when they are triggered or produced by art and literature. In everyday life, the creativity is hidden by the largely unconscious and extremely swift nature of the myriad cognitive operations that enter into the simplest of our meaning constructions. It is also hidden by the necessary folk-theory of our everyday behaviour which is based quite naturally on our conscious experience rather than on the less accessible components of our cognition.

In this article, we look at some aspects of polysemy which derive from the power of meaning potential. More specifically, we focus on aspects linked to the operation of conceptual blending, a major cognitive resource for creativity in many of its manifestations.

Polysemy is pervasive in language and appears in many forms. It is not just an accident of history or of synchrony, but rather an essential manifestation of the flexibility, adaptability, and richness in meaning potential that lie at the very heart of what a language is and what it is for. It is also a symptom (rather than a primitive component) of the way in which various cognitive operations allow for creativity at many levels.

The diversity and wide range of polysemy, and the wealth of theoretical implications associated with it, are richly attested in the present volume. In this article we review a number of cases of polysemy associated with conceptual blending. A majority of these cases have been discussed in other contexts and for a variety of theoretical purposes. Rather than repeat the analyses *in extenso*, we will frequently refer the interested reader to the appropriate source for a more detailed treatment. In the sources, polysemy was seldom in itself the major focus. By bringing together a large number of cases in the present context, we hope to give an idea of the overall importance of blending in polysemy phenomena.

2. An example of blending: the history of the world record in the mile

On 8 July 1999, *The New York Times* reported that Hicham el-Guerrouj had broken the record for the mile, with a time of 3:43.13. The illustration that accompanied the article, reproduced in Figure 1, shows a one-quarter mile racetrack with six figures running on it, representing el-Guerrouj in a race against the fastest milers from each decade since Roger Bannister broke the 4-minute barrier in 1954. El-Guerrouj is crossing the finish line as Bannister, trailing everyone, is still 120 yards back. This illustration prompts us to construct a conceptual packet that blends together structure from six separate input mental spaces, each with a one-mile race in which the record is broken by a runner. The blend places all six of the runners on a single racetrack, with a single beginning time.

This blend has the familiar features of conceptual integration networks.

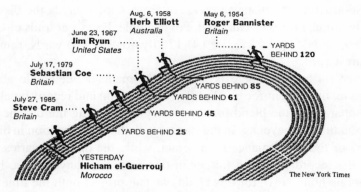

Figure 1. A comparison of world record times for the mile.

There is a cross-space mapping connecting counterparts in each of the six spaces: winners, racetracks, finish lines, the mile distance, and so on. There is a generic space containing the structure and elements taken to apply to all these spaces, which constitute the fairly rich frame of running the mile and breaking the record. There is selective projection to the blend: from each of the six input spaces, we project to the blend the entire frame of running the mile, but not, for example, a specific location for the race, or any of the runners except the winner. Some counterparts projected to the blend are fused, such as the racetracks. Others, such as the record breakers, are not. There is emergent dynamic structure in the blend, namely, structure that cannot be found in any of the inputs: the blend is a simulation of a mythic race between giants of the sport, most of whom in fact never raced against each other. In this mythic race, el-Guerrouj "defeats" Bannister by 120 yards.

This blend is immediately intelligible and persuasive, but its construction is remarkably complicated. Projecting to the blend el-Guerrouj, his location at the finish line, and his winning time as he crosses the finish line does not tell us how to locate the other runners behind him. Naturally, their historical records do not indicate where they were at time 3:43.13. Their location on the track at this time must be calculated separately. In this case, the calculation is made by assuming that each runner ran his race at a uniform speed, despite the fact that this never happens. We see therefore that the input mental spaces to the blend, however useful, are fictions that do not correspond to the real situations that occurred. With these fictions in place, it is easy to compute the distance each runner has travelled at time 3:43.13 as the product of 1 mile and the ratio of el-Guerrouj's winning time to the runner's winning time. Subtracting the distance travelled from 1 mile yields the distance by which the runner trails el-Guerrouj. For example, Bannister trails el-Guerrouj by [1760 yards] − [(3:43.13/3:59.4)(1760 yards)] = 120 yards, rounding to the nearest yard.

To see further that there is nothing automatic or inevitable about this blend as an instrument for highlighting competition and record-breaking, we can compare it to the blend for the history of breaking the distance record for a fixed time in bicycling. In the standard one-hour competition in bicycling, the time of the performance is invariant, while the distance varies. So one breaks the record by going farther in one hour than anyone else has ever gone in one hour. Now, for this blend, we can project both the time and the distance for each of the previous record holders without having to perform any calculation. We simply place all the record-holders on the same track, each at the distance he had achieved after one hour. In fact, the blend for the milers looks like the blend for the bicyclists, but in the first case some aggressive manipulations were required to achieve the blend. In the bicycle competition, the contestants in the inputs and in the blend all do in fact stop after an identical period of time has elapsed, namely one hour. In the mile race, the contestants in the blend effectively stop competing to win the moment the winner crosses the finish line, even though their counterparts in the input spaces continue to compete to win, to finish the mile, and in fact to break the record.

In the rest of this article, we will show how various kinds of polysemy occur as a result of blending. We will argue that the following principles guide the development of polysemy and furthermore that most polysemy is invisible:

(i)   Through selective projection, expressions applied to an input can be projected to apply to counterparts in the blend. In this way, blends harness existing words in order to express the new meanings that arise in the blend.

(ii)   Combinations of expressions from the inputs may be appropriate for picking out structure in the blend even though those combinations are inappropriate for the inputs. In consequence, grammatical but meaningless phrases can become grammatical and meaningful for the blend.

(iii) Terminology that naturally applies to the blended space ends up, through connections in the integration network, picking out meaning that it could not have been used to pick out if the blend had not been built.

(iv)   Blending provides a continuum for polysemy effects. Polysemy is an inevitable and routine outcome of blending, but it is only rarely noticed. The noticeability of polysemy is a function of the availability of certain frames through defaults, contexts, or culture.

The most obvious case of harnessing an existing word to express new meaning is category extension. Suppose we refer to a particular domestic relationship between two members of the same sex as a *same-sex marriage*. As we have analysed in Turner and Fauconnier (1995), this expression prompts us to create a conceptual blend that modifies the category "marriage". The expression "same-sex" comes from the mental space with the domestic relationship between the two adults of the same sex, while the word "marriage" comes from the mental space with the frame of conventional marriage. These expressions, attached to the inputs, are now used to evoke the blend, so "marriage" now picks out new meaning. Conceivably, this category modification could become so conventional for the entire linguistic community that one could without risk of appearing uncooperative refer to a same-sex marriage as simply a "marriage". By Principle (i), "marriage" applies to an element in the blend that is quite different from its counterpart in the inputs. By Principle (ii), "The brides married each other at noon" is a combination of expressions from the inputs that is now appropriate for the blend but impossible for the inputs.

The expression *computer virus* is a parallel example, where the new meaning is produced by technological innovation rather than social change. A conceptual blending network links the inputs of computer processes and health and medicine and the blended space of computer viruses, vaccines, disinfectants, and so on. By Principle (i), some vocabulary that applies to the inputs is projected to counterparts in the blend and so ends up expressing new meaning. In fact, in this case, the vocabulary has become conventional for the entire linguistic community, so one can say "I got a virus at the office", meaning a computer virus. This example, unlike *same-sex marriage*, is felt to be metaphorical, but the general blending mechanisms for creating polysemy are the same for *same-sex marriage* and *computer virus*. In fact, we point out below that on a continuum of blending networks, some are felt to be completely literal, some absolutely metaphoric, and others at various stages in between. In this way, the mechanism for extending meaning in the case of *computer virus* is not metaphor *per se*, although metaphor is a collateral feature of this particular blending network.

Complex numbers is a category extension in mathematics, analysed at length in Fauconnier and Turner (1998). One input space has the Euclidean plane and the other has real numbers. Before the invention of complex numbers, there was already a historical connection between the geometric line and the real numbers. Under blending, this connection was extended to involve the entire plane. In the blend, a complex number is both a number and a point. This point uniquely specifies a vector from the origin. By Principle (i), vocabulary from the geometric input is applied to this number, which is now said to have a magnitude and an angle (or argument); and vocabulary from the number input is applied to the complex number in the blend, so we can now speak of operations like "addition" and "multiplication". Clearly, the meanings of "angle", "product", "number", and "sum" – in a way, the meanings of all terms in number theory – have been extended and deeply modified. Vocabulary that applies to the inputs has been projected to pick out counterparts in the blend, and consequently applies to the new meaning that has been developed in the blend. By Principle (ii), it becomes mathematically correct to say that "the angle of the product of two numbers is the sum of the angles of the two numbers". This combination of expressions from the inputs becomes appropriate for the blend even though it does not apply to the inputs. Additionally, by Principle (ii) we can also refer to "the square root of negative one" for the blend, but not for the inputs.

In the case of *complex numbers*, the meaning extension is absolutely precise and rigorous. It defines an extension of mathematics itself. We see that it is not through linguistic or psychological properties of terms like "number" and "sum" that polysemy occurs. It occurs as a byproduct of the conceptual change brought about by the blending network. Given the connections in the network, by Principle (i), words like "number" or "angle" from the inputs come to apply to counterparts in the blend, producing a sharply different mathematical meaning. Mathematics loses none of its rigour by having words like "number" be polysemous. In some contexts, "number" refers to elements that do not have angles; in other contexts, "number" refers to elements that do have angles. "Number" retains all of its old meanings but acquires a new one to pick out elements in the complex number blend.

The examples we have considered are all traditionally considered to be category extension. For these cases, it is intuitively tempting to think that the category is extended by adding or deleting criterial features. But, as we have just seen with the example of complex numbers, category extension occurs by blending, which is not simply an operation of adding and deleting features. We now turn to an example where it does not seem even intuitively that the blend arises by adding or deleting features.

Coulson (1997) analyses *caffeine headache* as having two conventional readings, one in which the headache is caused by caffeine, the other in which the headache is caused by lack of caffeine. In this second case, we need an integration network involving a general schema for a headache and its cause, a present scenario in which the person with the headache has had no caffeine, and a counterfactual scenario in which someone has had caffeine and so has no headache. In the blend, the particular person with the headache has had no caffeine, the lack of caffeine is the cause of the headache, and the term "caffeine" has been projected from the all-important and desirable counterfactual scenario in which there is no headache. Although this looks and is intricate, it is an instance of a general pattern in which the integration network contains a fully activated and highly important mental space that is counterfactual to the blend, and the simple term for the blend is taken from the counterfactual scenario. For example, a *nicotine fit* is a fit caused by lack of nicotine, where the term "nicotine" is taken from the counterfactual scenario in which the person does not have the fit. *Easy error*, used in tennis to describe an error in making what should have been an easy shot, takes the modifier for the error from the counterfactual space. Perhaps most conventionally, a *money problem* activates a counterfactual space where there is money and no problem. In the blend, there is a problem, a causal relation, and a cause, namely, no money, but the term indicating the cause is taken from the counterfactual space in which there is money and therefore no problem.

We see that terms like *caffeine headache* have more than one meaning, being polysemous, because there is more than one blending possibility. The striking possibility pointed out by Coulson depends on the general availability of blending networks that have two highly active input spaces where one is directly counterfactual to the other in some crucial respect. For examples like *money problem* and *caffeine headache* that are licensed by such networks, it is very clear even at the intuitive level that the polysemy cannot be a result of adding and deleting semantic features attached to the two words. A caffeine headache situation, on the counterfactual reading, has no features of caffeine. In fact, its indispensable feature is a total absence of caffeine.

3.   Gradients of blending

In this section, we focus on a single word, *father*, to show how gradients of blending yield gradients of polysemy effects.

Consider an exceptionally simple limiting case in which a generic space in a conceptual integration network has two people and no relations. Take Input 1 in the network to be the *father–child* subframe of our more general kinship frame. And take Input 2 to consist only of two people with no relation between them, e.g. *Paul* and *Sally*. A simple cross-space mapping can link *father* and Paul, connecting them to one of the people in the generic space, and *ego* and *Sally*, connecting them to the other person in the generic space. Projecting *father* and *Paul* to the blend and fusing them there and *ego* and *Sally* to the blend and fusing them there yields a very simple network, in which the structure in the blend is almost entirely obtained by composition of the input structures. It is essentially equivalent to a Fregean composition, expressed in logical notation by something like

(1)   FATHER (Paul, Sally)

It is also equivalent to filling in slots in a frame (father, ego) with fillers (Paul, Sally). In English, this blend would be triggered by sentences like *Paul is the father of Sally*. Another way to think about the resulting blend is to view it as instantiating the projection of the kinship frame in Input 1 onto the situation in Input 2, consisting of Paul and Sally.

These are very simple networks, and if they were the only form of integration ever observed, there would be scant justification for setting up a theory of conceptual blending. Simple framing (or its Fregean equivalent) would suffice.

But in fact these simple networks are only the beginning of a long gradient of increasing complexity. Crucially, the same word (*father* for example) can operate in all the networks of the gradient. Superficially, the result is that the word appears to have many different meanings. On the contrary, the word is always playing the same role in inviting us to use our potential to construct meanings through mechanisms like conceptual integration. To show this, we will work through a series of cases along this continuum all using the word *father*. Consider:

(2)   *Zeus was the father of Sarpedon. He watched from Mount Olympus as his mortal son met his fated death.*

This example points to the fact that there was more pattern completion and projection from inputs in the *Paul* and *Sally* case than we had realized. In *Paul is the father of Sally*, we quietly projected from Input 1 a range of conventional knowledge, such as the mortality of the father and his normal paternal limitations. But it is a technical fact of blending that we can project equally from either input. So in the case of Sarpedon, the framing of the father's powers and limitations comes not this time from Input 1, but from Input 2.

Now consider:

(3)   *Zeus is the father of Athena. She was born out of his head, fully clad in armour.*

Now, from the kinship space, we bring in general schemas of human progeneration, such as the offspring's coming out of the body of a parent, but we bring in from our knowledge of divinity the possibility of unusual birth. We explicitly build in the blend, on the warrant of the second sentence, the particular kind of progeneration which involves neither a mother nor an infant.

The divinity in Input 2 allows for many wonderful blends, each of which contains a "father" and a creative method of progeneration. For instance, Zeus is also the father of Aphrodite, this time in virtue of having castrated Chronos and cast his genitalia into the ocean foam, whence Aphrodite is born.

Of course, the Zeus cases cannot be attributed to figurative speech or analogy. Zeus is still felt to be quite the father of Sarpedon, Athena, and Aphrodite. Family structure is inferred along with sentiments and emotions that come with it.

Now consider *Joseph was the father of Jesus.* In this case, in the blend, we do not project the usual structure of the father's role in procreation or the non-virginity of the mother. But we can project family structure and family sentiments and emotions. Again, this use of "father" is not felt to be metaphoric or analogical.

Now consider a neighbour who takes care of Sally for the day while Paul is away, carrying out fatherly duties like making her lunch, accompanying

her to school, reading bedtime stories. That neighbour can say to Sally: "I'm
your father for today". Like the Zeus and Joseph blends, some family structure
and genealogy is projected. As in the Joseph blend (but not the Zeus blends),
progeneration is not projected. Many of the typical aspects of the father–
offspring relationship are projected (routines, taking care, responsibility,
affection, protection, guidance, authority, and so forth). Compositionality is
no longer at all an option to account for this case. Too many properties felt
as central are missing. We have moved along the conceptual integration
network continuum from the pole of "Fregean" networks. But clearly, we
have not reached a point on the continuum that would be felt intuitively to
be metaphorical. Fatherhood is not a metaphor for what the neighbour is
doing. In fact, although some analogy has now contributed to the mapping,
the function of this blend is stronger than just analogy between the neighbour's actions and a father's actions. The neighbour in this local context is
really filling in the role of the father in relevant respects, not just doing
something "similar" to what the father does. The flexibility of blending with
selective projection and contextual elaboration allows for this intermediate
kind of situation which doesn't fit a prototypical semantic or pragmatic
characterization.

In the Zeus and Joseph cases, there are obvious Principle (i) and Principle
(ii) polysemy effects. By Principle (i), "father" is projected to the blend from
the *father–ego* input, but now picks out new meaning in the blend. By
Principle (ii), we can now refer in general, across all contexts, to Zeus as
"the parent of Athena", whereas, by contrast, Paul cannot be referred to in
all contexts as "the parent of Sally". We can refer to birth as "leaving Zeus's
head" in the way we normally refer to birth as "leaving the womb". Many
similar expressions, each using words that already apply to the inputs, can
be fashioned that pick out meaning only in the blend. We can also refer to
Joseph as "Jesus's mortal father", giving "mortal father" a contrastive rather
than redundant meaning, which is likewise inappropriate for the *father–ego*
input.

Consider further examples linked to *father*:

(4)   a.   *The Pope is the father of all Catholics.*
       b.   *The Pope is the father of the Catholic Church.*
       c.   *George Washington is the father of our country.*

They are further along the continuum. The first example still has people in both inputs. From the kinship input that provides the word "father", we project not progeneration at all but instead authority, size of the family, responsibility, leadership, social role. From the second input, we project specific properties of catholicism.

The second example arguably projects the role of a child to a single social entity (the Church). The blend reflects a type of socio-cultural model, in which a social entity (church, nation, community) is the "child" of its leader. The word "father" is now felt to have a different meaning, but not a particularly metaphoric one.

With the George Washington sentence, we go a little bit further by highlighting the causality in time between the parent and child, and between the founder and the nation. This abstraction increases the perceived difference between the two inputs and their domains. The impression of metaphor is undoubtedly stronger. And that subjective impression reaches a higher point when the two domains are even more explicitly distinguished, as in *Newton is the father of physics*. Physics, as opposed to church and country, does not even stand in metonymic relation to people and groups of people. Yet Newton and Washington as adult men have all the criterial biological features of possible fathers plus some of the stereotypical social ones (authority, responsibility ...). The conceptual integration networks directly bring in frame structure from both inputs.

Even more subjectively metaphorical are cases like Pound's *Fear, father of cruelty* (Turner 1987), where the two domains (emotions/qualities and people/kinship) have no literal overlap at all, and the projected shared schema is correspondingly abstract (causality). And finally, Wordsworth's acrobatic metaphor *The Child is Father of the man* comes around almost full circle by using background knowledge (children grow into men) to create emergent structure in the blend giving a rich instantiation to the abstract generic causal structure which maps kinship to the human condition in an unorthodox way. The oddness of its counterpart connections and the extensive drawing on the frames of both inputs to create a new organizing frame for the blend help make Wordsworth's line feel figurative. But the syntax and mapping scheme of *The Child is Father of the man* are the same as the syntax and the mapping scheme of *Paul is the father of Sally*.

The kinds of blend we have been talking about are often constructed using language. The reason language can prompt for blends that result in the same word's being used to pick out different meanings is that language does not represent meaning directly; it instead prompts for the construction of meaning in systematic fashion. All of the "father" examples are examples of the familiar XYZ construction ("*x* is the *y* of *z*") whose purpose is to prompt for blends in systematic fashion, in ways that naturally result in polysemy.

This gradient of polysemy for the word "father" falls out naturally as a consequence of the facts that (1) "father" is in each case attached to one of the inputs; (2) blending as a conceptual operation applies to those inputs; and (3) by Principles (i) and (ii), "father" comes to pick out elements in the blend and to participate in phrases that pick out structure in the blend but not the inputs. Polysemy is in this view not a property of words but a byproduct of the operation of conceptual integration and the fact that words are attached to its inputs. The cognitive operation of conceptual blending, with its mechanisms of selective projection and elaboration, is not restricted to linguistic examples. But a mind that can do blending, and that also knows language, will inevitably develop polysemy for words through blending. If words show up in inputs, they can be projected like any other element of an input. This will change their domain of application, unnoticeably in most cases, but noticeably when the emergent meaning in the blend to which they apply seems remarkably distant from the domain of the input from which they came. When we notice this distance, we call it by one of many names: extension, bleaching, analogy, metaphor, displacement. On our view, polysemy is a very common phenomenon, a standard byproduct of conceptual blending, but noticed only in a fraction of cases.

One way of thinking of language is as a system of prompts for integration. Since the conceptual structures to be integrated are many, each with ranges of words attached to them, an expression that prompts for their appropriate integration has to combine words, and language has to have forms to make these combinations possible. Obvious examples are predication (*this beach is safe*) and compounding (*likely story, possible solution, eligible bachelor, fake gun*). Consider, for example, *this beach is safe*. A common way of describing the meaning of this sentence is to say that a particular property, SAFE, is predicated of an object, BEACH, by means of the words "safe" and "beach". On this view, *this house is safe* asks us to apply the same particular property, SAFE, to a different object, HOUSE. So, "safe" just has one meaning, SAFE. It would be straightforward to say *the beach is safe* when we want to let a child play there. And in that situation, it would be equally true that *the child is safe*. But now we see the purported property SAFE attributed to the beach in *the beach is safe* and to the child in *the child is safe* would have to be two different properties, namely, on a first approximation, something like NOT

POTENTIALLY HARMFUL as opposed to NOT LIKELY TO BE HARMED. By the same token, the word "safe" in the sentence *the beach is safe* would have to apply many different properties on the readings that the beach is legally protected from development, has a statistically low number of drownings, is not a site of violent crime, is owned in such a way that its ownership cannot be taken away from the owner, is a vacation spot that can be proposed without problem to someone (as in a *safe bet*), and so on. In one sense, "safe" can mean many different things, but at the same time, there is no subjective apprehension of polysemy in these cases.

The details in these cases are actually surprising. They show that in order to make sense of "safe", we need to construct a counterfactual situation in which there is a victim, a location, instruments, possessions, and harm to the victim. In the case of the beach that is legally protected, the beach is the victim and the developers do harm to it. In the case of the beach with few drownings, the swimmers are victims and the beach (meaning by metonymy the water) does harm. In the case of the beach without crime, the vacationer is the victim and the criminals do harm. Alternatively, the owner of the beach can be the victim, or the person to whom we propose vacation spots can be the victim. We see that the noun to which "safe" is applied can point to many different roles in many different scenarios, not just the role of victim.

This leads, as shown elsewhere (Fauconnier and Turner 2002), to an analysis showing that, in order to do justice to the meaning of "safe", we must regard it not as applying a particular property but instead prompting for a particular kind of blend. The blend takes into account the frame of harm and the specifics of the situation referred to in the rest of the expression. We are required to blend them to create a counterfactual scenario in which there is specific harm, and to understand how the present situation is disanalogous to the specific counterfactual scenario. In fact, the linguistic expression singles out the disanalogous counterparts. For example, *the beach is safe*, meaning that the child will not drown, singles out a counterfactual counterpart beach with riptides, deadly waves, and so on, and asks us to understand that the beach in the present situation is disanalogous to it. If "safe" does have a meaning, it is something like "perform a conceptual integration, finding on your own appropriate connections, given the other words in the expression, and building a suitable counterfactual space on the basis of the harm scenario".

In fact, it is just like the caffeine example above that involved a counterfactual space of not having a headache and having had the caffeine, and understanding how that counterfactual space is disanalogous to the present situation. Here, too, the linguistic expression selects "caffeine" and "head-ache" in order to identify the disanalogous counterparts.

Now consider a word like "likely". Sweetser (1999) considers the case in which *likely candidate* means not someone likely to become a candidate or succeed as a candidate but, e.g., a candidate likely to grant an interview. As she writes, "So long as we can think up a scenario relative to the candidate in question, and evaluate that scenario for likelihood, *likely candidate* can mean the candidate who figures in the scenario we have labeled as likely." On her analysis, conceiving of such a scenario and evaluating it consists of finding a blend of the frame for likelihood, conceived of as probability of occurrence in a sequence, and the frame for candidate. Like "safe" above, "likely" prompts for a blend. Sweetser's examples make the point clearly that the scenarios necessary to do the appropriate blending may or may not be connected at all to the particular lexical items (e.g. "candidate"), as we see, for example, in the case where *possible textbook* refers to a textbook that might possibly be chosen as the one to be used in a college course. Just as the different meanings of "safe" may go unnoticed, so the different meanings of "possible" and "likely" may go unnoticed. But from a logical standpoint, a *possible textbook* in the sense of one that may be adopted is not the same as a *possible textbook* in the sense of one that might exist, or might be written, or a trade book that could double as a textbook. As before, in the cases of "likely" and "possible", blending opens the possibility of extensive polysemy in the logical sense, but which may go unnoticed. This is no accident, since the function of these linguistic forms, like the linguistic forms "Adj–Noun" and "Noun–Noun", is to prompt for blending.

4. Conclusion: the purpose of linguistic form

Human beings are confronted by a fundamental problem: conceptual systems are vast, rich and open-ended, while linguistic systems, impressive though they be, are relatively quite thin. How can a linguistic system be used to convey the products of conceptual systems, and how can these products find expression in language, given the stark mismatch in their respective infinities? If forms of language had to represent complete meanings, language could communicate very little. The evolutionary solution to this problem is to have systems of forms prompt for the construction of meanings that go far beyond anything like the form itself. The "of" found in a range of examples like

Paul is the father of Sally, Father of cruelty, Father of the Catholic Church, Vanity is the quicksand of reason, Wit is the salt of conversation, and so on does not single out any particular blend or even any particular projection; it only prompts for finding a way to construct a conceptual network that will have a relevant meaning. What we have to do to construct that network is nowhere represented in the linguistic structure. The single word "of" is thus associated with an infinity of mappings. Of course, this infinity of mappings is anything but arbitrary. It is constrained itself by the requirements on conceptual integration networks. Different grammatical forms prompt different infinities of conceptual mappings.

Because linguistic expressions prompt for meanings rather than represent meanings, linguistic systems do not have to be, and in fact cannot be, analogues of much richer conceptual systems. Prompting for meaning construction is a job they can do; representing meanings is not. As we have shown in this article, a byproduct of constructing conceptual integration networks will be massive, though often unrecognized, polysemy.

Notes

*   © Gilles Fauconnier and Mark Turner.

References

Coulson, Seana
    1997   Semantic leaps: the role of frame-shifting and conceptual blending in meaning construction. Ph.D. dissertation, University of California, San Diego.
Fauconnier, Gilles and Mark Turner
    1998   Conceptual integration networks. *Cognitive Science* 22(2): 133–187.
    2002   *The Way We Think: Conceptual Blending and the Mind's Hidden Complexities*. New York: Basic Books.
Sweetser, Eve
    1999   Compositionality and blending: working towards a fuller understanding of semantic composition in a cognitively realistic framework. In: Theo Janssen and Gisela Redeker (eds.), *Scope and Foundations of Cognitive Linguistics*, 129–162. The Hague: Mouton De Gruyter. (Cognitive Linguistics Research Series.)

Turner, Mark
    1987   *Death is the Mother of Beauty: Mind, Metaphor, Criticism.* Chicago:
                 University of Chicago Press.
Turner, Mark and Gilles Fauconnier
    1995   Conceptual integration and formal expression. *Journal of Metaphor
                 and Symbolic Activity* 10(3): 183–204.

Reconsidering prepositional polysemy networks: the case of *over*[*]

Andrea Tyler and Vyvyan Evans

1. Introduction

We focus here on the issue of semantic polysemy, the phenomenon whereby a single linguistic form is associated with a number of related but distinct meanings or *senses*. In particular, we consider how the notorious polysemy of the English preposition *over* might be accounted for in a principled, systematic manner within a cognitive linguistic framework. At base, we argue that the many senses of *over* constitute a motivated semantic network organized around an abstract, primary meaning component, termed a *protoscene*. The many distinct senses associated with *over* are accounted for by interaction of the protoscene with a constrained set of cognitive principles. Accordingly, our more general claim is that the lexicon is not an arbitrary repository of unrelated lexemes. Rather, the lexicon constitutes an elaborate network of form–meaning associations (Langacker 1987, 1991a, 1991b), in which each form is paired with a semantic network or continuum (Brisard 1997). This follows from two basic assumptions, widely demonstrated within the framework of cognitive linguistics. First, semantic structure derives from and mirrors conceptual structure (see, for example, Fauconnier 1994, 1997; Heine 1997; Jackendoff 1983; Lakoff 1987). Second, the kinds of bodies and neural architecture human beings have – how we experience – and the nature of the spatio-physical world we happen to live in – what we experience – determine the conceptual structure we have (Clark 1973; Evans 2000; Grady 1997; Heine 1993, 1997; Johnson 1987; Lakoff and Johnson 1980, 1999; Svorou 1993; Sweetser 1990; Talmy 1983, 1988, 1996, 2000; Turner 1991; Varela, Thompson and Rosch 1991).

This model of the lexicon generally, and the model of polysemy proposed here in particular, contrasts with traditional models in a number of ways. The traditional view holds that all regularity and productivity are in the syntax, with the lexicon serving as a repository of the arbitrary. Aronoff (1994) points out that Bloomfield articulated this perspective as early as 1933. More recently, Chomsky has reasserted this stance: "I understand the lexicon in a rather traditional sense: as a list of 'exceptions', whatever does not follow from general principles" (1995: 235). Models within this framework have tended to represent different word senses as distinct lexical items (Croft 1998). Polysemous forms are simply represented as an arbitrary list of discrete words that happen to share the same phonological form.

Over the years, this stand has been criticized for failing to account for systematic ways in which numerous forms are clearly related (Jackendoff 1997; Langacker 1991a; Levin 1993; Pustejovsky 1998). Croft (1998) notes that a number of linguists have argued for some type of derivation within the lexicon that would represent distinct senses as arising from a primary sense via a set of lexical operations. By and large, these analyses have focused on polysemy involving changes in the argument structure of verbs or alternatively in category changes, and have had little to say about the type of polysemy demonstrated by English prepositions in which syntactic category changes are often not involved.

In fact, most linguists (cognitive linguists excepted) have not paid much attention to the phenomena of polysemy. Pustejovsky notes that "The major part of semantic research ... has been on logical form and the mapping from a sentence-level syntactic representation to a logical representation" (1998: 33). The lexicon has been represented as a static set of word senses, tagged with features for syntactic, morphological and semantic information, ready to be inserted into syntactic frames with appropriately matching features. Within this tradition the lexicon has been viewed as "a finite set of [discrete] memorized units of meaning" (Jackendoff 1997: 4).

Cognitive linguistics takes a significantly different perspective on the nature of the mental lexicon. Of primary importance is the notion of *embodied meaning*: the meanings associated with many individual lexemes are instantiated in memory not in terms of features, nor as abstract propositions, but rather as imagistic, schematic representations. Such *image-schemas* are held to be embodied, in the sense that they arise from *perceptual reanalysis* of recurring patterns in everyday physical experience (see Johnson 1987; Mandler 1992, 1996 for a developmental perspective).[1] Perceptual analysis creates a new, abstract level of information – information tied to the spatiophysical world we inhabit but mediated by human perception and conceptualization. The central assumption of embodied meaning stands in stark contrast to approaches to the mental lexicon that represent lexical items as bundles of semantic, syntactic and morphological features.

A second distinguishing tenet of cognitive linguistics involves the representation of lexical items as natural categories involved in networks or continuums of meaning. Research into human categorization (Rosch 1975) strongly suggests that speakers distinguish between prototypical and peripheral members of a set, based not on criterial properties or features, but rather on how predictable a member is, based on a prototype (Lakoff 1987). Consequently, cognitive semantic accounts of polysemy (Brugman 1981; Brugman and Lakoff 1988; Lakoff 1987) have argued that lexical items constitute natural categories of related senses organized with respect to a primary sense and thus form semantic or polysemy networks. Hence, such accounts are strongly suggestive that the lexicon is much more motivated and organized than has traditionally been assumed (Dirven 1993; Lakoff 1987; see also Langacker 1991a; the work in *construction grammar* argues in a related vein, e.g. Fillmore, Kay and O'Connor 1988; Kay and Fillmore 1999; Goldberg 1995).

In the 1980s, Brugman conducted pioneering work in the polysemy of the English preposition *over* (1981 [1988]). This research was followed by Lakoff (1987), Brugman and Lakoff (1988), Dewell (1994) and Kreitzer (1997). Brugman and Lakoff treated prepositions as denoting a spatial relation between an element in focus (the figure), and an element not in focus (the ground).[2] The Brugman/Lakoff framework took a highly fine-grained approach to the semantics of prepositions. Accordingly, Lakoff (1987) provides a network that contains at least 24 distinct senses. More recently, work such as Evans (2000), Kreitzer (1997), Rice (1993), Ruhl (1989),[3] Sandra (1998), Sandra and Rice (1995), Tyler and Evans (2003), and Vandeloise (1990), has questioned whether such a fine-grained analysis is warranted, arguing that the Brugman/Lakoff analysis is methodologically unconstrained.

We will argue that a significant problem with previous approaches is that they fail to distinguish between what is coded by a lexical expression and the information that must be derived from context, background knowledge of the world, and spatial relations in general. That is, previous analyses fail to take account of meaning construction as a process which relies upon conceptual integration of linguistic and nonlinguistic prompts, guided by various global cognitive principles. Hence, we follow recent work in cognitive linguistics (Fauconnier 1994, 1997; Fauconnier and Turner 1998; Turner 1991, 1996), which posits that formal linguistic expression underspecifies for meaning. We will further argue that this failure stems in large part from the fact that previous approaches have not developed well-motivated criteria for (i) distinguishing between distinct senses within a network versus interpretations produced on-line and (ii) determining the primary sense associated with a preposition.

Our first objective in the present article is to outline what we term a "principled polysemy framework". This will anchor the semantic network of *over* to a foundational conceptual representation (our protoscene), deriving directly from uniquely human perceptions of and experience with the spatio-physical world. The protoscene we posit is a highly abstract representation of a recurring spatial configuration between two (or more) objects. Hence, details of the physical attributes of the objects involved in a particular spatial scene will be shown not to involve distinct senses (contra Brugman/Lakoff). We will argue that many of the distinct senses posited in previous approaches are produced on-line, as a result of a highly constrained process of integrating linguistic prompts at the conceptual level. Key to distinguishing our framework from previous ones will be outlining clear, motivated methodology for determining the protoscene associated with a preposition and distinguishing between senses that are instantiated in memory versus interpretations produced on-line. Our second objective is to demonstrate the usefulness of the framework by providing a complete account of the polysemy exhibited by *over*.

2. Previous approaches

2.1. *The full-specification approach*

The full-specification approach (e.g. Lakoff 1987) characterizes the polysemy network for *over* as subsuming distinct but related topographical structures at a fine-grained level. Each sense is represented by a distinct image-schema; each image-schema is related through various formal links and transformations. To see the level of granularity in this model, consider (1) and (2).

(1)   *The helicopter hovered over the ocean.*
(2)   *The hummingbird hovered over the flower.*

Following Langacker's *cognitive grammar* (Langacker 1987, 1991a, 1991b), figure–ground relations denoted by prepositions were described in terms of a *trajector* (TR) and a *landmark* (LM). Lakoff observed that in a sentence such as (1) *over* describes a relation between a TR, *the helicopter*, and a LM that is extended, *the ocean*, while in (2) the relationship is between a TR, *the hummingbird*, and a LM that is not extended, *the flower*. Lakoff argued that such differences in dimensionality of the LM should be represented as distinct senses in the semantic network associated with *over*. He termed this approach *full specification* (see Lakoff 1987 for full details and copious examples). From this view it follows that for a word such as *over*, there would be a vast number of distinct senses explicitly specified in the semantic network, including many of the metric characteristics of the variety of TRs and LMs, that can be mediated by the spatial relation designated by *over*.

While not in principle inconceivable,[4] in practice, as Kreitzer observed, the fine-grained distinctions between instances of *over* as in (1) and (2), along with the proposed links and transformations, provide a semantic network so unconstrained that "the model ... [allows] ... *across, through* and *above* all to be related to the polysemy network of *over*" (1997: 292). Sandra and Rice (1995), on the basis of their experimental findings, question whether the actual polysemy networks of language users are as fine-grained as suggested by models of the sort proposed by Lakoff. This view is echoed forthrightly in Vandeloise (1990).

Moreover, a Lakoff-type analysis fails to consider that detailed metric properties of LMs and TRs are often not specified by the lexical forms used by speakers in their utterances. For instance, the lexical form *flower* does not specify whether the entity should be construed as [+ vertical], as a tulip or calla lily might be, or [− vertical], as a lobelia or a water lily might be. Thus, in a sentence such as (2), *The hummingbird hovered over the flower*, it appears that verticality is not explicitly specified by the semantics of the LM. This indicates that there must be a sense of *over* in which the TR is higher than the nonextended LM and the verticality of the LM is not specified. Thus, Lakoff's account results in the highly questionable consequence of positing three senses of *over* in which the TR is located higher than a nonextended LM – one which specifies for a vertical LM, one which specifies for a nonvertical LM, and one which does not specify for verticality and hence subsumes the first two senses. Similarly, Lakoff's model would posit three additional senses involving a LM which is extended, one which specifies for verticality (e.g. *a mountain range*), one which specifies for nonverticality (e.g. *an ocean*), and one which does not specify for verticality (e.g. *the area*) and hence subsumes the first two.[5]

In essence, by building too much redundancy into the lexical representation, Lakoff's model vastly inflates the number of proposed distinct
meanings associated with a preposition such as *over*. An implicit consequence
of this representation is that real-world knowledge as well as discourse and
sentential context, which are used in the conceptual processes of inferencing
and meaning construction, are reduced in importance, as much of the information arising from inferencing and meaning construction is actually built
into the lexical representation.

2.2.   *The partial-specification approach*

Kreitzer's approach (1997), which we term *partial specification*, offers a
notable refinement of the Brugman/Lakoff approach because Kreitzer is able
to constrain the number of senses within a polysemy network, in a consistent,
motivated way. Building on work by Talmy (1983), Kreitzer posits that there
are three distinct levels of schematization inherent in the conceptualization
of a spatial scene: the component level, the relational level, and the integrative
level. The component level constitutes conceptual primitives, notions such
as LM, TR, PATH, contact between TR and LM, lack of contact, whether the
LM is extended, vertical, and so on. These combine giving the relational
level. Crucially, for Kreitzer "the relational level schema is taken as the basic
level of 'granularity' representing a sense of a preposition" (1997: 295).
Whereas for Lakoff each additional topographical component constituted a
distinct sense, Kreitzer claims that these individual components apply compositionally at the relational level. As such, image-schema transformations
(which allow new components to be added to the image-schemas) are no
longer taken as providing a new sense. Rather, image-schema transformations
simply serve to widen the applicability of a particular sense. Examples (3)
and (4) illustrate this point.

(3)   *The boy climbed over the wall.*
(4)   *The tennis ball flew over the wall.*

In (3) there is contact between the TR, *the boy*, and the LM, *the wall*,
whereas in (4) there is not. For Lakoff, this distinction warranted two distinct
senses. Kreitzer, by claiming that the sense provided by an image-schema is
defined at the relational level (rather than at the component level), is able to

argue that both usages represent only one sense of *over*. His insight is that the basic spatial relation between the TR and LM remains unchanged in (3) and (4), even though the components of the spatial scene may vary contextually. For Kreitzer, topographical features, such as contact and extendedness of the LM, are situated at the component level, and consequently do not delineate distinct senses or image-schemas.

Consequently, Kreitzer argues that the plethora of separate image-schemas posited by Lakoff can be represented by three image-schemas at the relational level. The primary sense, which he terms *over1*, is static, *over2* is dynamic, and *over3* is what Kreitzer terms the occluding sense. Examples of these are:

(5)   *The picture is over the sofa* [*over1*, static sense].
(6)   *Sam walked over the hill* [*over2*, dynamic sense].[6]
(7)   *The clouds are over the sun* [*over3*, occluding sense].

Although Kreitzer is successful in constraining Lakoff's analysis, his account faces a significant problem because his three basic senses of *over* are arbitrarily connected; they do not share a common TR–LM configuration. As Lakoff's model with a system of links and transformations has been abandoned, *over* now denotes three distinct relations, and it is difficult to see how Kreitzer's occluding sense of *over3* could be related to *over1* or *over2*. In order to appreciate the difficulty, consider (7) in relation to (5) and (6). In (7), *over* denotes a relationship in which the TR, *the clouds*, is beneath the LM, *the sun*. In (6), *over* denotes a dynamic relationship in which the TR is above the LM only at the midpoint of the TR, but in (5) the TR is stationed above the LM. It would seem that his claim to polysemy is undermined by three schemas so distinct as to have little in common. Moreover, he makes no attempt to account for how *over1* could give rise to *over2* and *over3* respectively.

Secondly, as with Lakoff's full-specification approach, Kreitzer's model fails to fully address the issue of the contributions of sentential context and background knowledge. Consider (8) for instance.

(8)   *The clouds moved over the city.*

Kreitzer posits that (8) has two construals as a result of his assumption that *over* has both a static and a dynamic relational schema. Construal 1 stipulates that the clouds moved above and across the city, such that they originated in a position not above the city, moved over the city, and came to be in a position beyond the city. Construal 2 stipulates that the clouds moved from a position in which they were not over the city, to a position such that they came to be directly over the city. These construals are diagrammed in Figures 1 and 2.

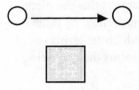

Figure 1. The clouds moved over the city: construal 1 (after Kreitzer 1997: 305).

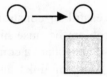

Figure 2. The clouds moved over the city: construal 2 (after Kreitzer 1997: 305).

Kreitzer argues that construal 1 is the result of *over2*, while construal 2 represents an integration of *move*, which contains a path schema as one of its components, and *over1*. On this view, the whole meaning of the sentence depends on which image-schema for *over* is taken.

In addition to these two construals posited by Kreitzer, however, there is a third construal in which the clouds move around but remain above the city. This is represented in Figure 3.

Based on Kreitzer's account, we would expect construal 3 to result from integration of *move* with *over1*, as the TR is always "above" the city. However, the problem for Kreitzer's account is that we have two construals, 2 and 3, which would thus not be distinguished image-schematically. How do we obtain distinct construals without such being coded?

Kreitzer's account is problematic because he is assuming that distinct construals either result from such being coded by a preposition at the relational level or arise at the integrative level. But the integrative level simply "conflates" the two linguistic codes. That is, the path schema of *move* is

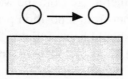

Figure 3.   The clouds moved over the city: construal 3.

added to the static schema of *over1*, resulting in a dynamic construal. Since we are able to distinguish construal 3 from construal 2, there must be a further level of integration at which linguistic codes are elaborated, such that linguistic underspecification is filled in, providing a variety of construals, limited only by our perceptual abilities and what is possible in the world. This is the level of integration we refer to as the conceptual level. Hence, a fundamental problem with Kreitzer's account (as well as with Lakoff's) is that it assumes that the rich understanding we obtain about spatial scenes is derived entirely from what is coded by formal linguistic expression. This represents a commitment to the view that conceptualization must always derive from linguistic antecedents. We argue that the ambiguity (given that there are three construals) arises precisely because *move* codes a path schema whereas *over* does not, and because of what we know about cities and clouds (cities, unlike walls, for instance, occupy an extended area). Accordingly, the elements can be integrated in at least three different ways, as indicated by the three construals. This is testimony to the highly elaborate and rich process of conceptual integration. The linguistic prompts themselves do not provide distinct interpretations; these come from our knowledge of what is possible in the world and our ability to integrate minimal cues to construct a complex and dynamic conceptualization of a spatial scene. Sentence (9) illustrates this point.

(9)   *The clouds moved over the wall.*

In (9) construals 1 (Fig. 1) and 3 (Fig. 3) are ruled out, not because *over* has both a dynamic and a static sense, but because walls are not extended landmarks (as noted in Lakoff's analysis), whereas cities are, and *moved* codes a path schema. Thus, when the sentential elements are integrated, the TR follows a path, as designated by *moved*, such that the TR occupies a position relative to the LM, as specified by the mental representation for *over*. The clouds move, neither away from the wall, nor in a vertical manner without crossing the wall, but from a position prior to the wall to a position beyond the wall. That this should be so follows from conceptual integration of the cues prompted by the linguistic elements in the sentence. Accordingly, we argue that a polysemy network needs to allow for the distributed contribution of meaning played by all sentential elements, as well as the constraints imposed by our experience of the world and our ability to construct a rich and highly dynamic conceptualization based on minimal linguistic cues.

Another problem with Kreitzer's account is that in attempting to constrain Lakoff's analysis he has significantly understated the amount of polysemy appropriately associated with *over*. For instance, many senses touched on by Lakoff are simply ignored by Kreitzer. We will provide a detailed examination of the semantic network for *over* in Section 4. Finally, neither Kreitzer nor Lakoff attempts a serious account of how he determined which sense of *over* should be considered the primary sense. We address this issue in detail in Section 3.2.

The spirit of our model is coherent with a number of previous analyses that have addressed the multiple meanings associated both with prepositions (Herskovits 1986; Vandeloise 1991, 1994) and with other linguistic forms (Cushing 1990, 1991). While these scholars differ from each other and from us in several key assumptions (e.g. the nature of lexical representation), they do entertain the possibility that the polysemy exhibited might be best modelled in terms of a central (or ideal) sense.[7]

3.   Principled polysemy: the basic framework

3.1.   *Methodology for determining distinct senses*

One of the problems with previous polysemy networks, as noted by Sandra and Rice (1995), is that there appear to be as many different approaches to how best to model a semantic network as there are semantic network theorists. While we accept that all linguistic analysis is to some extent subjective, we propose here to introduce methodology to minimize the subjective nature of our analysis. We do so in the hope that other scholars can employ our methodology and test the predictions made by our model. We aim to provide the basis for replicability of findings, a prerequisite for any theoretically rigorous study.

We suggest two criteria for determining whether a particular instance of a preposition counts as a distinct sense. Firstly, accepting the standard assumption that the primary sense coded for by prepositions is a particular spatial relation between a TR and a LM (although we will nuance what "spatial" means), for a sense to count as distinct, it must involve a meaning that is not purely spatial in nature and/or in which the spatial configuration between the TR and LM is changed *vis-à-vis* the other senses associated with a particular preposition.[8] Secondly, there must be instances of the sense that are context-independent, instances in which the distinct sense could not be inferred from another sense and the context in which it occurs. To see how this would work let us reconsider the sentences in (1) and (2). In (1), *over* designates a spatial relation in which the TR, coded by *the helicopter*, is located higher than the LM. In (2), *over* also designates a spatial relationship in which the TR, *the hummingbird*, is located higher than the LM, coded by *the flower*. Neither instance of *over* constitutes a nonspatial interpretation, hence neither use adds additional meaning with respect to the other. By virtue of our proposed methodology, these instances of *over* cannot be treated as two distinct senses.

In contrast, examples (10) and (11) do appear to constitute a distinct sense.

(10)   *Joan nailed a board over the hole in the ceiling.*
(11)   *Joan nailed a board over the hole in the wall.*

In these sentences the spatial configuration between the TR and LM designated by *over* is not consistent with the "above" meaning designated in examples (1) and (2). In addition, a nonspatial meaning appears to be part of the interpretation. That is, the meaning associated with *over* appears to be that of covering, such that *the hole*, the LM, is obscured from view by the TR. Clearly, this notion of covering and obscuring represents an additional meaning not apparent in examples such as (1) and (2). The fact that the usage in (10) and (11) brings additional meaning meets the first assessment criterion for whether this instance counts as a distinct sense.

In terms of the second criterion, we must establish whether the covering or obscuring meaning can be derived from context. If it can be, then this instance would fail the second assessment criterion and so could not, on the basis of the present methodology, be deemed a distinct sense. Assuming that the primary sense of *over* involves a spatial configuration between a TR and LM and that this configuration involves some sense of the TR being higher than the LM,[9] we see no way in which the covering meaning component associated with *over* in (10) and (11) can be derived from context. To see why this is so, contrast this instance with (12), in which the covering meaning is derivable from context.

(12)   *The tablecloth is over the table.*

The TR, the *tablecloth*, is higher than (and in contact with) the LM, *the table*. As tablecloths are typically larger than tables, and the usual vantage point from which such a spatial scene would be viewed is a point higher than the table, the result would be that a substantial part of the table would be covered and so obscured from view. The interpretation that the table is covered/obscured could be inferred from the fact that the tablecloth is *over* and hence higher than the table, in conjunction with our knowledge that tablecloths are larger than tables and that we typically view tables from above the top of the table. Such an inference is not possible in (10) as the spatial relation holding between the TR and the LM is one that would normally be coded by *below* (i.e. *the board is below the hole in the ceiling*), rather than by *over*, given the typical vantage point. Similarly, in (11) the spatial configuration between the TR and LM would normally be coded by something like *next to*. In short, unless we already know that *over* has a covering/obscuring meaning associated with it, there is no ready contextual means of deriving this meaning in sentences such as (10) and (11). From this, we conclude that the covering/obscuring meaning associated with *over* in (10) and (11) constitutes a distinct sense.

The two assessment criteria being proposed are rigorous and, in the light of future empirical research, may be shown to exclude senses that are legitimately instantiated in the language user's mental lexicon and hence would have to be adjusted. Nonetheless, without prejudging future findings, we suggest that this methodology predicts many findings that have already come to light, and so represents a reasonable approximation for assessing where we should draw the line between what counts as a distinct sense conventionalized in semantic memory, and a contextual inference produced on-line for the purpose of local understanding. The appeal of such methodology is that it provides a rigorous and relatively consistent way of making judgements about whether a sense is distinct, and provides methodology that can be used in an intersubjective way.

3.2. *Methodology for determining the primary sense*

An equally thorny problem is the question of what counts as the primary sense associated with a polysemy network. In previous studies of semantic networks, researchers have assumed that there is a single primary sense associated with a preposition and that the other senses are derived from this primary sense in a principled way. We share this assumption. Scholars, however, have often disagreed about which sense should be taken as primary (or central). Lakoff (1987) following Brugman (1981), argued that the primary sense for *over* is "above and across", and included a path along which the TR moves, as represented by sentences such as *The plane flew over the city*. Kreitzer (1997) disagreed, suggesting that the primary sense (*over1*) is something akin to an "above" sense, as in *The hummingbird hovered over the flower*. These decisions were primarily asserted rather than being argued for. Because linguists have simply asserted what constitutes the primary sense for a particular lexical category, appealing to intuitions and assumptions they often fail to explicitly articulate, we are in the unfortunate position that Lakoff (1987) and Kreitzer (1997) can offer equally plausible yet conflicting views of what the primary sense of *over* should be.

Sandra and Rice (1995) observed that given the current state of theoretical development, any analysis of a polysemy network, including what constitutes its primary sense, is relatively arbitrary, reflecting each analyst's own preferences (or indeed imagination). Langacker, however, has argued persuasively that there are various kinds of evidence to help us discover and verify the structure of a complex category (1987: 376). Building on his suggestions we advance a set of criteria that we believe provides a more principled, intersubjective method of determining the appropriate primary sense for individual prepositions. As with our criteria for determining distinct senses, we see these criteria as the beginning of a plausible methodology leading to replicability of findings. We hypothesize that some of these criteria may also be useful for other classes of words. But because of the particular nature of prepositions – that they code for spatial relations that may not have changed over many thousands of years (that is, the way humans perceive space seems not to have changed), and that they are a closed class – the nature of the primary senses associated with lexical forms is likely to be at least somewhat distinct from the primary senses associated with word classes such as nouns, adjectives, and verbs.

We suggest that there are at least four types of linguistic evidence that can be used to narrow the arbitrariness of the selection of a primary sense. We posit that no one piece of evidence is criterial but, taken together, they form a substantial body of evidence pointing to one sense among the many distinct senses being what Langacker (1987: 157) terms the *sanctioning sense*, from which other senses may have been extended. The evidence includes (i) earliest attested meaning; (ii) predominance in the semantic network; (iii) relations to other prepositions; and (iv) grammatical predictions (Langacker 1987).

Given the very stable nature of the conceptualization of spatial relations within a language, one likely candidate for the primary sense is the historically earliest sense. Having examined more than 15 English prepositions (see Tyler and Evans 2003), we found that the historical evidence indicates the earliest attested uses coded a spatial configuration holding between the TR and the LM (as opposed to a nonspatial configuration as in *The movie is over* [= complete]). Since English has historically drawn from several languages, not all prepositions entered the language at the same time and there are instances of competing, near synonyms, for instance, *beneath*, *below*, and *under*. In such cases, over a period of time the semantic territory has been divided among such competing prepositions, but even so, they retain a core meaning that directly involves the original TR–LM configuration. Unlike words from many other word classes, the earliest attested sense for many prepositions is still a major, active component of the synchronic semantic network of each particle. *Over* is related to the Sanskrit *upan* 'higher' as well as the Old Teutonic comparative form *ufa* 'above', that is, a spatial configuration in which the TR is higher than the LM (OED).

Turning to the notion of predominance within a semantic network, by this we mean that the sense most likely to be primary will be the one whose meaning components are most frequent in other distinct senses. We have identified 14 distinct senses associated with *over*. Of these, eight directly involve the TR being located higher than the LM; four involve a TR located on the other side of the LM *vis-à-vis* the vantage point; and three – covering, reflexive, and repetition – involve multiple TR–LM configurations. Thus, the criterion of predominance suggests that the primary sense for *over* involves a TR being located higher than the LM.

Within the entire group of English prepositions, certain clusters of prepositions appear to form compositional sets that divide up various spatial dimensions. *Above*, *over*, *under*, and *below* appear to form a compositional set that divides the vertical dimension into four related subspaces (see Tyler and Evans 2003). Other compositional sets include *in* and *out*, *on* and *off*, *up* and *down*. The linguistically coded division of space and spatial relations is relativistic in nature, depending largely on construal of the particular scene being prompted for (Langacker 1987; Talmy 1988, 2000). To a large extent, the label assigned to denote a particular TR–LM configuration is determined in relation to other labels in the composite set. So, for instance, what we label as *up* is partially determined by what we label as *down*. In this sense, the meaning of a preposition that participates in a compositional set is partially determined by how it contrasts with other members of the set. The particular sense used in the formation of such a compositional set would thus seem to be a likely candidate as a primary sense. For *over*, the sense that distinguishes this preposition from *above*, *under*, and *below* involves the notion of a TR being located higher than but potentially within reach of the LM. We expand on this argument in the next section.

The choice of a primary sense gives rise to testable grammatical predictions. So, for instance, if we recognize that what are now distinct senses were at one time derived from and related to a pre-existing sense and became part of the semantic network through routinization and entrenchment of meaning, we would predict that a number of the senses should be directly derivable from the primary sense. This is consistent with Langacker's (1987) discussion of a *sanctioning sense* giving rise to additional senses through extension. Any senses not directly derivable from the primary sense itself should be traceable to a sense that was derived from the primary sense. This view of polysemy explicitly acknowledges that language is an evolving, usage-based system. Grammatically, for any distinct sense that is represented as directly related to the primary sense, we should be able to find sentences whose context provides the implicature that gives rise to the additional meaning associated with the distinct sense. We have already discussed this notion briefly (Section 3.1) when we considered the additional meaning of covering/obscuring associated with *over* in (10)–(12). We argued that the use of *over* in (10) and (11) revealed additional meaning that could not be derived from sentential context, while the additional meaning of covering/ obscuring could be derived from context in (12). By the criterion of grammatical prediction, (12) constitutes evidence that a likely candidate for the primary sense associated with *over* involves the TR being located higher than the LM, as the distinct covering/obscuring sense can be derived from this primary sense and certain sentential contexts. Of course, the covering/ obscuring sense is only one of 14; all other senses would have to be tested against this same criterion.

3.3.   The protoscene

As we said earlier, we assume that English prepositions form polysemy networks organized around a primary sense. At the conceptual level, the primary sense is represented in terms of abstracting away from specific spatial scenes, that is, real-world scenarios such as described by (13a) and (13b), resulting in an idealized spatio-functional configuration.

(13)   a.   *The picture is over the mantel.*
        b.   *The bee is hovering over the flower.*

We call this abstracted mental representation of the primary sense the *protoscene*. It consists of a schematic trajector (TR), which is the locand (the element located, and in focus), and is typically smaller and movable; a schematic landmark (LM), which is the locator (the element with respect to which the TR is located, and in background), and is typically larger and immovable, and a conceptual configurational–functional relation which mediates the TR and the LM. In the case of *over*, the TR is conceptualized as being proximate to the LM, so that under certain circumstances, the TR could come into contact with the LM. The functional aspect resulting from this particular spatial configuration is that the LM (or the TR) is conceptualized as being within the sphere of influence of the TR (or the LM) (see Dewell 1994, and Vandeloise 1991, 1994 for a discussion of other prepositions).

In our label *protoscene*, the term *proto* captures the idealized aspect of the conceptual relation, which lacks the rich detail apparent in individual spatial scenes, while the use of *scene* emphasizes visual awareness of a spatial scene, although the information included in the image can contain information from other sense-perceptions. Because protoscenes are abstractions ultimately arising from recurring real-world spatial scenarios, we will diagram them.[10] In our diagrammatic representation of the protoscene posited for *over* (Fig. 4), the TR is portrayed as a dark sphere, the LM as a bold line.

The dashed line signals a distinction between the part of the spatial scene conceptualized as being proximal to the LM (i.e. within potential contact with the LM) and that which is conceptualized as being distal. The vantage point for construing the spatial scene is offstage, and external to the spatial scene. Crucially, the linguistic form *over* prompts for the conceptual spatial relation captured by the protoscene.

Two claims warrant more thorough investigation. The first is that the

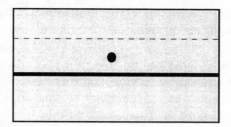

Figure 4. The protoscene for *over.*

spatial configuration holding between the TR–LM is correctly expressed by the description that *over* lexicalizes the protoscene depicted in Figure 4, namely that the TR is above but within a region of potential contact with the LM. This contrasts with the English preposition *above*, which we argue prompts for a conceptual spatial relation in which the TR is higher than but not within reach of the LM. The second claim warranting further scrutiny is that the TR and LM are within each other's sphere of influence.

Dealing with the first claim, using the criterion of relationship to other prepositions which form a compositional set, consider the instances of *over* and *above* in sentences such as (14).

(14) a. *She walked over the bridge.*
      b. *She walked above the bridge.*

The sentences in (14) are characteristic of the distinction in English between *over* and *above*. While in (14a) the conventional reading is one in which the TR, *she*, is above but within reach (in this particular case, the TR is in contact with the bridge), most native speakers of English would exclude possible contact from their reading of (14b). The TR, *she*, might constitute a ghostly presence capable of levitation, or the TR might be on a second bridge higher than the first, but generally English speakers would not interpret the bridge as the surface being walked upon. These examples strongly suggest that we are right in positing that *over* does designate a spatial configuration in which the TR is in potential contact with the LM.

We turn now to the functional aspect of the protoscene in Figure 4, namely the claim that the TR and LM are within each other's sphere of influence. A consequence of being within potential reach of the LM is that the TR can affect the LM in some way and *vice versa*. For instance, because of an independently motivated experiential correlation (Grady 1997), we conventionally understand power and control being associated with an entity who is higher than the entity being controlled (we will discuss this in more detail when we deal with the control sense for *over*). In physical terms we can only control someone or something, and hence ensure compliance, if we are physically proximal to the entity we seek to control. If, then, in recurring human experience, control, and hence the ability to physically influence someone or something, is dependent upon being higher than and physically close to the entity we seek to control, we would expect that these notions can be designated by *over* but not *above*. While both *over* and *above* designate spatial relations which are higher than, only *over* also designates the functional relation of influence, precisely because part of its spatial configuration involves the notion of potential contact between the TR and LM. Consider (15).

(15)   a.   *She has a strange power over me.* (Lakoff 1987)
        b.   *?She has a strange power above me.*

In terms of a control reading, while *over* in (15a) is perfectly acceptable, *above* in (15b) is decidedly odd. This suggests that the protoscene for *over* does indeed have a functional element of influence between the TR and LM, as a consequence of its spatial configuration designating potential contact between the TR and LM (see Vandeloise 1994 for a discussion of the functional nature of prepositions).

This relation places certain maximal constraints on what can count as *over*: a spatial relation should be prompted for using the preposition *over* only if the spatial relation ranges from a configuration in which there is TR–LM contact to one in which there is no contact but the TR can be construed as within potential reach of the LM. While there is strong evidence for defining *over* in this way, a review of the many interpretations regularly assigned to *over* by speakers of English shows that this representation alone is inadequate. Hence, there is a need to posit a set of cognitive principles of meaning construction and meaning extension that will account for the many additional senses associated with *over*.

3.4.   Cognitive Principles

3.4.1.   Perceptual analysis and reconceptualization

Mandler (1988, 1992, 1996) argues that a basic aspect of human cognition is the ability to submit salient (i.e. recurring) real-world scenarios and spatial scenes to perceptual analysis that gives rise to a new level of conceptualized information which is stored imagistically in the form of an abstract schematization, termed an *image-schema*.[11] Once stored, the image-schema is available for integration with other conceptualizations, further analysis, and reconceptualization.

Earlier, we used the term *conceptualization* in a nontechnical way. In order to distinguish our nontechnical usage from a more sharpened operationalization, we here introduce the term *complex conceptualization*. A complex conceptualization is a constructed representation,[12] typically (but not inevitably) produced on-line. A complex conceptualization represents our projection of reality (in the sense of Jackendoff 1983), and can represent static and relatively simple phenomena, e.g. *The cloud is over the sun*, or dynamic and relatively complex phenomena, e.g. *The cat ran over the hill and ended up several miles away*. Our claim is that the integration of linguistic forms with other cognitive knowledge prompts for the construction of a complex conceptualization.

In our model, the image-schemas representing the spatial configurations associated with prepositions are termed protoscenes.[13] The primary scene (i.e. the protoscene) associated with a preposition can be used, in conjunction with other linguistic prompts (i.e. within an utterance), to prompt for recurring spatial scenes and real-world scenarios.

Figure 5 represents the complex conceptualization which would be constructed in the interpretation of the recurring scenario prompted by sentences such as (16) and (17).

(16)   *The rabbit hopped over the fence.*
(17)   *The boy stepped over the pile of leaves.*

At some point, such recurring complex conceptualizations become subject to reanalysis and hence reconceptualization.[14] We posit that distinct senses arise as a result of the reanalysis of a particular aspect of such a recurring complex conceptualization. In other words, the recurring complex conceptualization from which a distinct sense originally arises is derivable from the

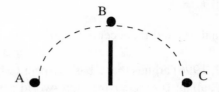

Figure 5.   Schematization of sentences of the type *The cat jumped over the wall.*

protoscene and thus the distinct sense is related to the protoscene in a principled manner.

On our analysis, while prepositions themselves do not prompt for dynamism, prepositions do participate in prompting for complex conceptualizations, which often are dynamic (in the sense that they include motion phenomena). Minimally varying static spatial scenes can be integrated at the conceptual level to provide a dynamic sequence. This is analogous to the way in which movie stills (static images) are flashed onto a screen in sequence to create the illusion of a moving image, a movie. Hence, we are arguing that prepositions prompt for nondynamic conceptual spatial relations, while maintaining that such relations can be integrated with other prompts, to create (dynamic) complex conceptualizations. In sum, we hold that while human conceptualization of spatial scenes is rich and dynamic, the available linguistic prompts underspecify such richness. Meaning is the result of integration of linguistic prompts at the conceptual level. Thus, the protoscene for *over* is integrated in the most felicitous way, given the sentential context, and given what we know about what is possible in the world.

3.4.2.   Ways of viewing spatial scenes

The notion of a vantage point mentioned in the discussion of the protoscene suggests that how a particular spatial scene is viewed will in large part determine the functional nature of a particular spatial scene, and thus in what way it is meaningful. Four distinct issues affect the functional nature of a particular spatial scene, based on the different ways in which such scenes can be construed (i.e. "viewed").

(i)   Every spatial scene is conceptualized from a particular vantage point.

The conceptualizer represents the default vantage point. Accordingly, the same scene can be construed from many different vantage points (Langacker [1987] divides this phenomenon into two aspects, *perspective* and *vantage point*).

(ii)   Certain parts of the spatial scene can be profiled (Langacker 1987, 1992). Thus, in the sentence *The cat is sitting in the middle of the circle*, the TR, *the cat*, is conceptualized as being surrounded by the LM, described by the circle; here the LM is being conceptualized as a container, and the space encompassed by the LM is being profiled. In contrast, in the sentence *Okay everybody, get in a circle*, the outer edge, or shape of the LM, is being profiled.[15]

(iii)   Related to (ii) is the fact that the same scene can be construed in a different way. For instance, in a spatial scene in which a large cloth is positioned in relation to a table such that the cloth covers the top of the table, the scene can be construed by focusing on contact between the cloth and the table. In this case, the scene is likely to be coded in English by the sentence *The tablecloth is on the table*. Alternatively, the relationship between the cloth and the table can be viewed as the cloth occluding the table from the observer's vantage point. In this case, the scene might be coded as *The cloth is over the table*. A less typical, but perfectly acceptable construal would be to place the table in focus, in which case the coding would be something like *The table is under the tablecloth*.

(iv)   The exact properties of the entities which are conceptualized as TR and LM can vary. In the sentence *The hot air balloon floated over New York City*, the LM is conceptualized as vertical and extended; whereas in the sentence *The plane flew over the ocean*, the LM is nonvertical and extended.

3.4.3.   Atemporality

In advancing the model of word meaning on which we will base our analysis of *over* in Section 4, we note, following Langacker (1987, 1991a, 1991b, 1992; see also Talmy 1988, 2000) that prepositions profile (i.e. designate) a spatio-functional relation that is scanned (i.e. apprehended) in summary fashion.[16] That is, they do not profile a relation that evolves through time, as is the case for example with verbs. Verbs profile processes that are scanned in serial fashion. For instance, in the sentence *The boy runs home from school*, the process profiled by *run* constitutes a process that integrates all the points occupied by the TR, *The boy*, which intervene between *school* and *home*, hence the process evolves through time by integrating these sequential components. The result is a sequential process. This contrasts with the relation described by a preposition, which does not evolve through time. Prepositions represent a conceptualized relation holding between two entities (a TR and a LM), independent of sequentially evolving interdependencies. In this sense, prepositions can be considered to profile atemporal relations.

3.4.4.   Inferencing strategies

We have argued that not all meanings assigned to a preposition, which arise from interpreting the particle within an utterance, are stored as distinct senses, and that previous models have often failed to recognize the contribution of encyclopaedic knowledge and inferencing involved in natural language processing. In deriving on-line interpretations we employ a number of inferencing strategies. Because of space constraints we will mention just three of the most important. In Section 4 we provide a detailed illustration of how these strategies enable us to produce meaning on-line.

(i)   Best fit. Only a tiny fraction of all possible spatial relations are coded by discrete lexical items. In linguistic terms, prepositions represent a closed class, that is, English speakers have a limited set of linguistic choices to represent a virtually unlimited set of conceptual spatial relations. Speakers choose the preposition that offers the best fit between the conceptual spatial relation and the speaker's communicative needs. The notion of best fit represents a crucial means for allowing us to fill in information about a particular spatial scene. To our knowledge, no other linguist has specifically discussed this notion, but it seems to be a logical extension of the notion of relevance (Grice 1975; Sperber and Wilson 1986).

(ii)   Knowledge of real-world force dynamics. Although a spatial scene is conceptual in nature, in the creation and interpretation of an utterance the speaker and hearer will assume that all elements in a spatial scene are subject to real-world force dynamics.[17] For instance, in the interpretation of a sentence such as *The cat jumped over the wall*, it is assumed the interlocutors will apply their knowledge of the world, which includes the information that entities cannot float in mid-air unless they possess the means or ability to do so. General knowledge of cats includes the information that they cannot hover above walls and that they are subject to gravity. Hence, any responsible account of the conceptual system and meaning extension must recognize the large body of real-world knowledge we bring to bear (often unconsciously) when constructing meaning. Vandeloise (1991) discusses this in terms of a naïve theory of physics that applies to how humans conceptualize spatial relations and use language to express those conceptualizations.

(iii)   Topological extension. This strategy involves the notion that the principles of Euclidean geometry do not hold at the level of conceptual structure (Talmy 1988, 2000). Conceptualized space and spatial relations are not held to be metric notions of fixed distance, amount, size, contour, angle, and so on. Rather, conceptualized space and spatial relations are topological in nature, that is they "involve relativistic relationships rather than absolutely fixed quantities" (2000: 170). Thus, a TR–LM configuration can be distorted conceptually, as long as the relation denoted by the protoscene remains constant. In applying this principle to prepositions, we argue that *over* denotes a relation in which the TR is above but within reach of the LM. This functional relationship has sometimes been referred to as the TR/LM being conceptualized as in each other's *sphere of influence* (Dewell 1994). The principle of topological extension allows us to account for examples in which, on first analysis at least, this relation does not appear to hold, e.g. *The plane flew over the city* (the plane is a considerable distance above the city, yet is being conceptualized as within potential reach).

3.5.   On-line meaning construction

How might on-line meaning construction apply to the protoscene (or indeed any distinct sense) to produce a contextualized interpretation of a preposition? To illustrate this process, we will consider the path sense posited by Lakoff (1987) and Kreitzer (1997). Lakoff termed this the above-across sense, while Kreitzer called it *over2*. Both Lakoff and Kreitzer sought to capture the intuition that *over* could be employed to designate a trajectory followed by a TR in which it moves from a position on one side of a LM so that it comes to be on the other side, as in (18).

(18)   *The cat jumped over the wall.*

Crucially, they suggested that *over* codes the trajectory or path as a distinct sense instantiated in semantic memory. Following the methodology previously suggested for determining whether a sense is distinct or not, we posit that in sentences such as (18) the interpretation that the TR follows a particular trajectory described by "above and across" can be inferred from context. Based on this methodology, *over* does not have a distinct above-across path sense associated with it.

The case for attributing an above-across sense to *over* in examples such as (18) relies on implied reasoning which runs as follows: (i) a spatial scene is conceptualized in which a cat starts from a position on one side of the wall and comes to be in a position on the other side; (ii) there is nothing in the sentence, other than *over*, which indicates the trajectory followed by the cat; (iii) therefore, *over* must prompt for an above-and-across trajectory. But this conclusion is a *non sequitur*. Simply because a trajectory is not prompted for by specific linguistic forms (formal expression) does not entail that such information is absent. To reach this conclusion is to assume that the lack of formal expression coding trajectory information implicates a lack of trajectory information *per se*. On this view, all elements that are salient in the interpretation of a scene must be coded linguistically.

We offer an alternative account that argues that the meaning assigned to any utterance is radically underdetermined by the lexical items and the grammatical structures in which they occur. That is, sentential interpretation is largely the result of various cognitive/inferential processes and accessing appropriate world knowledge. Consider the conceptualizations prompted for by the sentence in (18) and contrast this with (19).

(19)   *The tree branch extended over the wall.*

Lakoff's full-specification account for *over* would argue that (18) and (19) represent two different senses of *over*. For (19) he assumes that *over* has a meaning that can be paraphrased as "above" while in (18) *over* has a meaning, as already intimated, of "above and across". The implied reasoning for adducing that *over* in (19) is associated with a static "higher than" sense runs as follows: in the interpretation prompted for by (19), (i) no motion is involved hence there is no trajectory; (ii) the branch is located above the wall; and (iii) the only element that indicates the location of the branch in relation to the wall is the word *over;* hence, (iv) *over* must have an above sense.

We suggest that it is wrong to conclude that examples (18) and (19) represent two distinct senses. Rather than representing prepositions as carrying detailed information about each scene being described, we argue that they prompt for schematic conceptualizations (a protoscene and other distinct senses instantiated in semantic memory) that are interpreted within the particular contexts in which they occur. Under our analysis, a path (or its absence) is typically prompted for by the verb as it relates to other words in the sentence.[18]

In (18), the verb *jumped* does prompt for a conceptualization involving motion, which entails a trajectory. Hence, the interpretation of the above-across trajectory of the movement in (18) is not prompted for by *over* (i.e. the concept of the TR in motion is not a semantic attribute of the protoscene), nor for any of the other distinct senses associated with *over*, but rather arises from the integration of linguistic prompts at the conceptual level. Most of the information required to integrate the linguistic prompts and construct a mental conceptualization of the spatial scene is filled in by inferencing and real-world or encyclopaedic knowledge. In turn, this knowledge constrains the possible interpretations that *over* can have in this particular sentence. In the interpretation of (18), encyclopaedic knowledge (as adduced in part by the inferencing strategy pertaining to real-world force dynamics) includes (at the very least): (i) our understanding of the action of jumping, and in particular our knowledge of the kind of jumping cats are likely to engage in (that is, not straight up in the air as on a trampoline and not from a bungee cord suspended from a tree branch extending above the wall); (ii) our knowledge of cats (for instance, that they cannot physically hover in the air the way a hummingbird can); (iii) our knowledge of the nature of walls (that they provide vertical, impenetrable obstacles to forward motion along a path); and (iv) our knowledge of force dynamics such as gravity (which tells us that a cat cannot remain in mid-air indefinitely and that if the cat jumped from the ground such that the trajectory of its path at point B matches the relation described by *over the wall*, then it would have to come to rest beyond the wall, providing an arc trajectory). Thus, we argue that the interpretation regarding the above-across interpretation of the trajectory in sentence (18) is not prompted for by *over*, but rather arises from the integration of linguistic prompts at the conceptual level, in a way that is maximally coherent with and contingent on our real-world interactions.

We further suggest that part of the general understanding of this particular sentence involves the interpretation of *the wall* as an obstacle which *the cat* is attempting to overcome. There is an important conceptual connection between the TR, *the cat*, and the LM, *the wall*, that is, *the cat* and *the wall* are within each other's sphere of influence. Given this particular context and the functional element we have assigned the protoscene, the salient point is that the cat jumped high enough to overcome the obstacle. The exact metric details of a spatial relation in a specific spatial scene are filled in by application of inferencing strategies. These allow us to construct a likely interpretation, based largely on knowledge gained from recurring daily interactions with our environment. To make this point more concrete, reconsider Figure 5, which offers an approximate depiction of the complex conceptualization constructed in the interpretation of (18).

In Figure 5, the various positions occupied by the TR, *the cat*, along its trajectory are represented by the three spheres labelled A, B, and C. Notice that only point B – the point at which the cat is higher than but in potential reach of the wall – is explicitly mentioned in the sentence (i.e. this point in the trajectory is explicitly prompted for by the occurrence of *over*. Points A and C are inferred from what we know about jumping, cats and walls. The verb *jumped* codes self-propelled motion using a solid surface to push off from; thus, point A is implied as the initial point of the trajectory. The prompts are integrated in such a way that the trajectory initiated by the verb *jump* intersects with point B. Our knowledge of real-world force dynamics fills in position C. Put another way, if a cat begins at point A and passes through point B, then given our knowledge of gravity and the kind of jumping cats are able to do, point C is entailed.

Many spatial relationships exist between the TR and the LM in the complex conceptualization represented diagrammatically in Figure 5; thus, the speaker has many choices of which relationship between the TR and LM to mention. For instance, at both points A and C, the cat is beside the wall. The cat could also be described as jumping near the wall. But, none of these choices provides a sufficient cue for the construction of the relevant conceptualization that the cat jumped such that at one point in its trajectory it was higher than, but crucially within the sphere of influence of, the wall. Alternative prepositions fail to prompt for the key spatial configuration that prompts the listener to construct the complex conceptualization represented in Figure 5. Given the conceptualization the speaker wishes to convey, the speaker chooses from the closed class of English prepositions the one that best fits the relevant conceptual spatial relation between the TR and LM at one point in the cat's trajectory, which will, in turn, prompt the appropriate entailments or inferences. This inferencing strategy is the notion of best fit. Accordingly, we reiterate that a serious flaw in both the full- and partial-specification approaches is that neither fully distinguishes between formal expression in language, which represents certain information, and patterns of conceptualization, which integrate information prompted for by other linguistic elements of the sentence. *Over* does not itself prompt for an above-across sense, that is, for a path. We hypothesize that all path or trajectory information in the examples discussed results from conceptual integration of linguistic and other prompts, following the notion of best fit, which determines that the relation designated by the protoscene (and indeed other distinct senses) will not precisely capture a dynamic real-world spatial relation, which is constantly changing, but will provide a sufficient cue for conceptualization.

In order to illustrate the strategy of topological extension, we offer example (20).

(20)   *There are a few stray marks just above the line.*

Example (20) provides, on first inspection at least, a counterexample to the spatial configuration we proposed for the protoscene associated with *over* when it designates a spatial relation in which the TR is above but crucially within potential contact with the LM. On this view then, we would expect *over*, and not *above* to be employed in sentences such as (20), as this example is describing a spatial scene in which the TR, *a few stray marks*, is physically proximal to the LM, *the line*.

However, the inferencing strategy of topological extension places less significance on the absolute metric distance between the TR and LM than on the functional element associated with a particular sense. That is, the metric distance between the TR and LM can be extended or contracted if the functional element holds; in the case of *over* the TR and LM are understood as being within each other's sphere of influence. Although the *few stray marks*, the TR, are metrically proximal to *the line*, the LM, there is no contact and no potential for contact between them. The stray marks are distinct from the line and the LM is not within the sphere of influence of the TR. On the basis of sentences such as *She walked above the bridge*, in which no contact between the TR and LM is possible, we hypothesize that the functional element of the protoscene for *above* places the focus on the notion of non-bridgeable distance between the LM and TR. Thus, the relation in (14b) is best designated by *above*. This analysis is supported if we attempt to use *over* in place of *above*, as in *There are a few stray marks over the line*, which presents the ambiguous interpretation that the marks are in contact with the line and potentially obscuring parts of it. This interpretation arises from the covering sense, which we will address later.

Grice (1975) noted with his *maxim of manner* that in everyday conversation speakers generally try to avoid ambiguity, unless there is a purpose for the ambiguity. To avoid possible ambiguity, the inferencing strategy of attempting best fit in the choice of lexical item suggests that the speaker will choose the protoscene (or particular sense) that best facilitates conceptualization of the scene he or she intends the listener to construct. In light of the strategies of topological extension and best fit, we argue that *above* is the most felicitous choice to prompt for the complex conceptualization that involves a LM (a *line*), and a TR (*stray marks*) that is higher than and not in contact with the LM, as attested by (20).[19]

3.6. Pragmatic strengthening

Earlier we presented a method for establishing when a sense is distinct and hence putatively instantiated in semantic memory. Given our assumption that the distinct senses associated with a particular preposition are related to one another in a principled way, one of our purposes is to understand both how and why new senses associated with a particular preposition came to be derived. Since what are now conventionalized senses at one time did not exist, we seek to explain how they are related to the protoscene. Our hypothesis is that all the senses associated with the preposition *over* were at one time derived from the protoscene or from a sense that can be traced back to the protoscene for each individual preposition.[20]

Grady (1997) has shown in detail that tight correlations in experience can lead to conceptual associations between two quite distinct and otherwise unrelated concepts. For instance, on a daily basis we experience recurring correlations between quantity and vertical elevation. When a liquid is added to a container or when more objects are added to a pile, an increase in quantity correlates with an increase in height. Grady has suggested that correlations of this kind result in lexical items relating to vertical elevation developing a conventional reading in which they denote quantity, as in sentences such as *The prices have gone up*, where *gone up* refers not literally to an increase in vertical elevation, but rather to a quantificational increase.

A number of scholars who have investigated the meaning extension of lexical items have observed that inferences deriving from experience (analogous to the situation just discussed) can, through continued usage, come to be conventionally associated with the lexical form identified with the implicature (see e.g. Bybee, Perkins and Pagliuca 1994; Evans 2000; Fleischman 1999; Hopper and Traugott 1993; Svorou 1993; Traugott 1989). Following Traugott, we term this process *pragmatic strengthening*, and it results in the association of a new meaning component with a particular lexical form through the continued use of the form in particular contexts in which the implicature results. New senses derive from the conventionalization of implicatures through routinization and the entrenchment of usage patterns.

Recurring implicatures that come to be conventionalized can result either from independently motivated experiential correlations (as with quantity and vertical elevation) or from construing a spatial scene in a certain way, that is, from a new vantage point. Examples of each of these will be presented in Section 4.

Prepositions can also be employed to express figure–ground relations between nonphysical elements. In a sentence such as *A feeling of dread hung over the crowd*, the TR, *dread*, is an emotion rather than a physical entity. We argue that this use is possible because *over* conveys a specific relationship between an emotion, the TR, and the crowd, the LM; one in which the crowd is being affected by, or within the sphere of influence of, the feeling of dread. Being within the sphere of influence of a physical TR means the LM can potentially be affected by the TR, as in *Rain clouds hung over the city all week*. In *A feeling of dread hung over the crowd*, the TR is not physically located higher than the LM, but because *over* has the functional notion of a sphere of influence associated with it, *over* can be employed to designate relations between nonphysical entities.

3.7.   *The conceptual significance of syntax*

Our model takes the view that formal aspects of language, such as syntactic configurations, have conceptual significance. As syntax is meaningful, in principle in the same way as lexical items, it follows that differences in syntactic form reflect a distinction in meaning (Lakoff 1987; Langacker 1987, 1991a, 1991b; Sweetser 1990; Talmy 1988, 2000). We are using the generic term "preposition" to describe the linguistic forms we are studying. But this term subsumes a number of formal distinctions characterized by prepositions, verb–particle constructions (or phrasal verbs), adpreps (which are adverbial in nature, and do not overtly code a LM, e.g. *the race is over*; they are discussed in Section 4), and particle prefixes (bound spatial particles as in *overflow*, *overhead*, and so on).[21]

4.   Beyond the protoscene: additional senses in the semantic network

Our methodology for determining distinct senses points to the conclusion that in addition to the protoscene a number of senses must be instantiated in semantic memory (contra Ruhl's 1989 monosemy framework).[22] For instance, we see no direct way of deriving the interpretation of completion normally assigned to *over* in the sentence *The movie is over* (= finished), suggesting that such an interpretation is due to a distinct completion sense associated with *over* being stored in long-term memory. We now turn to a consideration of the distinct senses, other than the protoscene conventionally associated with the preposition *over*.

Figure 6 is a preview of the remainder of this paper; it represents our proposed semantic network for *over*, subsuming a total of 14 distinct senses, including the protoscene. Each distinct sense is shown as a dark sphere, which represents a node in the network; the protoscene occupies a central position indicating its status as the primary sense. In some instances our representation of the semantic network depicts a distinct, conventionalized sense arising from the conceptualization prompted for by another conventionalized sense, rather than directly from the protoscene. For instance, in the network represented in Figure 6, the "excess" sense is represented as arising from the conceptualization associated with the "more" sense rather than arising directly from a conceptualization in which the protoscene of *over* occurs. Figure 6 represents the claim that reanalysis of conceptualiz-

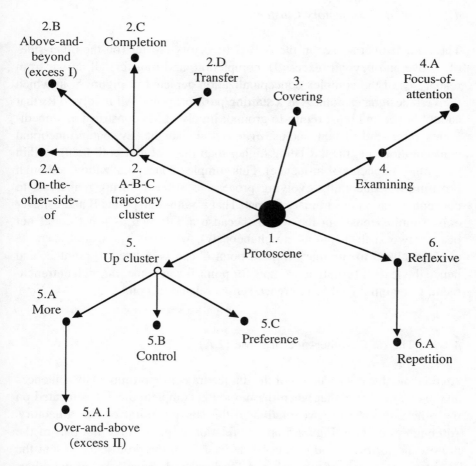

Figure 6.   The semantic network for *over*.

ations is potentially recursive and that a distinct sense can be the result of multiple instances of reanalysis. Moreover, we believe that a complex conceptualization, such as the one represented in Figure 5, can be submitted to multiple reanalyses and thus give rise to several distinct senses. When a complex conceptualization gives rise to multiple senses, we term the set of senses a "cluster of senses". A cluster of senses is denoted in our representation of a semantic network by an open circle. A single distinct sense is represented by a dark sphere.

4.1. The A-B-C Trajectory Cluster

The four distinct senses in the A-B-C trajectory cluster (on-the-other-side-of, above-and-beyond (excess I), completion, and transfer) all derive from reanalyses of the complex conceptualization depicted in Figure 5, in which the verb designates point A as a starting/push-off point. All involve TRs that cannot hover and must return to ground; involve LMs construed as impediments to forward motion; and use *over* to designate the key spatial/functional configuration (i.e. the TR being higher than the LM and both being within each other's spheres of influence). This complex conceptualization, although profiling a sequentially evolving process, is subject during reanalysis to conceptualization in summary format. That is, although points B and C never exist simultaneously in the world (because a TR such as a cat could not occupy two such positions simultaneously), when such a spatial scene is conceptualized in summary format, point C can be related to point B, and hence the lexical form that prompts for point B can come, through entrenchment, to be employed to reference senses related to point C.

4.1.1.   The on-the-other-side-of sense (2.A)

An unavoidable consequence of the unique trajectory prompted by sentences analogous to (18) is that when the motion is complete the TR is located on the other side of the LM relative to the starting point of the trajectory. Although point C in Figure 5 and its relation to point A are not part of the protoscene for *over* (and cannot be derived from the protoscene absent the particular properties of the verb and TR discussed above), the on-the-other-side-of sense has come to be associated with certain uses of *over* that are not derivable from context. Consider (21).

(21)   *Arlington is over the Potomac River from Georgetown.*

Notice in this sentence that the verb, *is*, fails to indicate any sense of motion. In our model, the verb typically codes for motion and hence prompts for a trajectory. Thus, the lack of motion coded by *is*, in turn, results in failure to prompt for a trajectory. If there is no trajectory, there is no beginning or endpoint, hence no principled way of deriving an on-the-other-side-of sense from this sentential context. Native speakers nevertheless will normally interpret this utterance such that Arlington is understood to be located on the other side of the Potomac River from Georgetown. Consequently, *over* must have a context-independent on-the-other-side-of sense associated with it. Accordingly, the two criteria for establishing that a sense is distinct have been met. The on-the-other-side-of sense adds meaning not apparent in the protoscene and the use in (21) is context-independent.

We hypothesize that this distinct sense came to be instantiated in memory as a result of reanalysis of the complex conceptualization represented in Figure 5, specifically, the privileging of the consequence of the jump – that the TR ends up on the other side of the LM. In addition, this conceptualization involves a shift in vantage point from being offstage (Langacker 1992) to being in the vicinity of point A. The default vantage point specified in the protoscene for *over*, Figure 4, is offstage. Previously, we noted that spatial scenes could be viewed from a number of possible vantage points, and these different vantage points could give rise to different construals of the same scene.

The on-the-other-side-of sense is illustrated in Figure 7. The eye icon on the left represents the vantage point, the vertical line the impediment and the dark sphere the TR.

Further evidence for this sense comes from examples like (22).

(22)   *Arlington is just over the river.*

The sentence in (22) is felicitous only if the construer (the vantage point) is located in the vicinity of point A (in Fig. 5) and Arlington is construed as point C. Thus, the reanalysis of *over* which results in the on-the-other-side-of sense involves two changes *vis-à-vis* the protoscene – the privileging of point C and interpreting it as the point at which the TR is located, and a shift in vantage point such that the construer is located in the vicinity of point A. While the on-the-other-side-of component (point C in Fig. 5) is correlated in experiential terms with arc-shaped trajectories and jumping *over* (i.e. higher than) obstacles by TRs such as cats, without the shift in vantage point this

Figure 7.   The on-the-other-side-of sense.

experiential correlation cannot be construed. We hypothesize that through the use of *over* in contexts where on-the-other-side-of is implicated, this meaning has come to be conventionally associated with *over* as a distinct sense, a process we term pragmatic strengthening.

The on-the-other-side-of sense is highly productive in English, as attested by the examples below. Notice that in neither of the following do we conventionally obtain the reading in which the TR is physically higher than the LM or that jumping or moving is involved.[23]

(23)   *The old town lies over the bridge.*
(24)   *John lives over the hill.*

Moreover, examples such as (24), which have been described as having *endpoint focus*, are reminiscent of the examples offered in Lakoff's (1987: 423) analysis for *over*, as evidence for an above-across sense.[24] We suggest that misanalysis of the on-the-other-side-of sense contributed to a path above-across sense being posited by earlier analyses.[25]

4.1.2.   The above-and-beyond (excess I) sense (2.B)

In (25) and (26) *over* is used as predicted by the protoscene but with the additional implicatures that the LM represents an intended goal or target and that the TR moved beyond the intended or desired point.

(25)   *The arrow flew over the target and landed in the woods.*
(26)   *Lissa just tapped the golf ball, but it still rolled over the cup.*

Given general knowledge of shooting arrows and targets, most speakers would assume that whoever shot the arrow intended to hit the target but aimed too high. The movement of the arrow, the TR, was above and beyond the LM, or in excess of what the agent intended. Similarly, given general knowledge of the game of golf and the goals of people who engage in the game, most speakers would assume that the agent (*Lissa*) intended that the movement of the *ball* (the TR), which she initiated with a tap, would result in the ball going into the *cup*, the LM. Thus the movement of the ball was above and beyond, or in excess of, what the agent intended.

The basic spatial configuration and trajectory followed by the TR is identical to that associated with the protoscene in the context of a verb depicting forward motion. But in sentences such as *The cat jumped over the wall*, the TR's movement beyond the LM is presumed to be intentional, while in sentences such as (25) and (26) the LM is construed as the target or goal and the presumed intention is to have the TR come into contact with the target. When the TR misses the target, it goes above and beyond the LM. Going above and beyond the target is conceptualized as going too far or involving too much. The implicatures of (i) the LM being construed as the target/goal and (ii) the TR passing *over* the LM as going beyond the target/ goal have been reanalysed, resulting in a distinct sense being added to the semantic network. Evidence for this sense being distinct comes from sentences such as (27), in which the sense cannot be derived from context.

(27)   *Your article is over the page limit.*

In this sentence, *over* cannot felicitously be interpreted as physically higher than, or even on-the-other-side-of. Rather, the interpretation seems to be that there is an established or "targeted" number of pages for the article and that the actual number of pages "went beyond" that target.

Figure 8 diagrams the above-and-beyond (excess I) sense, representing the LM as a bull's-eye target and highlighting the salient "beyond" portion of the trajectory. (Our analysis provides for a second source of an excess sense associated with *over*. This sense and its implication for the model are discussed later.)

We emphasize that we are not claiming that the semantic network contains criterial senses: that is, we are not suggesting that all uses of *over* will absolutely reflect one sense or another. Often, specific uses of a preposition will contain flavours of more than one sense, imbuing a particular reading with complex nuances of meaning and providing both intra- and inter-hearer differences in interpretation. Equally, we are not suggesting that application of the model outlined in Section 3 will mechanistically provide a single,

Figure 8.   The above-and-beyond (excess I) sense.

unique derivation for each distinct sense, based ultimately on the protoscene. We do not want to posit a simplicity rubric which claims that there is one correct analysis and deny that there may be many means of instantiating a distinct sense in memory. We find no strong evidence that human conceptualization and cognition is constrained by such a dictum (contra the widespread view adopted in formalist approaches to meaning in the generative tradition; for a critique of such views see Langacker 1991a: Chapter 10, and the discussion of the generality fallacy in Croft 1998).

At this point we see no principled reason to rule out the possibility that an excess interpretation might arise through an alternative route, as represented in the network by the over-and-above (excess II) sense (5.A.1). We in fact hypothesize that some speakers might derive an excess interpretation through one route while others arrive at it through the other. Still others may use both routes; the two resultant senses would then serve to inform each other in various ways. We further argue that it is inappropriate to treat this flexibility (or redundancy) as evidence that our model is flawed. Nor should an alternative analysis of the derivation of a particular sense be taken to constitute a counterexample to the overall model being posited. We see this flexibility (and redundancy) as an appropriate reflection of the richness of human cognition and the way in which experience is meaningful to us as human beings.

4.1.3. The completion sense (2.C)

When *over* is integrated into a complex conceptualization, such as described by Figure 5, the inferred shape of the trajectory has an endpoint C. The endpoint of any trajectory (which represents the process of moving) is commonly understood as representing the completion of the process.

We suggest that the completion sense associated with *over* has arisen as a result of the implicature of completion being reanalysed as distinct from the complex conceptualization represented in Figure 5. Once reanalysis has taken place, the final location resulting from motion correlates with the completion of motion, the distinct sense comes to be associated with the form *over* in the semantic network via pragmatic strengthening.

(28)   *The cat's jump is over* [= finished/complete].

We suggest that the meaning component of completion results from re-analysis of the spatial location of the TR as standing for an aspect of a process. In (28), for example, the endpoint of the motion through space over an impediment (i.e. the location at which the TR comes to rest) is interpreted as the completion of the movement. In this instance the completion sense is not describing a spatial relation but rather an aspect of a process. This is reflected syntactically by the fact that the completion sense does not mediate a TR–LM configuration in which the preposition is sequenced between the TR and the LM, as illustrated by example (28). The completion sense, in formal terms, is represented not by a preposition but rather by what we are terming an "adprep" (Bolinger 1971; O'Dowd 1998).[26]

The completion sense differs crucially from the on-the-other-side-of sense in that the latter focuses on the spatial location of the TR when the process is completed (see Fig. 9) while the former focuses on interpreting point C as the end of the motion or process. We tentatively hypothesize that an adprep will always arise when the reanalysis involves interpreting the location of the TR as an aspect of a process.

Figure 9 diagrams the completion sense. The dark sphere on the left represents the location of the TR at the beginning of the process. The large sphere on the right, which is in focus, represents the endpoint or completion.

Beginning   End

Figure 9.   The completion sense.

4.1.4.   The transfer sense (2.D)

A consequence of the conceptualization represented in Figure 5 gives rise to the transfer sense. Consider the following examples.

(29)   *Sally turned the keys to the office over to the janitor.*
(30)   *The teller handed the money over to the investigating officer.*

In these sentences, the conceptualization constructed is of a TR moving from one point to another. This follows from the conceptualization schematized in Figure 5, in which an implicature of transfer arises, a consequence of understanding the scene as one involving the transfer of a TR from one location, point A, to a new location, point C (see Fig. 10). We suggest that change in location of an entity is experientially correlated with transfer of the entity; change in position often gives rise to the implicature that transfer has taken place. Via pragmatic strengthening, this implicature is conventionalized as a distinct meaning component and instantiated in the semantic network associated with *over* as a distinct sense. As with the completion sense, the transfer sense involves the reanalysis of the trajectory or process. Again, in formal terms, *over* is represented not by a preposition but by an adprep. In Figure 10, the TR has been transferred from the left side of the impediment to the right side, as represented by the dark sphere, which is in focus.[27]

Figure 10.   The transfer sense.

4.2.   *The covering sense (3.)*

In our basic definition of TR and LM we noted that the typical situation is for the TR to be smaller than the LM, when the TR and LM are physical entities (although as we have seen, it is not inevitable that such is the case). All the senses and interpretations examined thus far have assumed that the TR is smaller than the LM. This default ascription is also represented in the protoscene we posited for *over*. However, there are instances in the real world in which the object that is in focus (the TR) is larger or perceived to be larger than the locating object (the LM). Such a situation is described by the sentence in (31).

(31)   *Frank quickly put the tablecloth over the table.*

Given our normal interactions with tables and tablecloths – we sit at tables or walk past them such that both the table and the tablecloth are lower than our line of vision – it follows that our typical vantage point is such that when a tablecloth is over the table we perceive it as covering the table. This being so, the vantage point is not that depicted in the default representation of the protoscene, in which the viewer/construer is offstage. Rather the vantage point has shifted so that the TR is between the LM and the construer or viewer. The perceptual effect of having the TR physically intervene between the viewer and the LM is that the TR will often appear to cover the LM or some significant portion of it.[28]

In accordance with the position outlined previously – that spatial scenes can be viewed from different vantage points – the covering interpretation results from having a particular vantage point from which the situation is construed. When a shift in vantage point occurs, the conceptualization constructed is likely to involve an additional implicature not part of the interpretation when the default vantage of the protoscene is assumed. In sum, we are arguing that the conceptualization constructed in the normal interpretation of (31) involves two changes from the default representation of the protoscene: first, the TR is perceived as being larger than the LM and second, the vantage point has shifted from offstage to higher than the TR.[29]

The covering implicature has been reanalysed as distinct from the spatial configuration designated by the protoscene (see Fig. 11). As noted with examples (10) and (11), when *over* prompts for a covering sense, the TR need not be construed as being located higher than the LM; hence, the covering sense must exist independently in semantic memory.[30]

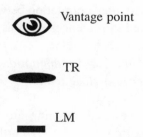

Figure 11.   The covering sense.

4.3. Above and proximal

4.3.1. The examining sense (4.)

As noted earlier, any spatial scene can be viewed from a variety of vantage points. The construal that gives rise to the examining sense is the result of a shift from the default (i.e. offstage) vantage point. In particular, we argue that in the scene associated with the examining sense, the vantage point is that of the TR, and further that the TR's line of vision is directed at the LM.

How might this construal arise? Consider the following sentence.

(32)   *Phyllis is standing over the entrance to the underground chamber.*

Here *over* is being used as designated in the protoscene and is mediating a spatial relation between the TR, *Phyllis*, and the LM, *the entrance to the underground chamber*, in which the TR is higher than but proximal to the LM. A consequence of Phyllis's being in this physical relation to the entrance is that she is in a position to carefully observe the entrance. An important way of experiencing and therefore understanding the act of examining is in terms of the examiner being physically higher than but proximal to the object being examined. Many recurring everyday examples of looking carefully at objects involve the human eyes being higher than the object being scrutinized, for example, examining tools, jewellery, a written text, or wounds on the body. Further, if an object is not proximal to the viewer, it is generally not possible to see the object clearly and therefore not possible to examine the object thoroughly. The experiential correlation between proximity and potential thoroughness is reflected in sentences such as (33) and (34).

(33)   *I'll give the document a close examination.*
(34)   *I'll give the manuscript a close read.*

Two experiential correlates of examining are the viewer being located above the LM and in proximity to the LM. Further, the functional aspect associated with the protoscene is that there is a conceptual connectedness between the TR and LM, i.e. the notion of sphere of influence. In this case, the connection is construed as that between the examiner and the examined. Because the protoscene for *over* contains these elements – a TR higher than a LM, proximity between the TR and LM, and a conceptual connectedness between the TR and LM – which match the physical correlates necessary for examination, *over* is a likely candidate for developing an examining sense.

But this is not the entire story. Notice that the use of *over* in (32) does not prompt for the interpretation that Phyllis is examining the entrance, only that she is located such that she could examine it. For the examining sense to arise, the scene must contextually imply examination. Put another way, examination must be an implicature deriving from the particular linguistic prompts in a given sentence. Consider (35).

(35)   *Mary looked over the manuscript quite carefully.*

The normal interpretation of this sentence is something like "Mary examined the manuscript". In this sentence, the TR, *Mary*, is physically higher than and in proximity to the LM, *the manuscript*. Thus, the TR and the LM are in the spatial configuration associated with the protoscene for *over*. In addition, the TR is construed as directing attention toward the manuscript. (This construal arises from our knowledge of the act of looking (it involves looking at something) and our knowledge of humans (often when they are looking, it is for some purpose).

This additional meaning element of directing attention towards the LM is essential to the examining sense (see Fig. 12). Now consider sentence (36).

(36)   *The mechanic looked over the train's undercarriage.*

The normal reading is that the mechanic examined the train's under- carriage, but for such examination to occur, *the mechanic*, the TR, must be physically underneath the train. In other words, in this conceptualization, the TR is under the LM. Clearly, in this situation, there is no way of predicting that *over* has associated with it an examination reading, given that the TR– LM spatial configuration does not correspond with that normally associated

Figure 12.   The examining sense.

with *over*, the very configuration that motivated the implicature of examination in the first place. This is good evidence, therefore, that the contextual implicature of examination has been instantiated as a distinct sense in the network via pragmatic strengthening. Hence, examination results from construing a scene in a particular way. This being so, speakers are free to use this examination-meaning component in the absence of the TR–LM configuration which gave rise to the implicature of examination initially.

4.3.2. The focus-of-attention sense (4.A)

Sentences (37) and (38) illustrate what we call the focus-of-attention sense. Notice that in (37) *over* can be paraphrased by *about*.

(37)   *The little boy cried over his broken toy.*
        (Cf. *The little boy cried about his broken toy.*)
(38)   *The senator presided over the opening ceremonies.*

In (37) and (38) the LM is the focus of attention. This sense is closely related to the examining sense from which it derives. In the examining sense, the vantage point is that of the TR, while the LM is physically below and proximal to the TR. We further posited that the TR must be construed as directing attention toward the LM. A natural consequence of the examining sense is that the object being examined, the LM, is the focus of the TR's attention. This natural consequence of examining has been privileged and reanalysed as distinct from the spatial scene in which it originally occurred (see Fig. 13), and via pragmatic strengthening, conventionalized as a distinct sense. (Fig. 13 differs minimally from Fig. 12; here the LM is in focus.)

Once this sense has been instantiated in memory, nonphysical TRs and LMs can be mediated by this sense.

Figure 13.   The focus-of-attention sense.

(39)   *The committee agonized over the decision.*
(40)   *The committee chair watched over the decision-making process.*

4.4. The vertical elevation or "up" cluster (5.)

Four distinct senses fall under this cluster, as can be seen in Figure 6. Each arises from construing a TR located physically higher than the LM as being vertically elevated, or up, relative to the LM. Being up entails a particular construal of the scene in which upward orientation is assigned to the TR (see Fig. 14).

Figure 14.   The up cluster.

This construal arises frequently in real-world experiences associated with the conceptual spatial relation *over*. For instance, in order to move over and beyond many LMs, movement from a physically lower location to a physically higher location is often necessary, i.e. vertical elevation of the TR occurs. Furthermore, an upward orientation is not typically construed in a neutral way. As Clark (1973) and Lakoff and Johnson (1980) have observed, an upward orientation is meaningful in human experience. An element in a vertically elevated position is often experienced as being positive or superior to an element in a physically lower position. Notice that there is nothing in the protoscene of *over*, i.e. of a TR being higher than the LM, that entails this construal: in the scene described by *The picture is over the mantel*, the picture is not construed as being in a better or superior position *vis-à-vis* the mantel.

4.4.1. The more sense (5.A)

As noted in the discussion of experiential correlation, vertical elevation and quantity are correlated in our experience. When there is an addition to the original amount of a physical entity, the height or level of that entity often rises. Because *over* can be construed as relating to a TR which is physically up with respect to a LM, and vertical elevation correlates in experiential terms with greater quantity, an implicature associated with having more of some entity is associated with being *over*. This implicature is conventionalized (via pragmatic strengthening), as attested by example (41).

(41)   *Jerome found over 40 kinds of shells on the beach.*

The normal interpretation of *over* in this context is "more than". The LM, *40 kinds of shells*, is interpreted as a kind of standard or measurement. The TR is not actually mentioned; in interpreting the sentence, we infer that the TR is shell types 41 and greater. If *over* were interpreted in terms of the protoscene in this sentence, we would obtain a semantically anomalous reading in which the additional shells would be understood as somehow being physically higher than the 40 kinds actually mentioned in the sentence. Again, we see no direct way in which this interpretation can be constructed from the protoscene and the sentential context alone. Moreover, there is no direct correlation between the concept of more types and vertical elevation. The concept here is more variety not greater quantity of shells. We argue that the "more" sense associated with *over* has arisen because of the independently motivated experiential correlation between greater quantity and greater elevation. Because of this experiential correlation, the implicature of greater quantity comes to be conventionally associated with *over* (which in terms of the designation prompted by the protoscene, has a greater height meaning, and hence also implicates greater quantity).

The implicature of greater quantity or more comes to be reanalysed as distinct from the conceptualization of the physical configuration that originally gave rise to it (see Fig. 15). Once reanalysis has taken place, the distinct sense comes to be associated with the form *over*, in the semantic network.

Figure 15. The more sense.

4.4.2. The over-and-above (excess II) sense (5.A.1)

The over-and-above (excess II) sense is closely related to the more sense. It adds an interpretation of "too much" to the "more" construal. We believe that a likely origin for this sense is the reanalysis of scenes involving containment, such as those described in (42) and (43).

(42)   *The heavy rains caused the river to flow over its banks.*
(43)   *Lou kept pouring the cereal into the bowl until it spilled over and onto the counter.*

In these scenarios the LMs are containers and the TRs are understood as entities held by the container. When the level of liquid or cereal (or whatever) that has been placed in the container is higher than but within reach of the top of the LM, then the amount constitutes more than the container can hold. A consequence of the capacity of a container being exceeded is that more of the TR becomes an excess of the TR, which results in spillage. In sum, more of the TR, *the water*, equals a higher level of water. Too much more of the TR results in a mess (see Fig. 16).

This node in the semantic network represents a second potential source for the general notion of excess associated with certain uses of *over*. We see subtle but distinguishable differences between the excess I sense, which seems to us to be more closely tied to motion along a path and the interpretation of

Figure 16. The over-and-above (excess II) sense.

going beyond a designated point, and the excess II sense, which seems to be more closely related to exceeding the capacity of containers and exceeding what is normal. For instance, in a compound such as *overtired*, it may be that the conceptualization involved is not that an expected level of tiredness is a goal that is missed, but rather, an expected or normal capacity for tiredness has been exceeded. Consider (44).

(44)   *The child was overtired and thus had difficulty falling asleep.*

In our interpretation of this sentence the child is conceptualized as having a certain capacity for activity; the child is conceptualized as a container and her or his activities are conceptualized as filling the container. When the activity level reaches that capacity, the child is tired and the normal response to that tiredness is to fall asleep. If the activity level exceeds the normal capacity, the child becomes too tired, which results in irritability and difficulty going to sleep.[31] In this example we might construct a "more" conceptualization for *over*, or we might construct an "excess" interpretation (which provides not just a more meaning, but the additional too-much-more meaning) for *over*.

4.4.3. The control sense (5.B)

A third experiential correlate associated with vertical elevation is the phenomenon of control or power. This meaning component associated with *over* is illustrated by (45) (from Lakoff 1987).

(45)   *She has a strange power over me.*

Clearly, this sentence does not mean that the TR, *she*, is higher than but within reach of *me*, the LM. Rather, the conventional interpretation derived from such an example is that the TR exerts influence, or control over the LM (as observed earlier). This meaning could not be derived from context, and is therefore suggestive, given our methodology, that this constitutes a distinct control sense instantiated in semantic memory. How then did the control sense derive from the semantic network associated with *over*? We suggest that this sense is due to an implicature becoming conventionally associated with *over*, from an independently motivated experiential correlation between control and vertical elevation.

For most of human history, when one person has been in physical control of another person, control has been experienced as the controller being physically higher. In physical combat, the victor, or controller, is often the one who finishes standing, in the up position; the loser finishes on the ground, physically lower than the controller. Hence an important element of how we actually experience control (and presumably from where the concept itself is derived) is that of being physically higher than that which is controlled.

(46)   *The fight ended with John standing over Mac, his fist raised.*

Further, within the physical domain, the physically bigger, up, often controls the physically smaller, down. Within the animal kingdom, a widespread signal of the acknowledgment of power or status is for the submissive animal to adopt a position in which its head is physically lower than the head of the dominant animal. In experiential terms then, control and vertical elevation are correlated. We suggest that because of an independently motivated experiential association between control and being vertically elevated, there is an implicature of control associated with *over*.

Nonetheless, if control were understood only in terms of vertical elevation, we would expect that the English preposition *above* should also implicate control. But as (47) demonstrates, this is not the case.

(47)   ?*She has a strange power above me* [control reading].

To exert control in order to affect the subject's actions and thus guarantee compliance, one must be physically proximal to the subject. In experiential terms, there are two elements associated with the concept control; the first is up, and the second is physical proximity. As we have argued throughout this article, while the protoscene for *over* designates a TR being physically higher and proximal to the LM, there is good evidence for supposing that *above* designates that the TR will be physically higher but precludes physical proximity. In linguistic terms, we would expect *over* to develop a control reading. The linguistic usage, then, accords with how we actually experience (see Fig. 17: the spiral shape denotes that the TR [sphere] controls the LM [vertical line]).

As we have been arguing, distinct senses, once instantiated in semantic memory, can be employed in situations that did not originally motivate them, as a consequence of being instantiated as distinct within the semantic network.

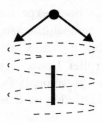

Figure 17. The control sense.

Accordingly, the control sense can be employed to mediate relations between nonphysical TRs and LMs. In examples (48) and (49), either or both the TR/ LM are nonphysical entities.

(48) *Camilia has authority over purchasing* [= the act of deciding what will be purchased].
(49) *Personality has more influence over who we marry than physical appearance.*

4.4.4. The preference sense (5.C)

In the preference sense, that which is higher is conventionally understood as being preferred to that which is lower.

(50) *I would prefer tea over coffee.*
(51) *I like Beethoven over Mozart.*

We suggest that the preference sense derives in the following way: being physically up in experiential terms can implicate greater quantity, which generally is preferred to a lesser quantity. In another experiential pattern being physically up is associated with positive states such as happiness (*He's feeling up today*), while being physically down is associated with being unhappy (*I'm feeling down today*) (see Lakoff and Johnson 1980). Given that happiness is normally preferred to unhappiness, this experiential correlation results in states associated with positions of vertical elevation being preferred to those associated with a lower position. Hence, being *over* implicates a preferred state (see Fig. 18: the TR, which is higher, is to be preferred to the LM, which is hence not in focus).

This implicature of preference is conventionalized, allowing a preference interpretation (rather than a higher-than reading) in examples (50) and (51).

Figure 18. The preference sense.

4.5.   Reflexivity

4.5.1.   The reflexive sense (6.)

Spatial reflexivity (first noted by Lindner 1981) is the phenomenon whereby a single entity which occupies multiple positions is conceptualized such that two salient positions occupied by the entity are integrated into a TR–LM spatial configuration. A preposition such as *over* is then used to mediate a spatial relation between the two positions, even though the same entity cannot simultaneously occupy two distinct spatial positions in the world. The dynamic character of experience is reanalysed as a static spatial configuration. Langacker (1987) discusses this gestalt-like static conceptualization of a dynamic process as summary scanning. Consider (52).

(52)   *The fence fell over.*

In (52), the TR – the initial (upright) position of the fence – is distinguished from the final position, in which the fence is lying horizontally on the ground. We see the fence fall through a 90-degree arc and from this experience a conceptual spatial relation is abstracted (via summary scanning), mediating the two temporally situated locations into a single spatial configuration. In the world, no such spatial configuration exists; after all, the same fence cannot be in two locations at the same time, but by conceptualizing the fence reflexively, the same entity can be both the TR and the LM (see Fig. 19).

Additional examples of the reflexive sense are given in (53) and (54).

Figure 19.   The reflexive sense.

(53)   *He turned the page over.*
(54)   *The log rolled over.*

This sense arises from reanalysis of a process. As noted previously, when *over* is used to profile a process, it is coded as an adprep.

4.5.2.   The repetition sense (6.A)

The repetition sense adds an iterative meaning component to the use of *over*, a meaning component that could not be predicted from the protoscene alone (or from any other sense considered so far). In examples (55) and (56), *over* can be paraphrased by *again* or *anew.*

(55)   *After the false start, they started the race over.*
        (Cf. *After the false start, they started the race again/anew.*)
(56)   *This keeps happening over and over.*

Many native speakers have informed us that sentences such as (56) prompt for a conceptualization of a wheel or cycle, which seems to be evoked by the notion of repetition. We hypothesize that the repetition-meaning component associated with *over* may be the result of iterative application of the reflexive sense (i.e. the 90-degree arc is repeated such that the TR passes through 360 degrees returning to its original starting point).

Such an analysis is consistent with the intuition that repetition is conceptualized as cyclical in nature (Fig. 20). An alternative derivation may be due to an iterative application of the A-B-C trajectory, such that when the endpoint or completion of the trajectory is reached the process begins again.[32] A third possibility may be that the notions of completion and reflexivity are conceptually integrated forming a conceptual blend (in the sense of Fauconnier and Turner 1994, 1998, 2002). We remain agnostic about which of these

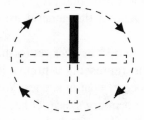

Figure 20.   The repetition sense.

routes led to the instantiation of the repetition sense in the semantic network for *over*.

5.   Conclusion

Previous polysemy accounts of *over* offer analyses that are too fine-grained. These accounts fail to distinguish between coding in formal expression and a level of conceptualization that integrates linguistic prompts in a way maximally coherent with sentential context and real-world knowledge. The selection of a linguistic prompt is, we argued, motivated by a principle of best fit. That is, given that prepositions represent a closed class they cannot possibly code the infinite array of all conceptual spatial relations. The speaker selects the preposition which, given the scene being described, is closest to accurately describing the key spatial relation. Conceptual integration results from such underspecified cues being used to construct a complex conceptualization, which elaborates the relatively impoverished linguistic input. A sentence such as *The cat jumped over the wall* results in a dynamic complex conceptualization in which the cat moves above and across the wall, not because this trajectory is coded for linguistically but because this is the most coherent and reasonable conceptualization, given the particular prompts, and given what we know about cats and walls.

In addition, we distinguish between constructed meanings and senses. The former are constructed on-line in the course of constructing a conceptualization of a specific scene prompted by a particular utterance, whereas senses are instantiated in memory, and can be recruited for the process of conceptual integration. While complex conceptualizations result from the process of conceptual integration taking account of motion and hence temporal frames, it does not follow that prepositions themselves code dynamism. Accordingly, we maintain the general assumption that prepositions code atemporal relations.

Within the polysemy network for *over* set forth here, the primary sense is termed the protoscene, and represents a highly idealized abstraction from our rich recurring experience of spatial scenes. We set forth a set of explicit criteria for determining the primary sense. Other distinct senses instantiated in the polysemy network for *over* result from pragmatic strengthening, i.e. reanalysis and encoding. We recognize a use as distinct only if its interpretation involves a change in the spatial configuration between the TR and LM and/or additional nonspatial information is involved. The polysemy network for *over* contains 14 distinct senses. Other interpretations derive from conceptual integration constrained by the cognitive principles discussed in Section 3.

The results of our study provide a means for distinguishing between distinct senses and the process of on-line meaning construction, which is primarily conceptual in nature. Clearly, a recognition of this distinction is imperative for future research into the nature of semantic networks, and provides additional insight into (i) the fundamentally non-arbitrary quality of the mental lexicon; (ii) the highly creative nature of the human conceptual system; and (iii) the fact that the way we experience renders spatio-physical interactions meaningful, which in turn gives rise to emergent conceptual structure.

Acknowledgements

Our thinking has benefited greatly from conversations with a number of colleagues. We would particularly like to thank Joseph Grady, Elizabeth Lemon and the members of the Georgetown Metaphor Group. We also thank Mark Aronoff, Steven Cushing, and two anonymous *Language* referees for their detailed comments and suggestions. We are grateful to Angela Evans for her assistance with the diagrams throughout, and for supplying us with many of our linguistic examples. Andrea Tyler would like to acknowledge the many insights and persistent questions raised by the students in her classes on pedagogical grammar and applying cognitive linguistics. Vyvyan Evans has benefited from detailed discussions with Craig Hamilton, and owes special thanks to Mark Turner for his insight and encouragement.

Notes

* This article was first published in slightly different form in *Language*, Volume 77, Number 4 (2001), 724–765. Reprinted by kind permission.
1. Johnson's (1987) pioneering work argues that image-schemas are representations of recurring aspects of bodily sensory–motor experience, such as verticality, containment, and so on, which are stored in long-term memory. Hence, they are not "mental pictures", but rather abstractions from rich experience. See also Cienki (1998) for an analysis of a single image-schema: *straight*.
2. The figure–ground notions were developed by the cognitive linguist Leonard Talmy (e.g. 1978), and are derived from gestalt psychology.
3. Ruhl (1989) has elegantly argued against a polysemy position, championing instead a monosemy framework. Monosemy holds that each lexical item is associated with a single highly abstract sense. On this view, the sense is so abstract that its precise meaning is filled in by context in conjunction with pragmatic knowledge. We will demonstrate (Section 4) that some senses cannot be predicted by context alone, a strong argument against a monosemy position.
4. Future empirical analysis might find that speakers make such fine-grained distinctions, but the evidence to date does not bear this out. Although we cannot definitively prove Lakoff's full-specification model is wrong, it does result in questionable consequences, both in terms of its linguistic representations and in terms of the little experimental evidence that is available.
5. The variations among just the two attributes of + / – or unspecified extended, and + / – or unspecified vertical, result in nine distinct senses. Each time another attribute is added to the model, the list of distinct senses multiplies accordingly – consider Table 1. The predictions become even more questionable when one considers that five of the nine senses involve attributes being unspecified.

   Analogous arguments can be made for specification of the exact, metric relationship between the TR and LM in terms of the presence or absence of contact, as Kreitzer (1997) underscores with the example *Sam went over the wall*, in which the precise manner of passing over the wall, either jumping or crawling, is unspecified, therefore the presence or absence of contact is unspecified.

Table 1.   Topographical features (after Lakoff 1987).

	+ Vertical	– Vertical	Unspecified
+ Extended	S	S	U
– Extended	S	S	U
Unspecified	U	U	U

S = specified; U = unspecified.

6. In order to motivate the distinction between *over1* and *over2*, Kreitzer appeals to Langacker's notion of *summary scanning* (Langacker 1987, 1991a). Langacker posits that summary scanning provides a means of integrating points occupied by a TR along a path into a construal of motion along a path. The path is reified at the conceptual level, even though it never actually exists in the world. Kreitzer argues that the dynamic *over2* describes a relation between a TR and a LM in which it is the path that is the TR.

7. The term *ideal meaning* is from Herskovits 1986: Chapter 4.

8. It is important to note that some central (= most basic, to be explicated) senses associated with prepositions will crucially involve a coordinate system along the vertical or horizontal axes, while others will not. We will argue that the primary sense associated with *over* does involve such a system in which the spatial relation of the TR being located higher than the LM is essential. But this should not be interpreted as a claim that all prepositions prompt for such a system. While the English prepositions *over* and *under* regularly code respectively for the TR being in a higher-than or lower-than position relative to the LM, the preposition *out* appears to be insensitive to this dimension. Thus, we find sentences like *The rain poured out of the sky* (in which the TR is lower than the LM) and *The water bubbled out of the hot springs* (in which the TR is higher than the LM) which do not affect the basic interpretation associated with *out*. Whether a particular preposition is sensitive to the horizontal or vertical dimensions is part of its basic lexical entry.

9. Although there has been disagreement about the appropriate representation of the primary sense associated with *over*, all published analyses accept these two basic assumptions. Synchronically, evidence that the basic spatial configuration prompted for by *over* is something like a TR in a higher-than position relative to the LM comes from sentences with clearly contrasting interpretations: *Nicole decided to walk over the bridge* versus *Nicole decided to walk under the bridge*. Having argued that the primary sense for *over* involves a spatial configuration in which the TR is higher than the LM, we readily acknowledge that in many instances this spatial configuration is not prompted for by *over*. Our analysis attempts to model how these non-canonical spatial configurations have come to be associated with the form *over*.

10. It should be noted that our diagrammatic representations of protoscenes are made for ease of explication. They should not be interpreted as making any serious claim about the neurological nature of imagistic representation.

11. An image-schema, as Mandler uses the term, constitutes a representation distinct from purely perceptual information. As such, it constitutes a rudimentary "theory" as to the nature of a particular object or relation between objects. The image-schema relating to containment, for instance, is a concept as opposed to a perceived entity, insofar as it constitutes a means of understanding the functional aspects of a particular spatial configuration.

12. This is akin to what Jackendoff (1983: 29) refers to as the *projected world*, and

is constructed at what Fauconnier (1997: 36) terms the *cognitive level* or *level C*.

13. In terms of specifics our claim is as follows: a particular spatial scene is a rich real-world scenario, mediating two objects (TR and LM) via a conceptual spatial relation. Recurring spatial scenes perceived as resembling each other are stored as an abstract protoscene. The aspect of the protoscene coded by a preposition is the spatial relation mediating the TR and LM, and not the whole protoscene. From this, it follows that a preposition presupposes a TR and a LM (as the conceptual spatial relation holds by virtue of mediating a relation between a TR and a LM). In minimal terms, a preposition prompts for a TR and LM, which are typically supplied linguistically, e.g. *The picture* [TR] *is over the mantel* [LM].

14. The reanalysis of an aspect of a particular complex conceptualization results in privileging a different aspect or perspective on the complex conceptualization. Yet, because the pertinent complex conceptualization is first prompted for by the use of *over*, as in Figure 5, the derived sense is coded by the same linguistic form, namely *over*.

15. Cruse (1986) discusses this in terms of modulation of a lexical item. For instance, various parts of *the car* are highlighted in the following sentences: *The car needs to be washed* (where *car* is interpreted as the exterior body of the car) versus *The car needs to be serviced* (where *car* is interpreted as the engine) versus *The car needs vacuuming* (where *car* is interpreted as the interior). This constitutes modulation or highlighting different parts and backgrounding others.

16. Langacker (1992) discusses the atemporal nature of prepositions in terms of the relationships they profile. "With *before* and *after*, time functions as the domain in which the profiled relationship is manifested. Its role is consequently analogous to that of space in the basic sense of *in*, *on* or *near*. A verb, on the other hand, is said to be temporal in a very different way ... the profiled relationship is conceived as evolving through time and is scanned sequentially along this temporal axis. It is by incorporating this further level of conceptual organization that *precede* and *follow* differ from the prepositions *before* and *after* ... [Verbs] specifically track [a process] through time ... A preposition can thus be characterized as profiling an atemporal relation that incorporates a salient landmark" (1992: 292).

17. Unless the world being discussed is explicitly designated as science fiction.

18. In sentence (19) the lack of motion is the result of integrating what is coded by the verb *extended* with our knowledge of trees. In particular, the interpretation of lack of motion depicted by (19) is the result of the interpretation of *extended* as it relates to a tree branch. We understand trees to be slow-growing plants such that humans do not perceive the growth of a branch as involving motion. Thus, we interpret *extended* to depict a state. Notice that the stative interpretation of *extended* is contingent upon the precise sentential context in which it occurs. *Extended* can also be interpreted to convey motion as in *He extended his arm towards the door*. Since there is no sense of motion prompted for by the verb in the sentential context provided in (19), no path or trajectory is projected for the TR.

19. We hasten to acknowledge that there are contexts in which two prepositions appear to be interchangeable and virtually synonymous: *Susan hung the picture over the mantel* versus *Susan hung the picture above the mantel*. We hypothesize that such substitutability arises because the semantic networks associated with each preposition represent continuums and at certain points the interpretations of two continuums can overlap. In addition, for *over* and *above* we find a close diachronic relationship, with *over* initially being used as the comparative form of *above*. The diachronic link may surface in these overlapping uses.

20. In terms of synchronic polysemy networks, the empirical work by Sandra, Rice, and their colleagues suggests that it may not be the case that a particular lexical form has a single primary sense from which language users perceive all other senses being derived. Their empirical work raises questions about the view that we can define polysemy as a strictly synchronic phenomenon in which speakers are consciously aware of a relationship holding between distinct senses of a particular lexical form. This is an empirical question for which we do not yet have sufficient evidence to determine the answer. If extensive experimental evidence shows that language users systematically and consistently fail to perceive some senses as being related, then we must question whether what we term polysemy constitutes a phenomenon that is wholly synchronic in nature. While we believe all the senses in a particular semantic network are diachronically (and perhaps developmentally) related, in terms of the adult lexicon, there may be differences in the perceived relatedness between distinct sets of senses, due to routinization and entrenchment, obscuring the original motivation for the derivation of senses from pre-existing senses such as the protoscenes for language users (see in particular Rice, Sandra and Vanrespaille 1999).

21. In formal terms, the particle in a verb–particle construction (VPC) is a more grammaticized preposition in that the LM is linguistically covert, that is, it is contextually understood without being linguistically coded (Lindner 1981; O'Dowd 1998). Such particles form part of a verb–particle construction with a verbal element, and each unit (the particle and the verb) contributes to the meaning of the whole unit (see Goldberg 1995 for a construction grammar approach, Morgan 1997 for a study of verb–particle constructions). We introduce the term adprep to describe a spatial particle which has adverbial meaning, that is, certain usages of the form *over* are adverbial in nature, describing an aspect of a conceptual process, as in *The movie is over* (= finished). Each formal component – preposition, particle (in a VPC), particle prefix, or adprep – contributes different kinds of meaning.

22. Recall that we are using the term "sense" for distinct meanings instantiated in memory (i.e. in the semantic network associated with each preposition).

23. It is worth pointing out that sentences such as (21)–(25) offer strong evidence against a monosemy theory of word meaning. Monosemy (see Ruhl 1989), as noted previously, posits that all interpretations of a linguistic form, such as a preposition, are contextually derivable from a highly abstract primary sense. However, as can be seen from the on-the-other-side-of sense, neither of the

original aspects of the spatial configuration hold – the TR is not above the LM and the TR is not proximal to the LM. The nature of a primary sense that would derive both these senses simply from contextual cues would need to be extremely abstract. We cannot see how a representation so abstract would also be constrained enough to distinguish among many other English prepositions.

24. Lakoff (1987: 422–423) represents sentences such as *Sam lives over the hill* as an example of schema 1.VX.C.E. (above-across, with a vertical, extended LM, contact between the TR and LM, and endpoint focus).

25. There is arguably a distinct sense which is derived from the on-the-other-side-of sense. In examples such as

(57)   *The festival will take place over the weekend*;
(58)   *The friendship remained strong over the years*;
(59)   *Let's take a look at changes over time*;

over mediates a temporal relation of concurrence between a process or activity and the times during which the process or activity elapses. This sense is likely to have developed from the on-the-other-side-of sense, when the physical LM is extended, as, for example, in *The boy walked over the hill*, *The cable runs over the yard*, and *The bridge stretches over the river*. In such situations the activity is concurrent with the duration required for the activity. Because of pragmatic strengthening, a duration sense may have become associated with *over*.

26. This is consistent with Langacker (e.g. 1987) who argues that grammatical class is determined by virtue of what is profiled. For instance, the relationship profiled by adverbs crucially differs from the relationship profiled by prepositions in that an adverb takes a relationship as its TR and does not have a salient LM. In contrast, a preposition takes an entity as its TR and elaborates a relational LM.

27. Nonphysical entities can be identified as TRs or LMs, if they are construed as focal and backgrounded respectively, and if a relation holds between them. As *over* has a conventionalized transfer sense associated with it, the relation between nonphysical TRs and LMs cannot be spatio-configurational, but as in *The government handed its power over to the newly elected officials*, it can involve the notion of transfer. This further illustrates that transfer must be a distinct sense: it could not be derived from context in such sentences. There is a conventional reading in which the members of the government transfer their authority, i.e. their mandate to govern, to a new set of officials. In literal terms, nothing is physically transferred, as the TR, *power*, is a nonphysical entity. Nonetheless, to say that power is a nonphysical entity is not to say that the concept "power" is without foundation in real-world experiences. In fact, the concept of power derives from a variety of very real experiences: physical forces, socially constructed relationships and hierarchies, and social interactions such as taking, issuing and following orders, commands, edicts, and so on. In this sense, we

each experience power in a real way, although the variety of experiences subsumed by the concept of power does not have physical substance or spatial dimensionality in the same way that a chair or a table has. Accordingly, it makes sense that power can be transferred, thus licensing the use of the transfer sense.

28. Again, following our argument that metric properties concerning the relationship between the TR and LM are filled in on-line, *over* can be used to prompt for this covering interpretation when there is contact between the LM and TR, as in (31), or when there is no contact between the TR and the LM, as in *The fibreglass protector was put over the drained swimming pool for the winter*.

29. These two changes are closely intertwined in everyday experience. We are often involved in real-world scenarios where the TR is physically larger than the LM and we normally view the TR–LM from above, as in *The cloth is over the table*. In this real-world scene, if the TR were smaller than the LM, the preposition of choice (best fit) would be likely to change.

(60)   ?*The small handkerchief was spread out over the table.*

(61)   *The small handkerchief was spread out on the table.*

However, there are also many real-world scenarios in which the TR is actually smaller than the LM but because of the construer's vantage point (the TR intervenes between the viewer and the LM), the TR appears larger than the LM. For instance, in *The dark clouds moved over the sun*, the clouds are not physically larger than the sun, but they appear larger to the earthbound viewer.

30. Lakoff (1987: 429) accounted for cases of the covering reading in which the TR is not higher than the LM by positing a *rotation transformation*. The covering schemas all have variants in which the TR need not be above (that is, higher than) the LM. In all cases, however, there must be an understood viewpoint from which the TR is blocking accessibility of vision to at least some part of the LM. We will refer to these as *rotated* (RO) schemas, though with no suggestion that there is actual mental rotation degree-by-degree involved. This is an extremely powerful transformation, potentially affecting all prepositions whose primary sense involves either a vertical or horizontal orientation. In a number of instances, the protoscenes for *over*, *wider*, *before*, and *after* would be essentially indistinguishable. And this analysis offers no explanation for why TR–LM configurations that do not match the protoscene would develop this reading.

A common consequence of the LM being covered by the TR is that the LM is occluded from the construer's view. Typically the scene described in (31) is that the tablecloth occludes the tabletop from the observer. As we see in examples such as the following, occlusion is not an inevitable consequence of covering.

(62)   *The mask is over her face.*

(63)   *She wore a transparent veil over her face.*

(64)   *The dark, heavy clouds are over the sun.*

(65)   *There are a few wispy clouds over the sun.*

In sentences (62) and (64) a consequence of the LM being covered by the TR is that the LM is no longer visible. In (63) and (65), however, covering does not obscure the object. We have not been able to find any instances of occluding which involve the use of *over1* that do not include a covering sense. Further, in the examples in which we can tease apart covering from occluding, the physical attribute of transparency/opacity of the TR must he specified. If the TR is not specified as transparent (65) the normal reading is that covering entails occlusion. Thus, we have concluded that the occlusion interpretation is a contextual implicature of the covering sense and real-world knowledge of the properties of objects such as tablecloths and blankets. Given the absence of contextually independent examples of occlusion – linguistic examples of *over* in which occlusion is not an implicature deriving from covering – our methodological procedure suggests that an occluding reading is an on-line interpretation.

31. In some cases, we see no clear way to determine which source is more appropriate. As we noted in our discussion of the excess I sense, specific uses of *over* (or any preposition) seem to contain "flavours" of more than one sense, which imbues a reading with complex nuances of meaning. For instance, consider the following.

(66)   *Hey! Why are you bringing in so many cases of motor oil? There must be a dozen cases here. That's well over the two cases I ordered.*

In this example we might construct a "more" conceptualization for *over*, or we might construct an "excess" interpretation (which provides not just a more meaning, but the additional too-much-more meaning) for *over*. In this latter case, the example could be derived from either the above-and-beyond (excess I) sense or the over-and-above (excess II) sense. On the one hand, *two cases* could be conceptualized as the target the customer was aiming for, and bringing in ten additional cases could be construed as going beyond the designated target. On the other hand, *two cases* could be conceptualized as the expected amount or level of goods, and the additional ten cases could be construed as going above the expected amount or level.

Alternatively, the hearer may construct a complex conceptualization in which all three senses are influencing the interpretation. This reflects our claim that there is a semantic network linking distinct senses, and that conceptualizations may be due to a semantic network constituting a meaning continuum, as discussed earlier. Accordingly, our network should be thought of as a semantic continuum, in which complex conceptualizations can draw on meanings from distinct nodes as well as the range of points between nodes, which provide nuanced semantic values. In addition, an important consequence of our claims

(i)   that the principles of meaning construction in conjunction with a distinct sense such as the protoscene (or any other distinct mental representation or sense), can be used to construct a wide range of conceptualizations;

(ii)   that any one conceptualization is subject to multiple construals (through, for instance, privileging a particular aspect of the scene or shifting the vantage point from which the scene is viewed);

(iii) that distinct senses can be extended to include nonphysical entities when such are perceived as focal (TRs) and backgrounded reference points (LMs);

(iv)   that semantic networks form an interrelated continuum of interpretations (rather than just a series of absolutely discrete points of meaning);

is that the model predicts that a particular sense may arise from more than one source.

In forms such as *overachieve, overkill, overdo,* and *overdress* we do not see a clear basis for arguing for the superiority of the above-and-beyond interpretation versus the over-and-above interpretation. As noted earlier, we do not consider this a flaw in our model; rather we see it as testimony to the richness and complexity of conceptualization. We also hypothesize that native speakers are likely to vary in their intuitions about these cases.

32. Lindstromberg (1997) offers a very similar explanation.

References

Aronoff, Mark
    1994   *Morphology By Itself: Stems and Inflectional Classes*. Cambridge, MA: MIT Press.
Bloom, Paul, Mary A. Peterson, Lynn Nadel and Merrill F. Garrett (eds.)
    1996   *Language and Space*. Cambridge, MA: MIT Press.
Bloomfield, Leonard
    1933   *Language*. New York: Holt, Rinehart and Winston.
Bolinger, Dwight
    1971   *The Phrasal Verb in English*. Cambridge, MA: Harvard University Press.
Brisard, Frank
    1997   The English tense-system as an epistemic category: the case of futurity. In: Marjolijn Verspoor, Kee Dong Lee and Eve Sweetser (eds.), *Lexical and Syntactical Constructions and the Construction of Meaning*, 271–286. Amsterdam: John Benjamins.
Brugman, Claudia
    1981 [1988] The story of *over*. M.A. thesis. Linguistics Dept, University of California, Berkeley. Published [1988] as *The Story of* Over:

Polysemy, Semantics and the Structure of the Lexicon. New York: Garland Press.

Brugman, Claudia and George Lakoff
1988   Cognitive topology and lexical networks. In: Steven Small, Garrison Cottrell and Michael Tanenhaus (eds.), *Lexical Ambiguity Resolution*, 477–507. Palo Alto, CA: Morgan Kaufmann.

Bybee, Joan, Revere Perkins and William Pagliuca
1994   *The Evolution of Grammar: Tense, Aspect, and Modality in the Languages of the World.* Chicago, IL: University of Chicago Press.

Chomsky, Noam
1995   Categories and transformations. In: *The Minimalist Program*, 219–394. Cambridge, MA: MIT Press.

Cienki, Alan
1998   *Straight*: an image schema and its metaphorical extensions. *Cognitive Linguistics*, 9(2): 107–150.

Clark, Herbert H.
1973   Space, time, semantics, and the child. In: Terence Moore (ed.), *Cognitive Development and the Acquisition of Language*, 27–64. New York: Academic Press.

Croft, William
1998   Linguistic evidence and mental representations. *Cognitive Linguistics* 9: 151–174.

Cruse, David A.
1986   *Lexical Semantics.* Cambridge, England: Cambridge University Press.

Cushing, Steven
1990   Prototypical considerations on modal meanings. In: Tsohatzidis (1990), 74–90.
1991   Explaining a missing modal meaning: ideology and paradigm as pragmatic parameter. In: Jef Verschueren (ed.), *Levels of Linguistic Adaptation*, 19–32. Amsterdam: John Benjamins.

Dewell, Robert
1994   *Over* again: image-schema transformations in semantic analysis. *Cognitive Linguistics* 5(4): 351–380.

Dirven, René
1993   Dividing up physical and mental space into conceptual categories by means of English prepositions. In: Cornelia Zelinsky-Wibbelt (ed.), *The Semantics of Prepositions: From Mental Processing to Natural Language Processing*, 73–97. Berlin: Mouton de Gruyter.

Evans, Vyvyan
2000   The structure of time: language, meaning and temporal cognition. Doctoral thesis. Linguistics Dept, Georgetown University.

Fauconnier, Gilles
1994   *Mental Spaces.* Cambridge, England: Cambridge University Press.

1997   *Mappings in Thought and Language.* Cambridge, England: Cambridge University Press.
Fauconnier, Gilles and Mark Turner
1994   Conceptual Projection and Middle Spaces. Dept of Cognitive Science: University of California, San Diego. Cognitive Science Technical Report No. 9401.
1998   Conceptual integration networks. *Cognitive Science* 22(2): 133–187.
2002   *The Way We Think: Conceptual Blending and The Mind's Hidden Complexities.* New York: Basic Books.
Fillmore, Charles, Paul Kay and Mary Catherine O'Connor
1988   Regularity and idiomaticity in grammatical constructions: the case of *let alone. Language* 64(3): 501–538.
Fleischman, Suzanne
1999   Discourse markers across languages: implications of a case study for historico-comparative and sociolinguistics. Paper presented at Georgetown University, November 1999.
Goldberg, Adèle
1995   *Constructions: A Construction Grammar Approach to Argument Structure.* Chicago, IL: Chicago University Press.
Grady, Joseph
1997   Foundations of meaning: primary metaphors and primary scenes. Doctoral thesis. Linguistics Dept, University of California, Berkeley.
Grice, Paul
1975   Logic and conversation. In: Peter Cole and Jerry L. Morgan (eds.), *Syntax and Semantics, Volume 3: Speech Acts,* 41–58. New York: Academic Press.
Heine, Bernd
1993   *Auxiliaries: Cognitive Forces and Grammaticalization.* New York: Oxford University Press.
1997   *Cognitive Foundations of Grammar.* New York: Oxford University Press.
Herskovits, Annette
1986   *Language and Spatial Cognition: An Interdisciplinary Study of the Prepositions in English.* Cambridge, England: Cambridge University Press.
Hopper, Paul and Elizabeth Closs Traugott
1993   *Grammaticalization.* Cambridge: Cambridge University Press.
Jackendoff, Ray
1983   *Semantics and Cognition.* Cambridge, MA: MIT Press.
1997   *The Architecture of the Language Faculty.* Cambridge, MA: MIT Press.
Johnson, Mark
1987   *The Body in the Mind.* Chicago, IL: Chicago University Press.

Kay, Paul and Charles Fillmore
1999   Grammatical constructions and linguistic generalizations: the *what's X doing Y?* construction. *Language* 75(1): 1–34.

Kreitzer, Anatol
1997   Multiple levels of schematization: a study in the conceptualization of space. *Cognitive Linguistics* 8(4): 291–325.

Lakoff, George
1987   *Women, Fire and Dangerous Things: What Categories Reveal about the Mind*. Chicago, IL: Chicago University Press.

Lakoff, George and Mark Johnson
1980   *Metaphors We Live By*. Chicago, IL: Chicago University Press.

1999   *Philosophy in the Flesh: The Embodied Mind and its Challenge to Western Thought*. New York: Basic Books.

Langacker, Ronald
1987   *Foundations of Cognitive Grammar, Volume 1*. Stanford, CA: Stanford University Press.

1991a   *Concept, Image and Symbol*. Berlin: Mouton de Gruyter.

1991b   *Foundations of Cognitive Grammar, Volume 2*. Stanford, CA: Stanford University Press.

1992   Prepositions as grammatical(izing) elements. *Leuvenese Bijdragen* 81: 287–309.

Levin, Beth
1993   *Towards a Lexical Organization of English Verbs*. Chicago, IL: University of Chicago Press.

Lindner, Susan
1981   A lexico-semantic analysis of English verb–particle constructions with *out* and *up*. Doctoral thesis. Linguistics Dept, University of California, San Diego. Distributed [1983] by the Indiana University Linguistics Club.

Lindstromberg, Seth
1997   *English Prepositions Explained*. Amsterdam: John Benjamins.

Mandler, Jean
1988   How to build a baby: on the development of an accessible representational system. *Cognitive Development* 3: 113–136.

1992   How to build a baby: II. Conceptual primitives. *Psychological Review* 99(4): 587–604.

1996   Preverbal representation. In: Bloom, Peterson, Nadel and Garrett (1996), 365–384.

Morgan, Pamela
1997   Figuring out *figure out*: metaphor and the semantics of the English verb–particle construction. *Cognitive Linguistics* 8: 327–357.

O'Dowd, Elizabeth
    1998   *Prepositions and Particles in English: A Discourse-Functional Account*. New York: Oxford University Press.
Pustejovsky, James
    1998   *The Generative Lexicon*. Cambridge, MA: MIT Press.
Rice, Sally
    1993   Far afield in lexical fields: the English prepositions. In: Michael Bernstein (ed.), *ESCOL '92*: 206–217.
Rice, Sally, Dominiek Sandra and Mia Vanrespaille
    1999   Prepositional semantics and the fragile link between space and time. In: Masako Hiraga, Christopher Sinha, and Sherman Wilcox (eds.), *Cultural, Psychological and Typological Issues in Cognitive Linguistics*, 107–127. Amsterdam: John Benjamins.
Rosch, Eleanor
    1975   Cognitive representations of semantic categories. *Journal of Experimental Psychology: General* 104: 192–233.
Ruhl, Charles
    1989   *On Monosemy: a Study in Linguistic Semantics*. Albany: State University of New York Press.
Sandra, Dominiek
    1998   What linguists can and can't tell you about the human mind: a reply to Croft. *Cognitive Linguistics* 9(4): 361–378.
Sandra, Dominiek and Sally Rice
    1995   Network analyses of prepositional meaning: mirroring whose mind – the linguist's or the language user's? *Cognitive Linguistics* 6(1): 89–130.
Sperber, Daniel and Deirdre Wilson
    1986   *Relevance: Communication and Cognition*. Cambridge, MA: Harvard University Press.
Svorou, Soteria
    1993   *The Grammar of Space*. Amsterdam: John Benjamins.
Sweetser, Eve
    1990   *From Etymology to Pragmatics: Metaphorical and Cultural Aspects of Semantic Structure*. Cambridge, England: Cambridge University Press.
Talmy, Leonard
    1978   Figure and ground in complex sentences. In: Joseph H. Greenberg (ed.), *Universals in Human Language, Volume 4*, 625–649. Stanford, CA: Stanford University Press.
    1983   How language structures space. In: Herbert Pick and L. Acredelo (eds.), *Spatial Orientation: Theory, Research and Application*, 225–320. New York: Plenum.

1988   Force dynamics in language and cognition. *Cognitive Science* 12: 49–100.

1996   Fictive motion in language and "ception". In: Bloom, Peterson, Nadel and Garrett (1996), 211–276.

2000   *Toward a Cognitive Semantics, Volumes I and II.* Cambridge, MA: MIT Press.

Traugott, Elizabeth Closs

1989   On the rise of epistemic meanings in English: an example of subjectification in semantic change. *Language* 65(1): 31–55.

Tsohatzidis, Savas L. (ed.)

1990   *Meanings and Prototypes: Studies in Linguistic Categorization.* London: Routledge.

Turner, Mark

1991   *Reading Minds.* Princeton: Princeton University Press.

1996   *The Literary Mind.* New York: Oxford University Press.

Tyler, Andrea and Vyvyan Evans

2003   *The Semantics of English Prepositions: Spatial Scenes, Cognition and the Experiential Basis of Meaning.* New York and Cambridge: Cambridge University Press.

Vandeloise, Claude

1990   Representation, prototypes and centrality. In: Tsohatzidis (1990), 403–437.

1991   *Spatial Prepositions: A Case Study in French.* Chicago, IL: The University of Chicago Press.

1994   Methodology and analyses of the preposition *in*. *Cognitive Linguistics* 5(2): 157–184.

Varela, Francisco, Evan Thompson and Eleanor Rosch

1991   *The Embodied Mind.* Cambridge, MA: MIT Press.

Polysemy as flexible meaning: experiments with English *get* and Finnish *pitää*

Jarno Raukko

1. Introduction

It is common to view polysemy as a collection or network of several inter-related meanings that is fairly stable, fairly unproblematic to segment and establish, and fairly well agreed upon by different speakers. Yet there are also opponents (of at least two kinds) who either wish to reduce polysemy to depend only upon contextual specifications, or simply claim that polysemy is irrelevant to the study of communication.[1] One way to build a bridge between these camps is to see polysemy as patterns of flexibility in (lexical) meaning in much the same way as it is accepted that situational (utterance or discourse level) meaning is nonfixed, inexact and negotiable. This does not imply that word-specific descriptions of semantic variation would be unnecessary, but it leaves room for dynamicity and open-endedness in categorization as well as for intersubjective disagreements about the structure of the poly-semy of a given word. I want to demonstrate the advantages of this view with an analysis of some of the results from polysemy experiments with nonlinguist informants.

Even if semantics is nonfixed, flexible, imprecise and in a pessimistic sense intangible, language users believe that much of what is communicated is based on a significant degree of intersubjective agreement. They need to believe in such an agreement in order to believe in the value of communi-cation (see Raukko 1996). A truly intersubjective type of experiment to investigate this phenomenon might involve a manufactured dialogical situ-ation where the linguist could, e.g., observe meaning negotiations between the participants over the meaning of a polysemous word in a specific context. So far I have employed a more modest "mock-intersubjective" framework where informants can creatively produce their own representations of the polysemy of a word, and I will in my analysis perform the "intersubjective shuttling" between the responses.

The two words whose polysemy provides the example cases in this article are two verbs, one from English (*get*, meaning e.g. 'obtain', 'receive', 'arrive', 'take', 'become', 'make', 'have', 'understand', 'answer', 'must' and 'be allowed to') and the other from Finnish (*pitää*, meaning e.g. 'like', 'must', 'hold', 'keep', 'consider', 'organize', 'wear' and 'not leak'). In most cases these verbs are not translational counterparts; the reason for selecting them lies mainly in the shared complex type of polysemy. The section on *get* concentrates on the results from an experiment called the *production test* and uses some secondary findings from the results of a so-called *difference evaluation test* (also known as the *similarity rating test*). The section on *pitää* focuses on the results of a third type of test, the *sorting test*.

2. Variability, flexibility, fuzziness and methodological needs

2.1. Flexibility and fuzziness

A new dynamic view of meaning gained ground by the end of the 19th century (Nerlich 1992: 100). Instead of a one-to-one relationship between word and idea, meaning was already seen as flexible, elastic, adaptable and open to change; "imperfect", so to speak. Such notions were at least presented in Germany (Erdmann 1910; Paul), France (Bréal 1868; Nyrop 1913; Paulhan), England (Gardiner) and the United States (Whitney 1867).

It could be said that mainstream semantics in the 20th century lost track of the notion of flexible meaning as the driving force of semantics in general and polysemy in particular. Structuralist semantics paid more attention to the difference between *homonymy* and *polysemy*[2] than to the ubiquity of polysemy. Indeed, many semanticists, including so-called cognitive semanticists (e.g. Geeraerts 1993; Tuggy 1993), have paid much attention to another tripartite division, namely *ambiguity*, *polysemy* and *vagueness*. Still, much of that literature rests on a notion of vagueness as a fairly static property of lexical meaning.

One recent addition is offered by Zhang (1998), who draws attention to the concept of *fuzziness* in this four-partite framework: *fuzziness*, *vagueness*, *generality* and *ambiguity*. (For Zhang, polysemy is closest to vagueness.) Her framework is Gricean, and her view of polysemy does not seem to allow for ambiguities that are left unresolved by the context. In her view only fuzziness is not "resolvable with resort to context" and "is closely involved with language users' judgments" (Zhang 1998: 13). After discussing syntactic and semantic tests for fuzziness, Zhang introduces some pragmatic tests. Whereas for Zhang (i) *bank* is ambiguous irrespective of people's judgements; (ii) *person* is general in that it does not specify sex, height or nationality; (iii) *good* is vague as to whether it refers to the goodness of a student, food or legs; (iv) *beauty*, by contrast, is fuzzy owing to the fuzziness of the concept it denotes, to the fuzzy nature of language users' perceptions of its referential boundary (1998: 27). Zhang calls such factors psychological, but does not explicate if her understanding of "semantic cognition" would also involve a more socially based procedure of "wanting to believe that interlocutors agree on meanings" in place of truth conditions and Grice's maxims.

2.2. *Flexibility and variability*

All words and morphemes display polysemy to a greater or lesser extent. In addition, polysemy reflects semantic flexibility. All discourse deals with this fuzzy state of affairs, and because virtually nothing is monosemous and fixed, there is no solid way to explain polysemy away by processes of contextual specification. Therefore, all investigations of linguistic meaning and linguistic function have to deal with semantic flexibility. Polysemy (flexibility) becomes the default, and it affects everything we say about syntax, semantics, pragmatics, text and discourse.

Semantic flexibility, semantic variability, and polysemy are to me in some sense three ways of talking about the same thing. However, in the following I shall concentrate on polysemy as one type of semantic variability. I am partly following Raukko (1997) where I contrasted a mainstream "traditional view" with an "alternative view".

Variability is different from variation (see Östman 1988). Variability has to do with a process, with a potential, with an inherent quality. Variation is rather a product, a materialized state of affairs, a descriptive quality. In research, variation is more like a top-down phenomenon: linguists first decide what language is, and what is a relevant linguistic feature, and then see how language varies according to that feature. Variability is more bottom-up: it is a starting point for a theory, and only through building a theory of the phenomena in language does the linguist gradually build a notion of what language is and what a relevant feature is.

What then is semantic variability? I would like to suggest at least six (overlapping) shades of the idea.

(i)   *Nonfixedness.* We cannot claim that language has a lexicon with ready-made meanings and polysemous categories for words; nor does a person's cognition contain a mental lexicon in the sense of a storehouse of ready-made meanings and categories.

(ii)   *Fuzziness, unclarity, non-pinpointability.* We cannot aim at preciseness in communication nor in the analysis of meaning.

(iii)   *Flexibility.* Language is constituted by social conventions. These social conventions allow for change and flexibility, and some disagreement between speakers. Still, it is not a dead end to try to describe semantics; we just have to allow for loose ends, and for the possibility of change and flexibility.

(iv)   *Ambivalence.* Polysemous situations are not about two competing meanings at a time but (in principle) about an indefinitely large "number" of meanings. Whereas ambiguity is usually tied to intention, ambivalence is the idea that even speakers themselves do not (always) know what they intend to communicate (Östman 1988, 2000).

(v)   *Intersubjective differences* (this can also be about variation). When we describe semantics, it is wiser to be descriptive and open-ended than prescriptive and definitive. Of course the social conventions themselves are (governed by) norms, but it is a different thing for linguists to decide what is the correct meaning – or set of meanings – of a word.

(vi)   *Polysemy* (in "static semantics" this is about variation). The default is that words do not have just one fixed meaning. Therefore many practical things that we do, such as provide glosses for foreign language items, or make lists of contrastive vocabularies in different languages, are very problematic endeavours.

These six shades of variability cover and partly explain the meaning and place of polysemy and flexible meaning in semantics. The four Subsections 2.3, 2.4, 3.1 and 3.2 will show how I have operationalized variability and in particular flexibility in my overall methodology and in my experiments.

2.3.   Methodological consequences

When we want to address semantic questions, such as "What kinds of meanings can this word 'have'?" and "What is crucial in the distinctions and potentials of that polysemy?", and take into account the properties of semantics that I have spelt out above, we have to choose some methodology, and choose some concrete methods.

One method that has become something of a default in linguistics is the corpus method. The linguist looks at a large and somewhat pre-processed selection of text material and tries to find the relevant instances (instantiations, specimens) of the item that s/he wants to study. However, problems arise, because most semantic questions would require some knowledge about the meaning-maker, the human beings producing and receiving and understanding the text and all its bits. When using a corpus, one is basically by oneself when trying to determine what the bits mean. Of course one can use one's linguistic knowledge – as a native or fluent speaker and as a linguistic expert – in order to determine the meanings. However, it is not necessarily a very interesting, reliable, nor "scientific" way to deal with semantic questions. One reason is the ever-presence of semantic variability and flexibility. If meanings are not out there as fixed entities, but instead emerge in language use situations, we need to know more about the context and the participants of the communicative situation in order to say what is being meant. Also, if meanings are fuzzy, it is even more difficult to determine the meaning if we are not ourselves part of the context of the communicative situation. Moreover, if people can have different opinions on what something means, why would it be enough for a linguist just to look at a corpus and say what he or she finds there?

Another way might be to turn to a different scientific ideal, something closer to the natural sciences, for instance cognitive neuroscience. So, for instance, one could forget about questions that semanticians, pragmaticians and discourse analysts are interested in, and concentrate on things that you can see in the curves and measures that show features in the electrical activity of the brain. Or feed a computer large masses of text and see how it categorizes words and texts according to distributions. The problem here is that we are quite far from linguistically interesting questions and methods. And unlike natural scientists, semanticists should not even dream of finding definitive or objective answers.

Then there is a middle way: do something about the tacit assumptions and hence the procedure of scientific discovery and linguistic analysis. This is the road I am taking. I have chosen to try out what certain kinds of experimental methods, experiments, experimentations can do for us.

One field of linguistics where it has been customary to use experiments is psycholinguistics. Although two out of three test types that I am using have been employed by semantically-oriented psycholinguists, my experimental methodology as a whole is not exactly of psycholinguistic nature. I am trying out experiments that fall between pure armchair speculation and hard-core experimental methods with an ideal of objectivity. Some of these experiments leave room for the creativity of the informant who is participating in the experiment (and hence bear similarities with elicitation and interviewing). Although these experiments use artificial settings, an open-minded and non-objectivist semantician can use the experiments to make discoveries about semantic flexibility and variability, as there is openness in the questions and room for the informant's personal effort.

Section 3 will introduce the three types of experiments that I have been using in my research into polysemy. In Section 3.2 I will show how the six shades of variability mentioned in Section 2.2 are operationalized in the experiments.

2.4.   *Polysemy as dynamic mass*

For me polysemy, flexibility and variability are broad cover terms, and I do not even mind using them as covering one another. Polysemy is flexible meaning, and it covers referential polysemy, regular polysemy, lexical polysemy (see Deane 1988), vagueness, generality and fuzziness. I prefer to investigate all variants of "one form – not just one fixed meaning" with the same tool pack, rather than concentrate on a conceptual typology of these variants.

Cognitive linguists such as Langacker (1988a) use a specific network model to describe polysemy with nodes that are joined by semantically plausible links (see Seto, this volume). I have tried to develop a more flexible, loosely structured, and "contiguous" version of the model (Raukko 1994, 1997) where the nodes are only used as methodological tools and, in principle, a polysemous semantic range is (ontologically) more like a flexible "mass" than a "network".

Flexible meaning is not only about graded membership of categories, fuzzy boundaries of categories and continuum effects – characteristics of (at least ideal) prototype theory. It is also about the nonspecificity of meaning and meaning type category membership. In Section 4.2 we will see how within a given range of the polysemy of *get* some instances can be more reliably allotted to a category than others. Some instances are vague or fuzzy enough to simultaneously match two different categories, but we will find at least two versions of this phenomenon. In some cases one can interpret the same meaning in two methodological ways, and therefore the semantic instance falls into a double membership of these (contradictory) categories. In other cases one does not need to decide the proper category, although related examples would fall into distinctive (neighbouring but still contradictory) categories.

3. Experimental applications of flexible meaning

3.1. Experimental settings

I will here report on three types of tests in my experimental research on polysemy: (i) production tests, (ii) difference evaluation tests, and (iii) sorting tests. As this article concentrates on *get* and *pitää*, the reader can find in the Appendices reproductions of (i) the whole of the questionnaire of the *get* production test, (ii) the instructions part for the *get* difference evaluation test, and (iii) the translation of the instructions sheet for the *pitää* sorting test.

I have devised the production test myself; I used the first pilot version in Helsinki in 1991 (Raukko 1993). The mature version (used since 1994) contains four questions on a questionnaire, of which an example (the case of *get*) is reproduced in Appendix 1. The informant (or subject) is asked to produce examples (sentences or phrases) each containing the lexeme *get* (in any form) so that each example portrays the word *get* in a meaning different from all the rest that the informant produces. This is the outline of question No. 1 in the questionnaire, and question No. 4 provides the analyst with the crucial help of paraphrases of the respective examples in which the informant is asked to avoid using the word *get*.

The analysis is based on 329 informants' responses to the *get* production test. Most of these 329 informants were high school students in two schools: Putnam City North High School, Oklahoma City, Oklahoma, USA; and Rider High School, Wichita Falls, Texas, USA. There were also 23 university students of English at the Midwestern State University, Wichita Falls, Texas, and a few teachers from each school. The experiment was carried out in March and April 1994; I was guiding the experiment on location (see Raukko 1999 for further details).[3]

The difference evaluation test is also called the similarity rating test, and my version follows the traditional setup (Lehrer 1974; Caramazza and Grober 1976; Colombo and Flores d'Arcais 1984; Gibbs et al. 1994; Sandra and Rice 1995). The idea is to go through pairs of sentences which each contain two uses of *get* and evaluate the semantic distance between the two uses in each case. The function of this test is more confirmative in nature, and I consider its reliability far lower than that of the production test. The reason is that multiple choice tests require far less commitment, creative effort and explicit signs of successful understanding of the instructions from the informant than tests where one has to write down one's own sentences, comment on them and paraphrase them. Another reason is that when the informant faces pairs of two stimulus sentences one pair at a time, it is much easier not to take the question of semantic distance seriously than in the case of the sorting test (introduced next below), where one needs to look at the whole of 50 stimuli from the outset and work much harder on them. It is no surprise that the sorting test requires much more time and expertise from the informant than the difference evaluation test. However, Section 4 will make two short references to the results of the *get* difference evaluation test. The locus of the experiment was the same as in the production test, i.e. USA 1994, and I had 79 informants (see Appendix 2).

The sorting test also follows a tradition, although I have devised my own elaborate version for my research on the Finnish verb *pitää*. The idea of sorting stimuli is familiar from psychology and psycholinguistics, and for polysemy I have seen it used by at least Colombo and Flores d'Arcais (1984) as well as Sandra and Rice (1995). I have performed the production test and the difference evaluation test for *pitää* (in Helsinki, during 1995–1999) as well, but the main emphasis in Section 5 will be on the results of the sorting test (in Helsinki, during 1998). The design and usability of the sorting test draws heavily on the production test, starting from the fact that the stimulus sentences originate in the production test responses. As the two tests address the same problem of "how to categorize meanings of *pitää*" from two different perspectives, the analyses of the two types of experiments are necessarily interlinked. The *pitää* sorting experiment was conducted in October 1998 in Helsinki with 21 informants who were university students, either majoring in general linguistics or taking an introductory course in general linguistics. The English translation of the instructions part from the original Finnish questionnaire can be found in Appendix 3.

3.2. How the experiments and analyses operationalize flexibility

Let us see how the experiments, or tests, help us grasp the six shades of variability (listed in Section 2.2), or help us operationalize the research questions pertaining to flexible meaning. The following is an illustrative list of examples, not an exhaustive analysis.

(i)   *Nonfixedness.* In the production test, instead of giving the informants a ready-made selection of instances that would display different meanings of a word, I ask them to produce these instances. They create their own personal view of polysemy by means of giving examples, commenting on the centrality of and links between the instances, and giving paraphrases for the examples. Although ready-made examples are given to informants as stimuli in the sorting test, the quantitative and qualitative properties of the divisions (cf. meaning types) are not fixed in advance, but the informant can establish them by her- or himself.

(ii)   *Fuzziness, unclarity.* I am using three different test types because they approach the same issue from different angles, and even if we never quite get into the "meaning itself", we have three kinds of evidence suggesting certain trends. When I analyse the results, I do not aim at clear-cut boundaries or discrete categories that include all possible data, and I allow for uncertainty even in the final results of the data analysis.

(iii)   *Flexibility* is present in many details of the experiments and my analysis of the results. Firstly, I have not fixed the territory of the word under study too strictly in advance. If in the test for the word *get* there appear examples with *forget*, I accept them and they tell me something about the way my informants see boundaries between categories. Secondly, if in the tests for *back* and *date* (also performed in the USA in 1994) all possible word-classes and even compounds occur, such as *back-up*, then this is evidence that people feel that word-class boundaries do not form boundaries for semantic analyses of polysemous words, as many traditional schools of thought have believed.

(iv)   *Ambivalence.* Even if the setting of the production test makes the informants use a metalanguage to "translate" linguistic examples that they have produced on their own (in the form of the paraphrasing task), this does not guarantee disambiguation and nonflexibility. On the contrary, paraphrases can distort the "intentions" of the informants or lead interpretations astray or contradict with examples. Of course methodologically I have to build my analysis on the paraphrases, but in the end, paraphrases are not an omnipotent metalanguage. They are just as much subject to flexibility effects as the original examples.

(v)   *Intersubjective differences.* One of the main concerns of an experiment is the search for both similarities and differences in the responses. In some sense similarities – that is, intersubjective agreement – are more relevant for the presentation of the results, if the objective is to describe the most important aspects of the polysemy of a word. These are the most basic social conventions about the use of the word. However, differences must also be taken into account. They can tell us not only about differences of opinion, but also about different perspectives on the same matter. Some examples of the use of a word can have double membership on the "map" of the semantics of that word. Some examples are so fuzzy that it is no use trying to fix them into a certain point on that same map. The most reliable way to study intersubjective variability in practice is to set up an experiment with native informants.

(vi)   *Polysemy.* It is clear that all my experiments try to give a richer understanding of polysemy.

It is clear that semantic studies lose depth if variability is ignored. The acknowledgement of variability has important methodological consequences, and I have chosen to try out experimental methods for this end. Although they cannot be used any more objectively than any other method, they have important qualities which directly address facets of semantic variability.

4.   Flexibility effects in the polysemy of *get*

This section focuses on the "problems" in the analysis of the polysemy of *get*. After the introductory overview on the polysemy as a whole, it takes three excursions to specific parts of the polysemy. Even if the experiments are designed to pave the way for a richer analysis of polysemy, it should be kept in mind that the problems are intrinsic in nature and therefore partly insoluble. There is no escaping from the fact that in the polysemy of *get* there are several points where examples and instances do not fall into categories neatly. Categories can be seen as continuums, but they also overlap and yield insoluble categorization situations. And as pointed out in Section 2.4, flexible meaning is not only about borderlines of categorization: in many cases the semantics itself of the instances is so fuzzy that it is difficult to interpret in the context of the polysemy of a word. We shall view these "problems" as supporting the theory of flexible meaning instead of leaving us with an unsatisfactory outcome.

The polysemy of *get* forms an exceptionally abundant and complex network of meanings and ranges of flexible meaning. This abundant polysemy of *get* has been discussed by e.g. Kimball (1973), Niedzielski (1976) and Lindstromberg (1991), whose main goal has been to provide a neat reductionistic representation (or even matrix).[4] Lindstromberg points out (1991: 289), however, that while his analysis mainly aims at simplicity (i.e. the polysemy of *get* can be explained via extensions from the meanings 'obtain' and 'seize'/ 'take hold of'), his approach is also more prototype-based and cognitive-semantic in nature than that of Kimball and Niedzielski. I find Lindstromberg's analysis of fairly little use, because my aim is not explanatory simplicity but descriptive "relevance": I aim at concentrating on "central" and "crucial" features in the polysemy of *get* partly from the perspective of a speaker who has no training in linguistics (i.e. a typical informant of mine). Needless to say, I am looking at colloquial and nonstandard (American) English, and because my informants are mostly American teenagers, I do not make any claims with respect to regional and social coverage and generalizability (see Raukko 1999).[5]

To get a first taste of some delicious details in the polysemy of *get*, here are some introductory examples that in themselves are flexible in meaning.

(0)   a.   *I didn't* get *that. What did you say?* (Lindstromberg 1991: 289)
       b.   *Part of being a nation is* getting *the history wrong.*[6]

The instance of *get* in (0a) can be analysed at least as (i) 'understanding' in the sense of 'grasping the content'; (ii) 'understanding' in the sense of 'hearing the words'; and (iii) 'hearing the words' in the sense of 'catching' them. *Getting* in (0b) can refer to (i) 'understanding' the history wrongly; (ii) 'interpreting' the history wrongly; (iii) 'reconstructing' the history in a wrong form; and (iv) 'making' the history wrong, causing a change of state, creating an image of history that is wrong.

In order to understand the place of the meaning types that will be in focus in Sections 4.1–4.3, a brief overview of the major categories in the polysemy of *get* is necessary. This overview is the outcome of a long and complex analysis of the results of the 1994 *get* production test experiment (partly reported in Raukko 1999). The meaning types listed below are the result of the method used, and they concentrate on the most salient categories (and the most salient features of the categories), and are continually subject to processual changes.

In a very general and abstract manner, the polysemy of *get* can initially be divided into such large groups of meanings as (i) CHANGE OF POSSESSION; (ii) CHANGE OF LOCATION; (iii) CHANGE OF STATE; and (iv) static meanings.[7] However, when we look at the responses of the 329 American informants in the *get* production test, we can abstract out a slightly different pattern of four most salient high-level meaning types: (a) OBTAINING; (b) RECEIVING; (c) MOTION; and (d) CHANGE OF STATE; where (a) and (b) correspond to (i), (c) to (ii) and (d) to (iii). In the case of each type, at least 70% of the informants produced at least one instance of the type, and thus differentiated it from all other meaning types. When we go further down to the "basic-level" meaning types that these productions most often represent, we find four corresponding but specified types: (a') CONCRETE OBTAINING FOR ONESELF; (b') CONCRETE RECEIVING; (c') CONCRETE (non-causative) MOTION; and (d') EXPERIENTIAL CHANGE OF STATE. The following sentences are prototypical examples of these basic-level meaning types, respectively from (a') to (d'). They are prototypical in at least two senses: they have the same characteristics as a more abstract outline of a prototype of the given meaning type would have, and they are examples which frequently occurred either in identical form or in safely comparable forms.

(1)   *She had enough money to get a car.*
(2)   *What are you getting for your birthday?*
(3)   *Get out of here.*
(4)   *I'm getting tired.*

The meaning types behind these examples are the top salient meaning types in the polysemy of *get*. Some others, comparable to these but which are not part of the salient higher-level groups (a) through (d) are: (e) UNDERSTANDING; (f) STABLE POSSESSION; (g) OBLIGATION; and (h) ABILITY (or 'permission'). Examples of these are given in (5) to (8) respectively.

(5)   *I don't get it.*
(6)   *I've got a headache.*
(7)   *I gotta go.*
(8)   *I get to go to Dallas on Saturday.*

UNDERSTANDING and STABLE POSSESSION are related to the abstract type CHANGE OF POSSESSION, although they are more or less static in meaning. The modal uses OBLIGATION and ABILITY are also fairly static, and at least the latter is related to cases of CHANGE OF STATE with a verbal complement, such as STARTING (*Let's get going*) and REACHING A STAGE (*Getting to know a foreign language is hard work*).

But why should OBTAINING and RECEIVING be different meanings in such a salient way? Why should not STABLE POSSESSION be more closely linked to CONCRETE RECEIVING, as we can have (colloquial) cases such as *I got a car* where it may not be specified whether the speaker refers to a change or a state of her/his possessions. The answer to these questions is: categories leak; we cannot establish such meaning types too tightly. Section 4.1 focuses on the question of OBTAINING VS. RECEIVING. Section 4.2 tackles a continuum between two high-level abstract groups. In the group of CHANGE OF LOCATION, there are basically two parts: non-causative MOTION and causative CARRYING. Instances of the latter, however, can come very close to certain types of OBTAINING and even some other meaning types, and this is where we see the necessary continuum. Section 4.3 questions the independence of both ABILITY and OBLIGATION *vis-à-vis* verbal types of CHANGE OF STATE.

4.1. Obtaining vs. receiving

According to my findings, meaning types in the polysemy of *get* that have to do with 'possession' (and that it is plausible to distinguish) include OBTAINING, RECEIVING, CATCHING ETC., UNDERSTANDING and STABLE POSSESSION. While the last two are static, CATCHING ETC. is a special type of CHANGE OF POSSESSION: such types of meanings have to do with, e.g., CONCRETE CATCHING (*Get the ball*), ANSWERING (*I will get the door*) and HURTING/KILLING/PUNISHING (*I'm gonna get you punk*). Thus, I argue that UNDERSTANDING and CATCHING ETC. are specialized enough not to belong to the type METAPHORICAL RECEIVING, which is probably their historical source.

As for OBTAINING and RECEIVING, the two main poles of CHANGE OF

POSSESSION, I have suggested in Raukko (1993, 1995, 1999) a variety of subordinate meaning types. Table 1 presents these types in a matrix form, which is not an experimental result as such.

Table 1.   Types of RECEIVING and OBTAINING, in the core of CHANGE OF POSSESSION. All example sentences are taken from the production test responses.

	Beneficiary = subject		Beneficiary = (direct or prepositional) object
	Subject is non-agentive	Subject is agentive	
Concrete	CONCRETE RECEIVING *(What did you get for Christmas?)*	CONCRETE OBTAINING FOR ONESELF *(Let's go get some bread.)*	CONCRETE OBTAINING FOR SOMEONE ELSE *(Please get me a drink.)*
Meta-phorical	METAPHORICAL RECEIVING *(I never get my way* or *I got an A on the test.)*	METAPHORICAL OBTAINING FOR ONESELF *(Get a life!)*	METAPHORICAL OBTAINING FOR SOMEONE ELSE[8] [Not produced by my informants]

The actual responses of the informants do not form such a neat picture as Table 1 does. In particular, there were several informants who not only made differentiations among these five types, but also differentiations within one or more of these types. The clearest trend of all is that within METAPHORICAL RECEIVING there are three subtypes which are sometimes distinguished from one another rather systematically, namely 'receiving a grade', 'catching an illness' and 'other types'. The strong representation of 'receiving a grade' is of course explained by the composition of the informant population. Apart from METAPHORICAL RECEIVING, we find type-internal differentiations in many responses, but no clear patterns among informants.

The problem is more general: how do we find organization in the rather chaotic-looking, varied outcome of the responses? When addressing the problem of motivating the distinction between OBTAINING and RECEIVING, it is safe to base the hypothesis on the concrete basic-level types, CONCRETE OBTAINING FOR ONESELF and CONCRETE RECEIVING, which are often the source of vague interpretations.

In the data, as many as 199 informants (61% of the total population) produced at least one instance of CONCRETE OBTAINING FOR ONESELF. I need to say that this is an initial count, because this meaning type is at the very centre of the discussion of problematic categorization. As many as 47 informants produced more than one instance, so that the overall number of instances in this initial counting was 266. The most frequently used paraphrase was *buy*, which occurred 88 times. Other paraphrases that clearly indicate an agentive and intentional role on the part of the subject were *obtain* (20 instances), *purchase* (19), *pick up* (17), *retrieve* (13), *take* (9) and *grab* (3). Thus 169 instances (64% out of 266) would at least partially meet the criterion of prototypical agentive obtaining. Yet even some of these examples could well slide towards other meanings: *pick up* could be said to contain a possible CARRYING component (see Section 4.2).

On the other hand, 162 informants (49% of the total population) produced at least one instance of CONCRETE RECEIVING. Half of these (82 informants) used *receive* as the paraphrase. It turns out that as many as 104 of these informants (64% out of 162) produced both CONCRETE OBTAINING FOR ONESELF and CONCRETE RECEIVING, that is, they distinguished these meaning types from one another. We thus have 104 cases of a pair of sentences that can be seen to manifest a clear difference between the meanings. Let us take a look at two such pairs; (9a) and (9b) come from my *get* informant No. 19, and (10a) and (10b) from informant No. 259; (9a'), (9b'), (10a') and (10b') are the paraphrases written by the same informants, respectively.

(9)   a.   *I got a car when I turned 16.*[9]
      a'.   *I received a car when I turned 16.*
      b.   *I went to the store to get a CD.*
      b'.   *I went to the store to purchase a CD.*
(10) a.   *I got my prom dress in August.*
      a'.   *I bought a prom dress in August.*
      b.   *I have gotten three letters from a friend.*
      b'.   *I have recieved* [sic: her spelling] *three letters from a friend.*

Without the paraphrases it would be difficult to decide whether the examples refer to OBTAINING or RECEIVING. In examples like (9a) one gets extra hints from the context – when you turn 16 it is your birthday and it is customary to get presents then – but at least (10a) would be vague in this respect without the paraphrase.

Not surprisingly, the material is filled with examples that are not easy to classify, some of them because they lack a paraphrase, others because the object of getting, the paraphrase and the encyclopaedic knowledge about the things talked about are necessarily unclear with respect to the component of agentivity. Consider examples (11)–(13) (and the corresponding paraphrases) which were the only instances of any type of (CONCRETE) CHANGE OF POSSESSION that the particular informant (Nos. 124, 171 and 276 respectively) produced.

(11)   *Let's get this.*
(11')   *Let's acquire this.*
(12)   *I get a coke.*
(12')   *I picked up* [*sic*: past tense] *a coke.*
(13)   *I need to get a new car.*
(13')   *I need to acquire a new car.*

Acquire as such is as polysemous as *get* in this respect. One could argue that *Let's* more probably invokes an agentive reading than a non-agentive one; that *pick up* may be an American colloquial synonym for *buy*; and that *need* may bring into mind that the speaker is planning to do something agentive about the problem. But still we are on soft ground with examples like these: the distinction between OBTAINING and RECEIVING seems to start losing its relevance.

As a large proportion of the instances contain elements that make them unclear cases, the temptation to do away with the distinction OBTAINING vs. RECEIVING grows. Yet at the same time we find a great number of clearer cases, some of them providing us with neat pairs of prototypical examples of the two types, distinguished by the informant as different meanings of *get*. After all, distinguishing (examples of) meaning types was what the production task was all about, so if an informant comes up with more than one example of CHANGE OF POSSESSION, we always have to give at least some explanation and description of the similarities and differences between the two or more examples.

The field of OBTAINING and RECEIVING, as presented in Table 1, is so complicated that we have to deal with several parameters at once. Some informants may show us an example where they want to distinguish CONCRETE OBTAINING FOR SOMEONE ELSE from METAPHORICAL RECEIVING (for oneself), calling our attention to three differences at the same time: (i) concrete vs. metaphorical; (ii) agentive vs. non-agentive; and (iii) for someone else vs. for oneself. Yet we the analysts may be led to search only for one minimal difference in each pair of sentences that the informants have produced.

The other test type, difference evaluation, gives us some additional evidence for the fact that the distinction is a difficult one. The pair in (14), which contained CONCRETE OBTAINING FOR ONESELF and CONCRETE RECEIVING, was not only judged as relatively different in meaning (the tenth highest "different" rating among the tested 31 pairs, with average rating of 2.13 on a scale from 0 to 4), but the judgements also deviated quite remarkably: the standard deviation for this pair was the fifth highest among the tested pairs.[10]

(14)   a.   *I went to get a candy bar.*
       b.   *I got a car for my birthday.*

The analysis of particular points in the polysemy of *get* requires sensitivity for continuum effects, generality effects and other kinds of flexibility. Ultimately we also need to ask ourselves why so many informants seem to consider the distinction between (agentive) OBTAINING and (non-agentive) RECEIVING so important in the otherwise abundant and complex polysemy of *get*, even if the distinction is partly too flexible to establish. The methods I have used so far cannot answer that question.

4.2.   *Obtaining vs. carrying*

A nice example to demonstrate the intricate but tricky difference between OBTAINING FOR SOMEONE ELSE and CONCRETE CARRYING comes from Lindstromberg (1991: 291) who does not comment very much on the difference in meaning:

(15)   *I got the letter to her* [the letter, to her].
(16)   *I got her the letter* [the letter, for her].

Lindstromberg terms both of these instances 'change of possession'. (Cf. Givón and Yang's (1994) somewhat different treatise.) At first glance, it would seem that (15) has more to do with motion than (16), while in (16) change of possession is highlighted. However, a more careful look reveals that *both* of these sentences can easily mean both things. Both of them *could* be paraphrased as "I took/brought/carried the letter to her" and "I gave/handed/(made her have) the letter", but we usually tend to think that if one of them had more to do with 'motion' and hence CARRYING, it would be (15), maybe because of the partly locative preposition *to*.

Some of my informants produced examples and paraphrases that portray a possible difference between CONCRETE OBTAINING FOR ONESELF and CONCRETE CARRYING; the following come from my *get* informants Nos. 6 and 77. (17a) and (18a), which are incidentally both paraphrased with *take*, are the ones that I would like to classify as CARRYING.

(17) a.   *I am getting something out of the closet.*
      a'. *I am taking something out of the closet.*
      b.   *I have to get a new car.*
      b'. *I have to purchase a new car.*
(18) a.   *Get your hands off me!*
      a'. *Take your hands off me.*
      b.   *She will get the milk from the store.*
      b'. *She will pick the milk from the store.*

In my scheme, it is typical for OBTAINING not to have locative complements (as in [17a] *out of the closet*), but this is by no means impossible. In (18a) the locative phrase *off me* highlights the motion component clearly more than *from the store* in (18b), while (18b) may refer to a commercial transaction as well. In some sense, however, (17a) and (18b) are similar instances, and yet they have to be classified differently, because the contrasting instances are so different. Thus (17b) and (18a) are at the opposite ends of a scale, while (17a) and (18b) fall in the middle.

The difference evaluation test again brings us one relevant example pair whose meaning difference informants strongly disagreed upon.

(19) a.   *Could you come and get me after school?*
      b.   *I am getting something out of the closet.* (= 17a)

The average and standard deviation figures are almost identical to the ones for the evaluated pair OBTAINING VS. RECEIVING discussed in Section 4.1. Thus, informants again differ greatly in their opinion about the similarity or difference of the meanings of *get* in (19a) and (19b), which supports the analysis of OBTAINING and CARRYING as being idealized abstractions forming the ends of a continuum of flexible meaning where 'change of possession' and 'motion' are present to varying degrees. Even the component 'change of state' is sometimes present as well, but in cases like *getting something into shape* we are already dealing with METAPHORICAL CARRYING instead of the concrete one.

There are also situations where the informant has produced three related instances, and while two represent OBTAINING and CARRYING, the third one can be classified as CATCHING ETC. – e.g. *Get the ball*, or *I will get you*.

Yet there are many cases where the informant has produced only one example relating to our present discussion, and it is relatively impossible to try and firmly classify the meaning type as either OBTAINING, CARRYING or CATCHING ETC.

(20)   *He went to get his money from the drawer.*
(20') *He went to acquire his money from the drawer.*
(21)   *Get me that pen.*
(21') *Fetch me that pen.*
(22)   *Will you get your plate?*
(22') *Will you move your plate?*

All these examples have components of at least two abstract meaning types at the same time. Thus, they support the point about the importance of flexibility in the analysis of polysemy.

4.3.   *Ability vs. reaching a stage vs. obligation*

There are three basically distinct meaning types of *get* that all take an infinitival complement: ABILITY, REACHING A STAGE and OBLIGATION. The first is a technical term for meanings like 'permission' and 'ability', which were not usually distinguished by informants and therefore do not occur as separate meaning types in the analysis. REACHING A STAGE belongs to the macro-type CHANGE OF STATE, and hence its meaning is more dynamic than that of the two modals (OBLIGATION and ABILITY). Besides having obvious differences as to aspects of modality and semantics, the three types favour different verb forms of the main verb *get*. While OBLIGATION is supposed to be bound to the form *got* (which appears as *have got to*, *has got to*, *'ve got to*, *'s got to*, *got to*, *gotta*, *gots to* or *don't got to*), it is prototypical for ABILITY to occur in the simple present tense (or future), while REACHING A STAGE is the most flexible morphologically, and "syntactically more marked" instances like *I'm getting to ...* tend to be interpreted as such non-modal uses. In the following the first two examples and paraphrases (23a–b) show informant No. 246 making a distinction between ABILITY and REACHING A STAGE, and (24) is the most frequent instance of OBLIGATION in the *get* production test, with two frequently occurring paraphrases.

(23)　a.　*I get to be on Television* [*sic*: the informant's capitalization].
　　　　a'.　*I'm going to be allowed to be on television.*
　　　　b.　*I'm glad I "got to know you"* [*sic*: the informant's quotation marks].
　　　　b'.　*I'm glad we became acquainted.*
(24)　*I've got to go.*
(24')　*I need to go. / I have to go.*

The relationship between ABILITY and REACHING A STAGE is problematic and partially overlapping, so that there are again many cases that are difficult to classify. In informant No. 246's case the difference seems fairly clear: getting to be on television can be considered a rare occasion, something that is possible only because circumstances make it so, while getting to know someone is usually considered a more everyday process.[11] This analysis is supported by the paraphrases, which in general are the only basis for distinguishing between ABILITY and REACHING A STAGE. *Be able to* and *be allowed to* are, by default, likely paraphrases of ABILITY. *Be allowed to* occurs in 18 responses and *be able to* in 13 responses (together in 31 responses, or 53%, out of 58 instances of ABILITY in total). In contrast, the omission of *get* is a fairly typical way to paraphrase REACHING A STAGE. (E.g. one informant paraphrased her *I'd like to get to know you* as *I'd like to know you better.*) There is also a strong tendency in my informants' responses with ABILITY to take up a certain lexical complement, i.e. the verb *go*. Forms of *get to go* occurred in 41 responses out of 58 (71%). This collocation seems to be very central in teenage American English. The most difficult form of *get* in this context is *got*, because it can occur with all of the three meaning types. A suitable example is *I got to go*, where both intonation and the paraphrase might "disambiguate" the meaning into one of the three.

OBLIGATION is to a large extent bound to the form *got* (for variants, see above), although I claim that there is one exception in my production test data: informant No. 155 paraphrased *I get to go to school today* as *I had to go to school today*, and although there is some confusion with the tense choice, "going to school" would at least be a likely candidate for a complement of OBLIGATION. Moreover, although an example like *Why do I always get to do the dishes?* did not occur in the production test data, it could be seen as marking the path between REACHING A STAGE and OBLIGATION. I claim that these examples suggest variability for OBLIGATION, although the standard view limits this meaning type to the form *got*.

I hope to have shown that despite the significant semantic differences (on the surface) between the three meaning types with an infinitival complement, there is a continuum from ABILITY via REACHING A STAGE to OBLIGATION. Once we have a continuum, it will be difficult to neatly classify instances of *get* into meaning types. At least the distinction between ABILITY and REACHING A STAGE is hard to establish solidly, even if we have prototypical instances of both and see informants distinguishing the two meaning types. We have seen again that the relationship between these two meaning types is best understood in terms of flexible meaning, where there is no strict division into two isolated meaning types.

5.   Flexibility manifested in the polysemy of *pitää*

Pitää is a Finnish verb with extensive polysemy. Some of its meanings correspond to the polysemy of the English verbs *hold* and *keep*, but two other salient and fairly distinct uses can be translated as *like / be fond of* and *must / have to*. The latter items are more separable semantic nodes, they are more "monolithic", whereas the ones that partly intersect with the semantic spaces covered by *hold* and *keep* form an intricate network of flexible meaning.

In the case of *get*, we saw results of (primarily) the production test and (secondarily) the evaluation test. I have performed similar tests for *pitää*, but the main emphasis will now be on a third type of experiment, namely the sorting test, which was briefly introduced in Section 3.1.

I will first give a brief overview of the polysemy of *pitää* as a whole in the form of a list of glossed examples, and then concentrate on the areas where flexibility and fuzziness are prominent features. The broader overview is useful both for the understanding of the place of the flexible area in the polysemy as a whole and for the assessment of quantitative results in the general framework. The following set of examples (which were produced by informants in the production test and later used as stimuli in the sorting test) portrays a concise list of the most crucial meaning types in the polysemy of *pitää*. By "crucial" I refer to such salience factors as frequency and earliness of occurrence in the production test, while the indicators for distinguishing meaning types now mainly derive from the results of the sorting test.[12] The list starts with LIKING (in [25]) and OBLIGATION (in [26]) (one of the meanings shared by *get* and *pitää*) and ends with six types (30)–(35) that belong to the problematic area of very flexible meaning.

(25) *Mä   pidin   tosta   leffasta.*
      I-NOM   like-PAST-SG1 that-ELAT   movie-ELAT[13]
      'I liked that movie.'
      [LIKING]

(26) *Minun pitää   lähteä   töihin.*
      I-GEN must-SG3   leave-INF   work-PL-ILLAT
      'I must leave for work.'
      [OBLIGATION]

(27) *Minä   pidän   sinua   hulluna.*
      I-NOM   consider-SG1   you-PART   crazy-ESS
      'I consider you crazy.' / 'I think you are crazy.'
      [CONSIDERING]

(28) *Suksi   pitää   tänään   hyvin.*
      ski-NOM   grip-SG3   today   well.
      'The skis have a good grip today.'
      [MAINTAINING CONTACT]

(29) *Pidä   minua   kädestä.*
      hold-SG2-IMPER   me-PART   hand-ELAT
      'Hold my hand' or more literally 'Hold me by my hand.'
      [MANUAL HOLDING]

(30) *Mä   pidän   avaimia   taskussa.*
      I-NOM   keep-SG1   key-PL-PART   pocket-INESS
      'I keep my keys in my pocket.'
      [KEEPING IN A PLACE]

(31) *Pidä*   *suusi*   *kiinni!*
      keep-IMPER-SG2   mouth-ACC-your   shut (ADVERB)
      'Keep your mouth shut.'
      [KEEPING IN A STATE]

(32) *Se   pitää*   *outoja   vaatteita.*
      s/he   wear-SG3   odd-PL-PART cloth-PL-PART
      'S/he wears strange/weird/odd clothes.'
      [WEARING]

(33) *Mä   pidän*   *huomenna   juhlat.*
      I-NOM organize-SG1   tomorrow   party-PL
      'I'm having/giving a party tomorrow.'
      [ORGANIZING]

(34) *Pidä*   *kiirettä!*
      keep-IMPER-SG2   hurry-PART
      'Hurry up.'
      [UPHOLDING A CONDITION]

(35) *Minä   pidin*   *lupaukseni.*
      I-NOM   keep-PAST-SG1 promise-ACC-my
      'I kept my promise.'
      [METAPHORICAL RETAINING]

The presence of flexibility becomes apparent in the variation of informant behaviour in the sorting test. With the meaning types LIKING and OBLIGATION, informants are quite unanimous (i.e. most informants group the same stimuli in these groupings and name the groups in similar ways), whereas variance increases when we go down the list.

The relationship between sentences (31) and (34) is quite intriguing. Firstly, these sentences were grouped together by as many as 62% of informants (13 out of 21). Secondly, there is a risk that some informants may have looked at a combining criterion that has nothing to do with the meaning types in the polysemy of *pitää*, namely the imperative form; this criterion was mentioned by three informants out of the above 13. Thirdly, not only are these two sentences often grouped together, but they both tend also to be grouped with other, somewhat different, sentences, such as (36).

(36)   *Pidä*   *hauskaa!*
       keep-IMPER-SG2   fun-PART
       'Have fun!'

Sentence (36) was grouped with (34) by as many as 17 informants (81%), but with (31) only by nine informants (43%); the difference is statistically significant. In contrast, there were ten stimuli (out of 50) that were sometimes sorted with (31) but never with (34), and conversely, only two that were sometimes sorted with (34) but never with (31). I think all this shows that (31) is a much more difficult stimulus sentence than (34), even if on the surface (31) would seem less idiomatic and more "basic" in meaning than (34). Sentence (36), for its part, was surprisingly sorted together with (33) by as few as two informants, although "having fun" and "having a party" could have been easily thought of as attracting similarity judgements. One possible reason is that there were two other stimuli that were thought of as matching (33) so well that there was no demand for other group members.

Let us look at one more example, namely (37). The interesting finding is that (37) was sorted together with each of (38) through (40) by eight to ten informants, but (38)–(40) in turn were sorted with one another by only two to five informants. The hypothesis is that (37) seems to be a combining link between the other three instances (38), (39) and (40), while these three are not so easily linked without the presence of (37).

(37)   *Minä*   *pidän*   *sinut*   *vaikka*   *väkisin.*
       I-NOM   keep-SG1   you-ACC   even   by-force
       'I will keep you by force if needed.'

(38)   *Puut*   *pitävät*   *lehtensä*   *pitkälle*   *syksyyn.*
       tree-PL-NOM   keep-PL3   leave-ACC-their   long-ALLAT   autumn-ILLAT
       'Trees keep/retain their leaves till late in the autumn.'

(39)   *Minä*   *pidän*   *sinua*   *lukitussa*   *komerossa.*
       I-NOM   keep-SG1   you-PART   locked-INESS   closet-INESS
       'I (will) keep you in a locked closet.'

(40)   *Pidän*   *asian*   *salassa.*
       keep-SG1   matter-ACC   secrecy-INESS = 'in secret'
       'I (will) keep the matter secret.' or 'I will keep it as a secret.'

Thus (37) can be seen as a flexible channel or path between the other three. Moreover, (39) was sorted together with (30) by half of the informants – an expected result considering the seeming similarity between the two sentences – but (40) was grouped with (31) by only one informant, despite the seeming similarity between the two instances.

We are left with a very unpredictable and intricate network of interrelations within the area of flexible meaning which cannot be reduced to established categories.

6. Conclusions

There are two ubiquitous phenomena in linguistic semantics. One is polysemy: the phenomenon that one form can be used for more than one meaning. The other has to do with the indeterminacy, nonfixedness, fuzziness, negotiability, variability and flexibility of the semantic values of all linguistic units. My point is that these are different sides of one and the same problem. However, this insight is only rarely exploited by linguists, at least when they are performing their actual practice of linguistic analysis and theorizing. And yet within the cognitive linguistic framework it has become almost a truism to say that *all* lexical items are polysemous (see e.g. Langacker 1988b: 50–51).

If it is accepted that practically all morphemes have not just one meaning, we can rephrase this claim in the form that practically all morphemes have *flexible* meaning. Thus we are moving from the first ubiquitous phenomenon to the second one. The difference remains that, while polysemy is generally thought of as a more permanent property of the semantics of a language – a product, so to speak – semantic indeterminacy is usually seen as a processual phenomenon. I have chosen to try out experiments in search of a richer understanding of polysemy as flexible meaning, and whichever experiment one chooses, there will be flexibility effects in the results.

Appendix 1. The questionnaire of the *get* production test

April __, 1994
female/male
Senior/Junior/Sophomore/Freshman
age ____

Dear student of Putnam City North High School [Oklahoma City]. My name is Jarno Raukko; I am a researcher of linguistics at the University of Helsinki, Finland, and I am studying some aspects of everyday English. I very much appreciate your participation in this test.

(1) The verb **get** (*get, getting, got, gotten*) is very common in spoken American English, and it seems to be used in very many different ways. You might say that *get* has different meanings. Could you please write down examples of the ways in which you use the word *get* differently. Your examples can be full sentences, but they do not need to be. You do not have to fill in every blank from A to K; just produce as many examples as you can think of where the use of *get* still differs from every other use you have mentioned.

[Additional instruction: if I had to answer a similar question concerning the word *bank*, I might produce examples like the following:

A.   *He had enough money left in his **bank** account.*
B.   *She followed the man along the river **bank**.*]

Now please write down examples with *get*. Feel free to use casual and colloquial style! These examples will not be corrected!

A. _____
B. _____
C. _____
D. _____
E. _____
F. _____
G. _____
H. _____
I. _____
J. _____
K. _____

Please turn over when you have finished answering question No. 1.

(2) In your examples, would you say that one or some of the uses of *get* is more typical or central or important than the others? Is one of them the *most* central one? If you think so, please write down the letter(s) of the example(s). Also explain briefly why you think so.

(3) Do you think that the uses of *get* in your examples are somehow connected or

linked to one another? Is there a common idea? If you think so, please explain or specify briefly.

(4) Finally, would you please once again read each of your examples for question No. 1 and try to express the same idea in another way. In other words, for each example, write down an alternative way of saying the same thing so that you don't use *get* any longer.

[If I had to do this for "She followed the man along the river bank" and I had to avoid using the word *bank* again, I could write "She followed the man along the side of the river".]

Thank you very much for your help.

Appendix 2.   The questionnaire of the *get* difference evaluation test

April __, 1994

Dear student! My name is Jarno Raukko; I am doing my Ph.D. in linguistics at the University of Helsinki, Finland. I am studying some linguistic aspects of English, and I would need your help in making judgements about meaning difference and meaning similarity. Below you find sentences that were produced by American high school students in a test of a slightly different kind than this one. The sentences are grouped in pairs, and you have to compare two sentences at a time. Each sentence has the word *get* in it, and you are supposed to decide whether that word carries the same meaning or two different meanings in the sentences. Additionally, you can decide the degree of the difference (from 0 to 4). I give you an example of how I might understand meaning difference (= MD).

In these sentences *get* has the same meaning (MD = 0):
    I am getting tired.
    The dog got sick.

In these sentences *get* has a somewhat different meaning (MD = 2):
    I am getting tired.
    A guy got me pregnant.

In these sentences *get* has a very different meaning (MD = 4):
    I am getting tired.
    Did you get his joke?

Now I would like you to estimate the meaning difference between the uses of *get* in the following pairs of sentences:

MD

I got home late.
I got a new car.   0 1 2 3 4

Did you get any mail today?
Did you get his joke today?   0 1 2 3 4

[etc.]

Appendix 3.   The questionnaire of the *pitää* sorting test. (Translation)

RESEARCH QUERY ABOUT THE MEANINGS OF THE VERB *PITÄÄ*

initials _____
year of birth _____
female/male
main subject _____

1.(a) In the enclosed envelope you will find 50 cards, each with a sentence containing the word *pitää*. Could you please sort these instances of the meanings of the verb *pitää* into groups where each member shares a "similar enough" meaning. **Let the sorting be solely based on the meaning of the word *pitää*, not on the meaning of the sentence as a whole** – even if the meaning of *pitää* is understood on the basis of the sentential context. For the purposes of this research, it is not essential, either, e.g. which form the verb *pitää* occurs in.

(The sentences are numbered only in order for you to be able to refer to those numbers in some of the questions to follow.)

Sort the sentence cards into piles. A pile can consist of any number of sentences, and a pile can also consist of one sentence alone. When you have finished piling, join the cards in each pile with a small paper clip (found in the envelope), so that it will be easier for me to collect the piles in the end.

(b) If some sentences are especially **difficult** to sort, mark a "D" on such sentence cards.

(c) Can you think of **names** for these piles – i.e. for these types or classes of meanings? (For example, you can use some other Finnish verb, which roughly means the same as the meaning of the *pitää* in question.) In that case, write that name on the topmost card.

(d) When you were doing the pile sorting, did it occur to you that some meanings were quite close to one another but not as close as the members of one pile? Would you be able to **combine** some piles **into classes at an upper level**? Use the bigger paper clips for combining.

2. The piles that you sorted can be said to correspond to meaning classes. In your opinion, what are the three most important/central meaning classes? Refer to the names you used or to the number of the topmost card.

_____ and _____ and _____

(Can you specify, in case it is unclear, whether you refer to a bottom-level category or a higher-level category?)

3. Continuation to task No. 2: please choose one sentence (i.e. one card) out of each of the three most important classes which best represents the respective meaning class, in your opinion. Refer to the numbers on the cards.

_____ and _____ and _____

4. The term *polysemy* is usually used to mean that one word (or some other item) has several meanings which are "related to one another" in a plausible way. The meanings have in other words developed from one another in the course of time, and even the present-day speaker can in principle think of the connection between the meanings. Do you feel that all of the meanings of *pitää* that you dealt with are in this manner "related to one another", or is one of them / are some of them very much apart from the rest?

Yes, all meanings seem
to be related to one another.

A large proportion of the meanings
are probably related to one another,
but the following is/are very separate:

_____

_____

_____

(Can you specify, in case it is unclear,
whether you refer to a bottom-level
category or a higher-level category?)

Could you now place the card piles into the envelope together with this questionnaire.

Thank you very much for your help!

Notes

1. Roy Harris (personal communication) belongs to the latter type, who commented on Raukko (1997) that polysemy is a pseudo-problem in integrationist linguistics, because it is only a feature of *langue*. Although a possibly relevant point, the consequent discussion would ultimately concern the extension of polysemy, and I see my attempt to group together polysemy, flexibility, fuzziness, and situational variability as an attempt to bring polysemy also very much into the realm of *parole*.
2. Langacker for instance (1988a: 136) argues that the distinction between polysemy and homonymy is a matter of degree and cannot be reduced to a simple dichotomy.
3. I wish to express my gratitude to all the 329 anonymous informants as well as the people who helped me in organizing the 1994 experiments, especially Walter Bower, Harry Brown, Kit Johnson, Melanie McGouran and Jackye Plummer.
4. I would also like to point out interesting ongoing research on the development of the polysemy of *get* in children, done by Simone Duxbury (Monash University, Melbourne, Australia) and Brigitte Nerlich, Zazie Todd and David Clarke (see Nerlich, Todd and Clarke, this volume).
5. The American flavour is represented for example in the distinction between *have got* ('possess', 'must') and *have gotten* (for all other meanings) and in the American spelling used in all of the examples, which authentically come from my American informants.
6. This sentence was used as an article title by my Helsinki colleague Pekka Kuusisto, and the interpretations below reflect the discussion we had over the title.
7. Henceforth I will use SMALL CAPITALS to indicate technical terms that function as names of meaning types that my experiments and my analyses suggest. Less technical descriptions are given in single quotes, such as 'permission' a few lines below.
8. METAPHORICAL OBTAINING FOR SOMEONE ELSE is a fairly unimportant meaning type, if not virtually non-existent, and in this matrix it mainly serves analogy. None of my informants (neither [1991] in Helsinki nor [1994] in the USA) produced examples that I would like to interpret and classify as METAPHORICAL OBTAINING FOR SOMEONE ELSE; yet in dictionaries there are some possible candidates, such as *He got her a job with the telephone company* (Collins Cobuild English Language Dictionary [1987]: Reading 8.4), whose metaphoricity, however, is not very strong.
9. I have to explain an additional feature of informant No. 19's response, because it functions as an explicit proof that American high school students seem to have

a clue of what they are doing in my production test. Namely, she not only produced examples, but dictionary-type definitions. She explicated her first example (9a) as *To get is to receive something* and her example (9b) as *To get something is to go buy something or accomplish something.*

10. The average ratings ranged from 0.33 to 3.13, so that 2.13 is a relatively high difference rating. The standard deviation in the ratings for this pair was 1.35. The standard deviations ranged from 0.94 to 1.46.

11. Two orthographically identical cases of, e.g., *I'm glad I got to know you* can mean either ABILITY or REACHING A STAGE depending on the intonation: ABILITY has stress on *got*, REACHING A STAGE on *know*. (I thank Diana ben-Aaron for pointing this out.) Needless to say, my method fails to account for prosody.

12. As in the case of the *get* production test, most *pitää* production test informants provided me with paraphrases of these examples (e.g. where they had to replace *pitää* with another word) so that I did not have to rely only on my native speaker intuition in order to interpret the meanings of *pitää* from the sentential context, but to save space I will not show these paraphrases and their glosses.

13. Explanations of the abbreviations for the suffixes referred to in examples:

NOM	nominative	INF	infinitive
GEN	genitive	IMPER	imperative
PART	partitive	PAST	past tense
ACC	accusative	SG	singular
ESS	essive	PL	plural
INESS	inessive	1	first person
ELAT	elative	2	second person
ILLAT	illative	3	third person
ALLAT	allative		

References

Bréal, Michel
1868   *Les idées latentes du langage. Leçon faite au Collège de France pour la réouverture du cours de grammaire comparée*, le 7 déc. 1868. Paris: Hachette.
Caramazza, Alfonso and Ellen Grober
1976   Polysemy and the structure of the subjective lexicon. In: Clea Rameh (ed.), *Semantics: Theory and Application.* Georgetown University Round Table on Languages and Linguistics 1976, 181–206. Washington, D.C.: Georgetown University Press.
Colombo, Lucia and Giovanni B. Flores d'Arcais
1984   The meaning of Dutch prepositions: a psycholinguistic study of polysemy. *Linguistics* 22: 51–98.

Deane, Paul
    1988   Polysemy and cognition. *Lingua* 75: 325–361.
Erdmann, Karl Otto
    1910   *Die Bedeutung des Wortes*. Aufsätze aus dem Grenzgebiet der Sprach-
                psychologie und Logik. 2. Aufl. Leipzig: Avenarius.
Geeraerts, Dirk
    1993   Vagueness's puzzles, polysemy's vagaries. *Cognitive Linguistics* 4:
                223–272.
Gibbs, Raymond W., Jr., Dinara A. Beitel, Michael Harrington and Paul E. Sanders
    1994   Taking a stand on the meanings of *stand*: bodily experience as moti-
                vation for polysemy. *Journal of Semantics* 11: 231–251.
Givón, Talmy and Lee Yang
    1994   The rise of the English GET-passive. In: Barbara Fox & Paul J.
                Hopper (eds.), *Voice: Form and Function*, 119–149. Amsterdam and
                Philadelphia: John Benjamins.
Kimball, John
    1973   Get. In: John Kimball (ed.), *Syntax and Semantics* 2, 205–215. New
                York: Seminar Press.
Langacker, Ronald
    1988a   A usage-based model. In: Rudzka-Ostyn (1988), 127–163.
    1988b   A view of linguistic semantics. In: Rudzka-Ostyn (1988), 49–90.
Lehrer, Adrienne
    1974   Homonymy and polysemy: measuring similarity of meaning. *Language
                Sciences* 32: 33–39.
Lindstromberg, Seth
    1991   *Get*: not many meanings. *International Review of Applied Linguistics
                in Language Teaching* 29: 285–302.
Nerlich, Brigitte
    1992   *Semantic Theories in Europe 1830–1930: From Etymology to Con-
                textuality*. Amsterdam and Philadelphia: John Benjamins.
Niedzielski, Henry
    1976   Semantic considerations of *get* and some of its Polish equivalents.
                Papers and Studies in Contrastive Linguistics 5: 219–238.
Nyrop, Kristoffer
    1913   *Sémantique*. Vol. IV of his *Grammaire historique de la langue
                française*. Copenhagen: Gyldendalske Boghandel Nordisk Forlag.
Östman, Jan-Ola
    1988   Adaptation, variability, and effect: comments on IPrA Working Docu-
                ments 1 and 2. *IPrA Working Document* 3: 5–40. University of
                Antwerp: International Pragmatics Association.
    2000   Merkityksen ajankohtaiset haasteet yleiselle kielitieteelle [The current
                challenges of meaning for general linguistics]. In: Anu Airola, Heikki

J. Koskinen and Veera Mustonen (eds.), *Merkillinen merkitys* [The mystery of meaning], 69–84. Helsinki: Gaudeamus.

Raukko, Jarno

1993   *Get* examined. A cognitive semantic study of the polysemy of *get* as a dynamic network of meanings. Unpublished M.A. thesis, Department of English, University of Helsinki.

1994   Polysemia: merkitysten verkosto – merkityksen verkko [Polysemy: the network of meanings – the net of meaning]. In: Pentti Leino and Tiina Onikki (eds.), *Kieli 8. Suomen kielen kognitiivista kielioppia 2. Näkökulmia polysemiaan* [Cognitive grammar of Finnish 2: perspectives to polysemy], 36–69. Helsinki: The Department of Finnish at the University of Helsinki.

1995   What do we get for *get* in Finnish? *The New Courant* 3: 170–180. [University of Helsinki, Department of English.]

1996   "No more polysemy", says the nationalist language police. The paradoxical battle between semantic flexibility and normativism. *Pragmatics, Ideology, and Contacts Bulletin* 3: 36–44. [University of Helsinki, Department of English.]

1997   The status of polysemy in linguistics: from discrete meanings to default flexibility. In: *SKY 1997: The 1997 Yearbook of the Linguistic Association of Finland*, 145–170.

1999   An "intersubjective" method for cognitive-semantic research on polysemy: the case of *get*. In: Masako K. Hiraga, Chris Sinha and Sherman Wilcox (eds.), *Cultural, Typological, and Psycholinguistic Issues in Cognitive Linguistics. Selected papers of the bi-annual ICLA meeting in Albuquerque, July 1995*, 87–105. [Current Issues in Linguistic Theory 152.] Amsterdam and Philadelphia: John Benjamins.

Rudzka-Ostyn, Brygida (ed.)

1988   *Topics in Cognitive Linguistics*. Amsterdam and Philadelphia: John Benjamins.

Sandra, Dominiek and Sally Rice

1995   Network analyses of prepositional meaning: mirroring whose mind – the linguist's or the language user's? *Cognitive Linguistics* 6: 89–130.

Tuggy, David

1993   Ambiguity, polysemy, and vagueness. *Cognitive Linguistics* 4: 273–290.

Whitney, William Dwight

1867   *Language and the Study of Language: Twelve Lectures on the Principles of Linguistic Science*. New York: Scribner, Armstrong.

Zhang, Qiao

1998   Fuzziness – vagueness – generality – ambiguity. *Journal of Pragmatics* 29: 13–31.

Metonymic polysemy and its place in meaning extension

Ken-ichi Seto

1. Introduction

The last quarter of a century has seen a rising concern with metonymy. The literature, from Nunberg's (1978) pioneering exploration to Radden and Koevecses' (1999) penetrating investigation, by way of Lakoff and Johnson's (1980) influential work, has shown that metonymy is not only as pervasive as metaphor but also no less important in the daily use of language. In spite of the continuing expansion of the metonymic realm as is shown in Panther and Radden (1999) and Barcelona (2000), however, the core notion of metonymy is, so far as I can see, not yet established. I shall argue specifically (i) that there has been no satisfactory definition of metonymy yet, owing to confusions about the difference between entities and categories; (ii) that the ultimate reason why those confusions so often occur resides in the (inevitable) spatial representation of categorical relations; and (iii) that the network model (the prototype–extension–schema triangle), which is supposed to deal with polysemy, does not work because metonymy has no proper place in the model. After these arguments I shall offer a new way of looking at polysemy: a cognitive triangle whose vertices are metaphor, metonymy, and synecdoche.

2. Why metonymy is still a vague notion

In classical rhetoric metonymy and synecdoche have been defined, respectively, as: "the substitution of a word denoting an attribute or adjunct of a thing for the word denoting the thing itself" and "a figure of speech in which a more inclusive term is used for a less inclusive one or *vice versa*, as a whole for a part or a part for a whole" (*The New Shorter Oxford English Dictionary*). However, since 1956, when Jakobson wrote a classic paper on metaphor and metonymy, the concept of contiguity has often been used to define metonymy. But what does "contiguity" involve? So far as I can see, this is the most important question to ask when defining metonymy. Does it mean the contiguity of entities alone? Or does it also mean the contiguity of categories? If the inclusive definition were taken, what would the contiguity of categories mean? In other words, is metonymy concerned only with a referential transfer between entities, or also with a nonreferential transfer between a more comprehensive category and a less comprehensive category? On the other hand, if one chose not to use the term "contiguity", at least in some cases, then what should be the defining characteristic of metonymy? To answer these questions, I shall first offer a new definition of metonymy which departs in some crucial respects from traditional views.

2.1.   The definition of metonymy

A new definition of metonymy can be given as follows:

(1)   Metonymy is a referential transfer phenomenon based on spatio-temporal contiguity as conceived by the speaker between an entity and another in the (real) world.

This is coupled with a new definition of synecdoche:

(2)   Synecdoche is a categorical transfer phenomenon based on semantic inclusion as conceived by the speaker between a more comprehensive and a less comprehensive category.

These two definitions are a declaration of independence for metonymy and synecdoche from the centuries-old, rhetorico-cognitive Western tradition. The major differences are:

(i)   While the traditional notion of metonymy has kept synecdoche as its servant, under the new definitions (1) and (2), synecdoche is independent of metonymy.
(ii)   Whereas traditionally metonymy is a mixed category, in that it covers entities and categories alike, the definition of metonymy in (1) makes it clear that metonymy is a coherent category that only comprises entity-based referential transfers and excludes categorical transfers.

(iii)   Synecdoche now comprises only category-based nonreferential transfers, leaving entity-based whole–part transfers to metonymy. As a
result, synecdoche also becomes a coherent category.

(iv)   Both definitions, (1) and (2), avoid theoretical confusions caused by
the ambiguity (see below) of "whole" and "part", which permits both
referential and categorical interpretations.

(v)   The new demarcation between metonymy and synecdoche makes it
possible to allocate "partonomy" (the "part-of" relation) to metonymy
along with other entity-based relations, and "taxonomy" (the "kind-
of" relation) exclusively to synecdoche.[1]

This division of work is not just notational but also substantial, because it
is supported on lexico-semantic grounds. Metonymy is concerned with reference; synecdoche is associated with (extensional and intensional) sense;
"partonomy" denotes a referential relation which holds, for example, between
a windmill and its sails (the sails are a part of a windmill); and "taxonomy"
(hyponymy) signifies a categorical relation which holds, for example, between
a ticket and a traffic ticket (a traffic ticket is a kind of ticket). Thus under the
new definitions (3a) is a metonymy, and (3b) is a synecdoche (in a parking
situation).

(3)   a.   *The windmill is turning.*
       b.   *I got another ticket.*

This distinction is so clear that it may seem hardly necessary to emphasize
the point because it is not a semantic practice to treat partonomy and taxonomy under the same heading. However, the realm of metonymy appears to
be a different world where partonomy and taxonomy have sat side by side
for centuries. Even Radden and Koevecses (1999), who provide the most
penetrating analysis of metonymy, do not raise questions about this matter.
For them, metonymy is sometimes referential and sometimes categorical.
Neither Lakoff and Johnson (1980) nor Lakoff and Johnson (1999) show
interest in the problem, although one of their great concerns is to define
what a category actually is. What makes them insensitive to this matter?

2.2. *The return of Lakoff and Johnson*

It is a curious fact that while partonomy and taxonomy are distinguished in lexical semantics, in research into metonymy they are lumped together. In this respect, Lakoff and Johnson (1999) is no improvement on Lakoff and Johnson (1980). For them metonymy is as partonomical as it is taxonomical. What, then, is the essence of metonymy? Is it a coherent category? Apparently so. Because taxonomy often looks like partonomy. Take the following two figures (Fig. 1 and Fig. 2).

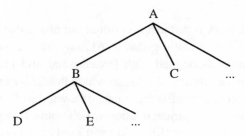

Figure 1.

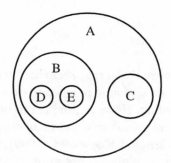

Figure 2.

Which figure represents partonomy and taxonomy better? Actually, this is a pseudo-question because there is no substantial difference in representability between the two figures. One figure can represent partonomy or taxonomy just as well as the other. For example, Figure 3 is a rough sketch of the taxonomy of things in the world (see Chomsky 1965: 83).

However, Figure 1 can also represent the partonomy of a tree (Fig. 4).

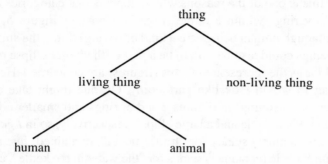

Figure 3.

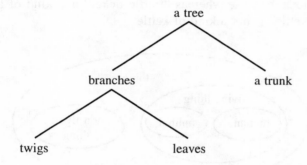

Figure 4.

Hence, Figure 1 is called a "tree" diagram. Note that once the taxonomy of things is represented by Figure 1, it would become "a tree". And a tree as an entity, not tree as a category, is composed of different parts such as a trunk, branches, roots, and so on. Likewise, each node below the top (thing) in Figure 3 would be interpreted as one of these parts. Therefore, taxonomy would become partonomy! But, of course, this is fallacious reasoning. Where are we going wrong? A pitfall is contained in the representation of Figure 3 itself. The moment the framework of Figure 1 is adopted to represent a taxonomical relation, it automatically forces us to reason along the above line and to conclude that there is no substantial difference between taxonomy and partonomy because each node is a part of a whole tree. Confusion of this kind, which may be called the partonomy–taxonomy fallacy (or the PT fallacy), is pervasive and it is caused by a specific spatial metaphor such as a tree diagram, as in Figure 1.

Perhaps this is one of the reasons why it appears that categories are better represented by rings within a circle (Fig. 2). Consider Figure 5, but note again that although human beings are a kind of (living) thing, the small ellipse of human beings could also be said to be a part of the larger ellipse of (living) things in so far as the represented forms (figures) are concerned. Here taxonomy once again would look like partonomy. Or, one might take a slightly different line of reasoning: in Figures 2 and 5, rings and smaller ellipses are rather contained in a circle and a large ellipse, respectively, so in *I got another ticket*, ticket (container) stands for "traffic ticket", contained, just as in *The kettle is boiling*, kettle (container) stands for "the water in the kettle", contained. Container-for-contained is a regular pattern of metonymy. Consequently, one might conclude that (3b) is an instance of metonymy. But this reasoning, too, is fallacious, because whereas "traffic ticket" is a kind of ticket, "the water in the kettle" is not a kind of kettle.

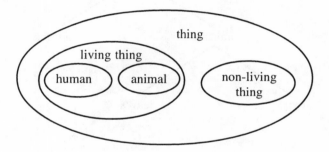

Figure 5.

Lakoff and Johnson (1999: 51) apparently succumb to the force of the PT fallacy (see also Lakoff 1987, Chapter 5). They point out that there is a conceptual metaphor A CATEGORY IS A CONTAINER. The primary experiential basis of the metaphor is, according to them, that "things that go together tend to be in the same bounded region (correlation between common location and common properties, functions, or origins)." I do not deny that there is such a conceptual metaphor because in fact there is one, not only in English but also in Japanese and perhaps many other (possibly all) languages. Thus we ask, for example, "Are tomatoes *in* the fruit or the vegetable category?" However, it is this conceptual metaphor that is the ultimate cause of the PT fallacy because it blurs the distinction between folk understanding and expert knowledge. It is necessary in the analysis of metonymy (as a piece of expert knowledge) as well as in lexical semantics to tell "things that go together" referentially from "things that go together" categorically.[2]

This blurred distinction between folk understanding and expert knowledge may also occur in other fields. For example, Reddy's classic paper on metaphor and thought (Reddy 1979) points out that the folk understanding of communication is dominated by the conduit metaphor so that, when talking about communication, we can hardly avoid using the metaphor. For instance, *get the idea across*, *put each concept into words very carefully*, and *extract coherent ideas from that prose*, are all expressions based on this metaphor. Reddy's (1979) most valuable finding, however, is not that the entire metalingual apparatus of the English language is largely (at least 70%) determined by the conduit metaphor, though this is a major discovery, but that this conceptual metaphor distorts the true picture of what is happening in communication. For the model of communication based on the metaphor "objectifies meaning in a misleading and dehumanizing fashion" (Reddy 1979: 308); we "have the mistaken, conduit-metaphor influenced view that the more signals we can create, and the more signals we can preserve, the more ideas we 'transfer' and 'store'," (p. 310); and we "neglect the crucial human ability to reconstruct thought patterns on the basis of signals and this ability founders" (p. 310). The conduit metaphor, which belongs to folk understanding, does not adequately capture the reality of communication.

Metaphors thus necessarily lead and mislead us. The conduit metaphor has contributed to establishing a distorted picture of how communication actually works. Whereas the picture given by the conduit metaphor is not wrong by one standard (folk understanding) because it is a picture we live by, it is wrong by another standard (expert knowledge) because it fails as a model of communication. This line of argument also applies to the conceptual metaphor A CATEGORY IS A CONTAINER. It is a metaphor we live by, a metaphor deeply entrenched in our minds, but it should not be so as part of the theory of metonymy, because it has a strong numbing effect and obscures the difference between partonomy and taxonomy. We should be careful to keep from putting both partonomy and taxonomy under the same heading of metonymy because, as Cruse (2000: 47) correctly distinguishes, "[s]eeing something meronymically [i.e. partonomically], i.e. as a whole consisting of parts (cf. Pustejovsky's 'constitutive role')" is one thing, and "[s]eeing something taxonomically, i.e. as a kind, in contrast with other kinds (cf. Pustejovsky's 'formal role')" is quite another.[3]

One might, however, argue that the definition of synecdoche previously raised in (2) also makes use of the metaphor A CATEGORY IS A CONTAINER. This is true, for "inclusion" and "comprehensive" are based on the A CATEGORY IS A CONTAINER metaphor. The two words might therefore better have been omitted in the definition. Compare a revised definition (4) with (2):

(4)   Synecdoche is a categorical transfer phenomenon based on hyponymy as conceived by the speaker between a genus and a species.

However, this improvement is only apparent because it has just hidden "inclusion" and "comprehensive" behind technical terms such as "hyponymy", "genus" and "species". Ask what a genus is, and we would have to answer that it is a more "comprehensive" or "inclusive" category, or we would come up with another technical term such as a "higher-order" category. The reason why a real improvement is next to impossible is simply that there seem to be no metalinguistic terms precise enough to describe the true nature of categories, no terms that are not (even potentially) contaminated with the A CATEGORY IS A CONTAINER metaphor or other closely related spatial metaphors. Four points may be worth noting.

(i)   Categories are in the mind (i.e. represented in the brain) but are very hard to access by way of (meta)language, perhaps because the nature of categories resists verbalization. Categorization (e.g. edible vs. non-edible) is an essential function of living things from human beings down to amoebas. There is no doubt that amoebas can categorize for this feature, edible vs. non-edible, but from this no-one would infer that they have the A CATEGORY IS A CONTAINER metaphor. Categorization itself is possible without language.[4]

(ii)   The force of the A CATEGORY IS A CONTAINER metaphor is compelling. More generally, the pressure of spatialization metaphors is so high that the moment one tries to talk about categories, the A CATEGORY IS A CONTAINER metaphor or any other closely related spatial metaphor is ready on the tip of the tongue.[5]

(iii)   Perhaps a rare linguistic tool that is appropriate for describing the true nature of categories, and is relatively free from the bias of folk understanding, is "kind of". "Kind of" can be used to distinguish between taxonomy and partonomy (e.g. a traffic ticket is a kind of ticket, not a part of a ticket; a leg is a part of a table, not a kind of table). Thus (4) may again be paraphrased: synecdoche is a categorical transfer phenomenon based on a "kind of" relation as conceived by the speaker between a genus and a species.

(iv)   It is only a step from the PT fallacy to the entity–category fallacy (or the EC fallacy, i.e. to interpret categories in terms of entities) because partonomy is just a kind (not a part) of entity-based contiguous relation. In short, metonymy is an E(ntity)-related transfer and synecdoche is a C(ategory)-related transfer. E-relation and C-relation are the bases of two different routes of thought.

2.3.   Langacker and the network model

Langacker's concern with metonymy started with "active zone" (Langacker, 1984), a usage-level metonymic fluctuation phenomenon, rather than lexical metonymy based on regular semantic shifts. This is why when Langacker (1990) presented the network model, a model supposed to capture meaning extension from a prototypical sense, there was no place for metonymy. Figure 6 is a slightly modified version.[6]

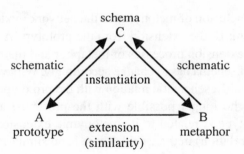

Figure 6.

Figure 6 shows that the extension from the prototype is exclusively metaphoric and that the schema C is the extraction of the commonality of A and B. Since a schema corresponds to a genus, a prototype to a species, and a metaphor to another species (in a domain different from the domain to which the prototype belongs), the schematic relation (i.e. the species-to-genus relation) and the instantiating relation (i.e. the genus-to-species relation) mean what we call the C-relation. If we interpret the schema as another extension, it corresponds to synecdoche (the species-to-genus type) in our sense. Now it is clear that whereas metaphor and synecdoche hold their places in the network model, there is no place for metonymy.

Langacker started to change his position later, gradually and tantalizingly, until he finally decided to give metonymy a place in the network model when he referred to "*extension* (generally metaphorical and metonymic)" (Langacker 1995b: 111).[7] A new version of the network model may be shown in Figure 7.

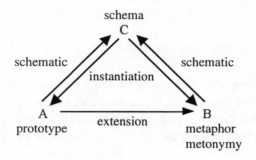

Figure 7.

However, the inclusion of metonymy in the network model poses a serious theoretical problem: B, the extension from the prototype A, is not a uniform node because the extension processes of metaphor and metonymy are different, so the status of schema has to change accordingly. While node C continues to be able to maintain a schematic relation with the prototype and a metaphor, such a relation is no longer possible with the prototype and a metonymy, because the prototype is related to its metonymic extension on the basis of contiguity (the E-relation) in the world. There is no similarity to be extracted from the two. Therefore, so far as metonymy is concerned, the network model stops working.

For example, see the notorious example of metonymy in (5) (Nunberg, 1978: 22):

(5)   *The ham sandwich is getting restless at table 20.*

"The ham sandwich" refers to "the customer who ordered it" in a restaurant situation. It is obvious that there is no sense relation (lexical or nonlexical) between "The ham sandwich" and "the customer"; they are only referentially connected by sharing the same space–time. It is therefore not possible to extract a schema (i.e. abstract semantic commonality) from "The ham sandwich" and "the customer". The same applies to the next example, a case of "active zone" or metonymic contextual fluctuation.

(6)   *She slipped her hand through his arm.*

In a normal, non-bloody situation, "his arm" metonymically refers to "the space between his arm and the side of the body". Again, there are no (meaningful) common semantic features to be extracted from the two referents in question. And although the metonymies in (5) and (6) are contextual in nature, things do not change with lexicalized metonymies:

(7)   *He is always chasing skirts.*

"Skirts" are not similar to "the girls who wear them", but only contiguous with them. Of course, ultimately any two things can be said to be similar in one respect or another, but that is not the point here.

One merit of the network model in Figure 7 is that three major extension patterns, metaphor, metonymy, and synecdoche, are all present, provided that synecdoche is substituted for schema. Metaphor is based on the similarity relation (the S-relation), metonymy on the E-relation, and synecdoche on the C-relation. They make up the three vertices of what is called the cognitive triangle.

3.   The cognitive triangle and its implications

A theory of polysemy should attach equal weight to metaphor, metonymy, and synecdoche. These are the major routes of meaning extension both synchronically and diachronically.[8] They also influence and partly stipulate the ways we think and act.

3.1.   The cognitive triangle

Figure 8 shows a simplified model of how a prototype extends its meaning.

P, the prototype, extends its meaning in three major directions: metaphor (the S-relation), metonymy (the E-relation), and synecdoche (the C-relation),

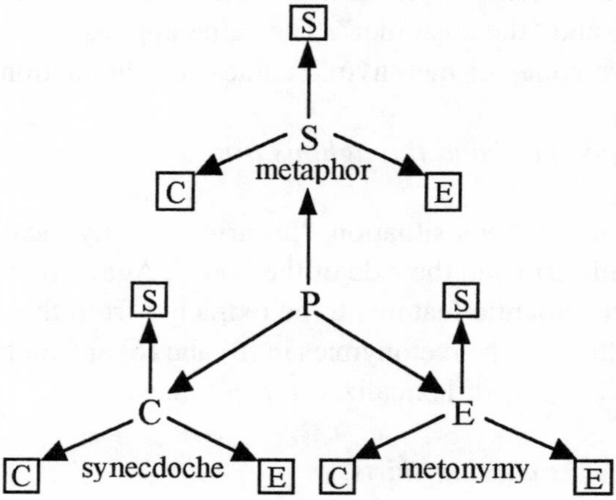

Figure 8.

which together make up the cognitive triangle. And each vertex extends a newly acquired meaning again in the three directions. Metaphor is similarity-based, metonymy is entity-based, and synecdoche is category-based. The extension to C is of two kinds: one is the species-to-genus type as in (8a) and the other is the genus-to-species type as in (8b).

(8)   a.   *Will you ship the goods by rail?*
       b.   *I have a temperature.*

"Ship" in (8a) extends its sense from "send something by ship" to "send something by any means of transportation". "Temperature" in (8b) extends its sense from "the temperature of the body" to "fever". In the latter example, "extends" is used in an extended (i.e. species-to-genus, or schematic) sense. Metonymy is of three types depending on the kinds of entities: spatial (e.g. book), temporal (e.g. earthquake), and abstract (e.g. beauty) (for details and examples, see Seto 1999).[9]

Another important point to make about the cognitive triangle is that metonymy and synecdoche belong to different cognitive domains.[10] See Figure 9.

Metonymy works in the E-domain, which is associated, typically, with the real world where entities are arranged concentrically. We tend to see two entities as closely connected if they are in a closer position than others. The

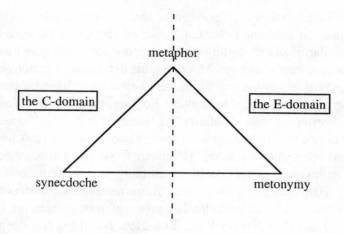

Figure 9.

whole–part relation in the sense of partonomy may be the closest relation of all the relations based on contiguity in the world. On the other hand, the C-domain is in the mind, where a lot of categories, some stable and some unstable, are arranged so that they may reflect how we group the things in the world. Synecdoche works in the C-domain. And metaphor, the third category, it may be said, does not have its own proper domain which might be called the S-domain. Rather, it straddles the E-domain and the C-domain, sometimes serving as a bridge to connect the two different domains, some-times connecting two faraway entities or two distant categories in a single domain. I shall have to leave the details to another paper.

3.2. *The classical quartet vs. the modern trio*

The cognitive triangle also explains semantic changes along the time axis. When speaking of the classification of diachronic semantic changes, Geeraerts (1994) refers to "the classical quartet of specialization, generalization, metonymy, and metaphor." Since specialization and generalization largely correspond to the two aspects of synecdoche used in our sense, that is, the genus-to-species transfer and the species-to-genus transfer respectively, the classical quartet can be collapsed into the modern trio of synecdoche (specialization and generalization), metonymy and metaphor. The cognitive triangle works both for diachronic semantic development and for synchronic semantic extension.

This tripartite theory of polysemic sense extension is obviously an improvement on Ullmann (1962), a classic of semantics, because Ullmann regards similarity and contiguity (thus metaphor and metonymy) as the two basic axes of semantic change. Moreover, his definition of metonymy based on contiguity is too broad and vague, and he seems to have no clear vision separating synecdoche from metonymy. For him, metonymy is "founded on some relation other than similarity" (Ullmann 1962: 78), "based not on similarity but on some other relation between two terms" (p. 163), and "based on relations other than similarity" (Ullmann 1964: 83). On other occasions, however, Ullmann is more specific: contiguity is a relation "between two references" (Ullmann 1951: 240). Thus, "Some metonymic transfers are based on spatial relations", while "[a]nother group of metonymies are based on temporal relations" (Ullmann 1962: 218–219). But there is a deep flaw in Ullmann's idea of contiguity, since in his writing contiguity sometimes means "sense-contiguity" (Ullmann 1951: 222, 243): "contiguity between the senses" (p. 231). He, too, commits the EC fallacy.

Thus as he discusses pejorative and ameliorative developments of senses, Ullmann refers to "fortune", a semantically neutral word, which comes to have an exclusively positive value "when used metonymically in the sense of 'wealth' " (Ullmann 1962: 235). This is a sense-relation, a special type of semantic specification, or narrowing, special in the sense that the change in evaluation is definitely ameliorative. This is a case of synecdoche in our sense, a categorical transfer, where the neutral "fortune" (genus) stands for the narrower "fortune (wealth)" (species). It is clear that, in the world, the neutral "fortune" is not contiguous with the narrower "fortune (wealth)"; they are just categorically related. Unfortunately, many later semantic theorists and others share the EC fallacy or the PT fallacy with Ullmann in the discussion of metonymy and categories in general. But some are more cautious. Tversky (1990), for example, makes a clear distinction between partonomy and taxonomy, and so do Lyons (1977), Cruse (1986), and Nerlich (to appear). The cognitive triangle, standing on secure semantic ground, promises a better way of looking not only at synchronic polysemy but at diachronic semantic change as well, as it is able to explain patterns of meaning extension and meaning change better than other models do.

4.   Conclusion

The main points can be summarized as follows:

(i)   Metonymy is an E-transfer, i.e. a referential transfer based on the contiguity between an entity and another in the world, as conceived by the speaker.

(ii)   Synecdoche is a C-transfer, i.e. a categorical transfer based on a "kind of" relation between a genus and a species, as conceived by the speaker.

(iii)   Metaphor is an S-transfer, i.e. a structural transfer based on the similarity between an entity or category and another entity or category, as conceived by the speaker.

(iv)   The PT fallacy is to confuse partonomy (the entity-based "part of" relation) and taxonomy (the category-based "kind of" relation) and to interpret taxonomy in terms of partonomy.

(v)   The EC fallacy is to confuse entities and categories and to interpret categories in terms of entities. The PT fallacy is a kind of EC fallacy.

(vi)   Folk understanding and expert knowledge should be distinguished in scientific discussion.

(vii)   Categorization is possible without language.

(viii) Langacker's network model is flawed because metonymy has no proper place in it.

(ix)   The cognitive triangle can be a model to describe not only synchronic polysemy but also diachronic semantic change.

(x)   In the cognitive triangle, metonymy belongs to the E-domain, synecdoche to the C-domain, and metaphor straddles both domains.

Notes

1. For the distinction between partonomy and taxonomy in relation to metonymy see Seto (1999); see also Cruse (1986) and Tversky (1990). As to the classification of whole–part relations, see Tversky and Hemenway (1984), Cruse (1979) and Winston, Chaffin, and Herrmann (1987). Note that partonomy is just one kind of referential relation which metonymy may exploit; there are many others, such as container-for-contained, cause-for-result, and so on (Seto 1999).
2. Lakoff (1987: 79) says: "[A] part (a subcategory or member or submodel) stands for the whole category – in reasoning, recognition, etc. Within the theory of

cognitive models, such cases are represented by metonymic models." For him, things that go together referentially and things that go together categorically can both be the basis of metonymy. Thus Lakoff (1987: 90) claims: "In short, a cognitive model may function to allow a salient example to stand metonymically for a whole category". Radden and Koevecses (1999), following this statement, refer to specific "category" metonymies such as STEREOTYPICAL MEMBER FOR A CATEGORY, CATEGORY FOR THE STEREOTYPICAL MEMBER, IDEAL MEMBER FOR THE CATEGORY, and CATEGORY FOR THE IDEAL MEMBER. All these fit the definition of synecdoche given in (2).

3. Cruse (2000: 50) notes further that "Pustejovsky does not really explain why he opts for four qualia roles … Croft (p.c.) sees no justification for four roles, or any definite number; if there were any super-domains, he would opt for just two, the taxonomic and the meronymic, the latter subsuming the constitutive, telic and agentive roles." While I agree with Cruse (and Croft) in dividing Pustejovsky's four qualia roles into two "super-domains" (the formal qualia and the other three), it seems hardly justified to squeeze the constitutive, telic and agentive roles into one and the same category of meronymy, at least under Cruse's definition of the term. Rather, these three roles may naturally be put into the category of spatio-temporal contiguity which essentially characterizes metonymy, with the constitutive qualia related to spatial contiguity, and the agentive and telic qualias to temporal (i.e. causal) contiguity (see Seto 1999 for further discussion and examples). Accordingly, Pustejovsky's formal qualia role may be associated with synecdoche in my sense, and the other three with metonymy. Although the latter three qualia roles do not exhaust the metonymic resources, the formal qualia does exhaust the synecdochic relations (genus-for-species, and species-for-genus).

4. Since Rosch (1973, 1978), the term "prototype" has become very popular. In fact there may be little doubt of the psychological reality of the prototype structure of categories. But how are categories prototypically structured? Taylor (1995) points out that "[t]here are two ways in which to understand the term 'prototype'. We can apply the term to the *central* member, or perhaps to the cluster of *central* members, of a category. … Alternatively, the prototype can be understood as a schematic representation of the conceptual *core* of a category" (emphases added). Note that the prototypical understanding of the term "prototype" is based on the centre–periphery metaphor. This may have partly contributed to the genesis of the A CATEGORY IS A CONTAINER metaphor even on the expert knowledge level.

5. Barcelona (personal communication) points out that another undesirable consequence of the A CATEGORY IS A CONTAINER metaphor is that it may mislead one into a belief that categories are discrete, since containers such as bowls and cups have discrete contours.

6. Langacker's (1990: 271) original figure is shown in Figure 10. In this, "[t]he process of extension occurs because a speaker perceives some *similarity* between the basic value (i.e. the local or global prototype) and the extended value. This

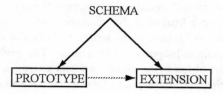

Figure 10.

similarity perception represents the *commonality* of the basic and extended values, so it constitutes a schema having the two for instantiations" (p. 271, emphases added). From this it is clear that Langacker's extension in the network model is exclusively metaphoric in nature (at the time the paper was written) because it is only in metaphoric extension that some schematic commonality can be extracted from a prototype and its extension, such as a real mouse and a computer mouse; on the other hand, it is virtually impossible, unless by force, to draw similarity perception from one sense – whether it is a prototype or not – and its metonymic extension, because a metonymic extension is associated with a prototype by way of contiguity, not similarity. It would be absurd, for example, to see some meaningful similarity between "long hair" *per se* and "a person with long hair" or between "a kettle" and "water in the kettle".

7. Langacker's (1984) "active zone" clearly constitutes part of metonymy, but there is no mention of metonymy there. The relationship between "active zone" and metonymy seems to have grown slowly. The first reference to metonymy is made in Langacker (1991: 456 footnote). Then Langacker (1993: 31) observes: "Metonymy largely overlaps with what I have called active zone phenomenon." The relationship between the two then develops rapidly into the total inclusion of "active zone" in the metonymy category in Langacker (1995a: 27): "Specifically, they [active-zone/profile discrepancies] represent a special case of METONYMY".

8. When dictionaries are compiled on the principle of clarifying the semantic networks of lexical entries, instead of describing their historical sense developments or current sense frequencies, they should seriously take into account the distinction between metaphor, metonymy, and synecdoche. In this regard, *The New Oxford Dictionary of English* is worth mentioning because it identifies three major extension patterns: "figurative extension of the core sense", "specialized case of the core sense", and "other extension or shift in meaning, retaining one or more elements of the core sense". It is obvious that "figurative extension" is metaphoric and that "specialized case" corresponds to one of the two kinds of synecdoche (unfortunately, no mention is made of generalization). However, the third category is plainly miscellaneous, although, judging from the examples cited there (p. x), there is no question that metonymy (along with some others) comes into this third category.

9. An earthquake is a temporal entity, so we can say, for example, that "there was"

an earthquake yesterday. An earthquake acquires the status of entity through an ontological metaphor, a kind of spatial metaphor. So does an abstract entity. For instance, when "beauty" is used in the sense of a beautiful woman, it is supposed that "beauty" is a salient property of that woman. The woman has this property, as it were, as a part of her body. To take another example, suppose that there is a woman at the other end of the phone whose voice is soft and whose name you don't know. You might refer to her in your mind as "Miss Softly". This is a metonymy. And "softly" here becomes an abstract entity to characterize the softly-voiced woman. Here again the property, as an abstract entity, is referentially related to the woman.

10. For different notions of the term "domain", see, among others, Lakoff (1987), Croft (1993) and Barcelona (2002).

References

Barcelona, Antonio
2000   (ed.) *Metaphor and Metonymy at the Crossroads: A Cognitive Perspective*. Berlin: Mouton de Gruyter.
2002   Clarifying and applying the notions of metaphor and metonymy within cognitive linguistics: an update. In: René Dirven and Ralph Poerings (eds.), *Metaphor and Metonymy in Comparison and Contrast*. Berlin: Mouton de Gruyter.
Browm, Lesley (ed.)
1993   *The New Shorter Oxford English Dictionary*. New York: Oxford University Press.
Chomsky, Noam
1965   *Aspects of the Theory of Syntax*. Cambridge, MA: MIT Press.
Croft, William
1993   The role of domains in the interpretation of metaphors and metonymies. *Cognitive Linguistics* 4: 335–370.
Cruse, David A.
1979   On the transitivity of the part–whole relation. *Journal of Linguistics* 1: 29–38.
1986   *Lexical Semantics*. Cambridge: Cambridge University Press.
2000   Aspects of the micro-structure of word meanings. In: Yael Ravin and Claudia Leacock (eds.), *Polysemy: Theoretical and Computational approaches,* 30–51. New York: Oxford University Press.
Geeraerts, Dirk
1994   Historical semantics. In: Ron E. Asher (ed.), *The Encyclopedia of Language and Linguistics,* 1567–1570. Oxford: Pergamon Press.

Jakobson, Roman
  1971 [1956] Two aspects of language and two types of aphasic disturbances. In:
       Roman Jakobson (ed.), *Roman Jakobson Selected Writings Volume
       2: Word and Language*, 239–259. The Hague: Mouton.
Lakoff, George
  1987   *Women, Fire, and Dangerous Things: What Categories Reveal About
       the Mind*. Chicago, IL: The University of Chicago Press.
Lakoff, George and Mark Johnson
  1980   *Metaphors We Live By*. Chicago, IL: The University of Chicago Press.
  1999   *Philosophy in the Flesh: The Embodied Mind and its Challenge to
       Western Thought*. New York: Basic Books.
Langacker, Ronald W.
  1984 [1990] Active zone. In: Ronald W. Langacker, *Concept, Image, and Symbol:
       The Cognitive Basis of Grammar*, 189–201. Berlin: Mouton de Gruyter.
  1990   A usage-based model. In: Ronald W. Langacker, *Grammar and
       Conceptualization*. Berlin: Mouton de Gruyter.
  1991   *Foundations of Cognitive Grammar. Volume II: Descriptive Applic-
       ation*. Stanford, CA: Stanford University Press.
  1993   Reference-point constructions. *Cognitive Linguistics* 4: 1–38.
  1995a   Raising and transparency. *Language* 71: 1–62.
  1995b   Cognitive grammar. In: Jan-Ola Östman, Jef Verschueren, Jan
       Blommaert and Chris Bulcaen (eds.), *Handbook of Pragmatics*, 105–
       111. Amsterdam: John Benjamins.
Lyons, John
  1977   *Semantics*. 2 volumes. Cambridge: Cambridge University Press.
Nerlich, Brigitte
  (to appear) Synecdoche: a trope, a whole trope, and nothing but a trope. In:
       Armin Burkhardt and Brigitte Nerlich (eds.), *Reflections on Tropes
       and Truth*. Berlin: Mouton de Gruyter.
The New Oxford Dictionary of English
  1998   *The New Oxford Dictionary of English*, edited by Judy Pearsall. New
       York: Oxford University Press.
Nunberg, Geoffrey D.
  1978   *The Pragmatics of Reference*. Bloomington: The Indiana University
       Linguistics Club.
Panther, Klause-Uwe and Günter Radden (eds.)
  1999   *Metonymy in Language and Thought*. Amsterdam: John Benjamins.
Radden, Günter and Zoltan Koevecses
  1999   Towards a theory of metonymy. In: Panther and Radden (1999),
       17–59.
Reddy, Michael J.
  1979   The conduit metaphor: a case of frame conflict in our language about

language. In: Andrew Ortony (ed.), *Metaphor and Thought*. Second edition 1993, 164–201. Cambridge: Cambridge University Press.

Rosch, Eleanor
1973   Natural categories. *Cognitive Psychology* 4: 328–350.
1978   Principles of categorization. In: Eleanor Rosch and Barbara B. Lloyd (eds.), *Cognition and Categorization*, 27–48. Hillsdale: Lawrence Erlbaum.

Seto, Ken-ichi
1999   Distinguishing metonymy from synecdoche. In: Panther and Radden (1999), 91–120.

Taylor, John R.
1995   *Linguistic Categorization: Prototypes in Linguistic Theory*. Second edition. New York: Oxford University Press.

Tversky, Barbara
1990   Where partonomies and taxonomies meet. In: Savas L. Tsohatzidis (ed.), *Meanings and Prototypes: Studies in Linguistic Categorization*, 334–344. London: Routledge.

Tversky, Barbara and Kathleen Hemenway
1984   Objects, parts, and categories. *Journal of Experimental Psychology: General* 113: 169–191.

Ullmann, Stephen
1951   *The Principles of Semantics*. Glasgow: Jackson.
1962   *Semantics: An Introduction to the Science of Meaning*. Oxford: Blackwell.
1964   *Language and Style: Collected papers*. Oxford: Blackwell.

Winston, Morton E., Roger Chaffin and Douglas Herrmann
1987   A taxonomy of part–whole relations. *Cognitive Science* 11: 417–444.

Synchrony/diachrony approaches

Polysemy in derivational affixes

Adrienne Lehrer

1. Introduction

The question of whether lexical elements and grammatical elements are semantically similar has been debated. Some linguists, e.g. Beard (1988, 1990, 1992), argue that lexemes and affixes, especially derivational affixes, are quite different, while others, such as Baker (1988), Lieber (1992), Lehrer (1993, 1996, 1999), and Panther and Thornburg (2002) show they are similar in that they are signs. Derivational affixes and lexemes share many semantic relations, such as synonymy, antonymy, and polysemy (the topic of this paper). Beard (1990) made an important observation about the semantics of derivational affixes (and function words), namely that the meanings expressed are limited to those concepts that also become grammaticalized: space, time, agency, possibility, animacy, etc.[1] Since the range of semantic concepts as well as most examples of metaphor and metonymy involve highly lexical (as opposed to grammatical) concepts, the question arises as to whether and/ or to what extent the polysemy found in derivational affixes parallels that found in lexemes. Yet even with limitations we expect to find the same types of polysemy that have been identified in the traditional studies of meaning change and in the works of many cognitive linguists interested in polysemy. If the concepts and relationships represented by words change and expand, then we should expect to find the same phenomenon in derivational morphemes too. So even if we do not find the range of polysemy reported in works like Apresjan (1974), Norrick (1981), Nerlich and Clarke (1992) and others, we should expect the polysemy we find in affixes to be a proper subset of regular polysemy.

A common structure of the relationship among senses is that of a central sense (Bloomfield 1933), which gives rise to a variety of different derived senses, where the derived senses are not necessarily related to each other (though they may be). *Radial structure* is the contemporary term for this relationship, and the suffix *-ship* (examined in Section 5) exhibits this structure, as do *over* (Brugman 1981; Lakoff 1987), and *-er* (Panther and Thornburg

2002). In some cases, however, the relationship of the senses has a different "shape", as Joos (1958) observed. His analysis of the word *code* had circular shape, and my analysis of -*ist* in Section 4 exhibits a chain-like structure, where sense A gives rise to sense B, which in turn gives rise to sense C.

Although this article deals only with English, it may serve as an example for similar studies of other languages. My main source is the classic study by Marchand (1966), supplemented by recent neologisms, which often reveal aspects of productive senses of words and morphemes that are not necessarily revealed in the conventional lexicon.

2. English prefixes

In the case of some English prefixes,[2] we find multiple meanings similar to those of full lexemes, namely the polysemy of space and time. Consider Table 1.

Table 1.   Spatial and temporal polysemy.

Prefix	Spatial	Temporal
ante-	antechamber	antebellum
fore-	foreground, forehead, foreplay	foreshadow
pre-	pre-abdominal	prenatal, prewar
post-	postfrontal	postwar, post-modern

Pre- and *post-* are predominantly temporal senses. The spatial senses are restricted to anatomy and zoology (Marchand 1966: 134), and this sense emerged in English later than the temporal one. The temporal sense of *pre-* also has a range of meaning, influenced in part by the word-class of the base. With nouns (*prewar, precontact, pre-election*) the time denoted is before the event or period named. With verbal bases (*preheat, preshrink, prepay*), the sense is "to perform some action before some pragmatically interpreted action". To *preheat the oven* is "to turn it on to a certain temperature before putting the food in". To *prepay* is "to pay [a bill] in advance of the due date or the service performed". There has been a gradual drift in words like *preboard* [an airplane] and *preregister* [for a class], where some individuals act before other individuals do the same thing. To *preboard/preregister* is "to board or register, not before some other action, but before the regular boarding or registration takes place".

Another domain in which we find a familiar instance of polysemy is in prefixes that denote hierarchies. Here the meanings include those of generality (versus specificity), quantity (more or less), and, in the case of *super-* and *sub-*, spatial orientation. See Table 2.

Table 2. The polysemy of quantity and generality.

Prefix	Generality	Quantity	Space
hyper-	hypernym	hyperactive	
hypo-	hyponym	hypothermal	
super-	superset	superactive	supertitle[3]
sub-	subset, subdivision	subnormal	subtitle

The sense involving quantity implies a contextual norm, and all four of the prefixes in Table 2 denote a quantity falling above or below that norm.

The prefix *arch-* shares some of the senses of the four items in Table 2. Its primary sense has to do with a social hierarchy, as in *archbishop* and *archduke*, but it has developed a sense of quantity as well. Here we find *arch-heretic* and *arch-villain*, where the meaning is "excessive". Marchand (1966: 144) suggests that the use is pejorative, which may explain why he has no examples like *arch-hero* and *arch-saint*.

Generalizing over the nine items above, we see a set of meanings ranging from space and time, and metaphorical extensions of spatial notions like *over* and *under*, to relationships of power and to quantity. Generality is a special case of quantity, since "more general" = "more inclusive".

3.   Diminutives

Another domain with well-known polysemy involves diminutives – affixes denoting small size, with a cluster of senses related to small size, such as young age and small quantity. In addition, there are extensions to meanings of affection and pejoration. Dressler and Merlini Barbaresi (1994) present a comprehensive analysis of Italian, German, and other European languages, where the diminutive is carried by suffixes. As Dressler and Merlini Barbaresi show, the meaning of *small* easily shifts to endearment – the affection we feel for small children and small animals, and also to pejoration, since *small* can denote "lesser importance". English has a few suffixes too (see Table 3), although their productivity is limited. Interacting with diminutives is at least one feminine suffix, *-ette*, which also carries diminutive meanings. I have included some questionable items, where the suffix carries the meaning listed, but the base is either meaningless or requires some re-interpretation. For example, although *booklet* can be glossed as "little book", *anklet* is not "a little ankle". However, the suffix *-let* still connotes "small size". A *hamlet* is a "small town", but the base, *ham-* (not the homonymous pork product) has no independent identifiable sense.

Table 3.   The polysemy of size and amount.

Prefix	Size–Amount–Age	Other senses
-ette	dinette, kitchenette	[PLACE] launderette, luncheonette
		[FEMININE] majorette
-kin(s)	napkin	[ENDEARMENT] babykins
-let	booklet, hamlet, anklet	[PLACE] anklet
	starlet[4]	[PEJORATION] kinglet
-ling	duckling, sapling	[ENDEARMENT] darling
		[PEJORATION] weakling
-y	baby, doggy, horsy	[ENDEARMENT, BABYTALK]

The metonymy of PLACE meanings for some of the items above are transfers of the whole word, not the suffix. *-ling*, with the exception of *darling*, is affectively pejorative, as in *weakling*, *trivling* "trivial, worthless", *giftling* "trivial gift", *witling* "one with small wit" (examples and glosses are from Walker [Dawson] 1936: 170–171). The meaning of the suffix *-y* is primarily "like", "characterized by", "full of" (Marchand 1966: 352); the diminutive sense is secondary. Two diminutive suffixes are widely found in personal names for girls, although speakers probably do not interpret them as diminutives: *Annette* and *Nancy*. However, the *-y* is productively used for nicknames: *Barby, Keithy, Tommy*.

4. Suffixes expressing agent/subject arguments

Another set of suffixes exhibiting polysemy are those for agent/subject arguments – suffixes that can be paraphrased as "one who is" or "one who does" (Table 4). The suffixes examined are *-an/ian*, *-ant/ent*, *-arian*, *-er*, *-ist*, and *-ite*.[5] Although each suffix has its own semantic structure, items tend to share some common meanings: MEMBER OF A CLASS, INHABITANT OF A PLACE, AGENT, INSTRUMENT, or FOLLOWER OF AN IDEOLOGY.

Table 4. Agentive suffixes.

Suffix	Agent	Member of a group	Inhabitant of	Instrument	Follower/ Ideology	Other
-an/-ian	logician	plebeian, reptilian	Persian, Arabian		Lutheran	HAS CHARACTER OF
-ant/-ent	servant, defendant			solvent		
-arian		sexagenarian			Unitarian, libertarian	
-er	teacher	commissioner	New Yorker, Berliner	toaster, lighter		CONNECTED WITH
-ist	pianist, chemist				Marxist, Calvinist	PREJUDICE
-ite		socialite			Mennonite	TECHNICAL

The suffix *-er* displays a traditional radial structure, with the AGENT sense in the centre (see Fig. 1). (See Panther and Thornburg 2002 for a more detailed analysis of the various senses of *-er* and their relationship.)

Of the agent suffixes other than *-er*, the agent sense is not necessarily central. Beard (1990) has described the frequency of agentive and instrumental polysemy in a number of languages, and such polysemy generally occurs by means of *-er* and *-ant/ent*. The technical senses of *-ite* are mostly from chemistry.

The suffix *-ist*, which is attached to nouns or bound bases, has three overlapping senses. The first is the agentive one, such as *violinist* or *physicist*. The second, which is related to *-ism*, describes a proponent of an ideology,

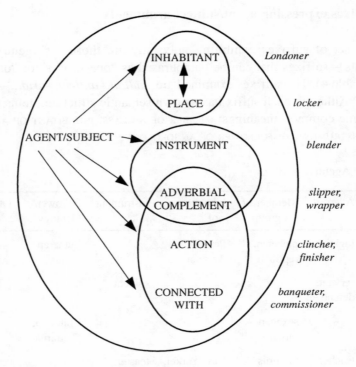

Figure 1. The polysemy of *-er*.

such as *federalist* or *capitalist*. The third is like the second, but it additionally adds a connotation of prejudice (Lehrer 1988, 1999). Historically, this sense evolved from the word *racist*, "one who believes in innate difference among races". But *racist* soon took on the sense "being unjustifiably prejudiced against a group on the basis of race" and the negative connotation transferred to the *-ist*, which expanded to *sexist*, *ageist*, *speciesist*, and other terms. This shift illustrates Traugott's analysis, where pragmatic implicatures give rise to conventional uses. "Semantic change ... involves specification, achieved through inferencing" (1988: 413). More interesting, however, is her observation that (in the case of metonymy) generally the meaning shifts to "the subjective belief state or attitude toward the situation" (p. 414). With *-ist*, the earlier sense, as in *federalist*, has a neutral connotation, while the newer sense, as in *sexist*, is negative and reveals the speaker's evaluation.

5.   Neologisms: a data source for semantic change in progress

One difficulty in determining the senses of derivational affixes (and lexemes for that matter) lies in the fact that although the productive meanings change over time, the language retains many items with older senses. For example, the current productive meaning of *-ster* is "an agent who does things that are bad or at least shady" (Lehrer 1999). Yet words like *spinster* and *youngster* obviously do not have this meaning.

One affix that I have been watching for several years is the prefix *meta-* (see Fig. 2). Numerous words with this prefix have existed in English for a long time, e.g. *metaphor*, *metaphysics*, and *metamorphosis*. There are also many scientific words with *meta-*, even new coinages based on analogy with existing scientific terms. The meanings glossed for these uses include "beyond" or "transcendental", and "situated behind" for some technical terms in anatomy and zoology, e.g. *metathorax* "hindpart of the thorax of an insect" and *metapodial* "one of the bones of the hand". Almost all of Marchand's examples of *meta-* are from this class, with subcategories based on the specific sciences (Marchand 1966: 125).

However, there are three related, newer productive senses, all of which were first recorded in the *OED* after 1925, and all have an umbrella sense of "second order representation". The specific overlapping (and not completely

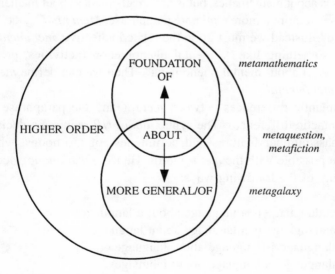

Figure 2.   The polysemy of *meta-*.

discrete) senses are: (i) "the foundations of a science or discipline", (ii) "aboutness", and (iii) "more general". (Some words incorporate two senses.)

The first meaning, "a foundational theory of X", is exemplified by *meta-history, metatheory, metapsychology, metamathematics,*[6] and *metalinguistics.* *Metasociology* can be paraphrased as "the foundations of the study of sociology"; *metalinguistics* is "the theoretical foundation of the study of language or linguistics".

The second sense, which is the most productive, can be glossed as ABOUT, and some words contain both meanings. For example, *metamathematics* is about mathematics, and *metalanguage* is about language, but the ABOUT sense of *meta-* contains a variable where the word in the base is repeated: "(an) X about (an) X".

> A metalanguage is a language about language(s).
> A metamovie is a movie about a movie (movies).
> Metacognition is cognition about cognition.
> A metarule is a rule about rules.
> A metamessage is a message about a message (messages).

So whereas *metalanguage* contains senses (i) and (ii), *metahistory* contains only the first sense, since it is not "history about history". Similarly, *meta-mathematics* is about mathematics, but is not "mathematics about mathematics".

Some cases require a more elaborate paraphrase. *Metamind* is not "a mind about a mind". Instead we must go to the related adjective, *metamental*, and define it as something like "a mental phenomenon (activities, processes, judgements, etc.) about mental phenomena". Then we can define *metamind* in terms of *metamental*.

Some semantic differences between *meta-X* and the paraphrase follow from the syntactic differences. The syntax *about NP* requires a decision on the count/mass/number features and definiteness of the nouns, where no contrasts are possible with the *meta-* words. Hence, *metalanguage* could be defined in any of the following ways:

> A metalanguage is a language about a language.
> A metalanguage is a language about languages.
> Metalanguage is language about language.
> Metalanguage is language about languages.

As in interpreting any utterance, pragmatic factors require fine-tuning based on contextual factors.

Let us turn now to the semantic requirements of the base of the second sense. One aspect of the meaning of these novel uses of *meta-* is the ABOUTNESS requirement. One can understand what a *metamovie* is – a movie about a movie – but it is perplexing to imagine what a *metapotato* might be, just as it is perplexing to interpret "a potato about a potato".

A primary class of items having ABOUTNESS properties are linguistic products of various sorts: speech acts, texts of various genres, concepts of linguistic analysis, and means of realization. Examples I have observed include *meta-question, metasentence, metawriting*, and *metajoke*. The *American Heritage Dictionary* has an entry for *metafiction*, "fiction that deals, often playfully and self-referentially with the writing of fiction or its conventions." In the domain of visual and performing arts we can have *metapicture, meta-documentary*, and *metamovie*. For example, Robert Altman's film *The Player* is not only a movie about a movie, but even a movie about itself. This sense of *meta-* can also be extended to bases denoting emotions, since emotions can have ABOUTNESS properties. Wilbur (1977) coined the term *metagrumbles* to describe "grumbling about [other people's] grumbling".

The third meaning of the prefix *meta-* is "more general, more inclusive". The earliest citation of this sense in the *OED* is *metagalaxy*, "cluster of galaxies" (1930). However, if this sense is glossed simply as "of", the overlap in meaning of ABOUT and OF is a natural development, as seen in the partial overlap/synonymy of phrases like *a book of birds* and *a book about birds*. This recent nuance is illustrated by words like *metapopulation* and *meta-invention*. A *metapopulation* is not "a population about populations", but rather "a higher-order population – a population OF populations". An article about microprocessors predicts that "it is not merely an invention but a *meta-invention*, which enables us to create yet other inventions" (*Modern Maturity*, Nov.–Dec. 1998: 65; emphasis added). In this example, a *meta-invention* is not "an invention ABOUT inventions", but "an invention OF [other] inventions". This use of *meta-* keeps the variable, but shifts the meaning from ABOUT to OF.

Of these three related senses, although the sense ABOUT is not the first recorded, it is synchronically central, lying between "foundation of" and "more general". (Geeraerts [1985] demonstrates how prototypicality can shift diachronically.)

The next three suffixes, *-dom, -hood*, and *-ship*, overlap in meaning in that they have a sense STATE or CONDITION, but in addition each has its own range of meanings.

-dom (see Fig. 3) is in fact a reduced form of a formerly independent word, with a central sense of "state" or "jurisdiction", as in *kingdom* or *Christendom*. This sense includes both concrete and abstract meanings, so we can have a phrase like *kingdom of God*, referring not to a physical place but to an abstract realm. From this meaning it is a short step to the sense of "territory", as in *kingdom* "place where the king rules", *dukedom*, and *sheikdom*. Also from the general sense of "state, condition" it is a natural shift to a special kind of condition illustrated by *stardom*, having the rank or being in the class of stars.

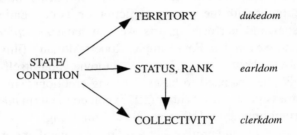

Figure 3.   The polysemy of *-dom*.

Marchand (1966: 262) lists others classes of meanings, such as humorous and pejorative senses, but these are not distinct senses. There are, rather, independent semantic dimensions that intersect with the meanings, and they can be found in any of the above senses: *dogdom, gangsterdom, autodom*.

-hood also has a general sense of "state" or "condition", but this sense includes "state of affairs", as in *falsehood* and *likelihood*, which leads to a sense of "status", e.g. *wifehood, widowhood*, which in turn leads to "time period connected with that state" as in *babyhood, childhood*. The first sense also develops into a collective body, as in *brotherhood, sisterhood*. See Figure 4.

The third item, *-ship*, has a more complex set of meanings (Fig. 5). The sense "state, condition" is found in items like *kinship* and *ladyship*, which blends into "office, rank" (*ambassadorship, editorship*), which is very closely related to "role, position" (*leadership, dictatorship*). Both of these latter two senses lead to "respectful designation" (*ladyship, lordship*). The general sense also yields senses of skill and art (*penmanship, marksmanship*) and also to

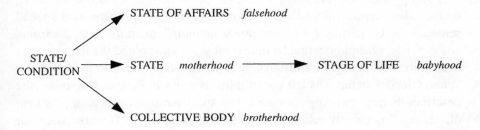

Figure 4.   The polysemy of *-hood*.

"community, collective" *(partnership, fellowship),* and finally, the sixth sense has developed into "stipend, financial benefit", in *scholarship, fellowship,* and *TAship (teaching assistantship).* However, this last may be limited to specific nouns, and may not be a feature of the suffix.

The last affixes to be discussed are three negative prefixes: *de-, dis-,* and *un-,* attached to verbs and participles. All three have a general meaning of producing the opposite state, usually by reversing an action or returning to an earlier state, but each has at least one other sense or nuance. In addition, there are many subtleties and complexities of meaning that I will not discuss here, since I am concerned only with polysemy.

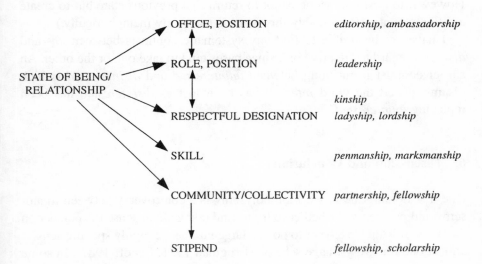

Figure 5.   The polysemy of *-ship*.

Examples of *de-* that show the sense of "reversing an action or state" include *decentralize, destalinize, decompress* and *decode*. But one special sense of *de-* is "getting rid of, remove something", as in *delouse, dethrone,* and *deforest*. One publication from several years ago coined the term *deNewt* to describe Newt Gingrich's resignation from the US House of Representatives. When Gloria Estefan was left out of a list of divas in *People Magazine*, she described herself as being *dedivaed*. The specialization of meaning "get rid of, remove" is closely related to the general meaning of "reverse state" or "undo action", since to remove something or someone involves a change of state, usually to a previous state. But an area can be *deforested* that has "always" been forest land (i.e. as long as anyone can remember).

The reversal sense of *dis-* is illustrated by *disarm* and *disappear*. In addition, this prefix can connote "refuse to, fail to" as in *disobey* and *disallow*. Some words require greater complications in their interpretation. For example, *disinherit* is not simply a reversal or negation of *inherit,* since a paraphrase of *Mr. Jones disinherited his children* is not a negation of *Mr. Jones inherited his children*. The syntactic frames of each verb are not parallel.

The last negative item is *un-*, whose reversal of state sense can be seen in *untie, unwind, unlace,* and *unbuckle*. (Marchand also lists *unfreeze*.) A closely related, specific sense is found in *unhorse, unsex,* and *unman*. To *unhorse* someone is to reverse a state, since that person is no longer on a horse. However, to *unsex* someone is not to return to a previous state but to create a different state. (Presumably this word is used only metaphorically.)

I have not been able to find any systematic contrasts between *un-* and *dis-* with regard to "deprive of", since bases tend to take one or the other. An earlier contrast in meaning between *uninterested* and *disinterested* (which disambiguated the word *interest*) has been lost as *disinterested* has been replacing *uninterested*.

6.   Discussion and Conclusions

One traditional issue in work on polysemy is a controversy between mono-semy and polysemy – whether to try to find one general sense (as pursued in the work of Ruhl [1989]) or to posit a large number of highly specific senses, almost one for every image schema (Brugman 1981; Lakoff 1987). In some cases, it is quite clear which way to go, since the traditional tests for ambiguity will give clear results (Geeraerts 1993; Cruse 1986, 1995). However, in many other cases, decisions are hard to make because the ambiguity tests are indeterminate. Ambiguity tests often fail where a general sense includes a specific sense, such as *egg* "reproductive body from various animals", "egg from a bird, with a yellow yolk, surrounded by a hard shell" [and other senses]. This type of polysemy has been termed *autohyponymous polysemy* by Cruse (1995).

In some of the affixes I have examined, neither solution – monosemy nor polysemy – seems optimal. Selecting monosemy leaves too much to the pragmatics and ignores the rather specific, contextually determined senses; speakers do not need to figure out that specific meaning each time they encounter a new use of the affix. Yet postulating many specific senses fails to capture the fact that there is a unity that connects the various meanings. In Figures 1 and 2, I have tried to capture both the general and specific senses. The general meaning includes the specific ones, but not necessarily exhaustively, and this in turn allows for the generation of nuances and innovations lying outside the specific senses. Tuggy's model (1993) is the closest one I have found to resolving the dilemma.

Tuggy, like Geeraerts (1993), shows that there is a continuum, not a sharp break, between ambiguity and vagueness. Moreover, diachronic factors blur the distinction even more. Tuggy shows how general schemas [general senses] and their elaborations [specific senses] co-exist in languages. Schemas or elaborations, or both, can become well-established through repeated usage and thereby become salient (Tuggy 1993: 279). When an elaborated sense becomes salient, it is considered prototypical. If the general sense is not salient but some of the elaborations [specific senses] are salient, the senses strike us as a case of ambiguity. However, if the general sense is salient, but the specific senses are not, we judge the item as exhibiting vagueness. When the general sense and at least one of the elaborated senses are salient, we are inclined to judge ambiguity. Tuggy's model of schema and elaborations does not require us to choose vagueness or ambiguity – we get both, along with an account of context and conditions that explain our judgements in clear cases and borderline cases.

Although the concepts represented by English affixes are limited, they show polysemy that is similar to that found in lexemes. There are metaphorical transfers of "space" and "time", "vertical position (superiority)", "generality", and "rank", and there is some metonymy, as in "a group or class of people" and "inhabitant of". Also there is the metonymic shift from "membership of a group" to "award for election to the group" to "financial support". Another similarity can be found in the structure of polysemy, which can be represented by radial categories, as exemplified by Brugman (1981), Lakoff (1987), and many other cognitive linguists. Figures 1 through 5 present a few of the affixes which show this pattern.

However, one claim by cognitive linguists is challenged by these data. It is assumed that the direction of change and innovation is from concrete to abstract, and specifically from space to time.[7] However, the prefixes *pre-* and *post-* primarily express temporal concepts, and the transfer to space is synchronically secondary and diachronically later. In any case, these examples challenge the assumption of necessary directionality. Yet given the fact that concepts that are expressed in affixes are already rather abstract, it could be argued that such examples are not serious counterexamples.

Notes

1. Mithun (1996) provides data from American Indian languages showing that the range of meanings of derivational affixes is larger than Beard claims.
2. Marchand (1966) lists all the items I discuss as prefixes, and I will follow him in this point. However, these morphemes differ as to their boundedness. Unfortunately, English spelling is no guide. Some items are usually spelt with a hyphen, some with a space before the base, and some are always part of the following word. Moreover, there are often inconsistencies in a given item.
3. Some opera companies call the translations of the text appearing above the stage *supertitles*; other call them *surtitles*. The prefix *sur-* is much less productive in English than *super-*.
4. *Starlet* suggests quantity – "a little bit of stardom" and possibly mild derogation. It also seems restricted to females, reinforcing an association of feminine and diminutive senses.
5. There are other agent/subject suffixes not dealt with here, some of which are discussed in Lehrer (1999).
6. The *OED* provides an 1853 citation of *metamathematics* as "beyond the scope of", but a 1926 citation is glossed as "pertaining to".
7. There is a whole scale from very concrete concepts expressed in words like *table* to extremely abstract ones, such as the meaning of *metaphysics*, with an indefinite number or points in between. Moreover, it is not always clear how to arrange concepts on this scale. Is time more abstract than space?

References

American Heritage Dictionary
    1992   Boston: Houghton Mifflin.

Apresjan, Jurij D.
    1974   Regular polysemy. *Linguistics* 142: 5–32.

Baker, Mark
    1988   Morphology and syntactic objects. A review of A. M. DiScillo and E. Williams, *On the Definition of Word. Yearbook of Morphology* 1: 259–284.

Beard, Robert
    1988   On the separation of derivation from morphology: toward a lexeme–morpheme based morphology. *Quaderni di semantica* 9: 3–59.
    1990   The nature and origins of derivational polysemy. *Lingua* 81: 101–140.
    1992   *Lexeme–Morpheme Base Morphology: A General Theory of Inflection and Word Formation*. Albany, NY: State University of New York Press.

Bloomfield, Leonard
    1933   *Language*. New York: Holt, Rinehard and Winston.

Brugman, Claudia
    1981   The Story of *Over*. M.A. thesis. Linguistics Dept, University of California, Berkeley.

Cruse, David A.
    1986   *Lexical Semantics*. Cambridge: Cambridge University Press.
    1995   Polysemy and related phenomena from a cognitive linguistic viewpoint. In: Patrick Saint-Dizier and Evelyne Viegas (eds.), *Computational Lexical Semantics*, 33–49. Cambridge: Cambridge University Press.

Dressler, Wolfgang U. and Lavinia Merlini Barbaresi
    1994   *Morphopragmatics: Diminutives and Intensifiers in Italian, German, and Other Languages*. (Trends in linguistics. Studies and Monographs 76). Berlin and New York: Mouton de Gruyter.

Geeraerts, Dirk
    1985   Cognitive restrictions on the structure of semantic change. In: Jacek Fisiak (ed.), *Historical Semantics, Historical Word Formation*, 127–154. Berlin: Mouton.
    1993   Vagueness's puzzles, polysemy's vagaries. *Cognitive Linguistics* 4: 223–272.

Joos, Martin
    1958   Semology: a linguistic theory of meaning. *Studies in Linguistics* 13: 53–71.

Lakoff, George
    1987   *Women, Fire and Dangerous Things*. Chicago: University of Chicago Press.

Lehrer, Adrienne
  1988   A note on the semantics of *-ist* and *-ism*. *American Speech* 63: 181–185.
  1993   Prefixes in English word formation. *Folia Linguistica* 2: 133–148.
  1996   Why neologisms are important to study. *Lexicology* 2: 63–73.
  1999   Are affixes signs?: The semantic relationships of English derivational affixes. In: Wolfgang U. Dressler, Oskar E. Pfeiffer, Markus A. Pöchtrager and John R. Rennison (eds.), *Morphologica 1996*, 143–154. (Papers from the Seventh International Morphology Conference, Vienna, Austria, February 1996.) The Hague: Holland Academic Graphics.
Lieber, Rochelle
  1992   *Deconstructing Morphology*. Chicago: University of Chicago Press.
Marchand, Hans
  1966   *The Categories and Types of Present-Day English Word Formation*. Birmingham: University of Alabama Press.
Mithun, Marianne
  1996   The meanings of roots and affixes. Papers from the Seventh International Morphology Conference, Vienna, Austria, February 1996.
Nerlich, Brigitte and David D. Clarke
  1992   Semantic change: case studies based on traditional and cognitive semantics. *Journal of Literary Semantics* 21: 204–225.
Norrick, Neal R.
  1981   *Semiotic Principles in Semantic Theory*. Amsterdam: John Benjamins.
Oxford English Dictionary
  1989   Oxford: Clarenden.
Panther, Klaus-Uwe and Linda L. Thornburg
  2002   The roles of metaphor and metonymy in *-er* nominals. In: René Dirven (ed.), *The Metaphor–Metonymy Continuum: The Ongoing Debate*, 279–319. Berlin: Mouton de Gruyter.
Ruhl, Charles
  1989   *On Monosemy*. New York: State University of New York Press.
Traugott, Elizabeth C.
  1988   Pragmatic strengthening and grammaticalization. *Berkeley Linguistics Society* 14: 406–416.
Tuggy, David
  1993   Ambiguity, polysemy, and vagueness. *Cognitive Linguistics* 4: 273–290.
Walker, John
  1936   *Rhyming Dictionary*, Revised and enlarged by Lawrence H. Dawson. New York: Dutton.
Wilbur, Ken
  1977   *The Spectrum of Consciousness*. Wheaton, IL: Theosophical Publishing House.

The role of links and/or qualia in modifier–head constructions

Beatrice Warren

1. The role of qualia in semantics

Whereas most publications on linguistic topics represent advances analogous to millimetres or at best inches, now and then there appears an article or monograph that represents a leap forward in terms of yards. Although it is too early to include Pustejovsky (1996) in this illustrious league, judging by the interest his model of generative semantics has raised, he may be considered a potential candidate.

The attraction of Pustejovsky's theory is that it suggests ways in which the flexibility of word meaning can be predicted. It is possible, he claims, to specify formally the generative devices "by which words can achieve a potentially infinite number of senses in context, while limiting the number of senses actually stored in the lexicon" (1996: 105).

As this quotation makes evident, he accepts, like so many semanticists in the last few decades, that word meaning is negotiable in context. However, unlike other proponents of flexible word meaning, he insists that something we can call default polysemy is "rule-governed". He accepts, again like many semanticists, that word meaning is componential, but rejects a simple list of features of meaning. Instead he argues for a rich representation involving argument structure (number and type of arguments associated with the word), event structure (type of event in which the word is involved) and qualia structure (a set of possible properties explaining the meaning of the word). These form the material on which generative devices operate in a well-defined manner to yield appropriate contextual interpretations of words.

Thus we appear to have a lexical parallel to syntactic rule-governed creativity, which would explain the allure of the theory. The introduction of qualia roles, which "not only structure our knowledge of words, but also suggest interpretation of words in context" (Pustejovsky 1996: 87) is a particular innovation, and a very audacious and strong claim. The origin of these roles, Pustejovsky informs us, is Aristotle's notion of modes of explanation. There are four roles:

(i)   CONSTITUTIVE: the relation between an object and its constituents, or
          proper parts.
(ii)   FORMAL: that which distinguishes the object within a larger domain.
(iii)   TELIC: purpose or function of the object.
(iv)   AGENTIVE: factors involved in the origin or "bringing about" of an
          object.

These four factors "drive our understanding of an object or a relation in
the world. They furthermore contribute to (or, in fact, determine) our ability
to name an object ..." (1996: 85). This brings to mind a theory by Clark and
Clark (1979: 789), which was inspired by Rosch and her colleagues' research
into the principles of human categorization, and which suggested that the
basis for categorization of objects includes (i) physical characteristics (cf.
the CONSTITUTIVE and FORMAL qualia), (ii) ontogeny (cf. the AGENTIVE quale)
and (iii) potential roles (cf. the TELIC quale). The qualia roles would in other
words represent the type of features which cause us to think of objects as a
kind, i.e. common constituent matter or parts, common *gestalts* (shape, size,
position, etc.), common origins, common functions. If we think of words as
category labels,[1] we would then have a rationale for the qualia roles – at
least for first-order entities[2] – which finds support in research into categorization. The question is: is there also empirical evidence that qualia structure
plays an important role in the description of meanings of words and in lexical
creativity giving rise to polysemy? The focus of the present contribution will
be that very question and we will turn to two different types of empirical
studies in search of an answer, first to a study dealing with defining components of meaning, and then to a collection of studies concerned with
relational meanings.

2.   Empirical evaluation

Some years ago Geeraerts presented ingenious studies of the particular features
that are salient in naming new objects. We get a detailed description of one
of these concerning a garment first used in Belgium in 1987, frequently
referred to by the English loan word *leggings* (1997: 32–47). The occurrence

of this word was examined in fashion magazines and mail-order catalogues, but only if a picture or drawing illustrated the referent. This made it possible to describe the referents of *leggings* according to the following six dimensions: the length of the garment (three possible "values": to the knee, below the knee, to the ankles); its width (tight-fitting, somewhat tight-fitting, loose-fitting); the presence of a crease (a clear crease, no crease); the material (finely woven or knitted, coarsely woven or knitted, transparent material, any other type); its function (upperwear or underwear); and finally the sex of the person wearing the garment. The results of the study showed that in 1988 the prototypical legging is long, tight-fitting, has no crease, is made of an elastic material and is worn by women like a pair of trousers. There are similar results for 1989, 1990, 1991 and 1992, but each successive year there appears an increasing number of referents which deviate from the prototype. These findings support the prototypical approach to semantics. That is to say, categories cannot be defined by a single set of necessary and sufficient attributes but exhibit a family resemblance structure, allowing definitions of words to expand along lines like the following: ABCD → BCDE → ACDE → ABC → BCD etc.

Pustejovsky's model does not address the changeability of criterial attributes. Nor does it account for the fact that defining features may be more or less salient. However, the referential features themselves, which were chosen by the investigators because they were felt to play a part in determining category members, appear to match the qualia fairly well. Length, width, crease could be said to represent FORMAL qualia; material a CONSTITUTIVE quale; the features "upperwear for women" arguably TELIC qualia.

Obviously a single example cannot support a theory in a decisive manner. There is, however, a collection of studies which could give substantial support. These studies are concerned with the semantics of modifier–head combinations and are relevant since an important point of Pustejovsky's theory is that it is when we combine words in utterances that the representational structures and the generative devices are activated to produce implicit, nonlisted meanings. The collection comprises the following (in particular): Ljung (1970), Brekle (1970), Aarts and Calbert (1979), Bartning (1980), Levi (1978), Warren (1978, 1984) and Leitzky (1989). They have in common the hypothesis that the interpretation of modifier–head constructions involves the retrieval of implicit links. That this would be so in the case of noun–noun compounds had generally been assumed: *silver spoon* "spoon *made of* silver", *apple tree* "tree *producing* apples", *cart wheel* "wheel *belonging to* cart", etc. Ljung's study, however, showed that adjectives also contain a link, or, more precisely, that the definition of adjectives typically involves a predicative verb and its complement, which is normally identical to the nominal stem in the case of denominal adjectives: *stony* "abounding in stones", *beautiful* "possessing beauty", *noisy* "producing noise". Aarts and Calbert (1979) formalized this mode of defining adjectives and stipulated that there are at least two types of semantic elements in adjectives: one with predicative and one with referential force.[3] The predicate links the referential content of the adjective with its head: *angry man* "man experiencing anger", *sad event* "event causing sadness". There is, they also postulated, a limited number of preferred links. Which of these is relevant depends on the nature of the referential content and the head of the adjective. Warren (1988) later illustrated that the variability of the link accounts for a certain type of polysemy in the case of adjectives. Consider Table 1.

Table 1. Variability of links in adjectives.

	Link	Referential content	Example
sad	experiencing	sadness	*sad girl*
	manifesting		*sad eyes*
	causing		*sad event*
healthy	having	health	*healthy child*
	causing		*healthy food*
smoky	emitting	smoke	*smoky fuel*
	containing		*smoky room*
	resembling		*smoky colour*

The studies listed above did not only have in common the assumption that the semantics of nominal modifiers could involve implicit links. As just indicated, they also postulated that there exists a list of preferred relations or, to use my terminology, default relations, which would naturally be invoked unless there was strong contextual evidence to the contrary (Warren 1985: 378–380, 1988: 132–134). Compare Pustejovsky's admission that a particular interpretation specified by the qualia structure may be overridden in certain contexts. For instance, *Bob finished the novels* could have two possible regular readings, i.e. "Bob finished reading the novels", in which case a feature in the Telic quale would be activated (novels are for reading), or "Bob finished writing the novels", in which case a feature in the AGENTIVE quale is activated (novels come about by being written). However, the interpretation "Bob finished wrapping up the novels" could be triggered in a case such as the following: Bob, we know, works at a publisher's firm and one of his jobs is to wrap and send various types of books – novels, textbooks, children's books, etc. Linguists have in the past not been interested in default values, possibly for ideological reasons, "all and only the grammatical constructions" being the goal. If Pustejovsky succeeds in persuading the linguistic guild of the validity of default values, this would amount to a minor breakthrough in my view, in particular in semantics.[4]

The lists of links presented in the studies cited are not identical, but strikingly similar, and could be said to be variations on a theme. My own version is shown in Table 2.

As we see from the above, the role combinations are reversible with the

Table 2.   Implicit links.

Link	Example	Role combination
		Compositional
consist of/constituted by	*electric power*	SOURCE–RESULT
constituting	*tragic event*	RESULT–SOURCE
		Possessive
belonging to	*facial skin*	WHOLE–PART
having	*rational creature*	PART–WHOLE
		Locative
occurring in/at/on	*polar climate*	PLACE–OBJ
	medieval games	TIME–OBJ
containing	*poisonous plant*	OBJ–PLACE
during which ... prevails	*happy times*	OBJ–TIME
		Causative
caused by	*nervous breakdown*	CAUSER–RESULT
causing	*noisy children*	RESULT–CAUSER
		Purpose
be for	*culinary utensils*	GOAL–INSTRUMENTS
		Resemblance
be like	*golden hair*	COMPARANT–COMPARED
be in accordance with	*normal behaviour*	NORM–ADHERENT

exception of the resemblance and the purpose relations. The reason for this, in the case of resemblance, is that although it is possible to compare the shape of a tulip to that of a bell (*bell tulip*) or *vice versa* (*tulip bell*), the referring item in this role combination automatically assumes the role COM-PARED. In the case of the purpose compounds, I found that they could be assigned two links and two role combinations: *tablecloth*: "cloth (OBJ/INS) which is for putting on tables (LOC/GOAL)"; *card table*: "table (LOC/INS) which is for playing cards (OBJ/GOAL) at"; *night-dress*: "dress (OBJ/INS) which is for wearing at night (TIME/GOAL)"; *dinnertime*: "time (TIME/INS) which is for having dinner (OBJ/GOAL) at"; *ball bat*: "bat (CAUSER/INS) which is for hitting balls (OBJ/GOAL) with"; *football*: "ball (OBJ/INS) which is for hitting with foot (CAUSER/GOAL)". As we see, the basic roles are reversible, but the superimposed purpose role is not.

There is quite substantial empirical support for the existence of these links. Ljung (1970), whose aim was to establish the meanings that denominal adjectivalization could express, examined the definitions of 218 adjectives ending in -*al*, -*ful*, -*ic*, -*ish*, -*ly*, -*ous* or -*y* in *Webster's Seventh New Collegiate Dictionary* and *Webster's Third New International Dictionary*. He found it possible to reduce the numerous definitions he had collected into a small number of types (gross definitions), either because they were synonymous or hyponymous. The present writer analysed 4,500 noun–noun compounds in context (types) and 291 adjectives (types) in altogether 12,890 contexts (Warren 1978, 1984) and found that, if there was a covert link,[5] it would with very few exceptions be one of those listed above.

An important discovery made by Ljung was that certain links ("meanings" in his terminology) are incompatible with *bona fide* adjectives, i.e. adjectives that could occur attributively (*sad girl*), predicatively (*girl is sad*), which could be graded (*very sad girl*), and which could tolerate insertions (*sad, anxious girl*). These links could, however, be found with modifiers which had the morphological make-up of adjectives, but which in all other respects were nouns: *glandular pain, sulphuric acid, continental capital*. These constructions he called N+aff N (noun+affix noun) compounds[6] and (obviously) he considered them types of compounds. He therefore suggested that certain links were restricted to *bona fide* adjectives and others to compounds, whether of the noun–noun or of N+aff N type. My own research into the semantics of nominal modifiers did not completely confirm this surmise. Instead I found that all the links that could occur in adjectives – also those compatible with *bona fide* adjectives – could occur in noun–noun compounds. The restriction was that not all links found in compounds could occur with *bona fide* adjectives, although they could be found in the so-called N+aff adjectives. Consider Table 3.

Table 3. Links which do not occur in *bona fide* adjectives.

Link	Example	Paraphrase
constituted by	*silver spoon*	"spoon made of silver"
	electric current	"current consisting of electricity"
	?smoky rings	"rings consisting of smoke"
belonging to	*family estate*	"estate belonging to a family"
	presidential home	"home belonging to the president"
	?flowery leaves	"leaves belonging to flowers"
occurring in/at/on	*city streets*	"streets in the city"
	suburban areas	"areas in the suburb"
	?beachy path	"path along the beach"
	afternoon tea	"tea served in the afternoon"
	nocturnal events	"events occurring in the night"
	?summery holidays	"holidays in the summer"
caused by	*hay fever*	"fever caused by hay"
	electric shock	"shock caused by electricity"
	?dusty allergy attack	"allergy attack caused by dust"
being for	*emergency telephone*	"telephone for emergencies"
	educational facilities	"facilities for education"
	?womanly doctor	"doctor for women"

I also found that the function of the modifier was a crucial factor as far as stress, syntactic behaviour, morphology and the semantics of the modifier are concerned. This was so in particular if the modifier was a classifier, in which case it combines with the head to form a referring unit, or if it was purely descriptive, in which case the modifier does not affect the meaning or reference of the head but contributes additional information about it (i.e. strictly speaking about the referent(s) of the head). Bolinger (1967) referred to this distinction as reference-modifying and referent-modifying, respectively. Referent-modifying modifiers, I found, are invariably *bona fide* adjectives, which – as just indicated – could only occur with certain links, viz. those in Table 4.

Table 4. Links in *bona fide* adjectives.

Link	Example	Role combination
constituting	*problematic case*	RESULT–SOURCE
causing	*harmful drug*	RESULT–CAUSER
having (possessive)	*rational man*	PART–WHOLE
having on (locative)	*dusty furniture*	OBJ–PLACE
resembling	*golden orange*	COMPARANT–COMPARED
in accordance with	*alphabetic order*	NORM–ADHERENT[7]

To a certain extent modifiers could be said to have a basic job description: nouns in the genitive are basically identifiers; uninflected noun modifiers (i.e. the modifier in noun–noun compounds) are basically restrictive (i.e. either identifiers or classifiers); non-derived adjectives and adjectives in *-y*, *-ful*, *-ish* and ?*-ly* are basically descriptors (*bona fide* adjectives); and adjectives in classical suffixes such as *-al*, *-an*, *-ar*, *-ary*, *-ic*, and *-ous* are basically classifiers *or* descriptors.[8] As we can see, certain functions can be connected to more than one type of modifier; notably uninflected nouns and adjectives in *-al*, *-an*, *-ar*, *-ary*, *-ic*, *-ous* etc. both have a basic potential classifying function, and the descriptive function can in principle be connected with both types of adjectives (i.e. the "native" and the "classical" types). From this it follows that there should not be a difference as to function between modifiers in noun–noun compounds and in combinations of *-al*, *-an*, and *-ic* adjectives plus nouns, both being basically classifiers. The examples in Table 5 appear to demonstrate this.

However, there should be a functional difference between the modifier in noun–noun compounds (basically nondescriptive) and in combinations involving *-y*, *-ful* and *-ish* adjectives (basically descriptive), which indeed seems to be the case, as illustrated in Table 6.

Table 5. Synonymous noun–noun and adjective–noun combinations.

Link	Noun–noun	Adjective–noun
consisting of	*metal ball*	*metallic ball*
part of	*moon surface*	*lunar surface*
be in/at/on	*coast road*	*coastal road*
caused by	*hand milking*	*manual milking*

Table 6. Non-synonymous noun–noun and adjective–noun combinations.

Link	Noun–noun	Adjective–noun
having	*beauty spot*	*beautiful spot*
	glamour girl	*glamorous girl*
	pepper sauce	*peppery sauce*
constituting	*problem child*	*problematic child*
	surprise party	*surprising party*
resembling	*gold fish*	*golden fish*
	silver paper	*silvery paper*

As I think the examples just given show, the meaning of the whole phrase is influenced by the function of the modifier. I will expand on this point later.

Another consequence of the distinction between basically *bona fide* adjectives (i.e. non-derived adjectives and those in *-y*, *-ful*, *-ish* etc.) and the potential N+aff adjectives (i.e. those in classical suffixes) is that the latter – being compatible with a greater number of links – should be polysemous to a greater extent than the former. This appears to be true, at least in principle. Consider Table 7, which deals with *musical*.

However, it should be pointed out in this connection that not all the *-al*, *-an*, *-ar*, *-ic* etc. adjectives occur with all the links in principle available for classifiers. Nor can all *bona fide* adjectives occur with all the links in principle

Table 7. The polysemy of an adjective with a classical suffix.

Link	Example	Role combination
constituting	*musical tones*	SOURCE–RESULT
constituted by	*musical composition*	RESULT–SOURCE
having (aptitude for)	*musical child*	PART–WHOLE
containing	*musical comedy*	OBJ–ABSTRACT PLACE
during which ... occurs	*musical soiree*	OBJ–TIME
belonging to	*?musical pitch*	WHOLE–PART
occurring within (the sphere of)	*musical term*	ABSTRACT PLACE–OBJ
causing	*?musical drumming*	RESULT–SOURCE
caused by	*musical shock*	SOURCE–RESULT
be for	*musical instrument*	GOAL–INSTRUMENT
resembling	*musical voice*	COMPARANT–COMPARED

available for these adjectives. There are of course natural notional restrictions: the referential content of *dusty* could hardly take on the role NORM, *musical* or *nervous* are hardly compatible with the role TIME, etc., but besides such natural limitations (which would be taken care of by qualia), there are numerous restrictions which must be characterized as idiosyncratic. For instance, *sad* is compatible with the PART role (*sad child*) and with the RESULT role (*sad news* "causing sadness"), but *hungry* is compatible only with the PART role (*hungry child*), not with the RESULT role (*?hungry smells* "causing hunger"); *nervous* can occur with the PART role (*my nervous sister*) and the CAUSER role (*nervous breakdown*), but not with the RESULT role (*?nervous news* "causing nervousness"); *sensational* is – contrary to expectation – incompatible with the experience link (*?sensational being* "having sensations").

3. Idiosyncrasy, conventionalization and compositionality

I have elsewhere (Warren 1988: 131–132) suggested that idiosyncrasies of this kind tend to develop to avoid cumbersome ambiguity and that a systematic investigation of restrictions may reveal two main types: (i) of some notionally possible links, only one will be favoured in connection with certain nouns; *sad*, e.g., strongly favours the link *experiencing* when modifying animate nouns, but may suggest *inducing, giving rise to* when combined with non-animates; (ii) the adjective is restricted to one link only, which in turn may give rise to "doublets" of, for instance, the kind listed in Table 8.

The fact that there are these idiosyncrasies has certain theoretical implications. For instance, we cannot plausibly assume that links of adjectives are computed according to context, their referential content, and heads, every time we come across them. Instead it seems that links in the case of adjectives often become conventionalized parts of their meanings. We find here a

Table 8.   Examples of "doublets".

Experiencing (manifesting)[9]	Causing
compassionate	*pathetic*
envious	*enviable*
hungry	*appetizing*
contemptuous	*contemptible*
furious	*infuriating*

difference between adjectives and modifying nouns. Links do not become conventionalized parts of the meaning of the modifiers in noun–noun compounds or in genitive constructions, blocking others from occurring in other combinations. Links in these cases are part of the whole phrase, not of a particular part of it, and they are typically not listed meanings, to use Pustejovsky's terminology. What could be listed – and often is in the case of compounds – is the whole construction.

One of the merits of Pustejovsky's model is that it highlights the existence of semantic elements which are not likely to be memorized. *Easy*, for example, by activating different quale roles would predictably suggest "read" when applied to *textbook*, "accomplish" when applied to *job*, "solve" when applied to *problem*, etc. None of these elements are likely to be stored. However, the above suggests that a clear distinction between nonlistable and potentially listable meanings would improve the model.

Pustejovsky seems to presuppose that meanings of phrases and sentences are compositional, possibly in the belief that no other position would be compatible with an approach the aim of which is to specify an infinite number of possible senses in context. In my experience, in the case of modifier–head constructions in which the modifier is a classifier, the meaning of the phrase is very frequently not compositional. This is a well-established observation in the case of compounds: *blackboard* does not refer to any board that is black; *frogman* does not denote any man that happens to be like a frog. Consider also expressions such as *black hole*, *compact disc*, *right angles*, etc. It is quite obvious that retrieving a link – if that is indeed what we do – does not necessarily amount to retrieving a definition of a modifier–head construction functioning as a referring unit. The source of the definition lies in the character of the referent. Working out the coiner's rationale for combining, say, *dirt* and *road* is one task for the interpreter; working out the *denotatum* of *dirt road* is another task. The accomplishment of the latter is what matters. It is perhaps possible to make Pustejovsky's model perform this two-stepped task. The qualia of *dirt* and *road* would produce the link; the class of referents of *dirt road* would supply this compound with its particular qualia. This would, however, mean allowing for the importance of the function of lexical items and – above all – for the influence of contextual referents on definitions. The above also demonstrates that semantic regularity does not presuppose compositionality, as is often assumed (on this, see also Warren 2001).

4. Referential metonymy

We have so far considered adjective–noun and noun–noun combinations and, in passing, genitive constructions.[10] There is, however, another construction which in my view could be considered to be a type of modifier–head construction, viz. referential metonymy. In these constructions we have not only an implicit link, but also an implicit head, as shown in Table 9.

Table 9. Metonymic patterns.

Implicit head	Implicit link	Explicit modifying noun	Referent
that which	consists of	*silver*	(cutlery)
that which	has	*beauty*	(beautiful lady/thing)
that which	is part of	*eye*	(iris, as in *blue eyes*)
that which	is in/at/on	*pocket*	(money, as in *out of pocket*)
place where ... occurs		*walkabout*	(road, Australian English)
that which	causes	*ecstasy*	(drug)
that which	is caused by	*hand*	(aid/applause)
that which	is/represents	*Ann*	(picture of Ann)[11]

There is not as much empirical evidence that metonymies would adhere to the above pattern as in the case of adjective–noun and noun–noun combinations. (I have at present around 100 randomly collected examples on which I base the above [see also Warren 1992: 64–73].) Nevertheless there are obviously very strong (and exciting) indications that whenever we have to work out the relation between two nouns, there is a common array of role combinations that we tend to choose from, although not all types of modifiers make use of all types of roles. If this is indeed correct, we have revealed the source of a fairly common type of polysemy. However, I bring up referential metonymy not only to strengthen my hypothesis concerning the basic semantic regularity in modifier–head constructions, but also because examples of referential metonymy very clearly demonstrate that we should distinguish between the "raw" semantic structure of modifier–head constructions and their definitions. The nature of the definition ultimately depends on the nature of referents. *Hand* used metonymically, and involving a producing link, need not mean "aid". It can also mean "applause", for example. The semantic structure merely constrains reference.

5. Evaluation

Let us finally examine whether the studies of relational elements in modifier–head constructions can be related to Pustejovsky's model and possibly support it. We find then that compositional and possessive links correspond well to CONSTITUTIVE qualia roles, that causative and purpose relations correspond equally well to the AGENTIVE and the TELIC qualia respectively. Locative relations would be a type of FORMAL qualia, which include according to Pustejovsky (1996: 85–86): (i) orientation, (ii) magnitude, (iii) shape, (iv) dimensionality, (v) colour, (vi) position. See Table 10.

Table 10. Matching links and qualia.

Links	Qualia
compositional and possessive →	CONSTITUTIVE
locative →	FORMAL
causative →	AGENTIVE
purpose →	TELIC

Admittedly, the FORMAL qualia seem poorly represented among the links since only one of the features specified by Pustejovsky is included. It should be remembered, however, that the other features would be involved in many PART–WHOLE combinations: *tall building* "building having great vertical length", *small house* "house having little size", etc. The resemblance relation, however, truly lacks a matching quale. A moment's reflection will establish that this is natural. Resemblance arises because some feature or features of COMPARED – one's intended referent – is reminiscent of some feature or features of COMPARANT – some other named entity: *foothill* "hill positioned like a foot", *frogman* "man having shape and function (i.e. diving) of a frog", *peanut* "nut growing (in pods) like peas", *puppet government* "government being manipulatable like puppets". As we see, resemblance in these constructions presupposes already-named entities which belong to distinct categories. It can therefore only be a relation, not a quale, which is what causes us to refer some entities or phenomena to a single category. (It is possible to make use of the resemblance relation to name something unnamed, in which case we have a nonliteral metaphorical use of a word. That is to say, the COMPARED (the intended referent) is implied and the COMPARANT is mentioned, assuming – but only apparently – the role of a referring item.)

This brings us to the question of whether we are dealing with a set of implicit links or latent qualia roles. Pustejovsky's position ought to be that the qualia give rise to the links: combining *silver* with *spoon* will highlight the FORMAL role of matter in *silver* and the AGENTIVE role of artefact in *spoon*, producing "made of"; combining *tea* and *spoon* will highlight the CONSTITUTIVE role of "liquid" in *tea* and the TELIC role of "for stirring" in *spoon*, giving the link "for stirring"; combining *apple* with *tree* will highlight the AGENTIVE role of "produced by tree" in *apple*, which then naturally links *apple* and *tree*; combining *seal* with *skin* will highlight the CONSTITUTIVE role of *skin*, i.e. part of animate, giving "skin of seal". Whether qualia roles could always be appealed to in this manner is an open question. What latent qualia in *apple* and *cake* are activated to give a locative have relation in *apple cake*, and similarly, in *victory* and *garden* to give "for promoting victory" in *victory garden*, or *frog* and *man* to produce "resembling" in *frogman*?

Assuming that we accept the existence of both default links and qualia, there seem to be the following possible hypotheses as to their relation: (i) links and qualia just happen to coincide, but are in fact quite unrelated; (ii) qualia are basic and give rise to links, which are not listed but completely dependent on qualia to be activated; (iii) qualia give rise to implicit links, but these, being frequently activated, become abstracted as grammatical types of meanings, and also become memorized and no longer necessarily dependent on qualia to be suggested; (iv) qualia and links are distinct because they have distinct functions but have a common conceptual basis.

Of these, I find the last two equally plausible, the second somewhat less plausible and the first implausible for the following reason: in view of the fact that modifier–head constructions pick out a referent – something we conceive of as a unit – just as single nouns do, the links and the qualia ought to reveal what constellations of entities or phenomena we tend to recognize as potentially unit-forming. Those which coincide in time and/or place (i.e. the relations involving composition, possession and location) are natural candidates. In the case of causal relations we seem to recognize that producer and product were once a unit. Consider *moonlight, piano sound*. We here seem to have revealed the cognitive basis for perceiving distinct elements which nevertheless are accepted as units. If this is indeed so, then links in modifier–head constructions, which denote units, and qualia in single nouns, which also denote units, ought to be of the same kind (with the natural exception of resemblance links). The fact that they are strengthens this surmise. It is also natural that we think of entities which are perceived as units for the same reason as forming a category.

Links and qualia are similar in that they become activated when words – in particular nouns – are combined. As we have seen, they are also strikingly similar as to type. Indeed it is remarkable that a deductively constructed model happens to agree so well with the results of empirical studies, the existence of which the constructor of the model was probably quite unaware of. Our conclusion must be that this agreement lends considerable support to the theory of qualia.

It would, however, be a mistake to think of Pustejovsky's model as a "finished product", as he himself points out. Above I have pointed out some weaknesses, e.g. that it seems to be restricted to first-order entities and that the fact that defining features may vary as to degree of salience is ignored. The main omission of the model is, however, that it fails to allow for the influence of contextual referents on word meaning. The fact is that the interpreter does not expect contextual referents invariably to agree with stored meanings and *denotata*.[12] There may be good enough matches, in which case we have non-prototypical senses. It may be possible to include the contextual referent in the conventional *denotatum* and yet other salient class-distinctive features suggest themselves, in which case we have the non-compositional meanings I have repeatedly exemplified above, i.e. *gold fish, glamour girl, beauty spot, black board, compact disc*, etc. It may be impossible to include the contextual referent in the conventional *denotatum*, in which case we have different types of nonliteral meanings. New meanings arise not only when words are combined, but above all when words are matched with referents. As we have seen, non-prototypical meanings, literal non-compositional meanings and most types of nonliteral meanings,[13] i.e. meanings which are truly polysemy-forming and invigorating factors in lexical semantics, are as yet not accounted for in Pustejovsky's model. Nevertheless, since Pustejovsky's model has opened our eyes to a possible basis for the semantic regularity we find in modifier–head constructions, to the distinction between listable and nonlistable polysemy, and to the difference between polysemy which arises when words are combined and the polysemy which arises when words are matched with contextual referents, it may very well turn out to be a substantial push forward within semantics.

Notes

1. I have elsewhere (Warren 1992: 18–20) argued that it is a mistake to think of words mainly as category labels and as invariably deriving from the formation of categories. Not all features of word meaning are criterial, i.e. serve to identify referents. There are also components of meaning, the basis of which is probably not category formation, and which serve to indicate speaker evaluation, which they can do *because* their application is free. Although semanticists acknowledge the difference in terms of denotation and connotation, they nevertheless tend to ignore all but criterial features in forming theories of word meaning. Qualia, too, must be seen as representing criterial features.
2. Although all (content) words have qualia structures in Pustejovsky's system (1996: 76), qualia must, I believe, be seen as primarily connected to first-order entities and only indirectly to second- and third-order entities. (For definitions of first-, second- and third-order entities, see Lyons 1977: 438–452.)
3. They also included negative elements as in *blind* ("not having sight"), *bare* ("having no cover") and quantifying elements as in *hot* ("having much heat"), *brief* ("having little duration"). Negative elements are obviously not part of all adjectives, but if they are, they always are. Positive quantifying elements are often not stable parts of meaning, but can appear or disappear as required by context. Consider: *the wall is tall* (*tall* contains a quantifying element) and *the wall is half a yard tall* (*tall* has no such element).
4. Downing (1977: 810–842) maintains that "the semantic relationships that hold between the members of these compounds (i.e. noun–noun compounds) cannot be characterised by a finite list of 'appropriate compounding relationships' " (p. 810). She makes this claim in spite of the fact that – on her own admission – only a small minority of the compounds she had collected and analysed did not fit any of the established compounding relationships. Her justification for rejecting a finite list is that virtually any relation is possible *in the right context*. This is correct. It is probably possible to think of a context in which *apple tree* could refer to the tree that people have thrown apples at. However, there is a price for rejecting a set of established relations, viz. the counter-intuitive claim that out of context, if encountered for the first time, *apple tree* would not suggest any compounding relationship, at least not any particular one. The introduction of default values saves the day. It allows us to recognize semantic regularity, even if it is not absolute, and to account for the fact that certain implicit meanings suggest themselves naturally, whereas others need contextual support. Personally,

I see default values as the outcome of two tendencies in human language, striving in opposite directions: constraints and rules on the one hand, which facilitate interpretation, and flexibility on the other, which promotes expressiveness.

5. Far from all adjective–noun combinations contain a covert link. For instance, there is no *implicit* predicate in nominalizations such as *national leader* ("somebody who *leads* nations") or *presidential appointees* ("people whom the president appoints"). In some adjectives functioning as adverbials, there is no link at all: *perfect fool* ("somebody who is perfectly foolish") (see Paradis 2000). (Pustejovsky accounts for these by means of selective binding [1996: 127–131].) Also, there are quite a number of adjectives which have conventionalized implied or figurative meanings. *Familiar*, e.g., can no longer mean "consisting of/belonging to/occurring in etc. family".

6. The term was originally coined by Lees (1960: 181).

7. That *bona fide* adjectives are restricted to these links is an intriguing discovery for which I have no good explanation.

8. *Basically* is a necessary qualification in this context, since it is possible to classify by describing (*short story, black coffee, white people*) or by identifying (*writer's cramp, clown's attire*), or identify by describing (*bring me the red box*), etc.

9. *Experiencing* is a type of possessive link which requires that the referential content of the modifier denotes some sensation and that the head denotes an animate. *Manifesting* is dependent on the *experience* link and requires that the referent of the head is thought of as a natural mediator of sensations: *(sad) eyes, (angry) face, (nervous) hands, (happy) smile, (furious) letter, (bitter) comments*. If this restriction is violated, we have what is sometimes referred to as transferred epithets or the Wodehouse effect, e.g. *a sad cigarette, a contemplative lump of sugar.*

   An alternative account of combinations of this kind sometimes suggested is to look upon them as metonymic: *happy face* "the possessor of the face experiences happiness"; *angry letter* "the author of the letter experiences anger".

10. For reasons of space I have refrained from discussing the semantics of genitive constructions. I will be content with the comment that the same type of default relations appear to be involved. Consider *Joan's picture* "picture that Joan owns" (possessive link), "that Joan made" (causal link), "that represents Joan" (compositional link).

11. For Pustejovsky's account of referential metonymy, see Pustejovsky (1996: 90–95).

12. Compare Nerlich and Clarke (2001), who point out that words keep recharging their semantic batteries because there always is and always will be a discrepancy, a fundamental incongruence, between the supply of words and our communicative demands.

13. Compare Kilgarriff (to appear), who also found that Pustejovsky's model failed to account for metaphors.

References

Aarts, Jan and Joseph Calbert
    1979   *Metaphor and Non-metaphor. The Semantics of Adjective–Noun Combinations*. Tübingen: Max Niemeyer Verlag.

Bartning, Inge
    1980   *Remarques sur la syntaxe et la sémantique de pseudo-adjectifs dénominaux en français*. Stockholm: Almqvist and Wiksell International.

Bolinger, Dwight
    1967   Adjectives in English: attribution and predication. *Lingua* 18: 1–34.

Brekle, Herbert E.
    1970   *Generative Satzsemantik und transformationelle Syntax im System der englischen Nominalkomposition*. München: Wilhelm Fink.

Clark, Eve and Herbert Clark
    1979   When nouns surface as verbs. *Language* 55(4): 767–811.

Downing, Pamela
    1977   On the creation and use of English compound nouns. *Language* 53(4): 810–842.

Geeraerts, Dirk
    1997   *Diachronic Prototype Semantics*. Oxford: Clarendon Press.

Kilgarriff, Adam
    (to appear) Generative lexicon meets corpus data: the case of non-standard word uses. Talk presented at the *Utrecht Congress on Storage and Computation in linguistics*, 19–21 October 1998.

Lees, Robert
    1960   *The Grammar of English Nominalizations*. The Hague: Mouton.

Leitzky, Eva
    1989   *(De)nominale Adjektive im heutigen Englisch*. Tübingen: Max Niemeyer Verlag.

Levi, Judith
    1978   *The Syntax and Semantics of Complex Nominals*. New York, San Francisco, London: Academic Press.

Ljung, Magnus
    1970   *English Denominal Adjectives*. Gothenburg Studies in English 21.

Lyons, John
    1977   *Semantics*. Cambridge: Cambridge University Press.

Nerlich, Brigitte and David Clarke
    2001   Ambiguities we live by. Towards a pragmatics of polysemy. *Journal of Pragmatics* 33: 1–20.

Paradis, Carita
    2000   Reinforcing adjectives: a cognitive semantic perspective on gram-

maticalization. In: Ricardo Bermúdez-Otero, David Denison, Richard M. Hogg and Chris B. McCully (eds.), *Generative Theory and Corpus Studies*, 233–258. Berlin, New York: Mouton de Gruyter.

Pustejovsky, James
1996   *The Generative Lexicon.* Cambridge and London: The MIT Press.

Warren, Beatrice
1978   *Semantic Patterns of Noun–Noun Compounds.* Gothenburg Studies in English 41.
1984   *Classifying Adjectives.* Gothenburg Studies in English 56.
1985   Making sense of making senses. In: Sven Bäckman and Göran Kjellmer (eds.), *Papers on Language and Literature,* 372–384. Gothenburg Studies in English 60.
1988   Ambiguity and vagueness in adjectives. *Studia Linguistica* 42(2): 122–172.
1992   *Sense Developments.* Stockholm: Almqvist and Wiksell International.
2001   Accounting for compositionality. In: Karin Aijmer (ed.), *A Wealth of English*, 103–114. Gothenburg Studies in English 81.

Polysemy and bleaching

Jean Aitchison and Diana M. Lewis

1. The problem

Fading meaning is a commonly mentioned type of semantic change, a process known variously as bleaching, desemanticization, weakening, depletion, distortion, even verbicide. The term "bleaching" is perhaps the most common, and may have originated with the German neogrammarian Georg von der Gabelentz, who noted that forms 'grow pale' (*verblassen*) and their colours 'bleach' (*verbleichen*) (Gabelentz 1891: 242). This paper argues that bleaching is more usefully regarded as a type of polysemy, and explores the bleaching/polysemy process.

In the past, many writers have been more concerned to censure bleaching than to study it, perhaps subconsciously echoing a 19th-century viewpoint that semantic change is undesirable:

> This tendency of words to lose the sharp, rigidly defined outline of meaning which they once possessed, to become of wide, vague, loose application instead of fixed, definite, and precise, to mean almost anything, and so really to mean nothing, is ... one of those tendencies, and among the most fatally effectual, which are at work for the final ruin of a language, and, I do not fear to add, for the demoralization of those that speak it (Trench 1856: 192).

According to Trench: "The causes which bring this mischief about are not hard to trace": words which get into general use are caught up "by those who understand imperfectly and thus incorrectly their true value". Consequently, words "become weaker, shallower, more indefinite; till in the end, as exponents of thought and feeling, they cease to be of any service at all" (1856: 193).

This disapproval has continued. In a guide for radio published in Britain in 1981 by the editor of the *Oxford English Dictionary*, for example, broadcasters were advised in a section labelled "Inflation or modishness of diction" to avoid the use of the word *tragedy* in sport by rephrasing (Burchfield 1981). Similarly, the author of a book on the social history of English vocabulary suggests that "Much verbicide seems to be an upper-class affectation" (Hughes 1988: 14).

These writers have apparently not taken into consideration the fact that the old, strong meaning often still exists alongside the newer, "weakened" meaning. We are therefore dealing with an important type of polysemy. From this viewpoint, the changes are not so much weakening as expansion, the development of multiple meanings: "meanings expand their range through the development of various polysemies ... these polysemies may be regarded as quite fine-grained. It is only collectively that they may seem like weakening of meaning" (Hopper and Traugott 1993: 100). Bleaching therefore must be regarded not only as a diachronic process, but also as a synchronic phenomenon, a type of polysemy which needs to be explored more fully.

Serious work on polysemy has recently escalated (e.g. Aitchison 2003; Aitchison and Lewis 1996; Geeraerts 1993; Geeraerts, Grondalaers and Bakema 1994; Gibbs 1994; Nerlich and Clarke 1997; Pustejovsky 1995; Pustejovsky and Boguraev 1996; Taylor 1995; Tuggy 1993), yet the facets investigated so far have been limited. In particular, the relationship between diachrony and synchrony has been sparsely explored, though with some notable exceptions (e.g. Sweetser 1988, 1990).

Bleaching is the semantic side of "grammaticalization" or "grammaticization", a term coined by Antoine Meillet, who defined it as "the attribution of a grammatical character to a previously autonomous word" (Meillet 1948: 131). In cases of "full" grammaticalization, words are demoted both semantically and syntactically (e.g. Bybee, Perkins and Pagliuca 1994; Heine, Claudi and Hünnemeyer 1991; Hopper and Traugott 1993; Traugott and Heine 1991). Typical examples are the English modals *can* and *will*, which were once main verbs meaning 'know' and 'want'. Full grammaticalization, then, is the final stage of a much wider phenomenon, which may affect a lexical item only partially, as when the meaning alone of a word is involved. The independence of semantic and syntactic aspects of grammaticalization has been pointed out by several linguists (e.g. Fischer 1997; Lightfoot 1979; Scott 1996).

Relatively little is known about the detailed stages of bleaching. Sweetser (1988, 1990) concentrated more on the overall direction of semantic change: she was particularly concerned with the move of modals from a root sense to an epistemic sense, for example. This paper therefore attempts to shed light on the "nitty-gritty" of the bleaching process.

2. Disaster nouns

Certain types of words are known to bleach/become polysemous fast, notably words relating to dire events, such as *catastrophe, disaster, tragedy*: *What a disaster! My new hat got wet*; pejorative adjectives, such as *awful, bad, dreadful, terrible*: *It was a terrible evening – Dulcie wouldn't stop talking*; and "violent" verbs such as *devastate, murder*: *I could murder a sandwich*.

English contains a number of nouns for a disastrous event: *calamity, catastrophe, disaster, tragedy*. Dictionaries mostly agree that these words describe serious misfortunes as their primary meaning, and provide overlapping definitions for them, as in the *The New Oxford Dictionary of English* (Oxford University Press 1998):

> **calamity**, *noun*, an event causing great and often sudden damage or distress; a disaster.
> **catastrophe**, *noun*, an event causing great and often sudden damage or suffering; a disaster.
> **disaster**, *noun*, a sudden event such as an accident or a natural catastrophe that causes great damage or loss of life ...
> **tragedy**, *noun*, an event causing great suffering, destruction, and distress, such as a serious accident, crime or natural catastrophe.

Of these words, only the entry for *disaster* includes the information that it may be used in less dire circumstances: "an event or fact that has unfortunate consequences ... *informal*, a person, act or thing that is a failure".

Yet investigation of the *British National Corpus* (*BNC*), a database which includes both spoken and written language, suggests that informal, humorous or figurative uses of all these words are extensive, alongside their more serious, older meanings. (The *BNC* contains approximately 100 million "w-units", roughly, lexical items, of which approximately 90 million are written, and around 10 million spoken.) Examples of (a) serious, and (b) trivial usages are given below:

(1)   a.   *This will make it much less likely that the entire human race will be wiped out by a* calamity *such as a nuclear war.*
       b.   *But what if ... you're out on the floor at some gay club, and you spot or (*calamity*) are spotted by some workmates ... what then?*

(2)   a.   *A large comet hitting the earth would mean* catastrophe.
       b.   *To fall in love with Alexander would be a* catastrophe.

(3)   a.   ... *the Hillsborough football* disaster *which killed 95 people.*

      b.   *To get a panama hat wet is to court* disaster. *The hat becomes limp and shapeless.*

(4)   a.   *259 passengers and crew ... were killed by a bomb. This was Britain's worst air* tragedy.

      b.   *The great* tragedy *of modern music is that ... the results are less and less significant from a human point of view.*

Of these similar-meaning words, *disaster* is by far the most frequent in the *BNC* (Table 1). It can therefore be regarded as the "prime" disaster word in English at the current time, and likely to shed useful light on the polysemy process.

Table 1.   Disaster nouns: frequency per million w-units.

	BNC Spoken	BNC Written
Calamity	0.6	1.5
Catastrophe	1.1	5.0
Disaster	22.3	32.1
Tragedy	6.3	19.3

As noted above, the dictionary entry labels non-serious uses of *disaster* as "informal", but does not give any indication of the relative quantities of the formal and informal usages, nor does it further characterize the informal ones. The polysemy question is therefore investigated in this paper by considering:

(i)   The scale of the disaster: what is the proportion of serious "real" disasters, to trivial inconveniences?

(ii)   The interpretation problem: how do speakers/hearers distinguish between the various meanings of the word?

(iii)   The development of polysemy: to what extent can this process be successfully characterized?

3. Scale of disaster

Disaster is widely used in both spoken and written language: the *BNC* contains over 3,000 examples. Of these, all the spoken ones were analysed for this paper, as well as 600 randomly selected written ones. Removal of unclear occurrences left 185 spoken and 589 written examples.

The proportion of "real" disasters to trivial inconveniences was assessed by dividing the *BNC* examples of *disaster* into serious (S), medium (M) and trivial (T) events. As a rough rule of thumb, an event which caused multiple deaths was classed as (S); one which involved one or two deaths, inflicted severe suffering on a small number of people, or caused environmental damage was listed as (M); one which caused social inconvenience was classed as (T). For example:

(5)   *At least 62 people were killed and 3,000 missing last night after an underwater earthquake sent 50 ft tidal waves crashing into the coast of Nicaragua. More than 227 people were injured in the* disaster. (S)
(6)   *But if all 22 million gallons escape, the* disaster *will be twice as bad as the 1988* Exxon Valdez *spill off Alaska.* (M)
(7)   *All other efforts to lose the fat from the offending areas proved to be a* disaster. *If I lost weight below 54 kg my bust disappeared, yet nothing went from my legs or posterior!* (T)

Table 2 shows how instances of *disaster* fell into the (S), (M) and (T) categories.

Table 2.   Disaster categories.

	Serious	Medium	Trivial
Spoken n=185	92 (50%)	27 (14%)	66 (36%)
Written n=589	255 (43%)	122 (21%)	212 (36%)

Superficially, Table 2 suggests that serious disasters outnumber trivial ones in both the spoken and written corpus. But these figures partly flatten out the data, in that an imbalance occurred between singulars and plurals: the singular examples tended to be more trivial than the plural ones, especially in the spoken corpus, where the ratio of trivial to serious disasters was 1.2:1

in the singular, but only 0.1:1 in the plural. This imbalance was less noticeable in the written corpus, where the ratio of trivial to serious disasters was 1:1 in the singular, and 0.4:1 in the plural.

Categorization into (S), (M) and (T) was a useful step, but proved to be oversimple: the (S), (M), (T) categorizations sometimes overlapped, in that the same event could seriously affect a huge number of people in one area, by definition (S), yet only a single person in some other area, by definition (M). We therefore subdivided the disasters into types which partly cut across the (S), (M), (T) categories.

The largest single group involved wars or serious accidents, which killed a large number of people. These were categorized as (S), as in (3a) and (5). Environmental disasters were mostly classed as (M), as in (6).

Social, political and economic disasters were split between the (M) and (T) classifications:

(8)   *If the tests prove positive, the flock is slaughtered: "For many farmers it spells financial* disaster ..." *the association's chairman said.* (M)

(9)   *The Tories were heading for* disaster *if they continued to delude themselves that only a little fine tuning of presentation was required to secure a fourth consecutive general election victory.* (T)

A subdivision of economic disasters involved the technical phrase "disaster recovery", a growth industry whose practitioners solve computer problems after a system breakdown. These were classed as (M):

(10)   *Comprehensive, tried and tested* disaster *recovery procedures can make the difference between getting vital computer systems up and running again within hours or days, and going out of business.*

Personal disasters were (M) when one or few people died or were injured:

(11)   *Then* disaster *struck. The first two men to exit from the following party were killed when their parachutes failed to open.*

But the majority of personal disasters were quite trivial (T), covering household inconveniences, sports losses, or minor social difficulties, as in (3b) and (7), and also (12), (13) and (14):

(12)   *The only reason I'm running up these debts is that now I've got so little capital left, that I've got to keep the capital for sheer* disasters *like the boiler.*

(13)   *The last wicket fell ... So it was another blackwash, another* disaster *for England.*

(14)   *There have been many* disasters *along the road, Yorkshire puddings you could sole your shoes with ... and last Christmas a chocolate log that disintegrated, the proud little Santa on top sinking without trace in a sea of chocolate gunge.*

The breakdown into the various categories is shown in Table 3.

Table 3.   Disaster by (S), (M), (T) and by type.

	Serious	Medium	Trivial	Total
War/Accident	342	4		346 (45%)
Environmental	3	28		31 (4%)
Soc/Pol/Econ	2	55	84	141 (18%)
Personal		62	194	256 (33%)
Total	347 (45%)	149 (19%)	278 (36%)	774

4.   Interpretation problem

How, then, do speakers use these words appropriately, and how do hearers interpret them in the way intended? Broadly speaking, the surrounding context clarified the level of disaster. Partly, this was explicitly specified, and partly, covert conventions operated, which are implicitly understood by English speakers.

The naming of a geographical location was the major clue that a serious incident involving multiple deaths had taken place, sometimes (though not necessarily) accompanied by further explanation of the type of disaster, as in: *the Bradford football disaster, the 1986 Chernobyl nuclear disaster, the Clapham disaster, the Clapham rail disaster, the Hillsborough disaster, the Hillsborough football crowd disaster, the Kegworth air disaster, the Lockerbie disaster, the Siberian pipeline disaster, the Stalingrad disaster, the Zeebrugge ferry disaster.*

For lesser events, the type of problem was often appended, as: *ecological disaster, economic disaster, electrical disaster, environmental disaster, financial disaster, the Great Onion disaster, industrial disaster, the poll tax disaster, political disaster.*

For trivial incidents, the cause of the problem tended to be specified, as in:

(15)   *The gravy's a* disaster. *It's got too much fat in it.*

(16)   *Newspapers love a good* disaster, *and a wedding where the bridegroom's trousers fell down at the altar would stand a far better chance of being reported than one that went without a hitch.*

Amidst this plethora of trivia, several topics recurred, especially cookery, as in (14), (15) and (17):

(17)   *My own efforts at making custard ... may have been forgotten by those who subsequently had to eat the awful stuff, but I am not likely to forget the watery culinary* disaster.

Sports losses were another common trivial disaster, as in (13), (18) and (19):

(18)   *His spell in Italian football was a* disaster *and he eagerly accepted the chance to join Manchester United for a record fee.*

(19)   *X must get through to him in the first six rounds or face* disaster.

The topics of food or sport therefore flagged that the disaster was a trivial event. The origin of food *disasters* is unclear, though use of *disaster* in sport has been attributed to Rudyard Kipling's *If*. One sports report explained this:

(20)   *Behind many a football club dressing room door, you'll find a copy of Rudyard Kipling's If pinned up, the poem that talks of "meeting triumph and* disaster *and treating those two imposters just the same".*

Nevertheless, it would be unwise to place too much emphasis on this, as other disaster words are also used to describe sport, presumably because of the difficulty of providing sparkling copy for events that are fundamentally repetitive:

(21)   *In a history of* disasters *stretching across 30 years, Scotland has been plagued by* calamity, *lapses in concentration and self-induced* tragedy. *The goalkeeper is always to blame and always will be.*

Food problems, however, were normally restricted to the word *disaster*, perhaps on the grounds that a food *tragedy* or *calamity* might be misunderstood as a case of food poisoning.

Collocational clues also helped to signal whether an event was a genuine disaster or a social hiccup. In particular, intensifiers often diminished the seriousness of the disaster: an *absolute disaster* mostly indicated a fairly trivial event, and so did a *total disaster*.

(22)   *The next morning was an* absolute disaster. *Loretta's hopes of a conciliatory chat with Bridget over breakfast were dashed.*

(23)   *England must pull itself together if a bitterly disappointing tour is not to become a* total disaster.

Similarly, *disaster strikes* and *disaster struck* often related to a trivial event:

(24)   *Even if* disaster strikes, *as it seemed to for one student of mine who dropped her nearly completed head on the concrete floor and an ear snapped off* [the wooden rocking horse she was carving], *don't let it worry you unduly. We simply glued the broken ear back in place.*

(25)   Disaster struck *again for the home side after 57 minutes.*

5.   The development of polysemy

A prerequisite for the development of polysemy may be that the word must be widely used. At first sight, this is a puzzle for *disaster*, in that serious disasters are relatively rare. Yet the word *disaster* was frequently used, primarily because many disasters discussed were potential, rather than actual. Only a proportion (about half) had happened, and the remainder were impending, avoided, or hypothetical, as in:

(26)   *The research station's scientists comment privately that only a big fire* disaster *will make the government look harder at fire research.*

(27)   *A second jet* disaster *was narrowly averted in Bogota on Thursday.*
(28)   *When you rescue the old Christmas tree lights from the loft for the umpteenth time, remember that they could be the cause of an electrical* disaster.

The potential, rather than actual, nature of many disasters is shown by the linguistic expressions used with them, as in: *avert, avoid, court, expect, face, foretell, head for, head off, predict, prevent, save from, warn of; imminent, impending, near, potential, brink of, chance of, doomed to, expectation of, fear of, recipe for; can be, could be, could have been, would be, would have been.*

The main characteristic of these hypothetical expressions was their diversity: in the written corpus, only *can, could* + verb, as in (28), and *will, would* + verb, as in (26), occurred more than ten times. The hypothetical nature of so many disasters, then, promotes bleaching, in that the word is used often in cases where no serious event has in fact occurred. Once a word is widely used in this way, bleaching/polysemy will escalate.

The word *disaster* therefore provides a blueprint for the birth of polysemy, and the characteristics noted here are likely to be found elsewhere.

First, words bleach at different rates in spoken speech and written language: spoken speech provides more bleached examples, as with *disaster*, and is normally ahead in the polysemy process.

Second, bleaching moves through a lexical item unevenly, in that different forms of the same word do not necessarily run parallel. *Disaster* (singular) was more bleached than *disaster* (plural).

Third, bleaching typically begins in particular topic areas. In the case of *disaster*, bleaching is especially frequent in sport (in common with other disaster words), and also in cookery (a feature of the word *disaster*, but not *tragedy*).

Fourth, collocation is an important factor: certain combinations tend to distinguish an event as serious or trivial. With disasters, an intensifier, as in *absolute disaster*, is likely to signify a non-serious event, though each disaster word has its own preferred intensifiers: an ?*absolute tragedy* or an ?*absolute calamity* is not impossible, it is just less idiomatic. Such "freezes" (i.e. frozen collocations) may provide the basis for a novel lexical item.

At first, "the persistence of older forms and meanings alongside newer forms and meanings ... leads to an effect that can be called 'layering' or 'variability' at any one synchronic moment in time" (Hopper and Traugott

1993: 123–124). But eventually, layering leads to full-blown polysemy, the splitting of an original lexical item into more than one. This decision is typically made by lexicographers. In the case of *disaster*, at least one dictionary (*NODE*) has opined that the phrase *disaster area* should be a headword, with its own independent lexical entry, away from its "mother" *disaster*:

> **disaster area**, *noun*, an area in which a major disaster has recently occurred: *the vicinity of the explosion was declared a disaster area. n* [in sing] *informal*, a place, situation, person or activity regarded as chaotic, ineffectual, or failing in some fundamental respect: *the room was a disaster area, stuff piled every-where | she was a disaster area in fake leopard skin and stacked heels.*

6. Conclusion

This paper has pointed out that words signifying catastrophic events are subject to bleaching, and consequently, the development of polysemy. It has provided a case study of the word *disaster*, noting that polysemy develops from layering, simultaneous different usages of the same word. Speech and writing, different forms of the same lexeme, different topic areas, and habitual collocations were explored and compared. These enabled the sources of the bleaching of *disaster* to be narrowed down and partially pinpointed. Only a fine-grained approach of this type can lead to a full understanding of the process of polysemy.

References

Aitchison, Jean
  2003   *Words in the Mind: An Introduction to the Mental Lexicon.* 3rd
              Edition. Oxford: Blackwell.
Aitchison, Jean and Diana M. Lewis
  1996   The mental word web: forging the links. In: Jan Svartvik (ed.), *Words*,
              39–47. Stockholm: Swedish Academy.
Burchfield, Robert
  1981   *The Spoken Word: A BBC Guide.* London: British Broadcasting
              Corporation.
Bybee, Joan L., Revere D. Perkins and William Pagliuca
  1994   *The Evolution of Grammar: Tense, Aspect and Modality in the
              Languages of the World.* Chicago: University of Chicago Press.

Fischer, Olga
    1997   On the status of grammaticalisation and the diachronic dimension in explanation. *Transactions of the Philological Society* 95(2): 149–187.
Gabelentz, Georg von der
    1891   *Die Sprachwissenschaft. Ihre Aufgaben, Methoden und bisherigen Ergebnisse.* Leipzig: Weigel.
Geeraerts, Dirk
    1993   Vagueness's puzzles, polysemy's vagaries. *Cognitive Linguistics* 4(3): 223–272.
Geeraerts, Dirk, Stefan Grondalaers and Peter Bakema
    1994   *The Structure of Lexical Variation: Meaning, Naming and Context.* Berlin: Mouton de Gruyter.
Gibbs, Raymond W.
    1994   *The Poetics of Mind: Figurative Thought, Language, and Understanding.* Cambridge: Cambridge University Press.
Heine, Bernd, Ulrike Claudi and Friederike Hünnemeyer
    1991   *Grammaticalization: A Conceptual Framework.* Chicago: University of Chicago Press.
Hopper, Paul J. and Elizabeth Closs Traugott
    1993   *Grammaticalization.* Cambridge: Cambridge University Press.
Hughes, Geoffrey
    1988   *Words in Time: A Social History of the English Vocabulary.* Oxford: Blackwell.
Lightfoot, David
    1979   *Principles of Diachronic Syntax.* Cambridge: Cambridge University Press.
Meillet, Antoine
    1912 [1948] *Linguistique historique et linguistique générale.* Paris: Champion.
Nerlich, Brigitte and David D. Clarke
    1997   Polysemy: patterns in meaning and patterns in history. *Historiographia Linguistica* 24(3): 359–385.
Pustejovsky, James
    1995   *The Generative Lexicon.* Cambridge, MA: MIT Press.
Pustejovsky, James and Bran Boguraev (eds.)
    1996   *Lexical Semantics: The Problem of Polysemy.* Oxford: Clarendon.
Scott, Biljana
    1996   Aspectogenesis and the categorisation of directionals in Chinese. D.Phil. dissertation, University of Oxford.
Sweetser, Eve E.
    1988   Grammaticalization and semantic bleaching. *Proceedings of the 14th Annual Meeting, Berkeley Linguistics Society*: 389–404.
    1990   *From Etymology to Pragmatics: Metaphorical and Cultural Aspects of Semantic Structure.* Cambridge: Cambridge University Press.

Taylor, John R.
1995   *Linguistic Categorization: Prototypes in Linguistics.* 2nd Edition. Oxford: Clarendon.
Traugott, Elizabeth Closs and Bernd Heine (eds.)
1991   *Approaches to Grammaticalization.* Volumes 1 and 2. Amsterdam: John Benjamins,
Trench, Richard Chenevix
1856   *English, Past and Present.* 3rd Edition. London: John Parker and Son.
Tuggy, David
1993   Ambiguity, polysemy, and vagueness. *Cognitive Linguistics* 4(3): 273–290.

Polysemy in the lexicon and in discourse

Andreas Blank

1. Introduction

A fundamental problem lexicologists – and indeed all speakers – have to face is the fact that the number of words we know is limited but that human imagination is virtually unlimited (Schlieben-Lange 1997: 242), and that the number of things, beings, processes and ideas that can be referred to is endless. There are two main strategies which allow us to cope with this discrepancy: first, we match the concrete referent with a lexicalized meaning of a word and actualize this meaning in the concrete context; second, if the first strategy cannot be applied or risks failure because there is no lexicalized meaning to cover the actual referent, we must create a lexical innovation, e.g. a semantic innovation, a new word-formation, a new idiom, or we must introduce a loan word (see Blank 2001a).

In the first case, the contextual meaning is located inside the range of an existing semantic invariant: a learned semantic rule is applied to a given context. In this paper I will try to define the criteria for this type of contextual variation (or "vagueness") and to distinguish it from different senses of one word, i.e. polysemy, and from different words having an identical signifier, i.e. homonymy (see Section 3). When we decide to use a word but transgress the traditional range of its semantic invariants, we create a semantic innovation. If this innovation is successful, it becomes, in turn, lexicalized as a new invariant of the word in question. The types of polysemy resulting from this diachronic process and the possible semantic relations linking them in synchrony will be discussed in Section 2. Finally, Section 4 deals with very regular types of polysemy which cannot be satisfactorily explained on the basis of more traditional theories of polysemy. This will lead us to a new view of polysemy as a complex multi-level phenomenon right at the crossroads where cognition, discourse, discourse rules and idiosyncratic lexicalization meet.

2. The synchrony of semantic change: types of polysemy

The term "polysemy" first appears in 1897 in Michel Bréal's fundamental *Essai de sémantique*:

> Le sens nouveau, quel qu'il soit, ne met pas fin à l'ancien. Ils existent tous les deux l'un à côté de l'autre. Le même terme peut s'employer tour à tour au sens propre ou au sens métaphorique, au sens restreint ou au sens étendu, au sens abstrait ou au sens concret ... A mesure qu'une signification nouvelle est donné au mot, il a l'air de se multiplier et de produire des exemplaires nouveaux, semblables de forme, mais différents de valeur. Nous appelons ce phénomène de multiplication la *polysémie*. (Bréal 1897: 154–155)

It is important to note that according to Bréal polysemy arises as a consequence of semantic change; it is the "synchronic side" of lexical semantic change. Bréal distinguishes various kinds of polysemy, using the types of semantic relation between the old sense and the new one as criteria (see also Fritz 1998: 57–58). Usually, these issues are not given the importance they merit (see, however, Sweetser 1990, but only with regard to metaphor) and most handbooks still define polysemy as being based on the existence of a semantic relation between lexicalized senses of a word without further explanation of the nature of this relation.[1]

To understand the diachronic background of lexical polysemy and how a semantic innovation can be related to a lexicalized sense, we need, first of all, a typology of semantic change. Such a typology, which is entirely based on associations between concepts, or concepts and linguistic signs, was suggested in Blank (1997) and is displayed in the left column of Table 1. This typology serves as a basis for a detailed description of types of polysemy based on associative relations in synchrony, presented in the right column of Table 1.

As one can see, there is no complete isomorphism between diachronic processes and synchronic states. Let us now briefly discuss the associative backgrounds of the types of semantic change and of their synchronic counterparts.

The best-known type of polysemy is metaphoric polysemy which derives in most cases from metaphor as a diachronic process. Both are based on a more or less salient similarity between two concepts that belong to different or even distant conceptual domains.

Similarity inside one and the same conceptual domain or folk-taxonomy

is the basis of co-hyponymous transfer, giving rise to co-hyponymous polysemy. These transfers probably occur because the speaker's knowledge of
the referential limits of the concepts involved is temporarily or permanently
blurred. This type of polysemy is limited to the same dialect or register. It is
quite unstable and tends to fade away.[2]

Types 3 and 4 are also based on similarity of concepts within the same
domain, as in most cases one of the two concepts involved in the semantic
change was conceived as a prototypical instance of the whole category and
therefore as a cognitive reference-point. In synchrony, however, we tend to
focus on the concomitant taxonomic relation between the two senses, one
being the hyperonym of the other. In this case, the associative relation
underlying the semantic change shifts to the background, while the taxonomic
inclusion of referential classes becomes dominant.[3]

Type 5, lexical ellipsis – or better, absorption – has two subtypes, depending
on which part of a given complex word *absorbs* the sense of this complex
word. Synchronically, however, absorption is identical either with the result
of semantic restriction, i.e. taxonomic polysemy, or with the synchronic effect
of metonymy. Thus, absorption as a diachronic process has no proper synchronic counterpart.

This leads us to metonymy (including meronymy) and to its analogous
synchronic counterpart. Both are based on conceptual contiguity, i.e. the
typical and salient co-occurrence or succession of elements in frames or
scenarios or of these frames themselves.[4] The same synchronic result is
produced by semantic change through popular etymology (with very few
exceptions). Diachronically, however, popular etymology necessarily combines conceptual contiguity with formal similarity.

Type 8 deals with the reciprocal connection of participants in a frame,
such as the HOST and the GUEST in the frame "RECEIVING GUESTS". When such
a converse relation develops within the same word, we call this auto-converse
change leading to auto-converse polysemy. Although this can be seen as a
classical instance of opposition (see Aristotle, *Categories* 10), this is rather a
special case of contiguity which one could also list under metonymy.

Opposite senses within one word develop in Types 9 and 10, too. Here,
however, the underlying association is *contrast*, either on the connotational
level (antiphrasis) or on the core content level, producing a kind of inner
antonymy. Both cases rarely become conventionalized and polysemy is often
"asymmetric" as it usually does not function in the same register.

An analogous type of semantic change is the imitation of an already

Table 1.

Types of lexical semantic change	Synchronic relation when conventionalized
1. Metaphor	**A. Metaphoric polysemy**
E *mouse* 'small rodent' > 'computer device'	E *mouse* 'small rodent', 'computer device'
It *afferrare* 'to grasp' > 'to understand'	It *afferrare* 'to grasp', 'to understand'
L *brevis* 'short' (spatial) > 'short' (temporal)	L *brevis* 'short' (spatial), 'short' (temporal)
2. Co-hyponymous transfer	**B. Co-hyponymous polysemy**
?*ratt-* 'rat' > F (reg.), It (reg.) 'mouse'	F (reg.) *rat*, It (reg.) *rat*, *ratta*, *ratto* 'rat', 'mouse'
Pt *aborrecer* 'to annoy s.o.' > 'to bore s.o.'	Pt *aborrecer* 'to annoy s.o.', 'to bore s.o.'
3. Semantic extension	**C. Taxonomic polysemy**[5]
MF *pigeon* 'pigeon raised for eating' > 'any kind of pigeon'	F *pigeon* 'pigeon raised for eating', 'any kind of pigeon'
Sp *tener* 'to hold' > 'to have'	Sp *tener* 'to hold', 'to have'
4. Semantic restriction	F *homme*, It *uomo*, Sp *hombre* etc. 'human being', 'man'
VulgL *homo* 'human being' > 'man'	F *blé* 'corn', 'wheat'
F *blé* 'corn' > 'wheat'	
5. Lexical ellipsis (absorption)	**D. Metonymic polysemy**
a) absorption into the *determinatum*	F *diligence* 'velocity', 'stage-coach'
Sp *coche* 'coach' > 'car' (< *coche automóvil*)	G *(der) Weizen* 'wheat', *(das) Weizen* 'beer made of wheat'
G *Schirm* 'shelter' > 'umbrella' (< *Regenschirm*)	
b) absorption into the *determinans*	
F *diligence* 'velocity' > 'stage-coach' (< *carose de diligence*)	
G *Weizen* 'wheat' > 'beer made of wheat' (< *Weizenbier*)	

6. Metonymy

L *lingua* 'tongue' > 'language'
L *defendere* 'to defend' > F *défendre* 'to forbid'
G *während* 'while' (temp.) > 'whereas' (advers.)

7. Popular etymology

F *forain* 'non-resident' > 'belonging to the fair' (< *foire*)
Lat *somnium* 'dream' > Sp *sueño* 'sleep' (< *somnus*)

8. auto-converse change

It *noleggiare* 'to lend' > 'to borrow'
L *hospes* 'host' > 'guest'

9. Antiphrasis

F *villa* 'country house' > F (argot) 'prison'
It *brava donna* 'honourable lady' > It (gergo) 'prostitute'

10. Auto-antonymy

E *bad* 'not good' > E (slang) 'excellent'
Sard *masetu* 'gentle' > 'irascible'

11. Analogous semantic change

F *polir* 'to polish', 'to steal', *fourbir* 'to polish' >
'to steal', *nettoyer* 'to clean' > 'to steal' etc.

L *levare* 'to lift up', 'to erect', Sp *alzar*, It *alzare*
'to lift up' > 'to erect'

L *lingua* 'tongue', 'language'
F *défendre* 'to defend', 'to forbid'
G *während* 'while' (temp.), 'whereas' (advers.)

E. auto-converse polysemy

It *noleggiare* 'to lend', 'to borrow'
F *hôte*, It *ospite*, Cat *hoste*, Occ *oste* 'host', 'guest'

F. Antiphrastic polysemy

F *villa* 'country house', F (argot) 'prison'
It *brava donna* 'honourable lady', It (gergo) 'prostitute'

G. Auto-antonymic polysemy

E *bad* 'not good', (slang) 'excellent'
Sard *masetu* 'gentle', 'irascible'

all relations possible, e.g.:

metaphoric polysemy

F *fourbir* 'to polish', 'to steal'

metonymic polysemy

Sp *alzar*, It *alzare* 'to lift up', 'to erect'

existing polysemy, be it metaphoric, taxonomic or metonymic, by another word, whose older sense is synonymous (or more rarely co-hyponymous or antonymic) with the word that serves as a model: thus, during the history of Romance languages, *?altiare* developed almost the same bundle of senses as *levare*, both being synonymous from the beginning (see Klein 1997: 134–137). As will be shown in Section 4, analogy may play an important role in cases of polysemy that cannot really be regarded as consequences of semantic change.

Types A–G in the right column of Table 1 represent synchronic relations between two senses of a word. The labels "metaphoric polysemy" etc. are therefore somewhat imprecise, as they do not describe the whole polysemy of a word. It is obvious that each of a pair of two related senses can establish semantic links to other senses of the word in question. When we say that a word is polysemous, this does not mean that all senses of a word are inter-related or have "something in common". Polysemy should rather be conceived as a chain or a network of senses. An application to lexicography leads inevitably to complex representations, but allows a precise characterization of the relations between the senses of one word, as shown in Figure 1 with E *man* and in Figure 2 with F *parler*:[6]

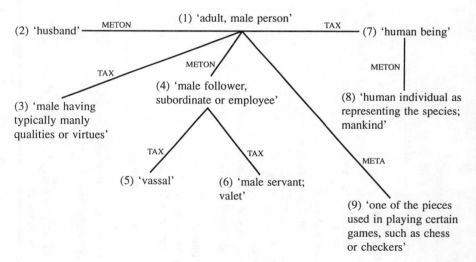

Figure 1. E *man* n.

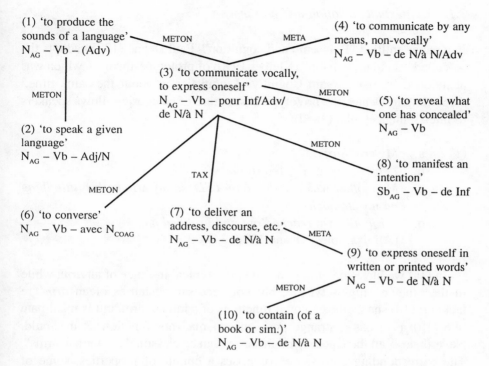

(1) 'to produce the sounds of a language' N_{AG} – Vb – (Adv)

METON

META

(4) 'to communicate by any means, non-vocally' N_{AG} – Vb – de N/à N/Adv

(3) 'to communicate vocally, to express oneself' N_{AG} – Vb – pour Inf/Adv/ de N/à N

METON

(5) 'to reveal what one has concealed' N_{AG} – Vb

METON

(2) 'to speak a given language' N_{AG} – Vb – Adj/N

(8) 'to manifest an intention' Sb_{AG} – Vb – de Inf

TAX

METON

(6) 'to converse' N_{AG} – Vb – avec N_{COAG}

(7) 'to deliver an address, discourse, etc.' N_{AG} – Vb – de N/à N

META

(9) 'to express oneself in written or printed words' N_{AG} – Vb – de N/à N

METON

(10) 'to contain (of a book or sim.)' N_{AG} – Vb – de N/à N

Figure 2. F *parler* vb.

3. Contextual variation – polysemy – homonymy

Polysemy as a concept of semantic description is distinct from but related to "contextual variation" (also called "vagueness") and "homonymy" (also known as "ambiguity"). Generally, it is difficult, if not indeed impossible, to make a clear-cut distinction between these three phenomena (see Geeraerts 1993: 263). Indeed, in real-life situations, words only occur in concrete utterances and not in their more abstract and somewhat idealized dictionary definition. Thus, one has to determine where contextual variation of one sense ends and where the semantic range of another sense starts – this is the distinction between vagueness and polysemy – and one also has to find ways of distinguishing polysemous words, whose senses are by definition related, from homonyms, i.e. two lexemes which are not semantically related.

3.1. *Contextual variation and polysemy*

In a paper entitled "Polysemy and cognition", Paul Deane (1988) adopts the so-called "standard version" (Kleiber 1990) of prototype-theory – which was abandoned by mainstream Cognitive Linguistics at about the same time.[7] According to Deane, the prototypical structure of categories allows speakers to utter sentences like (1a–d):

(1)   a.   *My* arm *hurts.*
      b.   *Look at the* arm *of the statue.*
      c.   *My mother was overdosed on LSD, so my* arm *is this little thing on my stomach.*
      d.   *A robotic* arm *reached out and grabbed me.*
           (All examples: Deane 1988: 347)

   In (1a) we have something like the prototypical instance of an *arm*, while in the other examples typical, but not necessary, features of an *arm* are lacking: (1d) shares the essential functions of a human arm, but is inanimate like (1b); (1c) has a strange position and may not function as it should. Nevertheless, all three peripheral instances can be classified as "human arms". The corresponding core sense comprises a bundle of properties, some of which can be suppressed and produce the variation found in (1). Deane calls this phenomenon "allosemy" and distinguishes this "non-distinct variation in the meaning of a word" (1988: 345) from polysemy by using a number of tests (for more details, see Deane 1988: 347–350).

   Other cases of what one could call "allosemy" or "contextual variation" are:

(2)   a.   *John washed the* car.
      b.   *The mechanic lubricated the* car.
           (Both examples: Cruse 1995: 33)

   There is, indeed, a kind of PART–WHOLE relation between (2a) and (2b), or rather between a general conception of a *car* and (2a) and (2b). On the other hand, there are no proper senses of E *car* corresponding to the exact readings in (2). They are, according to Cruse, "not even clearly conceptualizable" (1995: 33). In these cases the context allows us to focus on the relevant part or sub-domain of a complex concept.

In my view, it is important to make a clear distinction between the referential or extensional level and the level of semantic description: from a referential point of view, "vagueness" can only mean that a given referent is classified as a peripheral instance of a category, but still as a member of this category. If we want to deal with vagueness, or rather "contextual variation", semantically, it can only mean that in a given utterance the contextual meaning of a word is recognized as an actualization of a lexicalized sense of this word, although not all defining features are applicable to this context, e.g. [animate] or [human] to examples (1b) and (1d). This rather subjective intuition can be put to the test of *intersubjective relevance*: if two contextual meanings show a clear semantic overlap, e.g. the *arms* in (1), but nevertheless cannot be related properly by one of the seven semantic relations A–G, as defined in Section 2, then we are dealing with contextual variation of one sense.

If, on the other hand, two referents have to be considered as instances of two different extensional classes, we are beyond the limits of referential vagueness. If these two contextual meanings are instances of two lexicalized senses which are related by one of the seven synchronic semantic relations stated above, then we are dealing with polysemy, as in (3):

(3)   a.   *The* arm *of a coat.*
       b.   *The* arm *of a record player.*
       c.   *An* arm *of the sea.*
             (All examples: *WEUD*, s.v. "arm1")

The *arm* in (3a) is an instance of a CONTAINER–CONTENT metonymy; (3b) and (3c) are different types of metaphors, (3b) clearly sharing formal aspects with the human arm, (3c) being a kind of "landscape extremity". In contrast to (1), none of these referents is directly connected to the upper part of the human body or of a body built according to the human model: they are not arms but can be conceptualized as such.[8] If we adopt this point of view, it is clear that different extensional classes correspond to different concepts and senses which can all be related to one signifier. Metaphors, metonymies etc. do not extend an extensional or conceptual category, but relate a new extensional category and its concept to a given word.[9] If this metaphor or metonymy remains a singular contextual effect, i.e. an innovation, nothing happens, but if it is picked up by other speakers and eventually becomes conventionalized, a new sense is created within the lexical range of one word.

3.2.   *Polysemy and homonymy*

Using both the referential and the semantic criteria we can now distinguish polysemy from homonymy. Consider (4):

(4)   a.   *The* arm *on that statue looks better than yours.* (Deane 1988: 347)
       b.   *A special* arm *of the government is to investigate the matter.* (*WEUD*, s.v. "arm2")
       c.   *His religious convictions kept him from bearing* arms, *but he served as an ambulance driver with the Red Cross.* (*WEUD*, s.v. "arm2")
       d.   *Three lions passant gardant ... the Royal* Arms *of England.* (Porny, *Heraldry* [1787]; see *OED*, s.v. "arm2, IV014")

Referentially, all four examples belong to different extensional classes. Now, while (4b) is another lexicalized metaphor related to (4a), there is no proper reading of (4c) that allows us to establish a semantic relation to (4a) or (4b); here *arm* means 'weapon'. (4d) is metonymically linked to (4c), as indeed a noble's family crest was painted on a shield, i.e. on an *arm* (consider G *Waffen – Wappen*). We can thus conclude that (4a) and (4b) can be assigned to one polysemous word, and (4c) and (4d) to another, while there is no link between the first pair and the second: this is homonymy.

Polysemy results from the lexicalization of an associative process and therefore is semantic in nature, whereas homonymy, in the vast majority of cases, arises from phonetic clash, as was the case in our example E *arm*1 'upper limb of the human body' and the like vs. *arm*2 'weapon':

(5)   a.   OE *earm* 'upper limb of the body' > ModE *arm*1
       b.   OF *arme* 'weapon' > ME *arme* > ModE *arm*2

Divergent etymology is an important hint for the lexicographer and helps in understanding synchrony, but etymology should not be taken to *describe* synchrony. This is not only a question of methodological integrity; a description based on this criterion would not even succeed in explaining the following cases.[10]

(6)   a.   OF *voler* 'to fly' (itr.) [>METON> 'to hunt with falcons' (tr.) >METON> 'to catch the prey' >META>] 'to steal' (hence ModF *voler*1 'to fly' – *voler*2 'to steal')

    b.   MHG *sloz* 'lock' [>META> 'castle locking a valley or a pass' >EXTENSION>] 'castle, palace' (hence ModG *Schloss*1 'lock' – *Schloss*2 'castle')

(7)   a.   Lat *somnus* 'sleep' > Sp *sueño* – *somnium* 'dream' > Sp *sueño* (hence > Sp *sueño* 'sleep' –METON– 'dream')

    b.   OE *corn* 'grain' > ModE *corn* – OF *corn* 'horny induration on the foot' > ModE *corn* (hence ModE *corn* 'grain' –META– 'corn on the foot')

In (6) we should, diachronically, have polysemy, but the senses that linked the first and the last acceptation disappeared from usage (put into square brackets), so that there is no semantic relation between the remaining senses: this is "secondary homonymy". In (7), original homonymy is re-interpreted as polysemy by speakers who feel a semantic relation between the two senses in question: this is "secondary polysemy".

3.3. *Referential class and semantic relation: a double test for polysemy*

The last four examples have demonstrated that we need criteria that work exclusively in synchrony. A typology based on the features of referential class and semantic relation fulfils this need and helps us to separate homonymy from polysemy and the latter from mere contextual variation. See Table 2.

Contextual variation describes the semantic range of one lexicalized sense; thus, if there is a semantic difference, it is below the level of the semantic relations introduced in Section 2. Polysemy is a property of the semantic status of a word and describes a network of related senses of this word, as illustrated above with E *man* and F *parler*. Homonymy means that two words

Table 2.

	Word form	Referential class	Semantic relation A–G
Contextual variation ("vagueness")	Identical	Identical	No (below the level of semantic relation)
Polysemy	Identical	Different	Yes
Homonymy ("ambiguity")	Identical	Different	No (beyond the level of semantic relation)

are only phonetically identical; we are beyond the level of semantic relations.[11] The decision as to whether there is a semantic link or not is by no means fortuitous – as it sometimes may appear – but can, in most cases, be found by using the typology of semantic relations given above. This typology may be based on diachronic processes, but it is essentially a description of synchronic relations.

Considering finally the terms "vagueness" and "ambiguity", I would like to stress that it is not the senses of a word which are vague, but that sometimes contexts are vague when they allow different readings, and that often referents are vague insofar as they are difficult to attribute to an extensional category. But once we decide to attribute the "poor little thing on one's stomach" to the class of human arms, the word becomes fully linked to the corresponding concept and linguistic content. Prototypicality is thus a property of extensional classes and not of concepts or senses.

4.   Discourse rules, idiosyncrasy and lexicalization: levels of polysemy

4.1.   Typical recurrent polysemies

Up to now we have stood by Bréal's dogma that polysemy is the synchronic side of semantic change. A great number of lexicalized semantic changes support this view. It is, however, challenged by some types of polysemy which can be found in all languages, e.g. E *school* which, according to the context in which it is used, means 'building' (8a), 'a period of education' (8b), 'the body of pupils and of teachers' (8c), 'a course or a couple of courses' (8d) and 'department of a university' (8e):

(8)   a.   *The children are now at the* school.
       b.   School *starts at the age of six.*
       c.   *The entire* school *rose when the headmaster entered the auditorium.*
       d.   *After* school *the children rush home.*
       e.   *John now teaches at Harvard Medical* School.

Even more universal are the CONTAINER–CONTENT and the CAUSE–RESULT metonymies in (9) and (10):

(9)   a.   *I just bought Chomsky's latest* book [= CONTAINER].

      b.   *Chomsky's latest* book *is awful* [= CONTENT].

(10)   a.   *Mary is* sad [= STATE (AS RESULTING FROM SOMETHING)].

      b.   *Mary brings* sad *news* [= CAUSE].

Polysemy of this kind is quite common: the CONTAINER–CONTENT metonymy can be applied to all sorts of containers (see the semantic description in Copestake and Briscoe 1996: 30–31), the CAUSE–RESULT relation is generally found with emotional adjectives, and the different metonymies in (8) are common to a number of words referring to institutions with members in a building (e.g. *parliament, police station, church, country club*, etc.), and they are therefore highly predictable (see Bierwisch 1983: 82). To explain this kind of "regular" relation, we can choose between two approaches: monosemy (see Section 4.2) or a special type of polysemy which I will call "rule-based polysemy" (see Section 4.3).

4.2.   *Two-level-semantics and polysemy*

Let us first investigate the best-known monosemous approach to (8) and (9). In his "two-level-semantics", Bierwisch treats examples such as E *school* as conceptual shifts away from an abstract semantic representation, as a kind of world-knowledge guided semantic extension of a core sense in specific contexts (Bierwisch 1983: 85–88).[12] Bierwisch's monosemous interpretation leads to very complex or very abstract lexical entries (see his formalized notation). This is a problem at the level of metalanguage, but does not contradict monosemy as such. The "hard" problem with monosemy is that if we really had a core sense that is extended by conceptual information, the extension should work in all similar cases in one language and it should even work universally. This is not the case, as e.g. (8e) would not be possible in German, and (8d) would not allow insertion of E *police station* meaning 'duty hours':

(11)   a.   G ?*Hans lehrt jetzt an der Medizinischen* Schule *der Harvard-Universität.*

      b.   ?*After* police station *the policemen rushed home.*

A case where universality breaks down completely is transitivization:[13]

(12)   a.   E *John* sleeps *in this hotel. – This hotel* sleeps *100 guests.*
      b.   F *Jean* dort *dans cet hôtel. – ?Cet hôtel* dort *100 clients.*
      c.   G *Hans* schläft *in diesem Hotel. – ?Dieses Hotel* schläft *100 Gäste.*
(13)   a.   F *Marie* sort *de la maison. – Marie* sort *un pistolet de son sac.*
      b.   E *Mary* comes *out of the house. – ?Mary* comes *a pistol out of her handbag.*
      c.   G *Maria* kommt *aus dem Haus. – ?Maria* kommt *eine Pistole aus der Handtasche.*

(12) and (13) show that although transitivization is a general conceptual process, it is nevertheless highly idiosyncratic: e.g., in French, intransitive verbs for DIRECTION OF MOVEMENT (*sortir, entrer, monter, descendre*, etc.) have generally developed a causative sense (less commonly used with *entrer*, however), which is not the case in English and German. And even within one and the same language, a rule is not always applicable and idiosyncrasies occur, as demonstrated by the following examples taken from Pustejovsky and Boguraev (1996: 3–4).[14]

(14)   a.   *Sam enjoyed the* lamb.
      b.   *The* lamb *is running out in the field.*
(15)   a.   *?We ordered* cow *for dinner.*
      b.   *?The* frog *here is excellent.*

While E *lamb* admits the polysemy of 'animal' and 'meat prepared for cooking/eating', this is not allowed with *cow/beef*, and in (15b) a reference to the whole animal is excluded, since usually only hindlegs of frogs are eaten. If all these words had, on the intralinguistic level, a rather abstract core sense which allowed semantic extension based on encyclopaedic, extra-linguistic knowledge, the different idiosyncrasies would be very hard, if not impossible, to explain. Monosemy thus raises serious methodological problems and should be rejected as a semantic model.

We can conclude that the types of polysemy described in (8)–(14) result from profiling against a cognitive background, a process which can be used in similarly construed domains. Nevertheless these culture-specific rules are only actualized on the level of one language and thus have to be learned one by one (Schwarze and Schepping 1995). We have to learn their language-specific restrictions and their individual "areas of non-application".

4.3. Discourse rules and polysemy

We can now understand why polysemy in Bréal's sense does not provide a satisfying explanation for this kind of polysemy, as it is indeed difficult to explain the apparent regularities by pointing to a number of parallel semantic changes. Here again, an interesting distinction can be found in Deane (1988): Deane calls the nonpredictable, idiosyncratic polysemy (the "Bréal-type") "lexical polysemy", while polysemy as based on typical semantic relations, as discussed throughout the present section, is called "regular polysemy" (1988: 349–350). Deane's distinction in itself is ingenious; his terminology, however, is problematic as all polysemies treated here are "lexical" by nature.

Despite this imprecision, Deane was pointing in the right direction, as what he calls "lexical polysemy" is, as defined above in Section 2, a synchronic consequence of "lexicalized semantic change", while "regular polysemy" is obviously different. The first type can be illustrated with examples such as E *mouse* 'small rodent', 'computer mouse' or G *Schirm* 'shelter', 'umbrella' and will henceforth be called "idiosyncratic polysemy". Examples of the second type include E *book* 'printed work', 'contents of this work', and this type of polysemy will be called "rule-based polysemy", as the polysemy of *book* arises from the rule that metonymic transfers from the CONTAINER to the CONTENT are widespread in discourse. Using the term "conceptual metaphor" introduced two decades ago by Lakoff and Johnson (1980), we can call the CONTAINER–CONTENT relation a "conceptual metonymy" or a "contiguity schema" (see Blank 1999b). In fact, all examples cited in this section are instances of different conceptual metonymies, e.g. BUILDING–FUNCTION/GOAL (8b), BUILDING–AFFECTED PERSONS (8c), CAUSE–RESULT (10), CONTAINER–CONTENT (9, 12a), OBJECT–ACTOR (13a), ANIMAL–MEAT OF THIS ANIMAL (14).

We can now evaluate our typology of polysemy in the greater context of cognitive semantics. It is clear that not only conceptual metonymies but also conceptual metaphors lead to rule-based polysemy, as shown in the "extension" of the BUILDING–THEORY metaphor in (16b).

(16)　a.　*Is that the* foundation *of your theory?*
　　　b.　*His theory has thousands of little rooms and long, winding corridors.*
　　　　(Examples: Lakoff and Johnson 1980: 46, 53)

The central tenet of *Metaphors We Live by*, viz. that "our ordinary conceptual system, in terms of which we both think and act, is fundamentally metaphorical in nature" (Lakoff and Johnson 1980: 3), can easily be extended to metonymy. Conceptual metaphors are one way of structuring the world via language; conceptual metonymies represent another, maybe even more important way (see Seto, this volume). Less often, it seems, do we use taxonomic relations deriving from the relation between a prototypical instance of a category and the category itself.[15] It is obvious that we use all major strategies, metaphor, metonymy and hyponymy (what Seto, this volume, calls synecdoche) when we think and talk about the world.

This means that on the level of discourse we use conventional metaphors, metonymies (and taxonomies) and introduce innovations based on conventional conceptual metaphors and metonymies and on prototype–category relations. It is also rather uncontroversial that metonymies rely on fundamental contiguities – often anchored in frames and scenarios – and that metaphors result from perceptual or functional similarities between concepts or domains that are not directly related (see Croft 1993; Koch 1995; Blank 1997).

Two questions remain, however. On which level of knowledge are these conceptual metaphors and metonymies stored in our mind? And, why are there language-specific restrictions for the use of some words, while others do not have these restrictions, despite the fact that they are embedded in the same conceptual background (see the examples cited above)? It is obviously not enough to say that the latter are based on encyclopaedic knowledge and that the former is somehow idiosyncratic. At this point, it is necessary to add two further levels of linguistically relevant rules, i.e. the level of rules governing so-called "discourse types" or "discourse traditions" and the level of language rules that are specific to a particular language.

Discourse traditions are sets of rules for the correct production of a specific discourse, e.g. the set of metaphors and clichés of Renaissance poetry or the typical phrases and strategies used when buying a used car or presenting a paper at a conference (for details see Koch 1997). Although realized, of course, in a concrete language, a discourse rule is not language-specific: it characterizes a type of discourse and is common to speakers of all languages who use a discourse type in a specific way (e.g. the typical Petrarchian metaphors were known all over Europe during the 16th century, but only within a small group of connoisseurs). Language rules, on the other hand, are idiosyncratic and only govern the language use of a certain speech community or a geographically or socially defined group.

These two levels interact with encyclopaedic or conceptual knowledge, on the one hand, and with the actual discourse, on the other, as represented in Figure 3.

According to this model, innovations are either based on prominent encyclopaedic knowledge and have their psychological foundation in salient associations (e.g. salient similarity, contiguity or contrast), or speakers model them analogically on already-existing conceptual metaphors, metonymies or taxonomies which, of course, themselves have cognitive foundations. Innovations can be lexicalized directly as a specific language rule – an idiosyncratic metaphor, metonymy etc. (represented by the broken arrow) – or, and this seems to be more common, as a rule of the specific discourse type in which the innovation was first used. This innovation may later become lexicalized as a proper language rule.

In the case of metonymy, for instance, several conceptual contiguities are permanently highlighted and enable us to construe analogous metonymies for words that access the same, or a similarly construed, frame or the same discourse type. As we have probably not learned all these potential metonymies before, we must have learned the rules that underlie them, and their specific restrictions. Waltereit (1998: 14–19, 26–28) has demonstrated that these rules are mainly "discourse rules": every discourse type activates a set of conceptual metonymies that can be filled with concrete lexical metonymies. This explains why, e.g., (9) and (10) are very widespread types of contiguity corresponding to a rule in a large number of discourse types. The range of a conceptual metonymy is thus limited by the range of its discourse type(s), as shown in (17).

(17)   a.   *The* ham sandwich *is waiting for his check* [ORDERED DISH–CUSTOMER in waiters' discourse].

      b.   G *Ich werde verlängert* [EMPLOYEE–CONTRACT in discourses concerning work].

We can now understand why (10b) was odd: the contiguity schema PLACE OF WORK–TIME OF WORK is not a usual discourse rule, although it is fully understandable. The conceptual metonymy can be used creatively to produce analogous metonymies, but only when based on an activated discourse type. The same holds true for typical conceptual metaphors: once a similarity scheme is anchored in the mind as a rule of discourse types it can be productively filled with analogous metaphors, as exemplified in (18).[16]

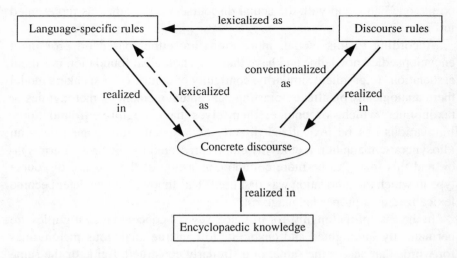

Figure 3.   Interaction of conceptual rules, language-specific rules, discourse rules
and discourse.

(18)   a.   E *The trigger word opens a* mental space [CONCEPTS–CONTAINERS
in linguistics].

b.   F *Je paragonne à ta jeune beaulté, Qui toujours dure en son
printemps nouvelle, Ce moys d'*Avril, *qui ses fleurs renouvelle ...*
(Ronsard, *Les amours* CIII [1552])

c.   *Thou art thy mother's glass and she in thee Calls back the lovely*
April *of her prime.* (Shakespeare, *Sonnets* III)

The use of F *avril*, E *April* in the sense of 'youth' is a metaphor restricted
to Renaissance poetry, but here again, analogous transfers were possible:

(19)   *For since mad* March *great promise made of me; If now the* May *of
my years much decline, What can be hoped my harvest time will be?*
(Sidney, *Astrophel and Stella* [~1580]. Cited after: Shakespeare, *Sonnets*,
edited by C. Knox. London: Methuen 1918: 6 fn.)

Restrictions based on a specific discourse type can also be found for
typical taxonomies, but here the situation remains less marked than in the
case of metaphor or metonymy and needs further investigation:

(20)   *I apprehended a* vehicle *on the* premises. [BASIC LEVEL CONCEPT–
SUPERORDINATE LEVEL CONCEPT in "police-speak"; see Nerlich and Clarke
1999].

Concrete metaphors, metonymies or taxonomies depend on rules of specific
discourses and exactly the same holds true for the conceptual metaphors,
metonymies and taxonomies that underlie them. They can be narrowly
restricted to a "small" discourse type or may function as a rule in a larger set
of discourse types. The specific character of the discourse type in which a
conceptual metaphor or metonymy is embedded also determines to what
extent we can apply this conceptual metaphor or metonymy to other words:
one cannot extend a conceptual metaphor or metonymy to a word that would
not be used in discourses where this rule is operative. The range of these
metonymies and metaphors is limited by cultural frames and the discourse
rules themselves, and can therefore vary from society to society.

Furthermore, it is possible for a metonymy, metaphor or a new hyponymous or hyperonymous sense to become lexicalized as a specific language
rule in a specific language.[17] At this point, we have an idiosyncratic lexicalization of a discourse rule (itself originally profiled against a cognitive
background). Parallel lexicalized metaphors and metonymies deriving from
such rules can then be interpreted as instances of "analogous semantic change"
(see Section 2).

4.4.   Four levels of polysemy

In order to summarize our findings, we can now revisit examples (8)–(19)
and determine their specific character, using the model of polysemy we have
developed. This leads to a fourfold typology of different levels of polysemy:

(i)   Rule-based, nonlexicalized polysemy.
        Ham sandwich 'customer who has ordered a ham sandwich'
    follows a discourse rule which is restricted to a very specific discourse
    type and which can only be applied to a limited number of contexts
    (Fauconnier 1984 speaks of a "closed connector"): name the customer
    by the meal he or she is eating. Within the framework of this discourse
    type this can be widely used. There seems to be no further lexicaliz-
    ation of this discourse rule or of one single instance of this metonymy

on the level of a specific language. It seems to be a discourse rule in the discourse of waiters and waitresses, probably all over the world. Roughly the same holds true for (17b), (18a–c) and (19).

(ii)   Rule-based and lexicalized polysemy with no or few idiosyncratic restrictions.

The polysemies of E *book* and *sad* derive from an encyclopaedic (maybe universal) cognitive background and are instances of rather unspecified discourse rules which allow us to refer to the content via the container, or to the cause via the effect, and so on. The examples are also institutionalized as language rules in their specific languages but, in contrast with the following types, they show almost no idio-syncratic restrictions of use and of transferability to analogous concepts.

(iii)   Rule-based and lexicalized polysemy with idiosyncratic restrictions.

a.   The different polysemies of E *school, to sleep, lamb, to operate*, as well as F *sortir*, all derive from a universal cognitive background and, as with the examples in (ii), they are instances of very wide discourse rules and are lexicalized as rules of the English lexicon. However, they are constrained by idiosyncratic restrictions of varying strength. This inhibits full transfer to analogous cases, which native speakers would regard as a violation of the language norm, despite the fact that they are completely systematic and understandable.

b.   E *mental space, vehicle* and maybe also *school* in (8e) belong to the same type as described in (iiia), but show furthermore a restriction to a specific stylistic or socio-linguistic level.

(iv)   Idiosyncratic lexicalized polysemy.

This last type covers cases of polysemy which have developed without the overt application of a conventional pattern, i.e. a conceptual metaphor, metonymy or taxonomy. Instances of this type cited in Section 1 are It *rat* 'mouse', 'rat'; Sp *coche* 'coach', 'car'; Sp *sueño* 'dream', 'sleep'; F *hôte* 'host', 'guest'; or Sard *masetu* 'gentle', 'irascible'. An intermediate stage of conventionalization as a discourse rule can not, however, be excluded. Idiosyncratic polysemy of this type seems to occur especially as a consequence of absorption, semantic extension, popular etymology, auto-converse change and contrast-based semantic change, i.e. types of semantic change which are based on general linguistic rules (e.g. expressivity or efficiency; see Blank

1999c), but not on conceptual patterns. They differ therefore from metaphor, metonymy and – less markedly – semantic restriction.

These different levels of conventionalization and idiosyncratic restrictions correspond, to a certain extent, to a speaker's awareness of a polysemy: type (i) appears to be completely normal in its context, but can easily be used to amuse or scandalize people when applied in an inappropriate discourse situation.[18] Type (iii b) can be used in many discourse types but should not be used in the wrong register. Type (iii a) is usually "inconspicuous", but can give rise to astonishment or reproof when transferred productively to non-lexicalized items. This gives innovative speakers a chance to produce a communicative effect. It is less easy to achieve a communicative effect in the case of type (ii) which is open to transfers. There is also evidence that with type (ii) speakers actually seem to have difficulties in distinguishing polysemous senses.[19] Type (iv) is too heterogeneous for generalizations: here everything depends on the individual instance of polysemy.

5.   Conclusion

In the previous section of this article I have tried to show that not all types of polysemy can be derived from types of semantic change. I had to modify Bréal's view in this respect. Polysemy as the *direct* lexicalized consequence of semantic innovation is only one type in a set of possibilities. Indeed, speakers seem to prefer to apply conceptual patterns anchored in discourse traditions and to create semantic innovations based on these patterns. Innovations can become conventional on the level of a discourse type and can eventually become lexicalized as a language rule with or without specific idiosyncratic restrictions of both use and transferability.

While even lay people can decide whether there is a semantic relation or not, polysemy has puzzled specialists for a long time. In this paper I have tried to develop a referential and semantic test that helps us to distinguish polysemy from contextual variation and homonymy. I have also discovered seven types of semantic relations between lexicalized senses of a word. This allows us to define lexical polysemy positively as a theoretical concept in semantics, and it can now be used with much more precision as a tool of semantic and lexicographic description. It should be noted, though, that the seven types of semantic relations and the distinction between polysemy, vagueness and ambiguity can obviously not be used to explain all concrete cases and to deliver explanations on which all those working in the field of semantics could agree. This is, in fact, due to the "interpretative nature of linguistic semantics" (Geeraerts 1993: 263).

Notes

1. See e.g. Cruse (1986: 80); Saeed (1997: 64); Taylor (1995: 99).
2. This type of relation can often be found across different dialects of one language, e.g. EurSp *tigre* 'tiger' vs. AmerSp *tigre* 'jaguar', or EurSp *león* 'lion' vs. AmSp 'puma'. These are, however, marginal cases of polysemy because they have no reality for speakers in ordinary life situations.
3. For a controversial discussion of this problem see Blank (1997: 191; 1999a: Section 3; to appear); Gévaudan (1997); Koch (2001).
4. See Blank (1999b); Koch (1999). For a different view of metonymy, see Seto (this volume).
5. Synecdochical polysemy according to the narrow definition of synecdoche in Nerlich and Clarke (1999).
6. Example taken from *WEUD* and *PR*. Abbreviations: meta = metaphor; meton = metonymy; tax = taxonomic relation; ag = agent; coag = counter-agent.
7. Polysemy is a core concept in newer studies in Cognitive Linguistics. According to Lakoff (1987), the different senses of a word correspond to the members of one single extensional cognitive category which, instead of having one proto-typical member, shows a certain number of "prototype effects". This rather naïve equation of "one word–one concept" not only turns out to be a typical mono-semous view of semantics, but leads to the puzzling interpretation of cases of clear homonymy, such as F *louer1* 'to rent' – *louer2* 'to praise', as a kind of monosemously conceived polysemy (e.g. in Geeraerts 1993: 234)! Cognitive semantics thus simply misses the main task of lexical semantics, i.e. to describe the senses of a word and the relations between them. For more details see Blank (2001b: Section 11).
8. This is probably the difference between (3b) and the robotic arm in (1d), which in fact *is* the arm of the robot, as it functions (and maybe looks) like a human arm, while the arm of the record player is not an arm but an artefact that can be perceived as an arm.
9. It is important not to equate *word*, *concept* and *extensional category* as is done in some directions of Cognitive Linguistics (especially Lakoff 1987; see the critique in Brown 1990: 23; Kleiber 1990: 147; Koch 1995: 37).
10. For further examples see Blank (1997: 430–433); Fritz (1998: 58); Ullmann (1962: 164–179); Widlak (1992).
11. The same set of criteria can be used to define other lexical relations such as

paronymy (word form: similar; referential class: different; semantic relation: no), *synonymy* (word form: different; referential class: identical; semantic relation: no, but senses differ only on the connotational level), *hyponymy* (word form: different; referential class: indifferent; semantic relation: yes).

12. For a more detailed discussion of (newer) approaches to monosemy see Koch (1998: 126–130). Other possibilities used in structural approaches are maximizing homonymy, which would override the semantic relations between the sense, or the shift of polysemy from the level of the "system" to the level of the "norm", as defined by Coseriu (1967). This direction is chosen by Dietrich (1997). In this case, however, the semantic system of the language degrades from a network of lexicalized word meanings to a mere "semantic potential". This systematic semantic potential would not really contain language-specific semantic knowledge but encyclopaedic knowledge, conceptual frames, rules of presuppositions etc. which permit deployment of this semantic potential on the level of lexicalized meanings. Such a "minimalist program of semantics" is suggested by Schlieben-Lange (1997: 244–247) (see the critique in Koch 1998). For a general critique of the monosemous view of word meaning in structural semantics as developed by Eugenio Coseriu and his disciples see Taylor (1999).

13. For further examples see Schwarze and Schepping (1995).

14. Examples of this kind not only challenge monosemous approaches to word meaning but also the decidedly polysemous approach advocated by Pustejovsky (1995): he has developed a complex semantic theory centred around four types of semantic features called qualia, which are modelled on the four types of causes as defined by Aristotle (see *Organon* IV, 2: Ch. 11). These qualia explain regular metonymic and taxonomic polysemy very well, but they do not explain exceptions as in example (13), and they seem to provide no explanation of metaphoric polysemy, as this type would require qualia or argument-structure mapping. Indeed, as Pustejovsky and Boguraev (1996: 4) admit: "the polysemy [in the case of *cow* or *frog*; AB] is the result of lexical rules rather than of alternations within the qualia of a single lexical item, such as with *door* [...]." An interpretation of these cases as "semi-productive polysemy" is given by Copestake and Briscoe (1996).

15. See Nerlich and Clarke (1999), who describe typical discourse types where taxonomic strategies are exploited.

16. There is, however, a greater number of very open conceptual metaphors (e.g. "orientational metaphors"); see Lakoff and Johnson (1980: 14).

17. According to Schwarze and Schepping (1995) this is even a necessary development.

18. Imagine someone talking about a restaurant where he/she has been for dinner saying: "And then this ham sandwich sitting next to us went off without paying."

19. This was the finding of the empirical study by Soares da Silva (1992): his Portuguese subjects had to classify the semantic relation of marked words in pairs of sentences from "0" (no relation) to "4" (identical). The highest scores in his test were actually given to Pg *livro* 'book' (CONTAINER–CONTENT) (3.92) and *triste* 'sad' (RESULT–CAUSE) (3.62), which means that many test subjects were not

fully aware of the polysemy, i.e. of the semantic difference. Instances of type (iii) were usually better classified as being polysemous (score between 1.5 and 3.5). See also Blank (1997: 418–419).

References

Aristotle
    1995   Categories; Organon IV. Both in: *Philosophische Schriften.* Volume 1.
                Darmstadt: Wissenschaftliche Buchgesellschaft.
Bierwisch, Manfred
    1983   Semantische und konzeptuelle Repräsentation lexikalischer Einheiten.
                In: Rudolf Ruzicka and Wolfgang Motsch (eds.), *Untersuchungen zur Semantik*, 61–99. Berlin: Akademie.
Blank, Andreas
    1997   *Prinzipien des lexikalischen Bedeutungswandels am Beispiel der romanischen Sprachen.* Tübingen: Niemeyer.
    1999a   Les principes d'association et leur importance pour la structure du lexique. *Studi italiani di linguistica teorica ed applicata* XXVIII.
    1999b   Co-presence and succession: a cognitive typology of metonymy. In: Günter Radden and Klaus-Uwe Panther (eds.), *Metonymy in Language and Thought*, 169–192. Amsterdam: Benjamins.
    1999c   Why do new meanings occur? A typology of the motivations for lexical semantic change. In: Andreas Blank and Peter Koch (eds.), *Historical Semantics and Cognition*, 61–89. Berlin, New York: Mouton de Gruyter.
    2001a   Pathways of lexicalization. In: Martin Haspelmath, Ekkehard König, Wulf Oesterreicher and Wolfgang Raible (eds.), *Language Typology and Universals: An International Handbook*, II, 1596–1608. Berlin, New York: De Gruyter.
    2001b   Semantik II. Neuere Entwicklungen in der lexikalischen Semantik. In: Günter Holtus, Michael Metzeltin, and Christian Schmitt (eds.), *Lexikon der Romanistischen Linguistik.* I, 1, 918–939.
    (to appear) Fondamenti e tipologia del cambio semantico. In: Giampaolo Salvi (ed.), *Semantica e lessicologia storica.* Rome: Bulzoni.
Bréal, Michel
    1897   *Essai de sémantique: Science des significations.* Paris: Hachette.
Brown, Cecil H.
    1990   A survey of category types in natural language. In: Savas Tsohazidis (ed.), *Meanings and Prototypes: Studies in Linguistic Categorization*, 17–47. London: Routledge.

Copestake, Ann and Ted Briscoe
  1996   Semi-productive polysemy and sense extension. In: James Pustejovsky
            and Branimir Boguraev (eds.), *Lexical Semantics. The Problem of
            Polysemy*, 15–67. Oxford: Clarendon.
Coseriu, Eugenio
  1967   Sistema, norma y habla. In: Eugenio Coseriu, *Teoría del lenguaje y
            lingüística general*, 11–113. Madrid: Gredos.
Croft, William
  1993   The role of domains in the interpretation of metaphors and metonymies.
            Cognitive Linguistics 4: 335–370.
Cruse, David A.
  1986   *Lexical Semantics*. Cambridge: Cambridge University Press.
  1995   Polysemy and related phenomena from a cognitive linguistic view-
            point. In: Patrick Saint-Dizier and Evelyne Viegas (eds.), *Compu-
            tational Lexical Semantics*, 33–49. Cambridge: Cambridge University
            Press.
Deane, Paul D.
  1988   Polysemy and cognition. *Lingua* 75: 325–361.
Dietrich, Wolf
  1997   Polysemie als 'volle Wortbedeutung' – gegen die 'Mehrdeutigkeit'
            der Zeichen. In: Ulrich Hoinkes and Wolfgang Dietrich (eds.),
            Kaleidoskop der Lexikalischen Semantik, 227–237. Tübingen:
            Niemeyer.
Geeraerts, Dirk
  1993   Vagueness's puzzles, polysemy's vagaries. *Cognitive Linguistics* 4:
            223–272.
Gévaudan, Paul
  1997   La polysémie verticale: hypothèses, analyses, interprétations. In: *Phin
            2* (www.fu-berlin.de/phin).
Fritz, Gerd
  1998   *Historische Semantik*. Stuttgart: Metzler.
Kleiber, Georges
  1990   *La sémantique du prototype*. Paris: Presses Universitaires de France.
Klein, Franz-Josef
  1997   *Bedeutungswandel und Sprachendifferenzierung. Die Entstehung
            der romanischen Sprachen aus wortsemantischer Sicht*. Tübingen:
            Niemeyer.
Koch, Peter
  1995   Der Beitrag der Prototypentheorie zur Historischen Semantik: eine
            kritische Bestandsaufnahme. *Romanistisches Jahrbuch* 46: 27–46.
  1997   Diskurstraditionen: zu ihrem sprachtheoretischen Status und ihrer
            Dynamik. In: Barbara Frank, Thomas Haye, and Doris Tophinke

(eds.), *Gattungen mittelalterlicher Schriftlichkeit*, 43–79. Tübingen: Narr.

1998   Saussures *mouton* und Hjelmslevs *træ*: zwei Schulbeispiele zwischen Semstruktur und Polysemie. In: Edeltraud Werner, Ricarda Liver, Yvonne Stork and Martina Nicklaus (eds.), *Et multum et multa. Festchrift Peter Wunderli*, 113–136. Tübingen: Narr.

1999   Frame and contiguity: on the cognitive basis of metonymy and certain types of word-formation. In: Günter Radden and Klaus-Uwe Panther (eds.), *Metonymy in Thought and Language*, 139–168. Amsterdam: Benjamins.

2001   Lexical typology from a cognitive and linguistic point of view. In: Martin Haspelmath, Ekkehard König, Wulf Oesterreicher, and Wolfgang Raible (eds.), *Language Typology and Universals: An International Handbook*, II, 1142–1178. Berlin, New York: De Gruyter.

Lakoff, George
1987   *Women, Fire and Dangerous Things: What Categories Reveal about the Mind*. Chicago: University of Chicago Press.

Lakoff, George and Mark Johnson
1980   *Metaphors We Live By*. Chicago: University of Chicago Press.

Nerlich, Brigitte and David D. Clarke
1999   Synecdoche as a communicative strategy. In: Andreas Blank and Peter Koch (eds.), *Historical Semantics and Cognition*, 197–213. Berlin, New York: Mouton de Gruyter.

OED
1989   *Oxford English Dictionary*. 2nd Edition. Oxford: Clarendon.

PR
1977   *Dictionnaire Alphabétique et Analogique de la Langue Française* par Paul Robert. Paris: Parmentier.

Pustejovsky, James
1995   *The Generative Lexicon*. Cambridge, MA: MIT Press.

Pustejovsky, James and Branimir Boguraev (eds.)
1996   *Lexical Semantics: The Problem of Polysemy*. Oxford: Clarendon.

Saeed, John I.
1997   *Semantics*. Cambridge, MA: Blackwell.

Schlieben-Lange, Brigitte
1997   Überlegungen zu einer einfachen Systematik der Zuweisung von (polysemen) Lesarten. In: Ulrich Hoinkes and Wolfgang Dietrich (eds.), *Kaleidoskop der Lexikalischen Semantik*, 239–247. Tübingen: Narr.

Schwarze, Christoph and Marie-Therèse Schepping
1995   Polysemy in a two-level-semantics. In: Urs Egli et al. (eds.), *Lexical Knowledge in the Organization of Language*, 283–300. Amsterdam, Philadelphia: John Benjamins.

Soares da Silva, Augusto
  1992   Homonimía e polissemia: análise sémica e teoria do campo léxico.
              In: R. Lorenzo (ed.), *Actas do XIX Congreso Internacional de*
              Lingüística e Filoloxía Románicas. Volume 2, 257–287. La Coruña:
              Fundación Pedro Barrié de la Maza.
Sweetser, Eve
  1990   *From Etymology to Pragmatics*. Cambridge: Cambridge University
              Press.
Taylor, John R.
  1995   *Linguistic Categorization: Prototypes in Linguistic Theory*. Oxford:
              Clarendon.
  1999   Structural semantics and cognitive semantics. In: Andreas Blank and
              Peter Koch (eds.), *Historical Semantics and Cognition*. Berlin, New
              York: Mouton de Gruyter.
Ullmann, Stephen
  1962   *Semantics: An Introduction to the Science of Meaning*. Oxford:
              Blackwell.
Waltereit, Richard
  1998   *Metonymie und Grammatik: Kontiguitätsphänomene in der*
              französischen Satzsemantik. Tübingen: Niemeyer.
WEUD
  1994   *Webster's Encyclopedic Unabridged Dictionary of the English Language*.
              New York: Gramercy.
Widlak, Stanislaw
  1992   *Fra lessicologia e stilistica. Problemi di lessicologia e stilistica*
              dell'italiano e di altre lingue romanze. Cracow: Universitas Cracovia.

Psycholinguistic approaches

Irony in conversation: salience, role, and context effects

Rachel Giora and Inbal Gur

1. Introduction

Much of what is going on in discourse comprehension and production depends on the very first moments of comprehension. Consider the following example:

Iddo and Omri (aged 7 years and 8 months, native speakers of Hebrew) are playing together. Iddo fetches himself a glass of juice out of the refrigerator.

(1)   Omri: I want to drink too.
        Mira (Iddo's mother): Iddo, *totci lo et ha-mitz* ('take the juice out [of the refrigerator] for him').
        Iddo (laughingly): ha ... ha ... **le-hotci lo et ha-mitz** ('to take/squeeze the juice out of him' – a Hebrew idiom meaning 'drive one crazy by imposing all kinds of hardships on her/him').

What this example illustrates is that speakers and comprehenders make use of what is available to them, regardless of contextual information or speaker's intent (see also Horton and Keysar 1996; Keysar et al. 1998; Keysar, Barr and Horton 1998). Though the idiomatic meaning of Mira's utterance in (1) was not the intended meaning, nor was it compatible with context, it was not ignored; contextual information did not inhibit its activation.

Why should contextually incompatible meanings be activated and infiltrate the ongoing discourse? Why doesn't context block unintended meanings? According to the graded salience hypothesis (Giora 1997, 2003), words' and expressions' salient meanings, i.e. meanings coded in the mental lexicon (whose relative salience is further affected by, e.g., frequency, familiarity, conventionality, or prototypicality) cannot be bypassed. Though prior context may be instrumental in enhancing a word's or an expression's meaning (e.g.

Forster 1989), it can hardly inhibit activation of salient meanings (cf. Tabossi 1988; Titone 1998; but see Martin et al. 1999; and Vu, Kellas and Paul 1998 for a different view). Salient meanings should always be accessed and always initially, regardless of contextual bias.

The question may need rephrasing, then. If contextual information is less able to affect preselection of the appropriate meaning when there are other equally or more salient competitors, why doesn't it suppress irrelevant meanings that surface only because of their availability? This may not be the right question either, because contextually inappropriate information does get suppressed (e.g. Gernsbacher 1990; Onifer and Swinney 1981; Swinney 1979). However, Gernsbacher and Robertson (1995) also showed that skilled and less skilled readers differ in their suppression abilities. While skilled readers did not outperform less skilled readers at the initial, access stage, they did at the later, suppression stage: Less skilled comprehenders were less capable of suppressing contextually irrelevant information (which must, therefore, interfere with their comprehension). But this will not explain the use Iddo made of the irrelevant meaning (in [1]). His laughter suggests that he computed both meanings (noticing their incongruity), deliberately choosing to use the contextually inappropriate meaning for a special purpose: to crack a joke.

Here, then, is an instance of an idiomatic meaning of an utterance, which though inconsistent with contextual information, was neither inhibited nor suppressed. Such behaviour is not explainable by an interactive approach to discourse comprehension, which allows contextual information to affect processing very early on so that only the contextually appropriate meaning of words and sentences becomes available (e.g. the Relevance Theoretic account proposed by Sperber and Wilson 1986/1995; Carston 1999; but see Giora 1998a for an alternative interpretation of this account). Moreover, activating inappropriate meanings after the appropriate meaning has been captured is not motivated by such models. Such behaviour is not explainable by the standard pragmatic model (Grice 1975; Searle 1979) either. According to this model, language comprehension always begins with the literal interpretation. If it is compatible with contextual information it is not revisited, and search is terminated. Upon this view, then, literally intended language is processed only literally. Since Mira's utterance was intended literally, this model cannot account for the involvement of the contextually irrelevant nonliteral meaning in Iddo's comprehension process (see also Gibbs 1980).

According to the graded salience hypothesis (Giora 1997, 2003), however, so-called irrelevant meanings are activated because they are salient. According to the retention hypothesis (Giora 1995, 2003; Giora and Fein 1999a), such meanings would, indeed, be attenuated or fade if they have no role in constructing the intended meaning. However, if they can be allocated some function in the construction of the discourse interpretation, they would be retained. Such is the case of the literal meaning of ironic utterances (e.g. Giora 1995; Giora, Fein and Schwartz 1998). According to the graded salience hypothesis, the contextually incompatible literal meaning of (the critical word of nonconventional) irony is activated because it is salient, i.e., stored in the mental lexicon. It is not dispensed with by contextual information, because it has a role in constructing the ironic meaning: it allows the comprehender to compute the difference between what is expected and what is (Giora 1995). For instance, when I say *What a lovely day for a picnic* on a stormy day, the literal meaning of the critical word *lovely* would be retrieved directly from the mental lexicon on account of its salience. Despite its contextual misfit, it would not be suppressed, because it is instrumental in deriving the ironic meaning ('lousy' or 'far from being lovely'). Indeed, in Giora, Fein and Schwartz (1998) we showed that the literal meaning of irony is made available immediately, and remains active even 2000 msec after offset of the target (ironic) sentence. However, after such a long delay, the same literal meaning is no longer active in literally biasing contexts. Having been accessed and integrated with contextual information, the literal meaning (of *lovely*) in the literal context (e.g. when *What a lovely day for a picnic* is said on a sunny day) has no further functions. It, therefore, begins to fade.

Similar findings are reported by Giora and Fein (1999a) regarding contextually inappropriate meanings of salient/conventional metaphors. In Giora and Fein's studies, the salient, literal meaning of utterances embedded in metaphorically biasing contexts was retained in spite of contextual misfit. However, the reverse did not hold: the salient metaphoric meaning of the same utterance embedded in a literally biasing context showed deactivation. For instance, concepts (e.g. 'rise') related to the literal meaning of conventional (Hebrew) metaphors (e.g. *Only now did they wake up,* meaning 'only now did they start doing something') were not suppressed in the metaphorically biasing context, even though they were contextually incompatible in that context. In contrast, the salient metaphoric meaning ('do') of the same conventional metaphor was less active in the literally biasing context, where it had no role in constructing the literal meaning of the utterance.

Such asymmetry has been shown to hold for balanced polysemous words as well (words having related meanings that are similarly salient). Where a contextually inappropriate meaning of a polysemous word was instrumental in sustaining the contextually appropriate meaning, it was retained. Where it was not, it was deactivated. In Williams (1992), (salient) central meanings (e.g. 'solid') of polysemous words (e.g. *firm*) were activated immediately and retained even after a long delay (of 859 msec) despite contextual misfit (e.g. *The school teacher was criticized for not being firm*). Such meanings are indeed conducive to the interpretation of less central interpretations. (Salient) less central meanings (e.g. 'strict'), however, were not found to be as context-resistant. Having been activated immediately, they were not retained after a long delay, when they were not compatible with contextual information (e.g. *The couple wanted a bed that was firm*). Though 'strict' may be related to *firm*, it is not conducive to the construction of its central meaning ('solid'). Therefore, it was not retained after it had been activated. However, 'solid' is conducive to the 'strict' interpretation of *firm*, and therefore it was not suppressed after being activated. This finding is consistent with the hypothesis that contextually incompatible meanings that are instrumental in the interpretation of the intended meaning are not suppressed (Giora 2003; Giora and Fein 1999a).

Salient meanings that have not been deactivated because they have some role in constructing the meanings currently being built, may be easily reused by the discourse participants on account of their availability (e.g. the idiomatic meaning in [1] above). To testify to the availability of the salient, though contextually incompatible, literal meaning of ironic discourse, we examine here the kind of response irony elicits in naturally occurring conversation. If irony is responded to literally, this would be consistent with both the graded salience hypothesis (Giora 1997) and the indirect negation view of irony (Giora 1995; Giora and Fein 1999b, 1999c) which assume that irony comprehension involves activation and retention of its salient, though contextually inappropriate, literal meaning. Such behaviour, however, is less compatible with the direct access view (e.g. Gibbs 1986) which assumes that in a rich context, irony is processed more or less directly, without having to go though a contextually incompatible interpretive phase. Such behaviour is also less compatible with the standard pragmatic model (Grice 1975; Searle 1979) which posits that the contextually inappropriate literal meaning activated initially should be rejected and replaced by the intended ironic meaning.[1] This suppression hypothesis (see also Gernsbacher, Keysar and Robertson 2001) predicts that immediately after the utterance has been comprehended, there should be no residue of the contextually inappropriate literal meaning.

We have chosen to focus on spontaneous speech because such discourse is less amenable to control and revision than written discourse. The assumption, then, that information available to interlocutors may play a major role in discourse comprehension and production must be particularly applicable to such discourse. It is not the case, of course, that spontaneous talk is not monitored (see, e.g., Zaidel 1987), or does not involve error correction. However, given the time constraints imposed on face-to-face interaction, spontaneous speech must be more "error" prone than written discourse, which is self-paced and can be revisited any time. If one wants to examine the extent to which contextually incompatible meanings are activated and manipulated in the course of discourse construction, spontaneous talk seems the natural environment to explore.

2. Irony and spontaneous discourse

So far, most of the research into the processes involved in comprehension was conducted in the laboratory. Findings showed that lexical access is hardly affected by contextual information (but see Martin et al. 1999; Vu, Kellas and Paul 1998). Ample evidence has been adduced supporting the view that lexical access is modular: lexical processes are autonomous and impervious to context effects (see Fodor 1983; Forster 1979). Upon one version of the modular view, lexical access is exhaustive; *all* the word's coded meanings are accessed initially upon its processing, regardless of contextual bias (e.g. Cairns 1984; Conrad 1974; Lucas 1987; Onifer and Swinney 1981; Picoult and Johnson 1992; Seidenberg, Tanenhaus, Leiman and Bienkowski 1982; Swinney 1979; Tanenhaus, Carlson and Seidenberg 1985; Tanenhaus, Leiman and Seidenberg 1979; Till, Mross and Kintsch 1988; West and Stanovich 1988 and references therein). Upon another (ordered) version, lexical access is exhaustive but frequency-sensitive: the more frequent meaning is accessed first, and a search for the intended meaning continues only in case the more frequent meaning is incompatible with the context (Bradley and Forster 1987; Duffy, Morris and Rayner 1988; Rayner and Frazier 1989; Rayner and Morris 1991; Sereno, Pacht and Rayner 1992; Simpson 1981; Simpson and Burgess 1985; Simpson and Foster 1986; Simpson and Krueger 1991; Swinney and Prather 1989; Tabossi 1988; for a review, see Gorfein 1989; Rayner, Pacht and Duffy 1994; Simpson 1994; Small, Cottrell and Tanenhaus 1988). Contextual information has only post-access effects, suppressing contextually inappropriate meanings and selecting the appropriate meanings (Swinney 1979).

The modular view of lexical access has been challenged by an interactive direct access hypothesis, according to which lexical access is selective. Contextual information directs access completely, so that only the appropriate meaning is made available for comprehension (e.g. Glucksberg, Kreuz and Rho 1986, Jones 1991; Martin et al. 1999; Schvaneveldt, Meyer and Becker 1976; Simpson 1981, Vu, Kellas and Paul 1998; but see Giora 2003 for a critique).

Evidence from research into figurative language comprehension accumulated in the laboratory seems consistent with the direct access view. Literal and figurative utterances have been shown to involve equivalent processes when embedded in supportive contexts (see Gibbs 1994 for a review). They were shown to be processed equally automatically (e.g. Gildea and Glucksberg 1983; Glucksberg, Gildea and Bookin 1982; Keysar 1989), to involve the same categorization procedures (see Glucksberg and Keysar 1990; Shen 1997), and to take equally long to read (Inhoff, Lima and Carroll 1984; Kemper 1981; Ortony et al. 1978). Irony was no exception: it was shown to take no longer to read than non-ironic discourse (see Gibbs 1986, 1994).

More recent findings, however, question the direct access hypothesis (and see Giora 1997, 1998b, 2003, for a critical review). For instance, utterances embedded in ironically biasing contexts took longer to read than when embedded in literally biasing contexts (Dews and Winner 1997; Giora, Fein and Schwartz 1998; Pexman, Ferretti and Katz 2000; Schwoebel, Dews, Winner and Srinivas 2000). They were also found to be processed literally first, and ironically later (Giora and Fein 1999c; Giora, Fein and Schwartz 1998). Even conventional ironies were found to be processed literally initially, in parallel to the ironic meaning (Giora and Fein 1999c). Further, reanalysis of Gibbs' findings (Giora 1995) is consistent with the view that irony comprehension involves a contextually incompatible (literal) phase (but see Gibbs 2002 for a different view). Would spontaneous speech support a modular based view which allows meanings to be activated regardless of context?

To test this we examined naturally occurring conversations. In particular, we looked at how irony affects text progression. Would it avail both the literal and ironic meaning for further discussion and elaboration, as predicted by the graded salience and retention hypotheses (Giora 1995, 1997, 2003)? Would it make available only the appropriate ironic meaning as predicted by the direct access view, the modular view, and standard pragmatic model?

To illustrate the way the contextually incompatible literal meaning of irony may avail itself for further elaboration, consider the following example (taken from Drew 1987) cited in Clark (1996: 374), in which the ironic/teasing turn is responded to literally (both in bold). In this example, Gerald has just bought a brand-new sports car, and is late for a meeting. He could respond to Lee's ironic reprimand by addressing the ironic meaning (the reprimand), saying, e.g., "I am sorry" or coming up with a real explanation. Instead, he proceeds along the lines proposed by Lee, thereby elaborating on the tease or irony (in bold), i.e., on the literal meaning of the ironic utterance (in bold):

(2)   Gerald: Hi how are you.
        Martha: Well, you are late as usual.
        Gerald: Eheh eheh eheh eheh.
        Lee: What's the matter **couldn't you get your car started?**
        Gerald: **Hehh. That's right. I had to get it pushed, eheh eheh eheh eheh.**

In our data, we looked for such responses to irony. Responses to the literal meaning of irony are predicted by the graded salience hypothesis (Giora 1997, 2003) and the retention hypothesis underlying the indirect negation view (Giora 1995). On the assumption that the literal meaning of (nonconventional) irony is the only one coded in the mental lexicon, it should be accessed once the irony is encountered. It should not be suppressed even when the ironic interpretation is derived, because it facilitates the computation of the difference between the expected and the derided situation.

2.1. Method

Participants: The participants were five Israeli friends (two women, three men) who spent a Friday evening together. They were 29–33 years old, native speakers of Hebrew, living in Tel Aviv.

Materials: Our data come from one-hour tape-recorded conversations among the participants. The conversations took place in Tel Aviv, in October 1997. They comprise 9,380 words. For illustration, consider an English translation of a Hebrew extract of the conversation (example [3] below, ironic utterances underlined), containing about 300 words, which partly revolves around Sara and Benjamin (Bibi) Netanyahu (the then Israeli Prime Minister and his wife), who, in a newspaper interview, complained about the press harassing them. The literal responses are in bold.[2]

(3)   1.   A: You don't understand one thing. You think they initiate these
                   things? This is maybe the first article they [wrote].

       2.   B: [They] stay home
                   and after them the paparazzi come ... and they are simply
                   [miserable].

       3.   A: [(They) **ruin] their lives**, what do you want?

       4.   B: I want to cite the last sentence of the article, yes, out of the
                   potency's (the word used in Hebrew is *heroism*) mouth
                   (meaning 'out of God's mouth', equivalent to the English
                   idiom 'out of the horse's mouth') [as they say].

       5.   A: [**Out of the baby's mouth**].

       6.   B: **Out of the hero's mouth**. In fact, it's not in this article, it's
                   in the, it's in the article that appeared in *Ma'ariv* (an Israeli
                   daily), but x Sara says that maybe following the tragedy of
                   Princess Diana they will begin to understand ... she and Diana
                   on the same level!

       7.   C: So, the last photograph, they chose the picture of Bibi and
                   Sara and their two kids on the beach in Caesaria and <xx>
                   ya'eni (a marker for irony) a spontaneous picture, but it's
                   obvious that this picture is carefully arranged: the big boy
                   with the father – the small one with the mother, and all this.

       8.   A: (0.1 second later) It's as if I take a picture of you (C) now,
                   say, you are sitting next to D (C's wife), because ... really,
                   come on!

       9.   C: One thing is certain, then ... the paparazzi photographers will
                   not catch them at the speed of 160 kph.

      10.   Everybody: @ (2 seconds).

      11.   D: So she cannot compare herself to Diana.

      12.   B: <xx> She is really miserable because they do her injustice.

      13.   A: Diana, my ass, this entire story, believe me, I feel like retching.

      14.   D: Yes.

      15.   A: Big deal! [<xx>]

      16.   C: [I don't feel] like retching at all, I feel like sharing
                   the profits.

17. D: [@@@@]
18. C: **[I feel like] sharing the profits.** Throw me some bone (equivalent to the English idiom 'throw me a scrap').
19. D: **Open a florist shop.**

2.2. A sample analysis

Speaker A (in [3.1]) sympathizes with the Netanyahus, while speaker B (in [3.2]) is critical of them. Speaker B describes them ironically as "miserable" – the literal sense – echoing their complaint and indicating that they are far from being miserable, and that they must be happy – the ironic meaning – about being so popular in the press. However, B (in [3.3]) elaborates on their "misery" – the literal sense of the irony – by retorting that their life is "ruined". Whether this response can be viewed as resonating with the literal meaning is dubious: it could be a repetition of that person's belief rather than a response to the previous utterance.

In (3.4), the reference to Bibi as God ("potency"/"heroism") is ironic. Both the following responses referring to him as either "baby" (sort of opposite) or "hero" in (3.6) are echoes of the literal meaning of the irony. The irony at the end of (3.6) remains uncommented on at this stage. D is going to refer to it later (in [3.11]), but it is hard to tell whether this is a response to the literal or ironic meaning of the irony here.

The ironical meaning 'spontaneous' in (3.7) is responded to by A in (3.8). A disagrees with C, i.e. with the ironical meaning, and attempts to defend the genuine spontaneity of the photograph of the Netanyahus (appearing in the press to affect "spontaneity" in order to support their claim that they are haunted by the press).

The irony in (3.9), which suggests the couple will never really run away from the paparazzo photographers, was responded to by a 2-second laughter.

The irony in (3.12) is a repetition of the topic of this conversation. It is a repetition of the literal meaning of the previous ironies, particularly those generated by the same speaker himself.

The irony in (3.16) is responded to by laughter in (3.17).

In (3.18), C echoes the literal meaning of his own irony, and in (3.19) the literal meaning of his irony is elaborated on by D.

2.3. Results and discussion

Fifty-six ironic utterances were selected, on which there was 100% agreement (as to their ironiness, reached at times after a discussion) between two native speakers of Hebrew who listened to the recording. One judge was a participant in the conversations. Of these 56 ironic utterances, 42 (75%) were responded to by reference to their literal meaning. The responses were judged as literal by the two judges as above. Only those on which there was 100% agreement that they were indeed responses to the literal meaning of the irony were counted.

These results suggest that the literal meaning of irony is accessed and retained by both speakers and addressees. The occurrence of irony in the conversations made its literal meaning available for further discussion and elaboration, as predicted by the graded salience hypothesis (Giora 1997, 2003) and indirect negation view (Giora 1995). However, they are partly inconsistent with the standard pragmatic model (Grice 1975; Searle 1979) and modular view (Onifer and Swinney 1981; Picoult and Johnson 1992; Seidenberg et al. 1982; Swinney 1979), attesting that the literal meaning was not suppressed as irrelevant. Further, they are incompatible with the direct access view, demonstrating that irony did not avail the ironic meaning exclusively.

It could be argued, of course, that tapping processes involved in understanding and producing naturally occurring conversations is not comparable to testing comprehension on-line. While the direct access view may be challenged on the basis of evidence about processes, evidence accumulated from conversational discourse may be telling only about products. While the challenge is valid, it is still important to note that these products are better explained by a graded salience view of comprehension rather than by a direct access view, which does not allow for any contextually incompatible interpretation to be activated initially. Recall, further, that these findings do not stand in isolation, but are consistent with previous findings attesting to processes attained by on-line measures such as reading times (Giora, Fein and Schwartz 1998; Pexman, Ferretti and Katz 2000; Schwoebel, Dews, Winner and Srinivas 2000) and lexical decision tasks (Giora and Fein 1999c; Giora, Fein and Schwartz 1998), showing that irony is not accessed ironically first.

Our findings can also be viewed as an instantiation of a more general phenomenon of "dialogic syntax" (Du Bois 1998). Dialogic syntax occurs when a speaker constructs an utterance based on an immediately co-present utterance. Du Bois discloses the ubiquity of dialogic syntax, showing that a vast array of linguistic elements such as syntactic, semantic, pragmatic, lexical, and even phonetic patterns in one speaker's discourse can be traced back to an immediately co-present utterance. This suggests that activation of any linguistic element makes it available for the same or next speaker to elaborate on, the literal meaning of irony included. Our findings indeed confirm that ironies avail their literal meaning, thereby allowing recurrence of the salient/literal meaning in the next discourse segment. Evidence of similar effects of a given utterance on adjacent ones (cf. Du Bois 1998) suggests that salience of meanings is a major factor in discourse comprehension and production.

3. Summary

According to the graded salience hypothesis (Giora 1997, 2003), salient meanings should always be activated initially, even when they are incompatible with contextual information. A meaning of a word or an expression is salient if it is coded in the mental lexicon (e.g. the literal meaning of less familiar irony but not its intended, nonliteral meaning made available by context). Factors contributing to degrees of salience are, e.g., conventionality, frequency, familiarity and prototypicality. Prior context may be instrumental as well, though its role is limited. It may be predictive and facilitate activation of a word's meaning(s), but it is less efficient in inhibiting activation of salient meanings. In this respect, the graded salience hypothesis is consistent with the modular model of lexical access (e.g. Rayner, Pacht and Duffy 1994; Swinney 1979), particularly with an ordered-access version of it that is frequency-sensitive (e.g. Hogaboam and Perfetti 1975; Simpson and Burgess 1985; Swinney and Prather 1989). It predicts that even rich and supportive contexts biased in favour of less salient meanings should not inhibit activation of salient meanings.

Indeed, previous research by Giora and her colleagues has demonstrated that nonsalient ironies activate their salient literal meaning initially (Giora 1999, 2003; Giora and Fein 1999c; Giora, Fein and Schwartz 1998): ironic utterances were shown to facilitate literally related concepts 150 msec after their offset, regardless of contextual bias. Similarly, salient ironies availed their salient ironic meaning initially, in parallel to their salient literal meaning. In contrast, nonsalient ironies facilitated ironically related concepts later –

1000–2000 msec after their offset. These findings support the graded salience hypothesis, but are inconsistent with the view that context affects comprehension significantly (e.g. Glucksberg, Kreuz and Rho 1986; Sperber and Wilson 1986/1995, but see Burgess, Tanenhaus and Seidenberg 1989 for a critique).

Previous research (Giora and Fein 1999c; Giora, Fein, and Schwartz 1998) has also demonstrated that, contra the standard pragmatic model (Grice 1975; see also Searle 1979) and the modular view (Swinney 1979), the contextually incompatible meaning of irony is not suppressed by contextually biased information. Both salient and nonsalient ironies retained their contextually incompatible literal meaning in spite of the availability of the ironic meaning (that emerged at a different temporal stage for the two types of irony). These findings support the indirect negation view (Giora 1995) which maintains that the contextually incompatible literal meaning of irony should be retained because it has a role in irony interpretation – it provides a reference point relative to which the ironicized situation is evaluated. Making the expected explicit allows for the computation of the difference between what is and what is looked for.

Spontaneous face-to-face talk can lend support to the retention hypothesis (Giora 1995, 2003; Giora and Fein 1999a) if it is found to abound in ironic utterances that get responded to literally. Indeed, having investigated irony reception in a spontaneous environment, we found that more often than not, irony is responded to by resonating with its salient, literal interpretation. These findings corroborate those of Kotthoff (1998), who shows that in friendly conversations, listeners very often respond to the literal meaning of the ironic utterance while at the same time making it clear that they have also understood the implicated meaning. Responding to the literal meaning demonstrates that this contextually incompatible meaning has neither been inhibited nor suppressed by contextual information.

Empirical research supporting the graded salience hypothesis (e.g. Giora 1998a, 1998b, 1999, 2003; Giora and Fein 1999a, 1999b, 1999c; Giora, Fein and Schwartz 1998; Pexman, Ferretti and Katz 2000; Schwoebel, Dews, Winner and Srinivas 2000) and indirect negation view (Giora 1995; Giora, Fein and Schwartz 1998) has so far focused on the processes involved in comprehension of written, often contrived discourses tested in the laboratory. In this study, we provide evidence in favour of the claim that salient meanings are involved in spontaneous discourse. In particular, we demonstrate that salient meanings are involved in text comprehension and production even when they are incompatible with the context or the intended meaning.

Acknowledgements

Support for this research was provided by grants from The Israel Science Foundation and Lion Foundation to the first author. Thanks are also extended to Ray Gibbs, John Du Bois and Brigitte Nerlich for their very helpful comments.

Notes

1. Even though Grice (1975) is not explicit about it, the processing model that follows from his assumptions is taken to be a replacement or substitution account (see, e.g., Levinson 1983: 157).
2. Legend (following Du Bois et al. 1993):

...	half a second break
..	a shorter break
[ ]	overlap
x	unclear word
<xx>	unclear utterance
@	laughter
( )	for words not appearing in the Hebrew text
underlining	ironic utterances
bold	responses to the literal meaning

References

Bradley, Dianne C. and Kenneth I. Forster
   1987   A reader's view of listening. *Cognition* 25(1–2): 103–134.
Burgess, Curt, Michael. K. Tanenhaus and Mark S. Seidenberg
   1989   Context and lexical access: implication of nonword interference for lexical ambiguity resolution. *Journal of Experimental Psychology: Learning, Memory and Cognition* 15: 620–632.
Cairns, Helen Smith
   1984   Current issues in language comprehension. In: Rita C. Naremore (ed.), *Recent Advances in Language Science*. San Diego: College Hill Press.
Carston, Robyn
   1999 (June) Linguistic meaning and literal meaning. International Pragmatics Conference on Pragmatics and Negotiation. Tel Aviv University and The Hebrew University of Jerusalem.

Clark, Herbert, H.
1996   *Using Language.* Cambridge: Cambridge University Press.
Conrad, Carol
1974   Context effects in sentence comprehension: a study of the subjective lexicon. *Memory and Cognition* 2: 130–138.
Dews, Shelly and Ellen Winner
1997   Attributing meaning to deliberately false sentences: the case of irony. In: Charlotte Mandell and Alyssa McCabe (eds.), *The Problem of Meaning: Behavioral and Cognitive Perspectives*, 377–414. Amsterdam: Elsevier.
Drew, Paul.
1987   Po-faced receipts of teases. *Linguistics* 25: 219–253.
Du Bois, John W.
1998   Towards a dialogic syntax. Ms. UC Santa Barbara.
Du Bois, John W., Stephan Schuetze-Coburn, Susanna Cumming and Danae Paolino
1993   Outline of discourse transcription. In: Jane A. Edwards and Martin D. Lampert (eds.), *Talking Data: Transcription and Coding in Discourse Research*, 45–87. Hillsdale, NJ: Lawrence Erlbaum Associates.
Duffy, Susan A., Robin K. Morris and Keith Rayner
1988   Lexical ambiguity and fixations times in reading. *Journal of Memory and Language* 27: 429–446.
Fodor, Jerry
1983   *The Modularity of Mind.* Cambridge: MIT Press.
Forster, Kenneth I.
1979   Levels of processing and the structure of the language processor. In: William E. Cooper and E. C. T Walker (eds.), *Sentence Processing: Psycholinguistic Studies Presented to Merrill Garrett*, 27–65. Hillsdale, NJ: Erlbaum.
1989   Basic issues in lexical processing. In: William Marslen-Wilson (ed.), *Lexical Representation and Process*, 75–107. Cambridge: MIT Press.
Gernsbacher, A. Morton
1990   *Language Comprehension as Structure Building.* Hillsdale NJ: Erlbaum.
Gernsbacher, A. Morton, Boaz Keysar, Rachel W. Robertson and Necia K. Werner
2001   The role of suppression and enhancement in understanding metaphors. *Journal of Memory and Language* 45: 433–450.
Gernsbacher, A. Morton and Rachel W. Robertson
1995   Reading skill and suppression revisited. *Psychological Science* 6: 165–169.
Gibbs, Raymond W., Jr.
1980   Spilling the beans on understanding and memory for idioms in conversation. *Memory and Cognition* 8: 449–456.

1986   On the psycholinguistics of sarcasm. *Journal of Experimental Psychology: General* 115: 3–15.

1994   *The Poetics of Mind.* Cambridge: Cambridge University Press.

2002   A new look at literal meaning in understanding what is said and implicated. *Journal of Pragmatics* 34: 457–486.

Gildea, Patricia and Sam Glucksberg

1983   On understanding metaphor: the role of context. *Journal of Verbal Learning and Verbal Behavior* 22: 577–590.

Giora, Rachel

1995   On irony and negation. *Discourse Processes* 19: 239–264.

1997   Understanding figurative and literal language: the graded salience hypothesis. *Cognitive Linguistics* 7: 183–206.

1998a   When is relevance? On the role of salience in utterance interpretation. *Revista Alicantina de Estudios Ingleses* 11: 85–94.

1998b   Irony. In: Jan-Ola Östman, Jef Verschueren, Jan Blommaert and Chris Bulcaen (eds.), *Handbook of Pragmatics*, 1–21. Amsterdam: John Benjamins.

1999   On the priority of salient meanings: studies of literal and figurative language. *Journal of Pragmatics* 31: 919–929.

2003   *On our Mind: Salience, Context and Figurative Language.* New York: Oxford University Press.

Giora, Rachel and Ofer Fein

1999a   Understanding familiar and less familiar figurative language: the graded salience hypothesis. *Journal of Pragmatics* 31: 1601–1618.

1999b   Irony interpretation: the graded salience hypothesis. *Humor* 12: 425–436.

1999c   Irony: context and salience. *Metaphor and Symbol* 14: 241–257.

Giora, Rachel, Ofer Fein and Tamir Schwartz

1998   Irony: graded salience and indirect negation. *Metaphor and Symbol* 13: 83–101.

Glucksberg, Sam, Patricia Gildea and Howard Bookin

1982   On understanding nonliteral speech: can people ignore metaphors? *Journal of Verbal Learning and Verbal Behavior* 21: 85–98.

Glucksberg, Sam and Boaz Keysar

1990   Understanding metaphorical comparisons: beyond similarity. *Psychological Review* 97: 3–18.

Glucksberg, Sam, Roger Kreuz and Susan H. Rho

1986   Context can constrain lexical access: implications for models of language comprehension. *Journal of Experimental Psychology: Learning, Memory, and Cognition* 12: 323–335.

Gorfein, S. David (ed.)

1989   *Resolving Semantic Ambiguity.* New York: Springer-Verlag.

Grice, H. Paul
    1975   Logic and conversation. In: Peter Cole and Jerry Morgan (eds.), *Speech Acts. Syntax and Semantics Volume 3*, 41–58. New York: Academic Press.

Hogaboam, Thomas W. and Charles A. Perfetti
    1975   Lexical ambiguity and sentence comprehension. *Journal of Verbal Learning and Verbal Behavior* 14: 265–274.

Horton, William S. and Boaz Keysar
    1996   When do speakers take into account common ground? *Cognition* 59: 91–117.

Inhoff, Alber Werner, Susan D. Lima and Patrick J. Carroll
    1984   Contextual effects on metaphor comprehension in reading. *Memory and Cognition* 12: 558–567.

Jones, Janet Lee
    1991   Early integration of context during lexical access of homonym meanings. *Current Psychology: Research and Review* 10: 163–181.

Kemper, Susan
    1981   Comprehension and interpretation of proverbs. *Journal of Psycholinguistic Research* 10: 179–183.

Keysar, Boaz
    1989   On the functional equivalence of literal and metaphorical interpretations in discourse. *Journal of Memory and Language* 28: 375–385.

Keysar, Boaz, Dale J. Barr, Jennifer A. Balin and Timothy S. Paek
    1998   Definite reference and mutual knowledge: process models of common ground in comprehension. *Journal of Memory and Language* 39: 1–20.

Keysar, Boaz, Dale J. Barr and William S. Horton
    1998   The egocentric basis of language use: insights from a processing approach. *Current Directions in Psychological Sciences* 7: 46–50.

Kotthoff, Helga
    1998   Irony, quotation, and other forms of staged intertextuality: double or contrastive perspectivation in conversation. *Interaction and Linguistic Structures* 5: 1–27.

Levinson, Stephen
    1983   *Pragmatics*. Cambridge, UK: Cambridge University Press.

Lucas, Margery M.
    1987   Context effects on the processing of ambiguous words in sentence context. *Language and Speech* 30: 25–46.

Martin, Charles, Hoang Vu, George Kellas and Kimberly Metcalf
    1999   Strength of discourse context as a determinant of the subordinate bias effect. *The Quarterly Journal of Experimental Psychology* 52A: 813–839.

Onifer, William and David A. Swinney
1981 Accessing lexical ambiguities during sentence comprehension: effects of frequency of meaning and contextual bias. *Memory and Cognition* 9: 225–236.
Ortony, Andrew, Diane L. Schallert, Ralph E. Reynolds and Stephen J. Antos
1978 Interpreting metaphors and idioms: some effects of context on comprehension. *Journal of Verbal Learning and Verbal Behavior* 17: 465–477.
Pexman Penny, Todd Ferretti and Albert Katz
2000 Discourse factors that influence irony detection during on-line reading. *Discourse Processes* 29: 201–222.
Picoult, Jonathan and Marcia K. Johnson
1992 Controlling for homophone polarity and prime target relatedness in the cross-modal lexical decision task. *Bulletin of the Psychonomic Society* 30: 15–18.
Rayner, Keith and Lyn Frazier
1989 Selection mechanisms in reading lexically ambiguous words. *Journal of Experimental Psychology: Learning, Memory, and Cognition* 15: 779–790.
Rayner, Keith and Robin K. Morris
1991 Comprehension processes in reading ambiguous sentences: reflections from eye movements. In: Greg B. Simpson (ed.), *Understanding Word and Sentence*, 175–198. Amsterdam: North Holland.
Rayner, Keith, Jeremy M. Pacht and Susan A. Duffy
1994 Effects of prior encounter and global discourse bias on the processing of lexically ambiguous words: evidence from eye fixations. *Journal of Memory and Language* 33: 527–544.
Schvaneveldt, Roger W., David E. Meyer and Curtis A. Becker
1976 Lexical ambiguity, semantic context, and visual word recognition. *Journal of Experimental Psychology: Human Perception and Performance* 2: 243–256.
Schwoebel, John, Shelly Dews, Ellen Winner and Kavitha Srinivas
2000 Obligatory processing of the literal meaning of ironic utterances: further evidence. *Metaphor and Symbol* 15: 47–61.
Searle, John
1979 *Expression and Meaning.* Cambridge: Cambridge University Press.
Seidenberg, Mark S., Michael K. Tanenhaus, James M. Leiman and Marie Bienkowski
1982 Automatic access of the meaning of ambiguous words in context: some limitations of knowledge based processing. *Cognitive Psychology* 14: 489–537.
Sereno C. Sara, Jeremy M. Pacht and Keith Rayner
1992 The effect of meaning frequency on processing lexically ambiguous

words: evidence from eye fixations. *Psychological Science* 3: 269–300.

Shen, Yeshayahu
1997   Metaphors and global conceptual structures. *Poetics* 25: 1–17.
Simpson, Greg B.
1981   Meaning dominance and semantic context in the processing of lexical ambiguity. *Journal of Verbal Learning and Verbal Behavior* 20: 120–136.
1994   Context and the processing of ambiguous words. In: A. Morton Gernsbacher (ed.), *Handbook of Psycholinguistics*, 359–374. San Diego, CA: Academic Press.
Simpson, Greg B. and Curt Burgess
1985   Activation and selection processes in the recognition of ambiguous words. *Journal of Experimental Psychology: Human Perception and Performance* 11: 28–39.
Simpson, Greg B. and Mollie R. Foster
1986   Lexical ambiguity and children's word recognition. *Developmental Psychology* 22: 147–154.
Simpson, Greg B. and Merilee A. Krueger
1991   Selective access of homograph in sentence context. *Journal of Memory and Language* 30: 627–643.
Small, Steven I., Garrison W. Cottrell and Michael K. Tanenhaus
1988   *Lexical Ambiguity Resolution: Perspectives from Psycholinguistics, Neuropsychology, and Artificial Intelligence.* San Mateo, CA: Morgan Kaufmann.
Sperber, Dan and Deirdre Wilson
1986/1995 *Relevance: Communication and Cognition.* Oxford: Blackwell.
Swinney, David A.
1979   Lexical access during sentence comprehension: (re)consideration of context effects. *Journal of Verbal Learning and Verbal Behavior* 18: 645–659.
Swinney, David A. and Penny Prather
1989   On the comprehension of lexical ambiguity by young children: investigations into development of mental modularity. In: David S. Gorfein (ed.), *Resolving Semantic Ambiguity*, 225–238. New York: Springer-Verlag.
Tabossi, Patrizia
1988   Accessing lexical ambiguity in different types of sentential contexts. *Journal of Memory and Language* 27: 324–340.
Tanenhaus, Michael K., Greg N. Carlson and Mark S. Seidenberg
1985   Do listeners compute linguistic representations? In: David Dowty, Lauri Kartunnen and Arnold M. Zwicky (eds.), *Natural Language*

Parsing: Psychological, Theoretical and Computational Perspectives. New York: Cambridge University Press.

Tanenhaus, Michael K., James M. Leiman and Mark S. Seidenberg
1979   Evidence for multiple stages in the processing of ambiguous words in syntactic contexts. *Journal of Verbal Learning and Verbal Behavior* 18: 161–167.

Till, Robert E., Ernest F. Mross and Walter Kintsch
1988   Time course of priming for associate and inference words in a discourse context. *Journal of Verbal Learning and Verbal Behavior* 16: 283–298.

Titone, Debra
1998   Hemispheric differences in context sensitivity during lexical ambiguity resolution. *Brain and Language* 65: 361–394.

Vu, Hoang, George Kellas and Stephen T. Paul
1998   Sources of sentence constraint in lexical ambiguity resolution. *Memory and Cognition* 26: 979–1001.

West, Richard F. and Keith E. Stanovich
1988   How much of sentence priming is word priming? *Bulletin of the Psychonomic Society* 26: 1–4.

Williams, John N.
1992   Processing polysemous words in context. Evidence from interrelated meanings. *Journal of Psycholinguistic Research* 21: 193–218.

Zaidel, Eran
1987   Hemispheric monitoring. In: David Ottoson (ed.), *Duality and Unity of the Brain*, 247–281. Hampshire: Macmillan.

Young children's and adults' use of figurative language: how important are cultural and linguistic influences?

Ann Dowker

For many years, it has been known that children – and adults – do not use language only for communication, or for referring to objects and events in the environment. Children's playful and nonliteral uses of language have been the subject of study at least since the end of the 19th century (e.g. Lukens 1894; Chamberlain and Chamberlain 1904; Trettian 1904; Jespersen 1922; Chukovsky 1925 [1968]; Weir 1962; Aimard 1977; Garvey 1977; Iwamura 1980; Sutton-Smith 1980; Schwartz 1981; Kuczaj 1982, 1983; Fox 1983, 1993; Schieffelin 1983; Nelson 1987; Dowker 1989, 1991, 1998; Joffe and Shapiro 1991; Johnson 1991; Crystal 1998). These nonliteral uses of language are very diverse, but one important feature that they share is their metalinguistic nature: they involve attention to and manipulation of aspects of language, rather than treating language as a means to the end of trans- mitting information. Children manipulate linguistic patterns and relationships, including phonological relationships (e.g. rhyme and alliteration); syntactic relationships (e.g. "modified repetition" as defined by Dowker 1991) and semantic relationships (e.g. simile and metaphor).

Metaphor and other forms of figurative language have been the object of considerable interest for researchers: partly because of their importance in the poetry and other literature – oral and written – of seemingly all cultures (Finnegan 1977); partly because of their relevance to the ways in which people form conceptual categories.

Metaphor subsumes a variety of devices. Simile and metaphor are disting- uished for several literary and psychological purposes (Kennedy and Chiappe 1999); and some researchers (Happe 1991; Nerlich, Todd and Clarke 1998) suggest that true metaphor emerges later and makes greater demands on theory of mind than does simile; but simile will here be treated as just one form of metaphor.

There have been numerous studies of the development and early use of metaphor (Gardner et al. 1978; Billow 1981; Fourment, Emmenecker and

Pantz 1987; Gentner, Falkenhainer and Skorstad 1988; Winner 1988; Caramelli and Montanari 1995).

Most of these studies suggest that some forms of metaphor begin very early. Billow (1981) found that it occurred frequently in the spontaneous play and conversation of children from 2½ to 6; and that it did not increase in frequency with age within that age range.

Gardner et al. (1978) and Winner (1988) also report extensive use of metaphor during the preschool period; though unlike Billow they found significant age differences. Metaphor increased during the preschool period and then declined with the onset of a "literal stage" at the age of about 6 or 7. It was suggested that during this period, children become more aware of linguistic rules and category boundaries and are reluctant to violate them. By adolescence, these rules and boundaries are more firmly defined, and the children are in complete control of them, and thus may be more ready to violate them for particular purposes. This may parallel the U-shaped relationships between expertise and strategy variability that Dowker et al. (1996) have proposed for other domains such as mathematics.

Later studies have mostly supported the view that young children are capable of comprehending and using metaphors, though there are some age differences in their frequency and predominant types. Numerous studies (Gardner et al. 1978; Dowker 1986; Gentner, Falkenhainer and Skorstad 1988) indicate that young children tend to use predominantly perceptual metaphors, e.g. *They* [children walking around the school] *sound like horses*. Older children and adults use a relatively larger number of cross-sensory metaphors, e.g. *Her dress is so loud that it shouts*, and psychological/physical metaphors, e.g. *fear like a seep of water* (from a poem by "Emma", quoted by Dowker, Hermelin and Pring 1996), and *I grasp your meaning*. For example, Caramelli and Montanari (1995) studied Italian children's use of animal terms as metaphors and found that they moved from basing metaphors predominantly on visual resemblance at age 6 to basing them predominantly on moral judgement at age 12.

There also appear to be age differences in the contexts in which people use metaphor, though this has not been studied as systematically. Children frequently use metaphor in the context of pretend play (Stross 1975; Billow 1981); while adults associate it strongly with poetry: an association that is possibly less strong for young children (Dowker 1986; Dowker et al. 1998).

When researchers attempt to distinguish between literal and figurative, including metaphorical, language, the distinction is often difficult to make.

Fass (1997: 2) points out that "it has proved extremely hard to develop precise criteria for distinguishing literal from nonliteral language". Lakoff and Johnson (1980) and Gibbs (1994) put forward the view that, in both children and adults, the distinction between figurative and literal language is less sharp than has sometimes been assumed. Gibbs (1994: 435–436) stated that "similar cognitive mechanisms drive our understanding of both literal and figurative speech"; that "people need not recognize figurative language as violating communicative norms and maxims in order to understand what those expressions figuratively mean"; and that "a great deal of our thinking is constituted by metaphorical mappings from dissimilar source and target domains". Examples of the latter include thinking of understanding as seeing (*That's very clear*; *I've got the picture*; etc.) or anger as heated fluid in a container (*He got all steamed up*; *I was boiling over*; *She hit the ceiling*).

Cross-cultural differences in metaphor use have only been studied to a limited extent from a psychological point of view, though they have also received attention from some other perspectives, e.g. the difficulties that they pose for translators. The ways in which metaphor is used are certainly influenced by pragmatics and cultural convention: for example, a British person would use the term *fox* to mean 'sly and cunning person', while a Canadian might use the same term to mean 'attractive woman'.

There have been some studies of the ways in which differences in metaphoric usage may reflect cultural differences in attitudes to and concepts of certain emotional, social and cognitive domains, such as anger (Gibbs 1994; Koevecses 2000a), emotions generally (Palmer, Bennett and Stacey 1999; Koevecses 2000b), and time (Zhou and Huang 2000; Moore 2001). Such studies have revealed considerable commonalities, revealing universal cognitive structures; for example both English and Wolof speakers have a tendency to map spatial vocabulary onto temporal concepts (Moore 2001). However, cultural differences are also found, and Moore concludes that "While there is a substantial amount of metaphor structure that is shared cross-linguistically, a full understanding of conceptual metaphor depends on properties of particular languages, communities of speakers, or individuals". Sometimes, even when a given type of metaphorical construction is found generally across cultures, it is given more emphasis in some cultures than others. For example, Yu (2001) points out that terms for the face are used metaphorically in both English and Chinese to refer to broader aspects of physical appearance (*she's not just a pretty face*), to emotion and character (*we must face up to this*), to interactions and relationships (*we had a face-to-*

face discussion), and to prestige and dignity (*he lost face*). However, such metaphors were used more richly in Chinese than English, reflecting cultural differences in the values attributed to the relevant concepts.

Far fewer studies have been carried out on the ways in which language or culture may affect the actual frequency of figurative language.

Some years ago, I carried out an analysis of spontaneous poems produced by children between the ages of 2 and 6 (Dowker 1986). The sources included Timothy Rogers' book *Those First Affections*, his extensive unpublished collection of poems by very young children, other published sources (e.g. Trettien 1894; Dixon 1930; Britton 1970; Griffin 1981; Heath 1983; etc.), and numerous personal communications from friends and acquaintances. In all, there were nearly 400 poems by English children: 398 to be precise, including 26 by 2-year-olds, 57 by 3-year-olds, 73 by 4-year-olds, 99 by 5-year-olds, 99 by 6-year-olds, and 44 by nursery-school children of unspecified age.

The English poems were compared with poems by French, Hebrew and Russian-speaking children of similar age-range. The 37 French poems were taken from various published sources (e.g. Aimard 1977; Chevalley 1982). Most of the 66 Russian poems come from Chukovsky (1970) with a few from other published sources. Some of the 19 Hebrew poems were unpublished and sent to me by friends and acquaintances; the rest come from Goldberg (n.d.) and Rivkai (1937).

The findings with regard to metaphor were as follows. One-sixth of the English poems contained metaphor. There was some increase with age from less than 10% of poems by 2- and 3-year-olds to 22% – just over a fifth – of poems by 6-year-olds. In all, 78 metaphors were produced. Most of the metaphors were similes; and about two-thirds of them were perceptually based; e.g. *When we walk around we look like shadows*; *The moon is just like a little white bird/Except that it hasn't got a little face*; *This man was so tall as the clouds*; *The sun is like a stove/Boiling water*; *Hands as soft as seal*. By contrast, only 7% were functionally or behaviourally based.

The poems by French children were more likely than those of the English children to contain metaphor. One third of their poems did so. Over half of the French metaphors were perceptually based (e.g. *Lune d'argent ... Etoiles d'or* [Moon of Silver ... Stars of gold]), though a somewhat higher proportion of the French metaphors did come into other categories, e.g. *Les oiseaux sont mignons/Malheureux/Comme les pauvres gens* [The birds are sweet/Unlucky/Like poor people].

If metaphors were commoner in the French than the English poems, they were much less common in the Russian and Hebrew poems. Only 8% of the Russian poems and none of the 19 Hebrew poems contained any metaphor.

The study of children's spontaneous poems is important in showing what they produce when not being actively directed by adults. However, there are some disadvantages in confining oneself to the study of spontaneous poems. They had to be noted down by adults, which may lead to selection bias: adults may choose to record poems which they consider to be particularly good or particularly funny or just particularly interesting. Moreover, these poems were produced over a very wide timescale, from the 1890s to the 1980s, and it is possible that children's poems could have changed somewhat over this period, perhaps in response to changes in children's literature. Therefore, a somewhat more controlled study was carried out, which involved eliciting poems from children.

Dowker et al. (1998) carried out a cross-linguistic study of poem production by young children. The participants were 122 English children, 59 French children, 148 Italian children, 118 Polish children and 118 Brazilian (Portuguese-speaking) children between the ages of 4 and 6 years.

The basic task involved the successive presentation of three pictures. After each picture was presented, the child was asked: "Could you tell me a story about this picture?" and his/her response was recorded on a tape-recorder and then played back to the child. The child was then told: "Now I'm going to tell you a poem, which is a bit like a story but not quite. And I'd like you to make up something like that." One of three poems dealing with the picture (a rhyming poem, an alliterative poem and a simile poem) was then presented as a stimulus, and the child was asked: "Can you make up something like that?" Once again, the child's response was recorded and then played back to him/her on the tape-recorder. The same procedure was followed with the next two pictures. (The instructions were, of course, translated into the relevant languages for the non-English children.) During this task, each child heard one rhyming poem, one alliterative poem and one simile poem.

Differences between the procedure as applied to the different groups were (i) that of necessity the stimulus poems were different, as the children of each group heard stimulus poems in their own language; (ii) the pictures sometimes differed between languages, as they had to permit the production of stimulus poems with the appropriate devices in a particular language.

There were some differences in the use of phonological devices. The Italian children made extensive use of both rhyme and alliteration; while the Polish children made considerable use of alliteration but less use of rhyme, and the English children used much rhyme but little alliteration. The French and Brazilian groups were the only groups in the study to use phonological devices in less than half of their poems. However, by far the most marked differences were in the use of simile and metaphor. Metaphor, almost always consisting of simile, was in general less common than the phonological devices; but there were extremely striking group differences. Only a tiny proportion of English, Italian or Polish children produced poems containing similes, whereas similes were much more common in the French and Brazilian poems.

It was inappropriate to investigate age differences in the use of simile in the English, Italian or Polish group, because of the very small numbers involved. They were nonsignificant in the Brazilian group ($\chi^2 = 0.45$; df = 2; p n.s.). In the French group, there was a significant increase with age ($\chi^2 = 8.82$; df = 2; $p < 0.05$).

The following are some examples of poems containing similes:

(1)   English poem by a girl of 4 years 6 months:

> It was quiet as the night.
> The rabbits were running across the street faster than the wind.
> They were hopping around so fast.
> We saw them run so fast
> That the badgers watched us.
> The trees were as big as a girl.
> And they could fall down
> Across the stream
> Into the woods of a chipmunk.

(2)   French poem by a 6-year-old boy:

> Le cochon est gros comme une armoire.
>
> [The pig is as fat as a wardrobe.]

(3)   Brazilian poem by a girl of 5 years 5 months:

> O gatinho e branquinho como nuvem.
> O gatinho e branquinho como o papel.

O gatinho gost de jogar bolinha e come
Leite feito um bebe.

[The kitten is white as clouds.
The kitten is white as paper.
The kitten likes to play with a ball, and drinks
Milk like a baby.]

Thus, contrary to what might have been predicted on the grounds that there are much greater phonological than semantic differences between languages, group differences were greater with regard to the use of metaphor and simile than with regard to the use of phonological devices. Whereas all the groups did make significant use of phonological devices in their poems, three of the five groups (English, Polish and Italian) used almost no metaphor in their poems.

The findings that metaphor was used more often, and phonological devices less often, by French than English children are in agreement with the results of the study of spontaneous poems. The spontaneous poems were not elicited by means of examples, making it unlikely that the cross-cultural differences in the studies were the artifacts of a particular methodology.

Both studies suggested a possible trade-off between the use of phonological devices and of semantic devices (e.g. simile and metaphor), in that the groups (French and Brazilian) that made the least use of phonological devices made the greatest use of metaphor. Dowker et al. (1998) also found that French and Brazilian children's poems outnumbered their stories, whereas the reverse was true of the other groups. This may indicate differences in the nature and sharpness of the division between the genres of stories and poems. Perhaps to French and Brazilian children, poems are "stories with rhythm", featuring semantic devices. For the other groups, poems may be more sharply distinguished from stories through their emphasis on phonological as opposed to semantic devices.

Do the group differences in poem production reflect differences in actual capacities for understanding or producing metaphor? Though it is difficult to answer this question with certainty, it appears unlikely that this is the case. Cross-cultural and cross-linguistic differences in metaphoric development have not been much studied; but much of the research on metaphoric development has been carried out with English-speaking children (e.g. Gardner et al. 1978; Billow 1981), and there is ample evidence that such children are capable of using metaphor and simile from an early age.

Thus, there is no evidence that the differences in metaphoric production are caused by or related to an inability to use or detect metaphor in certain groups.

Studies of the nature and extent of cultural differences in metaphor use bring up several issues. Metaphor may be influenced by nonverbal conceptual knowledge, by attitudes and emotions and by pragmatic context, and all of these may be influenced by both age and culture. In addition, however, metaphor may be influenced by factors within language itself.

As regards relationships between metaphor use and language development, there has been considerable discussion of the relationship between early metaphor use, and early literally-based overextensions of words. Numerous researchers (e.g. Vosniadou 1987) have warned against excessive readiness to label young children's utterances as metaphors, on the grounds that some "metaphors" are overextensions of meaning due to a lack of precise knowledge of word meanings, similar to the behaviour of an 18-month-old child who has just learned the word "doggie" and applies it to all four-legged animals (for discussion of this problem, see Vosniadou 1987). Gardner et al. (1978), Billow (1981) and others have attempted to guard against this possibility by only including renamings as "metaphors" if the children showed evidence of knowledge of the correct name for the renamed object, and of correct use of the term used in renaming.

Attempts to distinguish metaphor from overextension rest on the assumption that at least some overextension is due to a genuine belief that the term applies to the objects to which it is extended (or, at least, to the lack of a clear understanding that it is). However, overextensions in production need not be due to overextensions in comprehension (Fremgen and Fay 1980). Young children have a limited vocabulary. Despite realizing that a certain word is inappropriate to a certain referent, whose name (s)he does not know, a child may use the word because it is the most appropriate term that (s)he has available. Nelson et al. (1978) argue that overextensions based on perceptual similarities are really statements of analogy. The 18-month-old child, who is not yet capable of making a statement such as "This grapefruit looks like the moon" or even "This thing – I don't know it's name – looks like the moon" may point to a grapefruit and say: "Moon". Such utterances, according to Nelson et al., are a part of the child's emerging fascination with similarities and differences, which plays an important part in the early formation of categories.

If a child uses an inappropriate term, not because of overextension in comprehension, but as an imperfect substitute for the more appropriate term that (s)he lacks, then (s)he is doing one of the things that adults do when they use metaphor: expressing "the otherwise inexpressible". The adult who describes a state of depression as "a fog surrounding me", or who says "My love is like a red red rose" is presumably using the figurative expressions because (s)he cannot convey the meaning equally well by means of literal description. Indeed, Carabine (1991) has pointed out that both children and adults have "fuzzy boundaries" to the extensions of common word meanings, and that there is far more similarity between children and adults in their word extensions than is often recognized.

When word meaning extensions are or become standardized within a language, rather than idiosyncratic to a particular individual or occasion, they may be described as polysemy.

Polysemy has been defined (e.g. Ullman 1951) as the property of a word that has multiple but related meanings (e.g. *head* can mean 'upper part of the body', 'chief person in an organization', etc.). It is sometimes difficult to distinguish it from homonymy (the property of a word that has multiple unrelated meanings; e.g. *bank* can mean 'edge of a river' or 'financial institution').

Some linguists (Ullman 1951; Kinberg 1991) have suggested a continuum from figurative uses through polysemy to homonymy. Taking into account the above-mentioned findings concerning children's early semantic development, the following continuum is here proposed: overextension – figurative uses – polysemy – homonymy.

Such a view implies a close relationship between polysemy and figurative language; and indeed polysemy may be both a consequence and cause of figurative language use. Many of the extra, polysemous meanings that a word develops begin as metaphorical extensions of a primary meaning of that word: e.g. *head* in the sense of 'chief person' presumably originated as a metaphorical extension of *head* in its primary sense of 'upper part of the body'. This is not to say that all polysemous words have one clearly definable primary meaning; this is obviously not the case (Gibbs 1994). Other forms of figurative language such as metonymy, a form of indirect reference in which one word is replaced by a word referring to an entity closely associated with it, are also the sources of polysemous meaning (e.g. 'face' for 'person').

Polysemy may also influence nonliteral language use: especially in puns and riddles (Nerlich, Todd and Clarke 1998), but also metaphors and similes.

Since there appear to be cross-linguistic differences in metaphor use, and since polysemy and metaphor seem to be closely related, are there also cross-linguistic differences in polysemy? Do some languages have a greater incidence of polysemy; a greater number of meanings for the same word than do others? Sinha and Kuteva (1995) suggest that spatial locatives, such as *on* and *in* are polysemous in most or all languages, but are more so in some languages than in others. Hunt and Agnoli (1991) propose that English is more polysemous than Italian, and that Chinese and Japanese are more polysemous than either. This conclusion was, however, based on investigation of a relatively small number of words, e.g. 30 in English and 30 in Italian.

If there are cross-linguistic differences in polysemy, could this lead to cross-linguistic differences in the use of metaphor? It is difficult to answer this question, partly because of ambiguities in interpreting the direction of causation, and partly because such effects could be in either direction. If a culture has a strong tendency to use metaphoric expressions, then some of these could become completely or partially standardized, increasing the amount of polysemy in the language. On the other hand, explicit use of metaphor could serve as an alternative to polysemy.

According to Deane (1988: 325) "Human thought displays two complementary characteristics. While it displays flexible responses to novel situations, it is also highly structured, incorporating detailed information about the world" and (p. 358), "... viewed in cognitive terms, polysemy is a natural consequence of the interplay of cognitive flexibility and structure".

Figurative linguistic extension, literal linguistic overextension and polysemy overlap considerably with one another, and all appear to depend on the combination of flexibility and structure. In these respects, they do indeed resemble cognitive processes in numerous other domains. Arithmetic, for example, is a highly structured domain; but it also involves considerable flexibility and within-individual and between-individual variability of strategy use (Krutetskii 1976; Siegler and Jenkins 1989; Dowker et al. 1996; Siegler 1996; Baroody and Dowker 2003). A similar combination of flexibility and patterned structure characterizes children's drawing (Alland 1983; Karmiloff-Smith 1990).

Nerlich, Todd and Clarke (1998: 361) propose that "the ability to use polysemy in both metaphor and jokes facilitates the ability to play different roles in life and see things from different viewpoints and vice versa". They point out that both metaphor comprehension and the ability to form meta-representations are impaired in autism; it might be added that autistic individuals tend to be inflexible in their strategy use in many domains, and in language in particular.

The whole area of the relationship, especially in development, between figurative language and polysemy is still little understood. Fragments have been studied in isolation, but much research is still needed to bring the fragments together. We may conclude that:

(i)   Understanding of polysemous meanings of words improves with age.
(ii)   Metaphoric production and comprehension begin very early in child-hood, and become more sophisticated in adolescence and adulthood, possibly after a temporary dip in middle childhood (Gardner et al. 1978; Winner 1988).
(iii)   Polysemy, whether in the language development of an individual child or the historical development of a language, is in part based on meta-phoric extension (Nerlich and Clarke 1997; Nerlich, Todd and Clarke 1998).
(iv)   The existence of polysemy facilitates the use of certain forms of figurative language.
(v)   Most crucially, there are no clear boundaries between polysemy, over-extension and figurative language (Nelson et al. 1978; Gibbs 1994).

Clear-cut examples of metaphor, overextension, or literal polysemy without metaphoric overtones are probably rare; the categories share many character-istics and typically show significant overlap. The apparent divisions between them are due in part to the fact that they have frequently been studied separately, by researchers in different disciplines and subspecialities. Polysemy has tended to be the province of linguists and artificial intelligence researchers; overextension the province of developmental psychologists studying early language development; and metaphor the province of developmental psychol-ogists studying somewhat older children, of cognitive psychologists, and of students of literature. Moreover, metaphor and other forms of figurative language are frequently regarded as specialized poetic devices; though there is considerable evidence not only that everyday language is often figurative (Gibbs 1994) but that metaphor is less strongly associated with poetry in the early stages of its development than later on. Young children produce both poems and metaphors, but not necessarily in conjunction (Dowker et al. 1998).

However, one crucial gap in our knowledge is the question of the existence and extent of cross-linguistic differences in the frequency of use of either polysemy or metaphor. Even as regards age differences, although, as discussed above, some research has been done on developmental changes in metaphoric comprehension and production, very little research has been carried out on the development and use of polysemy. Only when both the developmental and linguistic influences on both polysemy and metaphor are better understood can we begin to fully understand the nature of these phenomena, and the undoubtedly close relationships between them.

References

Aimard, Paul
   1977   *Les Jeux de Mots de l'Enfant.* Villeurbanne: Simep-Editions.
Alland, Alexander
   1983   *Playing with Form: Children Draw in Six Cultures.* New York: Columbia University Press.
Baroody, Arthur and Ann Dowker (eds.)
   2003   *The Development of Arithmetical Concepts and Skills.* Mahwah, NJ: Erlbaum.
Billow, Richard
   1981   Observing spontaneous metaphor in children. *Journal of Experimental Child Psychology* 31: 430–445.
Britton, James
   1970   *Language and Learning.* London: Allen Lane.
Carabine, B.
   1991   Fuzzy boundaries and the extension of object-words. *Journal of Child Language* 18: 355–372.
Caramelli, Nicoletta and A. Montanari
   1995   *Animal Terms in Children's Metaphors.* Lund University, Sweden: Cognitive Science Research.
Chamberlain, Alexander and Isabel Chamberlain
   1904   Studies of a child, I and II. *Pedagogical Seminary* 9: 264–291 and 452–483.
Chevalley, Etienne
   1982   *Miracles de l'Enfance.* Paris: Guilde du Livre.
Chukovsky, Kornei
   1925 [1968] *From Two to Five.* Berkeley: University of California Press. 1968 translation by Miriam Morton of 1959 edition. First Russian edition published in 1925.
   1970 [1925] *Ot Dvukk do Pyati [From Two to Five].* Moscow: Narodnaya Asveta.
Crystal, David
   1998   *Language Play.* Harmondsworth: Penguin.
Deane, Paul
   1988   Polysemy and cognition. *Lingua* 75: 325–361.

Dixon, Catherine
    1930   *Children Are Like That.* New York: John Day.
Dowker, Ann
    1986   Language play in young children. Ph.D. thesis. University of London
                Institute of Education.
    1989   Rhyme and alliteration in poems elicited from young children.
                Journal of Child Language 16: 181–202.
    1991   Modified repetition in poems elicited from young children. *Journal
                of Child Language* 18: 625–639.
Dowker, Ann (ed.)
    1998   Language play in children. Special Issue of *Cahiers de Psychologie
                Cognitive/Current Psychology of Cognition* 17.
Dowker, Ann, Amanda Flood, Helen Griffiths, Louise Harriss and Lisa Hook
    1996   Estimation strategies of four groups. *Mathematical Cognition* 2:
                113–135.
Dowker, Ann, Beate Hermelin and Linda Pring
    1996   A savant poet. *Psychological Medicine* 26: 913–924.
Dowker, Ann, Grazyna Krasowicz, Giuliana Pinto, Antonio Roazzi and Anita Smith
    1998   Phonological and semantic devices in very young children: a cross-
                cultural study. *Cahiers de Psychologie Cognitive/Current Psychology
                of Cognition* 17: 389–416.
Fass, Dan
    1997   *Processing Metonymy and Metaphor.* London: Ablex.
Finnegan, Ruth
    1977   *Oral Poetry.* Cambridge: Cambridge University Press.
Fourment, Marie-Claude, Nelly Emmenecker, and Valerie Pantz
    1987   Etudes de la production de métaphores chez les enfants de 3 à 7 ans.
                Année Psychologique 87: 535–551.
Fox, Carol
    1983   Talking like a book: young children's oral monologues. In: Margaret
                Meek (ed.), *Opening Moves: Work in Progress in the Study of
                Children's Language Development.* University of London Institute
                of Education: Bedford Way Papers.
    1993   *At the Very Edge of the Forest: The Influence of Literature on Story-
                telling by Children.* London: Cassell.
Fremgen, Amy and David Fay
    1980   Overextensions in production and comprehension: a methodological
                clarification. *Journal of Child Language* 7: 205–211.
Gardner, Howard, Ellen Winner, Robin Bechhoffer and Dennie Wolf
    1978   The development of figurative language. In: Katherine Nelson (ed.),
                Children's Language, Vol. 1. Cambridge, MA: Gardner Press Inc.

Garvey, Catherine
    1977   Play with language and speech. In: Susan Ervin-Tripp and Claudia
                Mitchell-Kernan (eds.), *Child Discourse*. Academic Press.
Gentner, Dedre, Brian Falkenhainer and Janice Skorstad
    1988   Viewing metaphor as analogy. In: David Helman (ed.), *Analogical
                Reasoning*. London: Kluwer.
Gibbs, Raymond W., Jr.
    1994   *The Poetics of Mind*. Cambridge: Cambridge University Press.
Goldberg, Lea
    (not dated) *Between a Children's Writer and his Reader*. Tel Aviv: Sifriyat Hapoalim
                (in Hebrew).
Griffin, Elinor
    1981   *Island of Childhood: Education in the Special World of Nursery
                School*. New York: Teachers' College Press.
Happe, Francesca
    1991   The autobiographical writings of three Asperger syndrome adults:
                problems of interpretation and implications for theory. In: Uta Frith
                (ed.), *Autism and Asperger Syndrome*. Cambridge: Cambridge University
                Press.
Heath, Shirley
    1983   *Ways with Words*. Cambridge: Cambridge University Press.
Hunt, Earl and Franca Agnoli
    1991   The Whorfian hypothesis: a cognitive psychology perspective. *Psycho-
                logical Review* 98: 377–389.
Iwamura, Susan
    1980   *The Verbal Games of Preschool Children*. London: Croom Helm.
Jespersen, Otto
    1922   *Language: Its Nature, Development and Origin*. London: Allen and
                Unwin.
Joffe, Victoria and G. Shapiro
    1991   Sound-based language play in four language-impaired subjects. *The
                South African Journal of Communication Disorders* 38: 119–128.
Johnson, Janice
    1991   Developmental versus language-based factors in metaphor interpre-
                tation. *Journal of Educational Psychology* 83: 470–483.
Karmiloff-Smith, Annette
    1990   Constraints on representational change: evidence from children's
                drawings. *Cognition* 34: 57–83.
Kennedy, John and Dan Chiappe
    1999   What makes a metaphor stronger than a simile? *Metaphor and Symbol*
                14: 63–69.

Kinberg, Naphthali
    1991   Figurative uses, polysemy and homonymy in systems of tense, mood and aspect. *Lingua* 83: 319–338.

Koevecses, Zoltan
    2000a   The concept of anger: universal or culture-specific? *Psychopathology* 33: 159–170.
    2000b   *Metaphor and Emotion: Language, Culture and Body in Human Feeling.* Cambridge: Cambridge University Press.

Krutetskii, Vadim
    1976   *The Psychology of Mathematical Abilities in Schoolchildren.* London: University of Chicago Press.

Kuczaj, Stan
    1982   Language play and language acquisition. In: Hayne Reese (ed.), *Advances in Child Development and Child Behaviour 17.* London: Academic Press.
    1983   *Crib Speech and Language Play.* Berlin: Springer-Verlag.

Lakoff, George and Mark Johnson
    1980   *Metaphors We Live By.* Chicago: University of Chicago Press.

Lukens, Herman
    1894   Report on the learning of language. *Pedagogical Seminary* 3: 419–460.

Moore, Kevin
    2001   Spatial experience and temporal metaphors in Wolof: point of view, conceptual mapping and linguistic structure. *Dissertation Abstracts International, Section A: Humanities and Social Sciences* 61: 2685.

Nelson, Katherine (ed.)
    1987   *Narratives From the Crib.* Cambridge, MA: Harvard University Press.

Nelson, Katherine, Leslie Rescorla, Janice Gruendel and Helen Benedict
    1978   Early lexicons: what do they mean? *Child Development* 49: 960–968.

Nerlich, Brigitte and David Clarke
    1997   Polysemy: patterns of meaning and patterns of history. *Historiographia Linguistica* 25: 349–385.

Nerlich, Brigitte, Zazie Todd and David Clarke
    1998   The function of polysemous jokes and riddles in semantic development. *Cahiers de Psychologie Cognitive/Current Psychology of Cognition* 17: 343–365.

Palmer, Gary, Heather Bennett and Les Stacey
    1999   Bursting with grief, erupting with shame: a conceptual and grammatical analysis of emotion-tropes in Tagalog. In: Gary Palmer and Debra Occhi (eds.), *Languages of Sentiment: Cultural Constructions of Emotional Substrates*, 171–200. Amsterdam: Benjamins.

Rivkai, Yehuda
    1937   *Letters to Parents*. Jerusalem: Achiasaf (in Hebrew).
Schieffelin, Bambi
    1983   Talking like birds: sound play in a cultural perspective. In: Elinor Ochs and Bambi Schieffelin (eds.), *Acquiring Conversational Competence*. London: Routledge and Kegan Paul.
Schwarz, Judith
    1981   Children's experiments with language. *Young Children* 36: 16–26.
Siegler, Robert
    1996   *Emerging Minds: The Process of Change in Children's Thinking*. Oxford: Oxford University Press.
Siegler, Robert and Eric Jenkins
    1989   *How Children Discover New Strategies*. Hillsdale, NJ: Erlbaum.
Sinha, Chris and Tania Kuteva
    1995   Distributed spatial semantics. *Nordic Journal of Linguistics* 18: 167–199.
Stross, Brian
    1975   Metaphor in the speech play of Tzeltal children. *Anthropological Linguistics* 17: 305–323.
Sutton-Smith, Brian
    1980   *The Folkstories of Children*. Philadelphia: University of Pennsylvania Press.
Trettien, August
    1894   Psychology of the language interest of children. *Pedagogical Seminary* 3: 419–466.
    1904   Psychology of the language interest of children. *Pedagogical Seminary* 23: 113–177.
Ullmann, Stephen
    1951   *The Principles of Semantics*. Oxford: Blackwell.
Vosniadou, Stella
    1987   Children and metaphors. *Child Development* 58: 870–885.
Weir, Ruth
    1962   *Language in the Crib*. The Hague: Mouton.
Winner, Ellen
    1988   *The Point of Words: Children's Understanding of Metaphor and Irony*. Cambridge, MA: Harvard University Press.
Yu, Ning
    2001   What does our face mean to us? *Pragmatics and Cognition* 9: 1–36.
Zhou, Rong and Xiteng Huang
    2000   A cross-cultural study of the metaphorical representation of time. *Psychological Science – China* 23: 141–145.

Emerging patterns and evolving polysemies: the acquisition of *get* between four and ten years

Brigitte Nerlich, Zazie Todd and David D. Clarke

1. Introduction

The study of the acquisition of verbs has become central to developmental psycholinguistics (Tomasello 1992; Tomasello and Merriman 1995). This paper considers how the array of senses conventionally associated with the polysemic word *get* is acquired by children between the ages of 4 and 10 years (see Tomasello 1992 for the acquisition of *get* between the ages of 17 and 24 months). In the process it will investigate whether developmental psychology can shed light on recent developments in cognitive linguistics and *vice versa*.

Polysemic verbs are important, since it is a basic claim of cognitive linguistics:

> that a lexical item is typically polysemic – comprising a family of interrelated senses, forming a network centred on a prototypical value. Although the precise array of senses conventionally associated with the expression is not fully predictable, neither is it arbitrary – as the network evolves from the prototype, each extension is MOTIVATED in some cognitively natural fashion, and often in accordance with a general pattern or principle. (Langacker 1988: 392)

Although the developmental sequence of the acquisition of the senses of *get* is not fully predictable, neither can it be entirely arbitrary. Our central hypothesis is that the first senses to be acquired will be the most prototypical values of the word *get*, and that the developmental route followed from then on will be motivated by some cognitively natural pattern.

There are several other reasons why the verb *get* was chosen for this study. It is in the top five of the most common verbs in the English language, with nearly 125,000 citations (out of 100 million) in the *British National Corpus* (*New Oxford Dictionary of English* 1998: 770). It is also one of the first and most commonly used verbs in children's speech, along with other "general-purpose" or "light" verbs such as *put, make, go*, and *do* (Clark 1978).

Get is also one of the many highly polysemic verbs found in English. The *New Oxford Dictionary of English* (1998), a dictionary of modern usage, lists the following main senses and subsenses of *get* in current English usage:

(i)   come to have or hold (something); receive (experience, suffer, or be afflicted with something, receive as a punishment, contract a disease);

(ii)   succeed in attaining, achieving, or experiencing; obtain (move in order to pick up or bring [something]; fetch, travel by or catch a bus, train, obtain as a result of calculation, respond to a ring);

(iii)   enter or reach a specified state or condition; become (used with past participle to form the passive mood); cause or be treated in a specified way, induce or prevail upon [someone] to do something, have the opportunity to do, begin to be or do something;

(iv)   come, go or make progress eventually or with some difficulty (move or come into a specified position or state), succeed in making [someone or something] come, go or make progress;

(v)   have got; have;

(vi)   catch or apprehend (someone) (strike or wound [someone] with a blow, punish, injure or kill, be punished, injured or killed), annoy or amuse, baffle;

(vii)   understand.

Using the historical *Oxford English Dictionary* (1888–1924), it is possible to chart the development of the core senses of *get* over time. It seems that the main subcategories of senses were already well-established by the 1300s. The diachronic evolution of the sense of *get* can be roughly summarized as follows:

    1200: obtain possession
    1250: receive
    1300: seek out and take, procure (fetch)
    1350: succeed in coming or going
    1380: to receive knowledge
    1500: make oneself, become
    1897: to understand

Some questions that might be asked are: which senses are first learned by children and in which sequence? Does the developmental sequence of acquisition map onto the most prototypical synchronic spread of senses and/ or the diachronic spreading of senses?

In this paper, we use recent developments in cognitive linguistics to explore these questions. Some central tenets of cognitive linguistics and their implications for the developmental study of *get* are outlined below. This will provide the theoretical background for the study, but it will also allow us to spell out more clearly the various hypothetical scenarios which could be used to explain the acquisition of polysemous words by children.

2. Theoretical background

2.1. *Embodiment*

In recent years it has been proposed that meaning is grounded in the nature of our bodies and in our interaction with the physical, social and cultural environment we live in (see Lakoff and Johnson 1999). It is claimed that concepts are grounded in our bodily experience and then elaborated by structures of imagination, i.e. metaphor and metonymy. This means that metaphor and metonymy motivate sense extension in some cognitively natural fashion, as for example in expressions like *I got it* meaning 'I have understood it'.

The prototypical cognitive linguistic investigation focuses on the perceptual, visual bases of the emergence and change of word meanings. Meanings are seen as perceptually grounded. More recently researchers have also begun to study hearing and smell (see Ibarretxe-Antuñano 1999) as the source of our embodied conceptual structures which are again the basis for our construction of meaning. But the body's input into the construction of meaning is not only limited to our senses of vision, hearing and smell; we also interact with the world, and this much more actively, through our hands, through touch, grasping, gathering, giving and receiving. The prototypical and primordial experiential scene in which the word *get* is embedded can be said to be a situation in which somebody comes to have or hold something. From this underlying matrix *get*'s polysemous sense extensions seem to flow. In the case of *get* the scene, as illustrated in Figure 1, corresponds to the experiential Gestalt of a basic causal event in which an agent receives an object from another agent, which results in grasping or holding something:

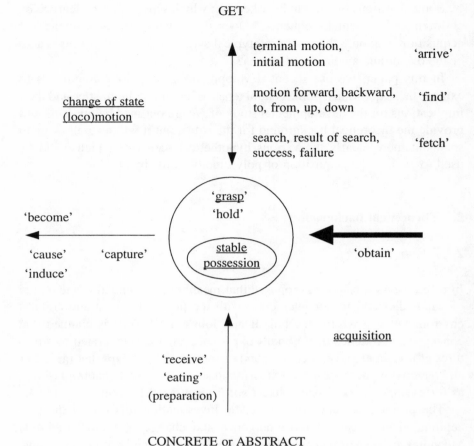

Figure 1. The prototypical scene associated with *get*.

someone causes something to be in somebody else's possession (see Tyler and Evans, this volume, for a discussion of protoscene).

2.2. Polysemy

Another central tenet of cognitive linguistics has been the polysemic structure of semantic categories. It has become clear that the study of the network of senses surrounding a word form is of fundamental importance for any study of language and cognition. Psycholinguists studying the mental lexicon have begun to ask questions like: are the meanings of a polysemous word "related to each other in some way, perhaps via a *core* concept ... ? ... Are the various meanings of words compartmentalized into many discrete and functionally independent units, or is the mental lexicon organized more economically with fewer but more highly structured lexical entries?" (Williams 1992: 194)

Some cognitive semanticists have investigated the polysemy verbs, such as *take* or *get*, in an intuitive way, relying on their own knowledge of a language (see Norvig and Lakoff 1987; Lindstromberg 1991). Others have studied the network of meanings surrounding a word form, such as *buy*, through the use of corpora (see Fillmore and Atkins 1992) and computerized semantic networks. Some have started to integrate research in cognitive linguistics with research in language acquisition and have begun to study polysemous verbs, such as *see* (see Johnson 1996, 1999).

Other cognitive psycholinguists have employed empirical methods to study the cognitive-semantic aspects of polysemy in adults. Gibbs, for example, analysed how subjects perceive the role of different image-schemas in the meaning of *stand* (Gibbs et al. 1994), and Sandra and Rice have examined the network of senses associated with certain prepositions using methods from experimental psycholinguistics (Sandra and Rice 1995; Rice 1996).

More recently still, research has begun in the study of the acquisition of *get* using the CHILDES database and applying Grady and Johnson's concept of "primary scene" (see Duxbury 1999 ms.; Grady and Johnson 1997). Also using CHILDES, Michael Israel has begun to chart the acquisition of *get* in the framework of an argument/construction grammar approach. He argues:

> that ultimately what children learn in acquiring these uses is a full set of constructions and not just a few idiomatic senses for a single verb. The study traces the emergence of these uses from a few verb-based formulae to a fully productive family of constructions. The evidence shows that these uses are not acquired in a random order, but rather are systematically linked to one another, with more complex constructions learned as extensions from simpler ones. (Israel, to appear)

In our study we use a lexically-based approach. Ideally, both approaches, the lexical-semantic and the grammatical-constructionist one should be combined.

Yet others are studying polysemy from an empirical point of view by using adult informants and applying production tests and similarity rating tests (Raukko 1999; see Raukko 1997; see also Lehrer 1974). Others still are investigating the acquisition of the *get*-passive using standard psychological experiments (Kerstin Meints, personal communication; see also Givón and Yang 1994).

Raukko (1999; see also Raukko, this volume) analysed the polysemous structure of the verb *get* by asking adult informants to fill in questionnaires where they were asked to produce sentence examples that manifest different meanings of *get*. His aim was to build up a picture of the intersubjective perception of the polysemy of *get*. He established that for young adults the senses of *get* cluster approximately around the following base senses: Obtaining, Receiving, Change of State, Motion, Understanding, Catching, Obligation, Stable Possession, Carrying, Ability. This conforms *grosso modo* to the main dictionary meanings of *get*, as well as to the diachronic evolution of *get* (except for *get* used in the sense of understanding, which had quite a high frequency in the examples produced by American high-school students; on the difficulties in categorizing the senses of *get*, see Raukko, this volume).

However, one should be aware of the fact (already noted by the father of the term *polysemy*, Michel Bréal, in 1884 – see Bréal 1991 [1884]):

> that the real meanings are often far more complex than the simple dictionary definitions would lead us to suppose. ... The primary dictionary meaning of words was often far adrift from the sense in which they were actually used. *Keep*, for instance, is usually defined as to retain, but in fact the word is much more often employed in the sense of continuing, as in *keep cool* and *keep smiling*. ... *Give*, even more interestingly, is most often used ... as 'mere verbal padding', as in *give it a look* or *give a report*. (Bryson 1990: 143)

Children learning a language might therefore be exposed to quite a different distribution of meanings than the dictionary one, and also quite different from what adults *believe* the distribution to be in theory, if not in practice (as captured by Raukko 1999, to some extent). In the case of *get* children would certainly be exposed to a high proportion of uses where *get* is mere verbal padding, is highly idiomatic, and where *get*, as part of a prefabricated semantic whole, has almost lost its own semantic value. Although this needs undoubtedly much further investigation, we shall see whether this parental influence is reflected in children's spontaneous production of sentences containing *get* or whether this production task elicits utterances based on an underlying knowledge of the prototypical core senses of *get* as found in dictionaries of common usage.

2.3. *Polysemic networks and pre-patterned chunks*

In the diachronic evolution of polysemic words there seems to be a certain point when the network of senses becomes saturated and begins to shed certain meanings. Either senses become so distant that they are perceived as unrelated (they become homonyms, such as French *voler* meaning 'to fly' and 'to steal'), or the word becomes part and parcel of a free-standing semantic conglomerate. Standing expressions such *Get a life, Get on with it,* and *Let's get out of here,* as well as phrasal verbs (a combination of a verb with an adverb or preposition that has a single meaning) develop, such as to *get into something, get over something, get out of something.* This corresponds to a general tendency for groups of words to settle into pre-packaged chunks (Deignan 1999: 34).

Most of these fossilized phrasal collocations of *get* are based on meta-phorical or metonymical mappings, or mappings of more concrete locative meanings onto more abstract mental meanings (see Brugman 1981; Lakoff 1987; Langacker 1987; Goddard 1998: 79; for a summary see Ungerer and Schmid 1996: Ch. 4). Examples of concrete uses are: *He got safely across the bridge*; *Driving carefully, she finally managed to get around the obstacle*; *I found the key and managed to get into the house*; and so on. Built on these are abstract uses such as: *I really couldn't get my idea across*; *The news is getting around quickly*; *To help get around this problem, some tanks are now equipped with radar*; *I finally got a remark in* [the conversation]; and so on (some of these examples are taken from *Cobuild* online).

Whereas research into the fossilization of metaphorically based col-locations helps us to understand some aspects of verbal polysemy, new research in construction grammar helps us to understand others. One of the foremost researchers in this field is Adèle Goldberg. She discusses the following examples:

(1)   *She sneezed a terrible sneeze.*
(2)   *She sneezed her nose red.*
(3)   *She sneezed her way to the emergency room.*
(4)   *She sneezed the foam off the cappuccino.*

Are we dealing here with four different senses of the verb *sneeze*? Goldberg (1998; see also Goldberg 1995) thinks not:

Instead of positing a new verb sense whenever a new syntactic frame is available, it makes sense to associate some aspects of meaning directly to the formal pattern itself. This allows us to account for the full semantic interpretation without positing implausible and ad hoc verb senses ... (Goldberg 1998: 205)

In her view "each of these formal patterns and its associated meaning(s) form a construction of the language" (Goldberg 1998: 205) and (argument structure) constructions encode certain archetypal forms of human experience. This has important implications for the study of language acquisition and the study of *get*.

Prefabricated chunks help us to build sentences up more quickly; argument structure construction provides us with ready-made blueprints for constructing sentences. Both should be important in language acquisition (see Hopper 1998: 166).

Goldberg (1998) has argued that light verbs such as *put*, *go*, *make*, *do* and *get* can be seen as "pathbreaking verbs", that is, as laying the foundations for the acquisition of more and more complex grammatical constructions. Some of these verbs are listed in Table 1.

Table 1.   Light verbs and constructional meanings they correspond to (reproduced from Goldberg 1998: 207).

Verb	Constructional meaning	Construction
put	X causes Y to move Z	Caused motion
make	X causes Y to become Z	Resultative
go	X moves Y	Intransitive motion
do	X acts on Y	Transitive
get	X acquires/possesses Y	Possessive

Goldberg claims that the initial meaning of a construction is a basic experiential Gestalt. This means that a basic pattern of experience is encoded in a basic pattern of the language (Goldberg 1998: 208). The scene for *get* was depicted in Figure 1.

As Slobin (1985) observed, children's first use of certain grammatical marking is applied to "prototypical scenes": "In Basic Child Grammar, the first Scenes to receive grammatical marking are 'prototypical', in that they regularly occur as part of frequent and salient activities and perceptions, and thereby become organizing points for later elaboration" (Slobin 1985: 1175).

We shall explore whether the same applies to the acquisition of verbs like *get*.

2.4. *Levels of polysemy*

In order to study the acquisition of the polysemous verb *get*, one has to be aware of three levels of polysemy:

(i)   A *primary* level of polysemy (based to a large extent on sense extensions which follow the path of the prototypical frame or scene in which *get* is embedded, as well as on metaphorical and metonymical extensions); here *get* can mean 'obtain', 'receive', 'fetch', 'reach', 'cause', 'induce', 'understand', and so on. Some of these senses are construction-based, such as the ditransitive *to get somebody something*.

(ii)   A *secondary* level of polysemy, where certain semantic conglomerates have formed, such as phrasal verbs and idioms.

(iii)   A *tertiary* level of polysemy, based again on metaphorical and metonymical extensions; here phrasal verbs derived from *get* have themselves become polysemous, as in *I got there in the end* (to a place) and *I got there in the end* (a task), *I got into the house* and *I got into trouble*, and so on.

3.   The acquisition of *get*

3.1.   *Hypotheses*

(i)   The first senses to be acquired will be the most prototypical values of the word *get* related to the primary scenario illustrated in Figure 1; then children will gradually work their way outwards to the more metaphorically and metonymically motivated meanings. This would be in contrast to a pattern in which random chunks are only later integrated into a conceptual whole roughly structured like the prototypical scene.

(ii)   The first senses to be acquired will stay on the primary level of polysemy.

(iii)   The synchronic spread of polysemes which cover the semantic area outlined by the word *get* reflects to a certain extent the diachronic spread of polysemes over time, and the developmental sequence in which *get* is acquired by children follows the same path.

(iv)   The conceptual frames associated with the various meanings of *get* are closely linked to children's primary situational knowledge in which the process of "getting" is integrated, of which the frame "obtaining a present" is the most central. This will be the starting point for a gradual exploration of the semantic and syntactic (argument structure) framework surrounding *get*.

This means that children should learn the major senses of *get* in the following sequence: 'obtain/receive', 'have', 'fetch', 'become', 'go/arrive', 'induce', 'having permission', 'understand'. We predict that the beginning and the endpoint in the sequence will be stable, whereas there will be quite a range of variation in the acquistion of the "intermediate" senses. We also predict that the children will produce only a small number of *get* instances from polysemy levels (ii) and (iii).

3.2.   Method

This study uses elicitation and ranking tasks in the hope of tapping competencies which do not normally show up in naturalistic tasks. We would like to stress, however, that analysing the use of *get* by children in natural settings is as important in the study of the acquisition of polysemy as using experimental data (see Duxbury 1999 ms.).

3.2.1.   Participants

Participants were recruited from local infant and junior schools. A letter was sent to all parents of children in the selected age groups, and all children who were given permission to take part in the study were used as participants. There were eleven 4-year-olds, twenty 7-year-olds, sixteen 8-year-olds, and twelve 10-year-olds.

3.2.2.   Materials

One Panasonic portable cassette recorder, cassette tapes, and some cards of postcard size on which the experimental sentences were typed.

3.2.3.   Design

The experimental stimuli consisted of a set of sentences using the word *get* that were chosen to represent the following core senses of the word: OBTAIN, FETCH, BECOME, GO, UNDERSTAND.[1] In order to keep the procedure simple enough for the 4-year-olds to understand, only one sentence was used to illustrate each meaning. The sentences were tested in a pilot study with ten children, as a result of which one of the sentences (OBTAIN) was changed to remove a possible desirability bias. The initial sentence involved getting a bicycle as a birthday present; many of the children commented that this was very boring and the sentence was replaced with a more neutral sentence about getting a cake. The letter to parents explained that the experimental sessions would be tape recorded and that all data would be kept anonymous and confidential. All children saw the same set of experimental sentences. The order of presentation of the sentences was randomized to prevent any order effects. The independent variable was age and the dependent variables were the sentences produced in the elicitation task and the rankings given for the experimental stimuli in the ranking task.

3.2.4.   Procedure

The experiment was conducted over a period of several weeks on the school site. Children were taken from the classroom one at a time to participate in the experiment. Children were told that the purpose of the experiment was to study the meaning of words and that there were no right or wrong answers. They were asked if they minded the cassette recorder being used and the machine was then turned on. Children were given an initial warm-up task to reduce shyness and then the experiment proper began. The production test method used by Raukko (1999, this volume) was adapted for use with young children and supplemented by a ranking task. Children were told that we were interested in the meaning of the word *get*, and asked if they could think of any sentences that used the word. (Raukko had asked participants to produce sentences showing as many different senses of *get* as possible; this was felt to be too difficult for young children and instead they were just asked to produce five different sentences.)

After the child had either produced five sentences or run out of ideas, the ranking task began. Children were told that they were going to hear five sentences using the word *get* and they would have to choose the one which was the best example of what the word meant. After the sentences were read out in a random order, the children were given the cards (in the same random order) to choose from. Once they had selected the best example, they were then asked to choose the best one from the remaining sentences, and so on until all five sentences had been ranked. Once all the sentences had been ranked, children were asked to give a reason for their best and worst choices. Experimental responses were recorded both on paper and on cassette. Once the experiment was over, children were thanked for their time, complimented on their answers, and returned to the classroom.

3.3. Results

The results fall into two sections – the qualitative production data and the quantitative rankings data.

3.3.1. Productions

To even out the numbers in each age group, data from five children were selected at random from the 7-year-old group, and discarded. (N.B. This applies to the production data only.) The productions were then categorized according to the kind of *get* produced and the syntactic frames used.

The typical frames in which utterances were produced are shown in Table 2. The numbers of utterances falling into each of the main senses is given in brackets. Not surprisingly, the 4-year-olds produced fewer utterances and also used a smaller range of types of *get*. This was also the only age group in which 'obtain/receive' was not the most popular *get* production. The 10-year-olds were the most creative in their production of sentences containing *get*. They produced nine different senses of *get*, including *get* as meaning 'induce somebody to do something', embedded in a wide variety of speech act types and argument structure frameworks. They are closely followed, however, by the 7-year-olds who produced eight different senses of *get*, including *get* as meaning 'become' and 'find'. The 8-year-olds produced seven senses of *get* and used less syntactic variety. However, they produced the only instances of *get* as idiomatic expressions, e.g. *Get a life!* and *Get lost*. This shows a gradual progression towards a mature competence in the use of *get* in its core senses, which accelerates at age 6–7. The use of *get* as "verbal padding", in phrasal collocations as well as idioms was, however, extremely rare.

As one can see from the prototypical objects and events listed in Table 2, the frames and scenes in which the utterances were implicitly embedded come mainly from the children's experiences with obtaining (more and more sophisticated) presents on the occasion of birthdays and at Christmas, of receiving pocket money and sweets, and of having, being in possession of, certain special toys or pets. This also ties in with the cognitive linguistic hypotheses about the embodiment of meaning, as the first senses children learn are related to their pleasure in having and holding something which is precious to them in some way.

3.3.2. Rankings

The rankings given to the different sentences by the children were collated. Since there were different numbers of children in the groups, the data is expressed as percentages in the graphs. The 20% level is equivalent to chance, since there were five choices.

Initially, the data were collated to see which sentences were ranked first, that is, as the best example of what the word *get* means. For the 4-year-olds, we can see (Fig. 2) that 'obtain/receive' was overwhelmingly selected as the first choice (by 45% of children in this age group). This is significantly different from chance ($p < 0.05$). This is not the case with the other age groups, where there is no sentence emerging as a clear first choice. We can see that for the 7-year-olds there is no clear leader. For the 8-year-olds, 'become' was never selected as first choice, but the others are ranked pretty much equal. For the 10-year-olds, again there is no overwhelming first choice.

The 4-year-olds' overwhelming choice of *get* 'obtain' as first choice becomes even clearer when we look at all the rankings that this sentence received. We can see (Fig. 3) that it was never ranked lower than in the top

Table 2. Typical frames of productions by children in the different age groups.

	4–5	6–7	7–8	9–10
Senses	have, fetch, obtain/receive	obtain/receive, fetch, buy, become, reach/go, have, retrieve, put on	obtain/receive, have, fetch, become, buy, put on, being allowed to do something	obtain/receive, fetch, buy, have, reach, retrieve, induce, find, being allowed to do something
Prototypical syntactic frames	[I] get X. Get X! Get me (some) X!	I get X. I'll get X. I can get X. I am going to get X. I (have) got X. Let's get X. Let's go and get X. Let's go to Y to get X. I want to get (some) X. I would like to get X. Can I/we get (some) X? Get (me) X! Can you get me X? Can you go and get me X? My mum told me to get X. I get X for you. Where shall I get X?	I got/get X. I went to get X. I am going to get X. I had to go and get X. My mummy got X. I got X. I have got X. Get X! Get me X! Can I get X? Could you go and get X? Y got X for Z. I got to do X.	I got/get X. I am going to get X. I went to get X. I want to get X. Y let me get X. Y needs to get X. Let's get X. Get X! Get X for Y! Can I get X? Can you get X? Y got me X. Y got some X from Z. Y got X for Z. I got X. I have got X. Y got more X than Z. Y got X to do Z.

	statement, order	statement, order, question	statement, order, question	statement, order, question
Prototypical speech acts				
Prototypical objects/events, prototypical conceptual frame	sweets, car, cat	sweets, toy, pocket money, play station, drink, shoes, cat	sweets, pocket money, pet, toy, ice-cream, bike, cat, drink, Christmas, birthday	sweets, pocket money, shoes, video, TV, drink, Christmas, birthday
Others	Get up!	get away from, get weighed, get ready	Get lost! Get a life! get ready, I got a long way to my birthday.	get told off, Got you!

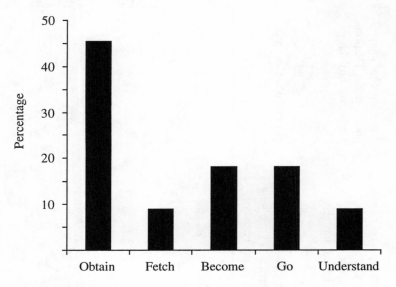

Figure 2.   Four-year-olds' first choice of meaning for *get*.

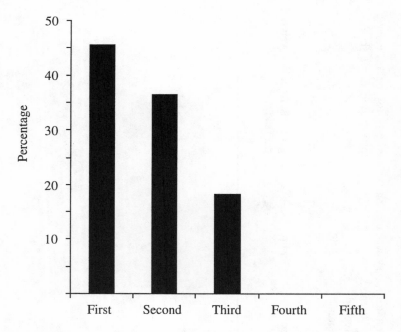

Figure 3.   Four-year-olds' rankings for 'obtain'.

three. This is quite unusual when compared to all the other rankings given across all age groups. The probability of this occurring by chance as first choice this many times is less than 0.005. Four-year-olds also tended to place 'understand' in the last two at a level significantly different from chance ($p < 0.05$).

For the 7-year-olds, the distributions are much flatter; there is no clear order to their rankings at all (see Fig. 4). In fact, the 7-year-olds gave the most undifferentiated responses out of the age groups surveyed, and none of the results are significantly different from chance. This could mean that 7-year-olds are simply guessing. It is, however, also possible that this result simply reflects the fact that they are aware of all the different meanings of *get*, and have no overall preferences about which is most central. In other words, they have learnt that 'obtain' is not necessarily a "better" example of *get*, but they have a pluralistic sense of the meaning of *get* and have learnt to embrace its alternative meanings without establishing particular preferences. This might also show that the process the acquisition of *get* is relatively slow but seems to accelerate around age 6, an age when children start to immerse themselves in word play, jokes, and metaphors, which for the most

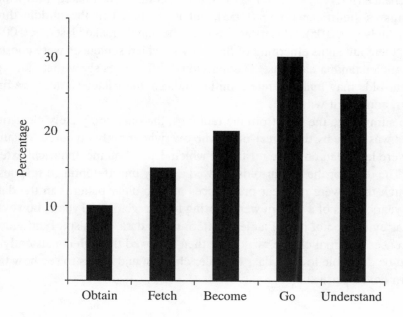

Figure 4.   Seven-year-olds' first choice of meaning for *get*.

part are based on the humorous exploitation of multiple meanings (see Nerlich, Todd and Clarke 1998).

The 8-year-olds also have fairly flat distributions, with no overall first choice, but a pattern is starting to emerge (see Fig. 5). 'Become' is ranked in the last two positions significantly more often than would be expected by chance ($p < 0.05$). 'Go' is ranked in the last two positions significantly less often than would be expected by chance ($p < 0.05$), and there is a tendency for it to be ranked third which just misses significance ($p = 0.055$). 'Understand' is significantly likely to be ranked last ($p < 0.01$). One could argue that they have achieved full competence and can produce all the various core senses of *get* and that they have reached the age at which, as some argue, metaphorical language goes underground (Gardner et al. 1978), a tendency that becomes even clearer with the 10-year-olds.

The picture becomes more interesting with the 10-year-olds (see Fig. 6). Here, a pattern is starting to emerge of the order in which sentences were chosen. Individual differences are also apparent, with children making a choice at the beginning and then following through in a pattern which is consistent with that choice. 'Obtain' is ranked second significantly more often than chance ($p < 0.05$). There is a trend for 'become' to be ranked third which just misses significance ($p = 0.053$), but it is ranked in the middle three significantly ($p < 0.05$). 'Understand' is overwhelmingly ranked last ($p < 0.001$). Thus, there are signs emerging of the order in which sentences were chosen, with 'understand' a clear last. The individual differences show that although 10-year-olds may make different initial choices, their later choices are in a pattern consistent with that.

To summarize the data from the rankings, the only completely clear first choice was made by the 4-year-olds, who overwhelmingly favoured 'obtain', and were less keen on those meanings which depend on metaphorical extension. The data for the 7-year-olds showed a fairly undifferentiated response, in which there were no clear preferences and no clear patterns in the data. By 8 years, signs of a pattern were starting to emerge. By 10 years, however, there is evidence not just of a clear pattern in the data, but also of individual differences in initial choice, which are then followed through consistently. It would be desirable to have data for older children and adults to see how this pattern develops further.

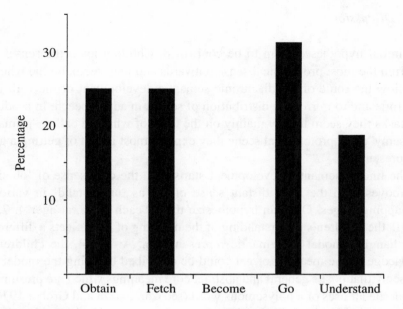

Figure 5. Eight-year-olds' first choice of meaning for *get*.

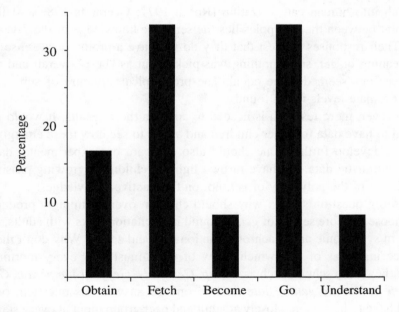

Figure 6. Ten-year-olds' first choice of meaning for *get*.

3.4.   Discussion

Our initial hypotheses seem to be confirmed. Children learn the senses of *get* from the most prototypical sense outwards and they seem, on the whole, to follow the route of the diachronic semantic development of the verb *get* over time and to mirror the distribution of senses in adult speech. In production tasks they seem to stay mainly on the level of what we called "primary polysemy". The prototypical scene they explore most is that of getting a gift or a present.

The line of semantic development starts with the core sense of 'obtain' and moves onto the most distant sense of *get* as 'understand' in various overlapping stages. One can hypothesize that at each stage, at ages 4, 7, 8 and 10, the children's understanding of the meaning of *get* reflects a different and changing model of semantic representation. At age 4, the children's knowledge of the meaning of *get* could be described by using the model of polysemy that posits general and abstract core meanings which are presumed to underlie all uses of a polysemous word (see Caramazza and Grober 1976), whereas the endpoint of the developmental process could be better described by a prototype model of semantic representation, inspired by Eleanor Rosch's research into human categorization (Rosch 1977; Geeraerts 1989). At the midpoint between the two poles lies the semantic knowledge of the 7-year-olds. Their responses suggest that they do not have a prototypical sense of the meaning of *get*, since nothing was picked out as "best" overall and all the meanings seemed to be equal. The prototypical structure of sub- and super-ordinate levels is not found.

However, more research is needed to confirm these results. It would be helpful to have data for older children and adults to see how these emerging patterns develop further. One should also compare our experimental data with naturalistic data. We have thrown light on children's growing passive knowledge of the polysemy of *get*, not on their active knowledge.

The big question still is: why should children overwhelmingly produce and choose the core senses of *get*, as found in elicitation tasks with adults, as found in synchronic and diachronic dictionaries and so on? Why don't they produce instances of *get*, which many of them must hear every morning before they go to school, such as *Get up*, *Get ready*, *Get your jumper on*, *Get on with it*, *We are getting late*, and so on? To answer this question, one would have to look more closely at adult and peer group input at every stage in lexical development between age 4, 10 and beyond.

This study has also shown the usefulness of an interdisciplinary approach which uses both psychology and cognitive linguistics. Developmental work in this field is important because it can show the gradual growth and structuring of the network of meanings surrounding a word form in language acquisition, and the relevance of the various frameworks of thinking and acting in which children learn certain words. We have seen how a pattern of semantic networks emerges at different stages of development, which seems to indicate that at different ages these patterns appear to map onto different theories of word representation. This article has also shown that the structure and organization of meanings around a polysemous word appear to change with age in a pattern roughly consistent with the diachronic change in word meanings and the spread of meanings in society.

Further research is needed to investigate whether the results found here would also apply to other polysemous verbs, and to explore the extent to which embodiment can be seen as motivation for word meanings. Finally, the theoretical approach explored here provides a useful framework for future research.

Notes

1. Sentences illustrating different meanings of *get*:

Oᴮᴛᴀɪɴ	Peter *got* a cake from the bakers.
Fᴇᴛᴄʜ	Can you *get* the milk out of the fridge?
Bᴇᴄᴏᴍᴇ	Francesca *got* really wet today.
Gᴏ	Let's *get* out of here.
Uɴᴅᴇʀsᴛᴀɴᴅ	The teacher spoke so fast I didn't *get* what she said.

References

Bréal, Michel
    1991 [1884] How words are organized in the mind. In: M. Bréal, *The Beginnings of Semantics. Essays, Lectures and Reviews*, 145–151. Edited and translated by George Wolf. London: Duckworth.
Brugman, Claudia M.
    1981   The Story of *over*. Trier: LAUT.
Bryson, Bill
    1990   *Mother Tongue. The English Language*. London and New York: Penguin Books.

Caramazza, Alfonso and Ellen Grober
    1976   Polysemy and the structure of the subjective lexicon. In: Cléa
                Rameh (ed.), *Semantics: Theory and Application*, 181–206.
                Georgetown University Round Table on Languages and Linguistics
                1976. Washington: University Press.
Clark, Eve V.
    1978   Discovering what words can do. Papers from the Parasession on the
                Lexicon, Chicago Linguistic Society, 34–57.
Deignan, Alice
    1999   Linguistic metaphors and collocation in nonliterary corpus data.
                Metaphor and Symbol 15(1): 19–36.
Duxbury, Simone
    1999 (ms.) *Get*ting the hang of multiple meanings – new perspectives on
                polysemy. Paper for the Theme session on language acquisition at
                the International Cognitive Linguistics Conference, Stockholm, July
                14, 1999.
Fillmore, Charles J. and Beryl Atkins
    1992   Towards a frame-based lexicon: the semantics of *risk* and its
                neighbors. In: Adrienne Lehrer and Eva Feder Kittay (eds.), *Frames,
                Fields, and Contrasts. New Essays in Semantic and Lexical
                Organization*, 75–102. Hillsdale, NJ: Lawrence Erlbaum Associates.
Gardner, Howard, Ellen Winner, R. Becchoffer and D. Wolf
    1978   The development of figurative language. In: Katherine Nelson (ed.),
                Children's Language, Vol. 1. Cambridge, MA: Gardner Press Inc.
Geeraerts, Dirk
    1989   Prospects and problems of prototype theory. *Linguistics* 27: 587–612.
Gibbs, Raymond W., Jr., Dinara A. Beitel, M. Harrington and P. E. Sanders
    1994   Taking a stand on the meanings of *stand*: bodily experience as
                motivation for polysemy. *Journal of Semantics* 11: 321–251.
Givón, Talmy and L. Yang
    1994   The rise of the English GET-passive. In: Paul J. Hoppe and Barbara
                Fox (eds.), *Voice: Form and Function*, 119–149. Amsterdam and
                Philadelphia: John Benjamins.
Goddard, Cliff
    1998   *Semantic Analysis. A Practical Introduction*. Oxford: Oxford
                University Press.
Goldberg, Adèle E.
    1995   *Constructions: A Construction Grammar Approach to Argument
                Structure*. Chicago and London: University of Chicago Press.
    1998   Patterns of experience in patterns of language. In: Tomasello (1998),
                203–220.
Grady, Joseph and Chris Johnson
    1997   Converging evidence for the notions of subscene and primary scene.

Proceedings of the 23rd Annual Meeting of the Berkeley Linguistics Society, 123–136. Berkeley, CA: Berkeley Linguistics Society.

Hopper, P. J.
1998   Emergent grammar. In: Tomasello (1998), 155–176.
Ibarretxe-Antuñano, Iraide
1999   Metaphorical mappings in the sense of smell. In: Gerard Steen and Raymond W. Gibbs Jr. (eds.), *Metaphor in Cognitive Linguistics*, 29–45. Amsterdam and Philadelphia: John Benjamins.
Israel, Michael
(to appear) Systematic idiomaticity in the acquisition of English 'get' constructions.
Johnson, Christopher R.
1996   Learnability in the acquisition of multiple senses: SOURCE reconsidered. In: J. Johnson, M. L. Luge and J. Moxley (eds.), *Proceedings of the 22nd Annual Meeting of the Berkeley Linguistics Society*, 469–480. Berkeley, CA: Berkeley Linguistics Society.
1999   Metaphor vs. conflation in the acquisition of polysemy: the case of *see*. In: Masako Hiraga, Chris Sinha and Sherman Wilcox (eds.), *Cultural, Typological and Psychological Perspectives in Cognitive Linguistics*, 155–169. Amsterdam: John Benjamins.
Lakoff, George
1987   *Women, Fire, and Dangerous Things*. Chicago: Chicago University Press.
Lakoff, George and Mark Johnson
1999   *Philosophy in the Flesh: The Embodied Mind and its Challenge to Western Thought*. New York: Basic Books.
Langacker, Ronald W.
1987   *Foundations of Cognitive Grammar, Vol. I. Theoretical Prerequisites*. Stanford, CA: Stanford University Press.
1988   Review of George Lakoff: *Women, Fire, and Dangerous Things*, Chicago: Chicago University Press. *Language* 64(2): 384–395.
Lehrer, Adrienne
1974   Homonymy and polysemy: measuring similarity of meaning. *Language Sciences* 32: 33–39.
Lindstromberg, Seth
1991   *Get*: not so many meanings. *International Review of Applied Linguistics* (IRAL) 29: 285–302.
Nerlich, Brigitte, Zazie Todd and David D. Clarke
1998   The function of polysemous jokes and riddles in lexical development. *Cahiers de Psychologie Cognitive/Current Psychology of Cognition* 17(2): 343–366.

New Oxford Dictionary of English
1998   Edited by Judy Pearsall; chief editor, current English dictionaries, Patrick Hanks. Oxford: Oxford University Press.

Norvig, Peter and George Lakoff
1987   Taking: a study in lexical network theory. *Proceedings of the 13th Annual Meeting of the Berkeley Linguistics Society*, 195–206. Berkeley, CA: Berkeley Linguistics Society.

Oxford English Dictionary
1888–1924 A new English dictionary on historical principles: founded mainly on the materials collected by the Philological Society / edited by James A. H. Murray ... with the assistance of many scholars and men of science. Oxford: The Clarendon Press. Introduction, supplement and bibliography published in 1933.

Raukko, Jarno
1997   The status of polysemy in linguistics: from discrete meanings to default flexibility. In: *SKY 1997: The 1997 Yearbook of the Linguistic Association of Finland*, 145–170.

1999   An 'intersubjective' method for cognitive-semantic research of polysemy: the case of *get*. In: Masko K. Hiraga, Chris Sinha and Sherman Wilcox (eds.), *Cultural, Typological and Psychological Perspectives in Cognitive Linguistics*, 87–107. Amsterdam: John Benjamins.

Rice, Sally
1996   Prepositional prototypes. In: René Dirven and M. Pütz (eds.), *The Construal of Space in Language and Thought*, 135–165. Berlin and New York: Mouton de Gruyter.

Rosch, Eleanor
1977   Human categorization. In: Neil Warren (ed.), *Studies in Cross-Cultural Psychology I*, 3–49. London: Academic Press.

Sandra, Dominiek and Sally Rice
1995   Network analyses of prepositional meaning: mirroring whose mind – the linguist's or the language user's? *Cognitive Linguistics* 6(1): 89–130.

Slobin, Dan Isaac
1985   Crosslinguistic evidence for the language-making capacity. In: Dan Slobin (ed.), *A Crosslinguistic Study of Language Acquisition, Vol. 2 Theoretical Issues*, 1157–1256. Hillsdale, NJ: Lawrence Erlbaum.

Tomasello, Michael
1992   *First Verbs. A Case Study of Early Grammatical Development.* Cambridge: Cambridge University Press.

Tomasello, Michael (ed.)
1998   *The New Psychology of Language. Cognitive and Functional*

Approaches to Language Structure. Mahwah, NJ and London: Lawrence Erlbaum.

Tomasello, Michael and W. E. Merriman (eds.)
1993   *Beyond Names for Things: Young Children's Acquisition of Verbs.* Hillsdale, NJ: Lawrence Erlbaum.

Ungerer, Friedrich and Hans-Jörg Schmid
1996   *An Introduction to Cognitive Linguistics.* London and New York: Longman.

Williams, John N.
1992   Processing polysemous words in context: evidence for interrelated meanings. *Journal of Psycholinguistic Research* 21(3): 193–218.

Computational approaches

"I don't believe in word senses"[*]

Adam Kilgarriff

1. Introduction

There is now a substantial literature on the problem of word sense disambiguation (WSD).[1] The goal of WSD research is generally taken to be disambiguation between the senses given in a dictionary, thesaurus or similar. The idea is simple enough and could be stated as follows:

> Many words have more than one meaning. When a person understands a sentence with an ambiguous word in it, that understanding is built on the basis of just one of the meanings. So, as some part of the human language understanding process, the appropriate meaning has been chosen from the range of possibilities.

Stated in this way, it would seem that WSD might be a well-defined task, undertaken by a particular module within the human language processor. This module could then be modelled computationally in a WSD program, and this program, performing, as it did, one of the essential functions of the human language processor, would stand alongside a parser as a crucial component of a broad range of Natural Language Processing (NLP) applications. This point of view is clearly represented in Cottrell (1989):

> [Lexical ambiguity] is perhaps the most important problem facing an NLU [Natural Language Understanding] system. Given that the goal of NLU is understanding, correctly determining the meanings of the words used is fundamental. The tack taken here is that it is important to understand how people resolve the ambiguity problem, since whatever their approach, it appears to work rather well. (Cottrell 1989: 1)

Word meaning is of course a venerable philosophical topic, and questions of the relation between the signifier and the signified will never be far from the theme of the paper. However, philosophical discussions have not addressed the fact of lexicography and the theoretical issues raised by sense distinctions as marked in dictionaries. We often have strong intuitions about words having multiple meanings, and lexicography aims to capture them, systematically and consistently. The philosophy literature does not provide a taxonomy of the processes underpinning the intuition, nor does it analyse the relations between the word sense distinctions a dictionary makes and the primary data of naturally occurring language. This is a gap that this paper aims to fill.

I show, first, that Cottrell's construal of word senses is at odds with theoretical work on the lexicon (Section 2); then, that the various attempts to provide the concept "word sense" with secure foundations over the last 30 years have all been unsuccessful (Section 3). I then consider the lexicographers' understanding of what they are doing when they make decisions about a word's senses, and develop an alternative conception of the word sense, in which it corresponds to a cluster of citations for a word (Section 4). Citations are clustered together where they exhibit similar patterning and meaning. The various possible relations between a word's meaning potential and its dictionary senses are catalogued and illustrated with corpus evidence.

The implication for WSD is that there is no reason to expect a single set of word senses to be appropriate for different NLP applications. Different corpora, and different purposes, will lead to different senses. In particular, the sets of word senses presented in different dictionaries and thesauri have been prepared, for various purposes, for various human users: there is no reason to believe those sets are appropriate for any NLP application.

2.   Thesis and antithesis: practical WSD and theoretical lexicology

2.1.   Thesis

NLP has stumbled into word sense ambiguity.

Within the overall shape of a natural language understanding system – morphological analysis, parsing, semantic and pragmatic interpretation – word sense ambiguity first features as an irritation. It does not appear as a matter of particular linguistic interest, and can be avoided altogether simply by treating all words as having just one meaning. Rather, it is a snag: if you have both river *bank* and money *bank* in your lexicon, when you see the word *bank* in an input text you are at risk of selecting the wrong one. There is a practical problem to be solved, and since Margaret Masterman's group started examining it in the 1950s (see, e.g., Sparck Jones 1986), people have been writing programs to solve it.

NLP has not found it easy to give a very principled answer to the question, "what goes in the lexicon". Before the mid-1980s, many systems made no claims to wide coverage and contained only as many words in the lexicon as were needed for the "toy" texts that were going to be analysed. A word was only made ambiguous – that is, given multiple lexical entries – if it was one that the researchers had chosen as a subject for the disambiguation study. This was clearly not an approach that was sustainable for wide coverage systems, and interest developed in dictionaries, as relatively principled, wide-coverage sources of lexical information.

As machine-readable versions of dictionaries started to become available, so it became possible to write experimental WSD programs on the basis of the dictionary's verdict as to what a word's senses were (Lesk 1986; Jensen and Binot 1987; Slator 1988; Guthrie et al. 1990; Véronis and Ide 1990; Guthrie et al. 1991; Dolan 1994). Looked at the other way round, WSD was one of the interesting things you might be able to do with these exciting new resources.

Since then, with the advent of language corpora and the rapid growth of statistical work in NLP, the number of possibilities for how you might go about WSD has mushroomed, as has the quantity of work on the subject (Brown et al. 1991; Hearst 1991; Gale, Church and Yarowsky 1992, 1993; McRoy 1992; Yarowsky 1992). Clear (1994), Schütze and Pederson (1995) and Yarowsky (1995) are of particular interest because of their approach to the issue of the set of word senses to be disambiguated between. Schütze and Pederson devised high-dimensionality vectors to describe the context of each occurrence of their target word, and then clustered these vectors. They claim that the better-defined of these clusters correspond to word senses, so a new occurrence of the word can be disambiguated by representing its context as a vector and identifying which cluster centroid the vector is closest to. This system has the characteristic that a context may be close to more than one cluster centroid, so at times it may be appropriate to classify it as more than one sense.

Both Clear (1994) and Yarowsky (1995) provide a mechanism for the user to input the senses between which they would like the system to disambiguate. They ask the user to classify a small number of statistically selected collocates which the algorithm can use to "seed" the process of learning the patterns which each sense is associated with. The user determines what the relevant set of senses is when deciding on the senses he or she will assign seed collocates to.[2] Clear then finds all the words which tend to co-occur with the nodeword in a large corpus, and quantifies, for a very large number of words, the evidence that it occurs with each of the seeds, and thus indirectly, with each sense of the nodeword. Disambiguation then proceeds by summing the evidence for each sense provided by each context word.

Yarowsky's method is iterative: first, those corpus lines for the nodeword which contain one of the seed collocates are classified. Then the set of corpus lines so classified is examined for further indicators of one or other of the senses of the word. These indicators are sorted, according to the strength of evidence they provide for a sense. It will now be possible to classify a larger set of corpus lines, so producing more indicators for each sense, and the process can be continued until all, or an above-threshold proportion, of the corpus lines for the word are classified. The ordered list of sense-indicators will then serve as a disambiguator for new corpus lines.

In the Semantic Concordance project at Princeton a lexicographic team has been assigning a WordNet (Miller 1990) sense to each noun, verb, adjective and adverb in a number of texts, thus providing a "gold standard" disambiguated corpus which can be used for training and evaluating WSD programs (Landes, Leacock and Tengi 1996).

In 1994–1995, there was an extended discussion of whether WSD should be one of the tasks in the MUC (Message Understanding Conference) program.[3] This would have provided for competitive evaluation of different NLP groups' success at the WSD task, as measured against a "benchmark" corpus, in which each word had been manually tagged with the appropriate WordNet sense number (as in the Semantic Concordance). Some trials took place, but the decision was not to proceed with the WSD task as part of the 1996 MUC-6 evaluation, as there was insufficient time to debate and define detailed policies. The theme has recently been taken up by the Lexicons Special Interest Group of the Association for Computational Linguistics (ACL), and a pilot evaluation exercise is taking place in 1998: a milestone on the road from research to technology.

2.2.   Antithesis

Since the publication of *Metaphors We Live By* (Lakoff and Johnson 1980) and *Women, Fire and Dangerous Things* (Lakoff 1987), there has been one approach to linguistics – cognitive linguistics – for which metaphor has been a central phenomenon. Metaphor is, amongst other things, a process whereby words spawn additional meanings, and cognitive linguists are correspondingly interested in polysemy. Lakoff's analysis of the polysemy of *mother* is hugely cited. Word sense ambiguity can often be seen as a trace of the fundamental processes underlying language understanding (Sweetser 1990). The structures underlying the distinct meanings of words are at the heart of the cognitive linguistics enterprise (Taylor 1989; Geeraerts 1990).

Working in this framework, Cruse (1995) gives a detailed typology of polysemy. He distinguishes polysemy, defined according to distinctness of meaning, from polylexy, which is where, in addition to distinctness of meaning, distinct lexical entries are required. A word is polysemous but not polylexic where its non-base meanings are predictable, so they can be generated as required and need not be stored. He also addresses where readings are antagonistic and where they are not, and the characteristics of the different semantic properties, or "facets", of a sense. He uses ambiguity tests to tease out a number of issues, and a full Cruse lexical entry would contain: a specification of polysemous senses; their lexical relations including their relations to each other; whether they were antagonistic or not; the facets, shared or otherwise, of each, and the extent to which distinct facets of meaning could operate autonomously, so approach the status of senses on their own. He considers several varieties of "semi-distinct" readings.

Lexical ambiguity has also moved centre-stage within theoretical and computational linguistics. Both AAAI (the American Association for Artificial Intelligence) and ACL have recently devoted workshops to the topic.[4] When Pustejovsky and others discuss the generative lexicon (Briscoe, Copestake and Boguraev 1990; Pustejovsky 1991), the generative processes they have in mind are, again, ones whereby words spawn additional meanings (or, at least, additional uses). Regular polysemy (Apresjan 1974) has recently been discussed, and computational mechanisms for addressing it proposed, by Ostler and Atkins (1991), and Copestake and Briscoe (1995), *inter alia*. Levin and colleagues have also been finding systematicity in lexical ambiguity, in relation to verb classes, their patterns of subcategorization, and their patterns of alternation (Levin and Rappoport Hovav 1991; Levin 1993; Levin, Song and Atkins 1997).

This combination of circumstances leads to an odd situation. Much WSD work proceeds on the basis of there being a computationally relevant, or useful, or interesting, set of word senses in the language, approximating to those stated in a dictionary. To the WSD community, word senses are, more or less, as the dictionary says. Sometimes not all the sense distinctions recognized in the dictionary are viewed as salient to the program. WSD researchers tend to be "lumpers", not "splitters"[5] (Dolan 1994). (This is not, of course, to say that WSD authors have not noted the theoretical problems associated with dictionarys' word senses.) WSD research has gone a long way on this basis: it is now common for papers to present quantitative comparisons between the performance of different systems. Meanwhile, the theoreticians provide various kinds of reason to believe there is no such set of senses. To get beyond this *impasse*, the question "what is a word sense?" needs to be considered more closely.

3.   What is a word sense?

"No entity without identity" (Quine 1969).

Or, to know what something is, is to know when something is it. To know what a word sense s_1 is, is to know which uses of the word are part of s_1 and which are not, probably because they are part of s_i where $i \neq 1$. If we are to know what word senses are, we need operational criteria for distinguishing them.

3.1.   Selection and modulation

A good starting point is Cruse's textbook on *Lexical Semantics* (Cruse 1986). "Lexical units" are the object of his enquiry, and he devotes two substantial chapters to specifying what they are. He states the heart of the problem thus: One of the basic problems of lexical semantics is the apparent multiplicity of semantic uses of a single word form (without grammatical difference). He addresses in some detail the difference between those cases where the context *selects* a distinct unit of sense, from those where it *modulates* the meaning. In the pair

(1)   *Have you put the money in the bank?*
(2)   *The rabbit climbed up the bank.*

the two sentences select different meanings of *bank*, whereas in

(3)   *He doesn't often oil his bike.*
(4)   *Madeleine dried off her bike.*
(5)   *Boris's bike goes like the wind.*

different aspects of the bicycle – its mechanical parts; its frame, saddle and other large surfaces; its (and its rider's) motion – are highlighted in each case. The meaning of *bike* is modulated differently by each context.[6]

3.2. Ambiguity tests

The selection/modulation distinction is closely related to the distinction between ambiguity and generality, also referred to as "vagueness", "indeterminacy" and "lack of specification".[7] Where a word is ambiguous, a sense is selected. Where a word-meaning is general between two readings, any particular context may or may not modulate the word-meaning to specify one or other of the readings. Thus, *hand* is unspecified between right hands and left hands; some sentences modulate the meaning to specify a right or left hand, as in *When saluting, the hand should just touch the forehead*, while others do not.[8]

Clearly, *bank* is ambiguous between the readings demonstrated above; *bike* is not. But for many reading-pairs, the answer is not clear:[9]

(6)   *I planted out three rows of beans yesterday.*
(7)   *Cook the beans in salted water.*

(8)   *The cottage was charming.*
(9)   *Our hosts were charming.*

(10)   *Bother! I was about to talk to John, but now he's disappeared!* (NOT-HERE)
(11)   *I can't find it anywhere, it seems to have disappeared.* (CAN'T-FIND)

A number of tests have been proposed for determining whether a word is ambiguous or general between two meanings. They are catalogued in Zwicky and Sadock (1975), Cruse (1986), ten Hacken (1990) and Geeraerts (1993). Here, I shall describe only one of the more successful tests, the "crossed readings" one.

(12)   *Mary arrived with a pike and so did Agnes.*

could mean that each arrived with a carnivorous fish, or that each arrived bearing a long-handled medieval weapon, but not that the one arrived with the fish and the other with the weapon. On the other hand, in

(13)   *Tom raised his hand and so did Dick.*

each might have raised a right hand, each might have raised a left, or one might have raised his right, and the other, his left. The question now is, in

(14)   *Ellen bought some beans, and so did Harry.*

is it possible that Ellen bought plants and Harry, food? If so, then the conclusion to be drawn from the test is that *bean* is ambiguous between the readings, and if not, then it is not.[10]

3.2.1.   Criticisms of the tests

The tests are generally presented with the aid of an unproblematic example of ambiguity and an unproblematic example of vagueness. This is done in order to demonstrate what the test is and what the two contrasting outcomes are. However, this is not to use the tests in anger. What we want of a test is that it is consistent with our intuitions, where our intuitions are clear, and that it resolves the question, where our intuitions are unclear. The cross-reading test fares tolerably well in meeting the consistency condition (though see Geeraerts 1993 for a contrary view). But do the tests help where intuitions are unclear? There is little if any evidence that they do. Here I discuss three classes of problems.

   Firstly, it must be possible to construct a plausible test sentence. The word in its two uses must be able to occur with the same syntax and the same lexico-grammatical environment. Consider the transitive and intransitive uses of *eat*, as in *John ate the apple* and *John ate*. Is this a case of ambiguity or vagueness?

(15)   *?Mary ate, and John, the apple.*

is unacceptable, but the reason is that elided constituents must have the same syntax and subcategorization in both their expressed and elided occurrences. It might be desirable to treat all words with alternative subcategorization possibilities as ambiguous. But whether or not that is done, the test still fails to elucidate on the topic of a word's meaning, where the word has different syntax in different uses. The test can only be posed where the two uses are syntactically similar.

The *disappear* example displays a different variant of this problem. The CAN'T-FIND and NOT-HERE readings have different aspectual characteristics: CAN'T-FIND is stative while NOT-HERE is a punctual "achievement" verb.

(16)   *Martha disappeared and so did Maud.*

does not permit a crossed reading, but that is because we cannot construct a viable aspectual interpretation for the conjoined sentence. Compare

(17)   ?*I evicted and knew her.*[11]

It is not evident whether there is a conclusion to be drawn regarding polysemy.

In general, one can apply more or less effort into trying to find a test sentence (and associated context) in which the crossed reading is plausible. A test is clearly flawed, if, the more ingenuity the investigator displays, the more of one particular outcome they will get. (The crossed reading test is the test which suffers least from this flaw, but it is nonetheless in evidence.)

The second point is more general and theoretical. A certain amount of interpretation of an utterance must have been undertaken before an acceptability judgement can be made. Three parts of the interpretation process are lexical access; parsing; and "pragmatic interpretation", the final stage of incorporating the new information into the discourse model. The premise behind acceptability judgements is that a subject can report on the outcome of the first two stages, irrespective of what goes on in the third. For a wide range of syntactic questions, the methodology is widely used and has proved its worth.

Nunberg's (1978) arguments illustrate the hazards of the premise for questions in lexical semantics. Consider the sentence

(18)   ?*The newspaper costs 25p and sacked all its staff.*

It is anomalous. We cannot place the origin of the anomaly in the lexicon unless we grant *newspaper* two lexical entries, one for a copy of the newspaper and one for the owner or corporate entity. Then the size of our lexicon will start to expand, as we list more and more of the possible kinds of referent for the word, and still it will never be complete. So the origin of the anomaly must be the interpretation process. But the anomaly seems similar to the anomaly that occurs with *bank*. In a case lying between *newspaper* and *bank*, how would we know whether the source of the anomaly was the lexicon or the interpretation process? In the general case the point at which the lexical process becomes a general-purpose interpretative one cannot be identified. There is no accessible intermediate representation in which lexical ambiguities are resolved (for acceptable sentences) but in which the contents of the sentence has not been incorporated into the hearer's interpretation of the discourse. Geeraerts (1993) presents an extensive critique of the tests along these lines, presenting evidence that the different tests give contradictory results, and that even if we constrain ourselves to looking at just one of the tests, they can all be made to give contradictory results by manipulating the context in which the item under scrutiny is set.

The third problem is simply the lack of evidence that the tests give stable results. It will sometimes happen that, for the same reading-pair, an informant will deem crossed readings possible for some test sentences and not for others. Or different informants will have conflicting opinions. There are, remarkably, no careful discussions of these issues in the literature. The merit of the method of acceptability judgements for syntax rests on the relative stability of their outcomes: they work (to the extent they do) because linguists agree where the question marks belong. Preliminary investigations into the stability of outcomes in lexical semantics suggest that it is severely lacking.

3.3.   *Psycholinguistics and "semantic priming"*

There is a set of findings in psycholinguistics which might allow us to base an account of "word sense" directly on the mental lexicon. The experimental paradigm is called "semantic priming". It is well-established that, if I have just heard the word *doctor* (the "prime"), and then a sequence of letters (the "target") is flashed upon a screen and I am asked to identify whether it is a word or not, I respond faster if it is a word and it is *nurse* than if it is a word but unrelated to *doctor*.[12] If an ambiguous prime such as *bank* is given, it turns out that both *river* and *money* are primed for.

If *bank* is presented in isolation, priming for both *river* and *money* is found for another second or two. In a context which serves to make only one of these appropriate, after something between 50 and 200 milliseconds a choice is made and after that only the appropriate target is primed for.

So, for ambiguous words, priming behaviour has a distinct "signature". Perhaps it is possible to identify whether a word is vague or ambiguous by seeing whether it exhibits this signature.

The hypothesis is explored by Williams (1992). He looked at adjectives, for example *firm*, for which the two readings were represented by *solid* and *strict*. After confirming that the prime, *firm*, in isolation, primed equally for *solid* and *strict*, he tested to see if *solid* was primed for when *firm* occurred in a *strict* context, and *vice versa*, after delays of 250, 500 and 850 ms.

His results were asymmetrical. He identified central meanings (*solid*) and non-central ones (*strict*). Where the context favoured the central reading, the non-central-sense targets were not primed for. But when the context favoured the non-central reading, central targets were. The experiments provide evidence that the various meanings of polysemous words are not functionally independent in language comprehension, and that not all senses are equal, in their representation in the mental lexicon. Williams discusses the asymmetrical results in terms of hierarchical meaning structures.

Priming experiments do show potential for providing a theoretical grounding for distinguishing ambiguity and generality, but more work needs to be done, and the outcome would not be a simple, two-way, ambiguous/general distinction. Also, the method would never be practical for determining the numbers of senses for a substantial number of words. The results of the experiments are just not sufficiently stable: as Williams says, the priming task "suffers from a large degree of item and subject variability" (p. 202).

4. Lexicographers, dictionaries and authority

What set of procedures do lexicographers have available to them to pin down those protean entities, 'meanings'? Faced with the almost unimaginable diversity of the language they are trying to describe, with the knowledge that what for the sake of convenience we are pleased to call a language is in many ways a synthesis of shifting patterns that change from year to year, from locality to locality, from idiolect to idiolect, how do they arrive at those masterpieces of consensus, dictionaries? How do they decide what, for the purposes of a dictionary, constitutes the meaning of a word, and where, in the case of polysemous words, one meaning ends and the next begins? (Ayto 1983: 89)

In the middle of this debate stand the lexicographers. The word senses that most WSD researchers aim to discriminate are the product of their intellectual labours. But this is far from the purpose for which the dictionary was written.

Firstly, any working lexicographer is well aware that, every day, they are making decisions on whether to "lump" or "split" senses that are inevitably subjective: frequently, the alternative decision would have been equally valid. In fact, most dictionaries encode a variety of relations in the grey area between "same sense" and "different sense": see Kilgarriff (1993) for a description of the seven methods used in *LDOCE* (1987).

Secondly, any particular dictionary is written with a particular target audience in mind, and with a particular editorial philosophy in relation to debates such as "lumping vs. splitting", so the notion of specifying a set of word senses for a language in isolation from any particular user group will be alien to them.

Thirdly, many are aware of the issues raised by Lakoff, Levin, Pustejovsky and others, with several lexicographers bringing valuable experience of the difficulties of sense-division to that literature (see below).

Fourthly, the weight of history: publishers expect to publish, bookshops expect to sell, and buyers expect to buy and use dictionaries which, for each word, provide a (possibly nested) list of possible meanings or uses. Large sums of money are invested in lexicographic projects, on the basis that a dictionary has the potential to sell hundreds of thousands of copies. Investors will not lightly adopt policies which make their product radically different to the one known to sell. However inappropriate the nested list might be as a representation of the facts about a word, for all but the most adventurous lexicographic projects, nothing else is possible.[13]

The division of a word's meaning into senses is forced onto lexicographers by the economic and cultural setting within which they work. Lexicographers are obliged to describe words as if all words had a discrete, non-overlapping set of senses. It does not follow that they do, or that lexicographers believe that they do.

4.1.   Lexicographical literature

Lexicographers write dictionaries rather than writing about writing dictionaries. Little has been written that answers the challenge posed by Ayto in the quotation above. Zgusta's influential *Manual* (1971), while stating that the specification of word meaning is the central task for the lexicographer (p. 23) and the division of a word's meanings into senses is a central part of that, gives little guidance beyond admonishments to avoid making too many, or too few, distinctions (pp. 66–67).

Ayto's own offering in the (1983) paper is the "classical" or "analytic" definition, comprising genus and differentiae. In choosing the genus term, the lexicographer must take care to neither select one that is too general – *entity* would not do as a genus term for *tiger* – nor too specific, if the specific genus term is likely to be unknown by the dictionary users. Where two meanings of a word have different genus terms, they need treating as different senses. The next task is to identify the differentiae required to separate out senses falling under the same genus term. He discusses *cup*, and argues that there are three senses, one for the "trophy" sense, one for the varieties standardly made of china or earthenware, and one for the prototypically plastic or paper varieties. But his consideration of the arguments for treating the second and third of these as distinct ends in a welter of open questions.

Stock (1983) is a response to Ayto's piece, and finds it wanting, firstly, in the circularity involved in using different genus terms to identify distinct senses – the lexicographer will only look for distinct genus terms after determining there are distinct senses – and secondly, in that the model cannot be applied to many words. She looks closely at *culture*, noting how different dictionaries have divided the territory that the word covers in quite different ways, and observes,

> It is precisely the lack of clarity in our use of the word *culture* which makes it such a handy word to have at one's disposal. It offers, as it were, semantic extras just because in most uses its possible meanings are not clearly disambiguated. What can the dictionary maker do to reflect this state of affairs? They do not, cannot by their very structure, show that there is slippage between some of the senses that they give but not between others. (p. 139)

Hanks (1994), looking at *climb*, and Fillmore and Atkins (1992), studying the semantic field centred on *risk*, make similar comments about the inadequacies of dictionary conventions, and appeal to prototype theory and frame semantics for richer frameworks to describe the relationships between the different ways a word (or word-family) is used.

Stock, Hanks, and Atkins were all involved in the early stages of the *COBUILD* project, which, in the early 1980s, broke new ground in lexicography through its use of very large computerized language corpora (Sinclair 1987). Good lexicographic practice had long used huge citation indexes, but being able to see hundreds of instances of a word in context, ordinary and extraordinary examples thrown together, was a radical development. It has changed how lexicographers think about meaning. Where Ayto's paper offers semantic analysis, Stock presents corpus evidence. The lexicographer's primary source of evidence for how a word behaves switches from subjective to objective; from introspection to looking at contexts.

4.2. A corpus-based model of word senses

This suggests a quite different answer to the question "what is a word sense?" Corpus lexicography proceeds approximately as follows. For each word, the lexicographer

(i)   Calls up a concordance[14] for the word;
(ii)   Divides the concordance lines into clusters, so that, as far as possible, all members of each cluster have much in common with each other, and little in common with members of other clusters;
(iii)   For each cluster, works out what it is that makes its members belong together, re-organising clusters as necessary;
(iv)   Takes these conclusions and codes them in the highly constrained language of a dictionary definition.

Putting the concordance lines into clusters is data-driven rather than theory-driven. The lexicographer may or may not be explicitly aware of the criteria according to which he or she is clustering. The interactions between the lexicographers' clusters and the automatic clusters produced for Information Retrieval purposes, and the potential for automating some of the clustering that the lexicographer performs, are subjects of current research. (It is a requirement for corpus lexicography software that it supports manual clustering [Atkins 1993; CorpusBench 1993; Schulze and Christ 1994].) Stage (iii) is just a fallible *post hoc* attempt to make the criteria explicit. The senses that eventually appear in the dictionary are the result, at several removes, of the basic clustering process.

Ambiguity tests failed to provide us with an account of what it meant for two uses of a word to belong to the same word sense. Once we operationalize "word sense" as "dictionary word sense", we now have a test that meets the challenge. The identity test for a word sense in a particular dictionary is that two usages of the word belong to it if and only if the lexicographer would have put them in the same cluster.[15]

We can now present a different perspective on the ambiguity/generality debate. Where a word's uses fall into two entirely distinct clusters, it is ambiguous, but where the clusters are less well-defined and distinct, "vague" or "unspecified" may be a more appropriate description. There is no reason to expect to find any clear distinction between the two types of cases.

5.   Use, frequency, predictability, and the word sense[16]

"Clustering" is a metaphor. It regards corpus lines as points in space with measurable distances between them. To give the account substance, more must be said about the ways in which corpus lines may be "close". In this section, I classify the types of relationships that hold between a word's patterns of usage, and consider how these considerations relate to lexicography.

There are five knowledge sources which come into play for understanding how a word contributes to the meaning or communicative intent of the utterance or discourse it occurs in. If a word in context is interpretable by a language user, it will be by virtue of these knowledge sources.

Whether a dictionary provides a word sense that matches an instance of use of the word, is dictated by considerations of frequency and predictability: if the instance exemplifies a pattern of use which is sufficiently frequent, and is insufficiently predictable from other meanings or uses of the word, then the pattern qualifies for treatment as a dictionary sense. A use is predictable, to the extent that a person reading or hearing it for the first time can understand it (in all its connotations). Clearly, different dictionaries have different thresholds of frequency and predictability.

To illustrate the various processes whereby new types of usage may be added to the repertoire for a word, let us consider the simple single-sense word, *handbag*: "a small bag, used by women to carry money and personal things (British; American English translation: purse)" (*LDOCE* 1995).

As the 715 examples in the *British National Corpus* (*BNC*)[17] make plain, typical uses involve things being put into, or taken out of, or looked for in handbags, or handbags being lost, found, stolen, manufactured, admired, bought or sold. But a couple of dozen examples stretch the limits of the definition or fall outside it altogether.

First, a proper name, and a reference to a unique object:

(19)   *the "Drowning Handbag", an up-market eatery in the best part of town*

(20)   *an inimitable rendering of the handbag speech in* The Importance of Being Earnest

Next, metonymy, visual metaphor, simile:

(21)   *She moved from handbags through gifts to the flower shop*

(22)   *"How about you? Did the bouncing handbag find you?"*[18]

(23)   *a weird, menacing building with bats hanging in the trees like handbags*

(24)   *Skin generally starting to age like old handbag or bodywork of car*

Next, Mrs Thatcher:

(25)   *from Edward Heath's hip-pocket to Margaret Thatcher's handbag and on to Mr Major's glass of warm beer*

(26)   *Thousands will be disgusted at the way she* [Thatcher] *is lining her handbag*

(27)   *send out Mrs Thatcher with a fully-loaded handbag*

(28)   *"If you want to define the Thatcher-and-after era in a single phrase,"* he muses, *" 'accountants with plenary powers' says it." Well now – I would have gone for something a little snappier: "A mad cow with a handbag," comes to mind as a first attempt.*

(29)   *She* [Thatcher] *cannot see an institution without hitting it with her handbag.*

The last of these is cited in another citation as the launching-point of verbal *handbag*. Of the three verbal citations, all were species of hitting and in two of them, Mrs. Thatcher was the perpetrator. This sense still survives in 1999 in the following passage from an article in *The Times* (21 July, 1999):

(30)   *Baroness Thatcher chose a Buckingham Palace garden party to demonstrate to William Hague her unswerving support for Michael Ashcroft, the embattled Tory treasurer. It was a classic Thatcher handbagging, according to witnesses who observed the encounters ...*

Next, and closely related to Mrs. Thatcher, "handbag-as-weapon":

(31)   *Meg swung her handbag.*
(32)   *determined women armed with heavy handbags*
(33)   *it was time to race the old ladies back to the village for the tea and scones of Beck Hall. I beat them, but only just – those handbags are lethal.*
(34)   *old ladies continue to brandish their handbags and umbrellas at the likes of Giant Haystacks*
(35)   *the blue rinse brigade will be able to turn out in force without having to travel and give poor Louis Gerstner the handbagging of his life.*
(36)   *Peterborough manager Chris Turner added: "Evidently one of their players caught one of our players and it was handbags at 10 paces and then someone threw a punch."*

The final, quite distinct group relates to discos, and the lexical unit *dance round your handbag*, a pejorative phrase for the behaviour of certain exclusively female groups at discothèques and dances where – prototypically – they dance in a circle with their handbags on the floor in the middle. The conversational speech subcorpus of the *BNC* provides two instances of the full form while in the written corpus, the two related corpus lines, both from music journalism, make only fleeting references to the collocation, and strikingly indicate a process of lexicalization:

(37)   *The shoot was supposed to be a secret, but word got out and Hitman regulars travelled down to Manchester. Two thousand couldn't get into the club, and tension mounted between trendy regulars (locked out of their own club) and the Hitman's handbag brigade (shut out of their programme).*
(38)   *New Yawk drawling rap over Kraftwerk's "The Model" just does not work, no way, no how. Handbag DJs will love it.*

All these uses can be traced back to the standard sense: the potential for using the word in the nonstandard way, is (in varying degrees) *predictable* from

(i)   Its standard meaning and use;
(ii)   General linguistic knowledge (e.g. of processes of metonymy, regular polysemy, and ellipsis, etc., and, in this case, the relation between words for goods and words for shops or departments of shops where those goods are sold);
(iii) General world knowledge (e.g. regarding Mrs. Thatcher, or juvenile female behaviour at discotheques) and
(iv)   Knowledge of related collocations (e.g. "lining their pockets", "WEAPON at NUMBER paces");
(v)   Taxonomic knowledge.

These five knowledge sources define the conceptual space within which lexical creativity and productivity, and the idea of a "word sense", are located.[19]

Needless to say, they frequently interact in complex ways. In *handbags at ten paces*, the speaker[20] assumes the addressee's awareness of handbag-as-weapon. Note that *?briefcases at ten paces* and *?shoulder-bags at ten paces* do not carry the same meaning. Although briefcases and shoulder-bags are just as viable weapons as handbags, the words *briefcase* and *shoulder-bag* do not carry the "weapon" connotations which make the citation immediately understandable. Handbag-as-weapon is a feature of the word, over and above the extent to which it is a feature of the denotation.

In the citation's context, there is no overt reason for a reference to *handbag*; the people involved are men, not women, so not prototypical handbag-users, and there is no other reference to femininity. It would appear that the speaker is aiming to both distance himself from and minimize the significance of the incident by treating it as a joke. The "duel" metaphor is itself a joke, and the oddity of handbag in the context of either football or duel, along with its associations with femininity and Mrs. Thatcher, contributes to the effect. Moreover, there is a sexist implication that the men were behaving like women and thereby the matter is laughable.

Interpreting *handbags at ten paces* requires lexical knowledge of handbag-as-weapon, collocational knowledge of both form and meaning of "WEAPON at NUMBER paces", and (arguably) knowledge of the association between handbags and models of masculinity and femininity.

The "music journalism" use displays some further features. *Handbag* was lexicalized in the clubbing world in *circa* 1990 as a music genre: the genre that, in the 1970s and 1980s, certain classes of young women would have danced round their handbags to.[21] The coinage emanates from the gay and transvestite club scene and is redolent with implications, from the appropriation of the handbag as a symbol of gay pride, to changes in the social situation of women over the last 20 years (and its expression in fashion accessories), to transvestite fantasies of being naïve 17-year-old girls in a more innocent age.

To restrict ourselves to more narrowly linguistic matters: the license for the coinage is via the *dance round your handbag* collocation, not directly from handbags. As shown by the spoken corpus evidence, the regular, non-ironic use of the collocation co-exists with the music-genre use. It is of much wider currency: all but two of a range of informants knew the collocation, whereas only two had any recollection of the music-genre use. Also, "handbag" music (or at least the use of that label) was a 1990–1991 fashion, and the term is no longer current: 1996 uses of it will probably refer back to 1990–1991 (as well as back to the 1970s and 1980s). Syntactically, the most information-rich word of the collocation has been used as a nominal premodifier for other nouns: in the music-genre sense, it is used as other music-genre words, as an uncountable singular noun, usually premodifying but potentially occurring on its own: "Do you like jazz/house/handbag?"

5.1. Frequency

These arguments make clear that there is a *prima facie* case for including handbag-as-weapon and handbag-as-music-genre as dictionaries senses, and *dance round your handbag* as an only partially compositional collocation. Each exhibits lexical meaning which is not predictable from the base sense. So why do the dictionaries not list them? The short answer is frequency. Around 97% of *handbag* citations in the *BNC* are straightforward base-sense uses. The music-genre sense is certainly rare, possibly already obsolete, and confined to a subculture. The collocation is partially compositional and occurs just twice in the corpus: for any single-volume dictionary, there will not be space for vast numbers of partially compositional collocations. Not only is a lexicographer "a lexicologist with a deadline" (Fillmore 1988) but also a lexicologist with a page limit.

5.2. *Analytic definitions and entailments*

The handbag-as-weapon sense is rather more common, and a further consideration comes into play. The denotations of base-sense handbag and handbag-as-(potential)-weapon are the same. Correspondingly, the lexical fact that there is a use of *handbag* in which it is conceptualized as a weapon does not render the *LDOCE* definition untrue. A lexicographer operating according to the classical approach whose goal was simply to provide necessary and sufficient conditions for identifying each word's denotation would say that the "weapon" aspect of meaning was irrelevant to his or her task. A more pragmatic lexicographer might also follow this line, particularly since space is always at a premium.

The situation is a variant on autohyponymy (Cruse 1986: 63–65), the phenomenon of one sense being the genus of another sense of the same word. The prototypical example is *dog* (canine vs. male canine). *Dog* is a case where there clearly are distinct senses. For *knife* (weapon/cutlery/bladed-object), Cruse (1995: 39–40) argues for "an intermediate status" between monosemy and polysemy, since, on the one hand, "bladed-object" is a coherent category which covers the denotation, but on the other, in a scenario where there was a penknife but no cutlery knife at a table setting, one might reasonably say "I haven't got a knife". *COBUILD* (1995) distinguishes "weapon" and "cutlery" senses, while *LDOCE* (1995) provides a single, analytically adequate, "bladed-object" sense.

In a discussion of the polysemy of *sanction*, Kjellmer (1993) makes a related observation. His goal is to examine how language breakdown is avoided when a word has antagonistic readings. Nominal *sanction* is such a word: in *sanctions imposed on Iraq* the meaning is akin to "punishment" ("PUN") whereas in *the proposal was given official sanction* it is related to "endorsement" ("END"). A first response is that the context disambiguates – punishment, not support, is the sort of thing you "impose", whereas "give" implies, by default, a positively-evaluated thing given. Syntax is also a clue: the plural use is always PUN, whereas determinerless singular uses suggests END. Kjellmer then finds the following instances:

> The process of social control is operative insofar as *sanction* plays a part in the individual's behaviour, as well as in the group's behaviour. By means of this social control, deviance is either eliminated or somehow made compatible with the function of the social group. ... Historically, religion has also functioned

as a tremendous engine of vindication, enforcement, sanction, and perpetuation of various other institutions. (Kjellmer 1993: 119)

Here the context does not particularly favour either reading against the other. In the second case, the co-ordination with both an END word (vindication) and a PUN one (enforcement) supports both readings simultaneously. How is this possible, given their antagonism? How come these uses do not result in ambiguity and the potential for misinterpretation? The answer seems to be that

> we may operate, as readers or listeners, at a general, abstract level and take the word to mean 'control, authority' until the context specifies for us which type of control is intended, if indeed specification is intended. In other words, faced with the dual semantic potentiality of the word, we normally stay at a higher level of abstraction, where the danger of ambiguity does not exist, until clearly invited to step down into specificity. (Kjellmer 1993: 120)[22]

Citations where *sanction* is unspecified for either PUN or END are rare, and there is no case for including the unspecified "control" sense in a dictionary.

The example demonstrates a relationship between a lexicographer's analytic defining strategy and the interpretation process. There are occasions where a "lowest common denominator" of the usually distinct standard uses of a word will be the appropriate reading, in a process analogous to the way an analytically-inclined lexicographer might write a definition for a word like *charming* or *knife*, which would cover the word's uses in two or more distinct corpus clusters. Some dictionaries use nested entries as a means of representing meanings related in this way.

6. Implications for WSD

The argument so far exposes a lack of foundations to the concept of "word sense". But, a WSD researcher might say, "so what?" What are the implications for practical work in disambiguation?

The primary implication is that a task-independent set of word senses for a language is not a coherent concept. Word senses are simply undefined unless there is some underlying rationale for clustering, some context which classifies some distinctions as worth making and others as not worth making. For people, homonyms like *pike* are a limiting case: in almost any situation where a person considers it worth their while attending to a sentence containing *pike*, it is also worth their while making the fish/weapon distinction.

Lexicographers are aware of this: the senses they list are selected according to the editorial policy and anticipated users and uses of the particular dictionary they are writing. WSD researchers have generally proceeded as if this was not the case: as if a single program would be relevant to a wide range of NLP applications.

The argument so far shows that there is no reason to expect the same set of word senses to be relevant for different tasks.

The *handbag* data show how various the nonstandard uses of *handbag* are. These uses are sufficiently predictable or insufficiently frequent to be dictionary senses (in a dictionary such as *LDOCE*). They are licensed by a combination of linguistic principles, knowledge of collocations, lexico-syntactic contexts and world knowledge. Only in a single case, the department store metonym, is there a plausible linguistic principle for extending the base meaning to render the nonstandard use interpretable. The data suggest that little coverage will be gained by an NLP system exploiting generative principles which dictate meaning potential. The nonstandard uses of words tend to have their own particular history, with one nonstandard use often built on another, the connections being highly specific to a word or lexical field.

The *handbag* data also indicate how the corpus dictates the word senses. The *BNC* is designed to cover a wide range of standard English, so is consonant with a general-purpose dictionary. The common uses in the one should be the senses in the other. But, were we to move to a music journalism corpus, the music-genre sense would be prominent. A 1990s music-journalism dictionary would include it. The practical method to extend the coverage of NLP systems to nonstandard uses is not to compute new meanings, but to list them. Verbal *handbag* can, if sufficiently frequent, be added to the lexicon as a synonym for *beat*; "WEAPON at NUMBER paces" as one for "have an argument". Given the constraints of the sublanguage of a given NLP application, and the usually much narrower confines of the knowledge representation (which defines the meaning distinctions the system can provide an interpretation for) the proliferation of senses is not a problem. For the medium term future, the appropriate language-engineering response to a use of a word or phrase, for which there is a valid interpretation in the knowledge representation but where the system is currently getting the wrong interpretation because use of the word or phrase does not match that in the lexicon, is to add another lexical entry.[23]

The implications of the account for different varieties of NLP application are addressed in Kilgarriff (1997a, 1997b).

7. Conclusion

Following a description of the conflict between WSD and lexicological research, I examined the concept "word sense". It was not found to be sufficiently well-defined to be a workable basic unit of meaning.

I then presented an account of word meaning in which "word sense" or "lexical unit" is not a basic unit. Rather, the basic units are occurrences of the word in context (operationalized as corpus citations). In the simplest case, corpus citations fall into one or more distinct clusters and each of these clusters, if large enough and distinct enough from other clusters, forms a distinct word sense. But many or most cases are not simple, and even for an apparently straightforward common noun with physical objects as denotation, *handbag*, there are a significant number of citations in which it does not straightforwardly mean what it standardly means. The interactions between a word's uses and its senses were explored in some detail. The analysis also charted the potential for lexical creativity.

The implication for WSD is that word senses are only ever defined relative to a set of interests. The set of senses defined by a dictionary may or may not match the set that is relevant for an NLP application.

The scientific study of language should not include word senses as objects in its ontology. Where "word senses" have a role to play in a scientific vocabulary, they are to be construed as abstractions over clusters of word usages. The nontechnical term for ontological commitment is "belief in", as in "I (don't) believe in ghosts/God/antimatter". One leading lexicographer doesn't believe in word senses. I don't believe in word senses, either.

Acknowledgements

This research was supported by the EPSRC Grant K18931, SEAL. I would also like to thank Sue Atkins, Roger Evans, Christiane Fellbaum, Gerald Gazdar, Bob Krovetz, Michael Rundell, Yorick Wilks and the anonymous reviewers for their valuable comments.

Notes

*   This article was first published in slightly different form in *Computers and the Humanities* 1997; 31(2): 91–113. Reprinted by permission. © 1997 Kluwer Academic Publishers.

    The title of this article is quoted from Sue Atkins (Past President, European Association for Lexicography; General Editor, *Collins-Robert English/French Dictionary*) responding to a discussion which assumed discrete and disjoint word senses, at The Future of the Dictionary Workshop, Uriage-Les-Bains, October 1994.

1. Since the paper was written, seven years ago, the exercise, christened SENSEVAL, has now taken place not once but twice, SENSEVAL-1 in 1998 (Kilgarriff and Palmer 2000) and SENSEVAL-2 in 2001 (Cotton et al. 2001; Edmonds and Kilgarriff 2002).

2. In Yarowsky's work, this is just one of the options for providing seeds for the process.

3. MUC is a series of US Government-funded, competitive, quantitatively-evaluated exercises in information extraction (MUC-5, 1994).

4. The AAAI Spring Symposium on Representation and Acquisition of Lexical Information, Stanford, April 1995 and the ACL SIGLEX Workshop on The Breadth and Depth of Semantic Lexicons, Santa Cruz, June 1996.

5. "Lumping" is considering two slightly different patterns of usage as a single meaning. "Splitting" is the converse: dividing or separating them into different meanings.

6. Cruse identifies two major varieties of modulation, of which highlighting is one.

7. See Zwicky and Sadock (1975) for a fuller discussion of the terms and their sources.

8. Also related to this distinction is the polysemy/homonymy distinction: when do we have two distinct words, and when, one word with two meanings? Most commentators agree that there is a gradation between the two, with the distinction being of limited theoretical interest. For some purposes, the distinction may be more useful than the vagueness/ambiguity one (Krovetz 1996). In practice, similar difficulties arise in distinguishing homonymy from polysemy, as in distinguishing vagueness from ambiguity.

9. Examples (6)–(11) are taken by comparing four state-of-the-art English learners' dictionaries (*CIDE* 1995; *COBUILD* 1995; *LDOCE* 1995; *OALDCE* 1995) and finding words where the lexicographers in one team made one decision regarding what the distinct word senses were, whereas those in another made another. This immediately has the effect of introducing various factors which have not been considered in earlier theoretical discussions.

10. For many putatively ambiguous reading-pairs, there are intermediate cases. A sprouting bean, or one bought for planting, is intermediate between food and plant. But the possibility of intermediate cases does not preclude ambiguity: whether

two readings of a word are completely disjoint, permitting no intermediate cases, is a different question to whether a word is ambiguous. This imposes a further constraint on ambiguity tests. A speaker might say: "Ellen and Harry must have bought the same kind of bean, unless, say, Ellen bought plants and Harry bought beans sold at the supermarket but which he was intending to plant". We should not infer that *bean* is vague. Rather, we must insist that both of the crossed readings are prototypical. (There are of course further difficulties in making this constraint precise.)

11. Eight out of ten informants found the related sentence, "I loved and married her", odd. The two who found it acceptable were reading "and" as an indicator of temporal sequence.

12. This is the "lexical decision" task in a mixed, visual and auditory procedure. It is one of a variety of versions of semantic priming experiments. The basic effect is robust across a number of experimental strategies.

13. The format of the dictionary has remained fairly stable since Dr. Johnson's day. The reasons for the format, and the reasons it has proved so resistant to change and innovation, are explored at length in Nunberg (1994). In short, the development of printed discourse, particularly the new periodicals, in England in the early part of the 18th century brought about a re-evaluation of the nature of meaning. No longer could it be assumed that a disagreement or confusion about a word's meaning could be settled face-to-face, and it seemed at the time that the new discourse would only be secure if there was some mutually acceptable authority on what words meant. The resolution to the crisis came in the form of Johnson's *Dictionary*. Thus, from its inception, the modern dictionary has had a crucial symbolic role: it represents a methodology for resolving questions of meaning. Hence "the dictionary", with its implications of unique reference and authority (cf. "the Bible") (Leech 1981). Further evidence for this position is to be found in McArthur (1987), for whom the "religious or quasi-religious tinge" (p. 38) to reference materials is an enduring theme in their history; Summers (1988), whose research into dictionary use found that "settl[ing] family arguments" was one of its major uses (p. 114, cited in Béjoint [1994: 151]); and Moon (1989) who catalogues the use of the UAD (Unidentified Authorising Dictionary) from newspapers' letters pages to restaurant advertising materials (pp. 60–64).

14. By "concordance" I mean a display which presents a line of context for each occurrence of the word under scrutiny in the corpus, with all occurrences of the key word aligned. Fuller details are, of course, system specific, but it has rapidly become evident that this kind of display is the basic requirement for any corpus lexicography system.

15. A psycholinguistic investigation along these lines is presented in Jorgensen (1990).

16. In a paper on this topic, it is critical to distinguish between uses of a word that are candidates for treating as distinct senses, and ones that are distinct senses in

an actual or idealized dictionary. Here and throughout the paper we use "use" for the former, and "sense" for the latter.

17. For the *BNC* see http://info.ox.ac.uk/bnc. Counts were: handbag 609, handbags 103, handbagging 1, handbagged 2.
18. This turns out to be a (sexist and homophobic) in-group joke, as well as a case of both metonymy and of a distinct idiomatic use of the word. Interestingly, in the text, "the bouncing handbag" succeeds in referring, even though the idiom is not known to the addressee, as is made explicit in the text.
19. In my thesis, in the context of an analysis of polysemy, I call the first four knowledge types homonymy, alternation, analogy and collocation. (Taxonomy is addressed separately.)
20. This is presented as a quotation of a football manager's spoken comment; quite whether it is verbatim, or the *Daily Telegraph* journalist's paraphrase, we shall never know.
21. Thanks to Simon Shurville for sharing his expertise.
22. Kjellmer implies that the further specification is a temporal process, there being a time in the interpretation process when the lexical meaning of the word is accessed but specified for "control" but not for either PUN or END. I see no grounds for inferring the temporal process from the logical structure.
23. A well-organized, hierarchical lexicon will mean that this need not introduce redundancy into the lexicon.

References

Apresjan, Juri D.
  1974   Regular polysemy. *Linguistics* 142: 5–32.
Atkins, Sue
  1993   Tools for computer-aided corpus lexicography: the Hector project. *Acta Linguistica Hungarica* 41: 5–72.
Ayto, John R.
  1983   On specifying meaning. In: Reinhard R. K. Hartmann (ed.), *Lexicography: Principles and Practice*, 89–98. Sidcup, UK: Academic Press.
Béjoint, Henri
  1994   *Tradition and Innovation in Modern English Dictionaries*. Oxford: Oxford University Press.
Briscoe, Edward J., Ann A. Copestake and Branimir K. Boguraev
  1990   Enjoy the paper: lexical semantics via lexicology. In: *COLING 90*(2): 42–47, Helsinki.
Brown, Peter, Stephen Della Pietra, Vincent J. Della Pietra and Robert L. Mercer
  1991   Word sense disambiguation using statistical methods. In: *Proceedings, 29th ACL*, Berkeley, California.

CIDE
1995   *Cambridge International Dictionary of English.* Cambridge: Cambridge University Press.

Clear, Jeremy
1994   I can't see the sense in a large corpus. In: Ferenc Kiefer, Gábor Kiss and Júlia Pajzs (eds.), *Papers in Computational Lexicography: COMPLEX '94*, 33–48, Budapest.

COBUILD
1995   *The Collins COBUILD English Language Dictionary.* 2nd Edition. Edited by John McH. Sinclair et al. London.

Copestake, Ann A. and Edward J. Briscoe
1995   Semi-productive polysemy and sense extension. In: James Pustejovsky and Branimir Boguraev (eds.), *Lexical Semantics: The Problem of Polysemy*, 15–67. Oxford: Clarendon.

CorpusBench
1993   *CorpusBench Manual.* Textware A/S, Copenhagen, Denmark.

Cotton, Scott, Philip Edmonds, Adam Kilgarriff and Martha Palmer (eds.)
2001   *Proceedings of SENSEVAL-2, Second International Workshop on Evaluating Word Sense Disambiguation Systems.* ACL, Toulouse, France.

Cottrell, Garrison W.
1989   *A Connectionist Approach to Word Sense Disambiguation.* London: Pitman.

Cruse, David A.
1986   *Lexical Semantics.* Cambridge: Cambridge University Press.
1995   Polysemy and related phenomena from a cognitive linguistic viewpoint. In: Patrick Saint-Dizier and Evelyne Viegas (eds.), *Computational Lexical Semantics*, 33–49. Cambridge: Cambridge University Press.

Dolan, William B.
1994   Word sense disambiguation: clustering related senses. In: *COLING 94*, Tokyo.

Edmonds, Philip and Adam Kilgarriff (eds.)
2002   Evaluating word sense disambiguation systems. *Journal of Natural Language Engineering* 8(4): 279–292.

Fillmore, Charles
1988   Keynote lecture, British Association of Applied Linguistics conference, Exeter, September 1988.

Fillmore, Charles J. and Beryl T. S. Atkins
1992   Towards a frame-based lexicon: the semantics of *risk* and its neighbors. In: Adrienne Lehrer and Eva Kittay (eds.), *Frames, Fields and Contrasts*, 75–102. New Jersey: Lawrence Erlbaum.

Gale, William, Kenneth Church and David Yarowsky
  1992   Estimating upper and lower bounds on the performance of word-
             sense disambiguation programs. In: *Proceedings, 30th ACL*, 249–
             156.
  1993   A method for disambiguating word senses in a large corpus. *Computers
             and the Humanities* 26(1–2): 415–539.
Geeraerts, Dirk
  1990   The lexicographical treatment of prototypical polysemy. In: Savas
             L. Tsohatzidis (ed.), *Meanings and Prototypes: Studies in Linguistic
             Classification*, 195–210. London: Routledge.
  1993   Vagueness's puzzles, polysemy's vagueness. *Cognitive Linguistics*
             4(3): 223–272.
Guthrie, Joe A., Louise Guthrie, Yorick Wilks and Homa Aidinejad
  1991   Subject-dependent co-occurrence and word sense disambiguation. In:
             Proceedings, 29th ACL, Berkeley, California.
Guthrie, Louise, Brian M. Slator, Yorick Wilks and Rebecca Bruce
  1990   Is there content in empty heads? In: *COLING 90*(3), 138–143, Helsinki.
Hanks, Patrick
  1994   Linguistic norms and pragmatic exploitations or, why lexicographers
             need prototype theory, and vice versa. In: Ferenc Kiefer, Gábor Kiss
             and Júlia Pajzs (eds.), *Papers in Computational Lexicography:
             COMPLEX '94*, 89–113, Budapest.
Hearst, Marti A.
  1991   Noun homograph disambiguation using local context in large text
             corpora. In: *Using Corpora: Proc. Seventh Ann. Conf. of the UW
             Centre for the New OED*, 1–22, Waterloo, Canada.
Jensen, Karen and Jean-Louis Binot
  1987   Disambiguating prepositional phrase attachment by using on-line
             dictionary definitions. *Computational Linguistics* 13: 251–260.
Jorgensen, Julia C.
  1990   The psychological reality of word senses. *Journal of Psycholinguistic
             Research* 19(3): 167–190.
Kilgarriff, Adam
  1992   Polysemy. Ph.D. thesis. University of Sussex, CSRP 261, School of
             Cognitive and Computing Sciences.
  1993   Dictionary word sense distinctions: an enquiry into their nature.
             Computers and the Humanities 26(1–2): 365–387.
  1997a   Evaluating word sense disambiguation programs: progress report. In:
             Robert John Gaizauskas (ed.), *Proceedings, SALT Workshop on
             Evaluation in Speech and Language Technology*, 114–120, Sheffield,
             UK, June.
  1997b   Foreground and background lexicons and word sense disambiguation

for information extraction. In: *Proceedings, Workshop on Lexicon Driven Information Extraction*, 51–62. Frascati, Italy, July.

Kilgarriff, Adam and Martha Palmer (eds.)
2000   Special issue on SENSEVAL: evaluating word sense disambiguation programs. *Computers and the Humanities* 34(1–2). Dordrecht: Kluwer.

Kjellmer, Goran
1993   Multiple meaning and interpretation: the case of *sanction. Zeitschrift für Anglistik und Amerikanistik* 41(2): 115–123.

Krovetz, Robert
1996   Surprises under the hood: an investigation of word meanings and information retrieval. To appear.

Lakoff, George
1987   *Women, Fire and Dangerous Things*. Chicago: University of Chicago Press.

Lakoff, George and Mark Johnson
1980   *Metaphors We Live By*. Chicago: University of Chicago Press.

Landes, Shari, Claudia Leacock and Randee Tengi
1996   Building semantic concordances. In: Christiane Fellbaum (ed.), *WordNet: An Electronic Lexical Database*. Cambridge, MA: MIT Press.

LDOCE
1987   *Longman Dictionary of Contemporary English*, New Edition. Edited by Della Summers. Harlow.
1995   *Longman Dictionary of Contemporary English*, 3rd Edition. Edited by Della Summers. Harlow.

Leech, Geoffrey
1981   *Semantics*. Cambridge: Cambridge University Press.

Lesk, Michael E.
1986   Automatic sense disambiguation using machine readable dictionaries: how to tell a pine cone from an ice cream cone. In: *Proceedings, 1986 SIGDOC Conference*, Toronto, Canada.

Levin, Beth
1993   *English Verb Classes and Alternations*. Chicago: University of Chicago Press.

Levin, Beth and Malka Rappoport Hovav
1991   Wiping the slate clean: a lexical semantic exploration. *Cognition* 41: 123–151.

Levin, Beth, Grace Song, and Beryl T. S. Atkins
1997   Making sense of corpus data: a case study of verbs of sound. *International Journal of Corpus Linguistics* 2(1): 23–64.

McArthur, Tom
1987   *Worlds of Reference*. Cambridge: Cambridge University Press.

McRoy, Susan W.
1992   Using multiple knowledge sources for word sense discrimination. *Computational Linguistics* 18(1): 1–30.

Miller, George
1990   Wordnet: An on-line lexical database. *International Journal of Lexicography* (special issue) 3(4): 235–312.

Moon, Rosamund
1989   Objective or objectionable? Ideological aspects of dictionaries. *English Language Research*, 3: Language and Ideology, 59–94.

MUC-5
1994   *Proceedings, Message Understanding Conference*. DARPA.

Nunberg, Geoffrey
1978   *The Pragmatics of Reference*. Bloomington, IN: University of Indiana Linguistics Club.
1994   The once and future dictionary. Presentation at The Future of the Dictionary Workshop, Uriage-les-Bains, France, October 1994.

OALDCE
1995   *Oxford Advanced Learner's Dictionary of Current English*, Fifth Edition. Oxford: Oxford University Press.

Ostler, Nicholas and Beryl T. S. Atkins
1991   Predictable meaning shift: some linguistic properties of lexical implication rules. In: James Pustejovsky and Susan Bergler (eds.), *Lexical Semantics and Knowledge Representation: ACL SIGLEX Workshop*, Berkeley, California.

Pustejovsky, James
1991   The generative lexicon. *Computational Linguistics* 17(4): 409–441.

Quine, Willard van O.
1969   Speaking of objects. In: Quine, Willard van O., *Ontological Relativity*, 1–25. New York: Columbia University Press.

Schulze, Bruno and Oliver Christ
1994   *The IMS Corpus Workbench*. Institut für maschinelle Sprachverarbeitung, Universität Stuttgart.

Schütze, Hinrich and Jan O. Pederson
1995   Information retrieval based on word senses. In: *Proceedings, ACM Special Interest Group on Information Retrieval*.

Sinclair, John M. (ed.)
1987   *Looking up: An Account of the COBUILD Project in Lexical Computing*. London: Collins.

Slator, Brian M.
1988   Lexical semantics and a preference semantics parser. *Technical Report MCCS-88-16*, Computing Research Laboratory, New Mexico State University, New Mexico.

Sparck Jones, Karen
    1986   *Synonymy and Semantic Classification*. Edinburgh: Edinburgh University Press.

Stock, Penelope F.
    1983   Polysemy. In: *Proceedings, Exeter Lexicography Conference*, 131–140.

Summers, Della
    1988   The role of dictionaries in language learning. In: Ronald A. Carter and Michael McCarthy (eds.), *Vocabulary and Language Teaching*, 111–125. London: Longman.

Sweetser, Eve
    1990   *From Etymology to Pragmatics: Metaphorical and Cultural Aspects of Semantic Structure*. Cambridge: Cambridge University Press.

Taylor, John
    1989   *Linguistic Categorization: Prototypes in Linguistic Theory*. Oxford: Oxford University Press.

ten Hacken, Pius
    1990   Reading distinction in machine translation. In: *COLING 90*, Helsinki.

Véronis, Jean and Nancy M. Ide
    1990   Word sense disambiguation with very large neural networks extracted from machine readable dictionaries. In: *COLING 90*(2), 389–394, Helsinki.

Williams, John N.
    1992   Processing polysemous words in context: evidence for interrelated meanings. *Journal of Psycholinguistic Research* 21: 193–218.

Yarowsky, David
    1992   Word-sense disambiguation using statistical models of Roget's categories trained on large corpora. In: *COLING 92*, Nantes.
    1995   Unsupervised word sense disambiguation rivalling supervised methods. In: *ACL 95*, 189–196, MIT.

Zgusta, Ladislav
    1971   *Manual of Lexicography*. The Hague: Mouton.

Zwicky, Arnold M. and J. M. Sadock
    1975   Ambiguity tests and how to fail them. *Syntax and Semantics* 4: 1–36.

Senses and texts

Yorick Wilks

1. Introduction

Empirical, corpus-based, computational linguistics (CL) has reached by now into almost every crevice of the subject, and perhaps pragmatics will soon succumb. Semantics, if we may assume the sense-tagging task is semantic, has shown striking progress in the last five years and, in Yarowsky's most recent work (Yarowsky 1995), has produced very high levels of success – over 90% – well above the key bench-mark figure of 62% correct sense assignment achieved at an informal experiment in New Mexico in about 1990, in which each word was assigned its first sense listed in the *Longman Dictionary of Contemporary English* (*LDOCE*).

A crucial question in this paper will be whether recent work in sense-tagging has in fact given us the breakthrough in scale that is now obvious with, say, part-of-speech tagging. Our conclusion will be that it has not, and that the experiments so far, however high their success rates, are not yet of a scale different from those of the previous generation of linguistic, symbolic-AI or connectionist approaches to the very same problem.

A historian of our field might glance back at this point to Small, Cottrell and Tanenhaus (1988), who surveyed the AI-symbolic and connectionist traditions of sense-tagging at just the moment when corpus-driven empirical methods began to revive, but had not been published. All the key issues still unsettled are discussed there and that collection showed no naïvety about the problem of sense resolution with respect only to existing lexicons of senses. It was realized that that task was only meaningful against an assumption of some method for capturing new (new to the chosen lexicon, that is) senses and, most importantly, that although existing lexicons differed, they did not differ arbitrarily much. The book further demonstrated that there was also strong psychological backing for the reality of word senses and for empirical methods of locating them from corpora without any prior assumptions about their number or distribution (e.g. in early versions of Plate's work, published later in Wilks et al. 1990; see also Jorgensen 1990).

My purpose in this paper will be to argue that Kilgariff's negative claims are wrong, and his errors must be combated, while Yarowsky is largely right although I have some queries about the details and the interpretation of his claims. Both authors, however, agree that this is a traditional and important task: one often cited as being a foundational lacuna in, say, the history of Machine Translation (MT), because of the inability of early Natural Language Processing (NLP) systems to carry it out. It was assumed by many, in that distant period, that if only word-sense ambiguity could be solved by the process we are calling sense-tagging, then MT of high quality would be relatively straightforward. Like many linguistic tasks, it then became an end in itself, like syntactic parsing; and now that it is, we would claim, firmly in sight (despite Kilgarriff) it is far less clear that its solution will automatically solve a range of traditional problems like MT. But clearly it would be a generally good tool to have available in NLP and a triumph if this long-resistant task of CL were to yield.

2. The very possibility of sense-tagging

Kilgarriff's (1993) paper is important because it has been widely cited as showing that the senses of a word, as distinguished in a dictionary such as *LDOCE*, do not cover the senses actually carried by most occurrences of the word as they appear in a corpus. If he can show that, it would be very significant indeed, because that would imply that sense-tagging word occurrences in a corpus by means of any lexical data based on, or related to, a machine-readable dictionary or thesaurus is misguided. I want to show here that the paper does not demonstrate any such thing. Moreover, it proceeds by means of a straw man it may be worth bringing back to life!

That straw man, Kilgarriff's starting point, is the "bank model" (BM) of lexical ambiguity resolution, which he establishes by assertion rather than quotation, though it is attributed to Small, Hirst and Cottrell as well as the present author. In the BM, words have discrete meanings, and the human reader (like the ideal computer program) knows immediately which meaning of the word applies (Kilgarriff 1993: 367), "given that a word occurrence always refers to one or the other, but not both" of the main meanings that a word like *bank* is reputed to have. In the BM, the set of senses available for a word does not depend on which particular dictionary you start with, but is somehow abstractly fixed. The main argument of Kilgarriff's paper is to distinguish a number of relationships between *LDOCE* senses that are not discrete in that way, and then to go on to an experiment with senses in a corpus. But first we should breathe a little life back into the BM straw man: those named above can look after themselves, but here is a passage from Wilks (1972: 12):

> ... it is very difficult to assign word occurrences to sense classes in any manner that is both general and determinate. In the sentences "I have a stake in this country" and "My stake on the last race was a pound" is "stake" being used in the same sense or not? If "stake" can be interpreted to mean something as vague as "stake as any kind of investment in any enterprise" then the answer is yes. So, if a semantic dictionary contained only two senses for "stake": that vague sense together with "Stake as a post", then one would expect to assign the vague sense for both the sentences above. But if, on the other hand, the dictionary distinguished "Stake as an investment" and "Stake as an initial payment in a game or race" then the answer would be expected to be different. So, then, word sense disambiguation is relative to the dictionary of sense choices available and can have no absolute quality about it.

QED, one might say, since the last sentences seem to show very much the awareness (a quarter of a century ago, but in the context of a computer program for sense-tagging) that sense choice may not be exclusive if defined, as it must be, with respect to a particular dictionary. Hence, in my view, the BM is no more than a straw man because writers of the dark ages of CL were as aware as Kilgarriff of the real problems of dictionary senses versus text occurrences.

In general, it is probably wise to believe, even if it is not always true, that authors in the past were no more naïve than those now working, and were probably writing programs, however primitive and ineffective, to carry out the very same tasks as now (e.g. sense-tagging of corpus words). More importantly, Wilks (1972), which created an approach called preference semantics, was essentially a study of the divergence of corpus usage from lexical norms (or preferences), and developed in the 1970s into a set of processes for accommodating divergent/nonstandard/metaphorical usage to existing lexical norms, notions that Kilgarriff seems to believe only developed in a much later and smarter group of people around 1990, which includes himself, but also, for example, Fass, whose work was a direct continuation of that quoted above. Indeed, in Wilks (1972) procedures were programmed (and run over a set of newspaper editorials) to accommodate such "divergent" corpus usage of one word to that of an established sense of a different word in the same text, while in Wilks (1978) programmed procedures were specified to accommodate such usage by constructing completely new sense entries for the word itself.

A much more significant omission, one that bears directly on Kilgarriff's main claim and is not merely an issue of historical correctness, is the lack of reference to work in New Mexico and elsewhere (e.g. Cowie, Guthrie and Guthrie 1992) on the large-scale sense-tagging of corpora against a machine-readable dictionary (MRD)-derived lexical database. These were larger-scale experiments whose results directly contradict the result he is believed to have proved. I shall return to this point in a moment. The best part of Kilgarriff's paper is his attempt to give an intuitive account of developmental relations between the senses of a word. He distinguishes "generalizing metaphors" (a move from a specific case to a more general one) from "must-be-theres" (the applicability of one sense requires the applicability of another, as when an act of matricide requires there to be a mother) from "domain shift" (as when a sense in one domain, like *mellow* [of wine], is far enough from the domain of *mellow* [of a personality] to constitute a sense shift).

It is not always easy to distinguish the first two types, since both rest on an implication relationship between two or more senses. Again, the details do not matter: what he has shown convincingly is that, as in the Wilks (1972) quotation, the choice between senses of a given word is often not easy to make because it depends on their relationship, the nature of the definitions and how specific they are. I suspect no-one has ever held a simple-minded version of the BM, except possibly Fodor and Katz, who, whatever their virtues, had no interest at all in lexicography.

The general problem with Kilgarriff's analysis of sense types is that he conflates:

(i)   Text usage different from that shown in a whole list of stored senses for a given word e.g. in a dictionary (which is what his later experiment will be about), with

(ii)   Text usage divergent from some "core" sense in the lexicon.

Only the second is properly in the area of metaphor/metonymy or "grinding" (Copestake and Briscoe 1991) work of the group in which he places himself, and it is this phenomenon to which his classification of sense distinctions summarized above properly belongs. This notion requires some idea of sense development, of senses of a word extending in time in a non-random manner, and is a linguistic tradition of analysis going back to Givón (1967). However, the straw man BM and the experiment Kilgarriff then does on hand-tagging of senses in text, all attach to the first, unrelated, notion which does not normally imply the presence of metonymy or metaphor at all, but simply an inadequate sense list. Of course, the two types may be historically related, in that some of the (i) list may have been derived by metaphorical/metonymic processes from a (ii) word, but this is not so in general. This confusion of targets is a weakness in the paper, since it makes it difficult to be sure what he wants us to conclude from the experiment. However, since I shall show his results are not valid, this distinction may not matter too much.

One might add here that Kilgarriff's pessimism has gone hand in hand with some very interesting surveys he has conducted over the internet on the real need for word-sense disambiguation by NLP research and development. And one should note that there are others (e.g. Ide and Véronis 1994) who have questioned the practical usefulness of data derived at many sites from MRDs. My case here, of course, is that it has been useful, both in our own work on sense-tagging (Stevenson and Wilks 2001; Cowie, Guthrie and Guthrie 1992) and in that of Yarowsky, using Roget and discussed below.

Kilgarriff's experiment, which has been widely taken to be the main message of his paper, is not described in much detail. He does not give the reader the statistics on which his result was based even though the text quite clearly contains a claim (p. 378) that 87% of (non-monosemous) words in his text sample have at least one text occurrence that cannot be associated with one and only one *LDOCE* sense. Hence, he claims, the poor old BM is refuted, yet again. One must note here that this is a claim about word *types*: so if 87% of them have at least one "defective" token, this could mean that a very small number of text words (i.e. *tokens*) are "defective".

So, Kilgarriff's claim (about word types) is wholly consistent with, for example, 99% of text usage (of word tokens) being associated with one and only one dictionary sense! Thus the actual claim in the paper is not at all what it has been taken to show, and is highly misleading.

But much empirical evidence tells also against the claim Kilgarriff is believed to have made. Informal analyses by Georgia Green (1989) suggested that some 20% of text usage (i.e. of word tokens) could not be associated with a unique dictionary sense. Consistent with that, too, is the use of simulated annealing techniques by Cowie, Guthrie and Guthrie (1992) at the Computing Research Laboratory (CRL) New Mexico to assign *LDOCE* senses to a corpus. In that work, it was shown that about 75%–80% of word usage could be correctly associated with *LDOCE* senses, as compared with hand-tagged control text. That figure was subsequently raised substantially by additional filtering techniques (particularly in Stevenson and Wilks 2001).

The two considerations above show, from quite different sources and techniques, the dubious nature of Kilgarriff's claim. Antal (1963) argued long ago (and some believe Wierzbicka 1989 maintains some version of such a position) that words have only core senses. On such a view, dictionaries/ lexicons should express that single sense and leave all further sense refinement to some other process, such as real world knowledge manipulations, AI if you wish, but not a process that uses the lexicon.

Since the CRL result suggested that the automatic sense-resolution procedures worked very well (near 80%) at the homograph level (i.e. the sense-cluster level, such as the *LDOCE* dictionary uses) rather than the ordinary sense level (the latter being where Kilgarriff's examples all lie), one possible way forward for NLP would be to go some of the way with Antal's views and restrict lexical sense distinctions to the homograph level. Then sense-tagging could perhaps be done at the success level of part-of-speech tagging. Such a move could be seen as changing the data to suit what you can accomplish, or as reinstating AI and pragmatics within NLP for the kind of endless, context-driven, inferences we need in real situations.

This suggestion is rather different from Kilgarriff's conclusion. He proposes that the real basis of sense distinction be established by usage clustering techniques applied to corpora. This is an excellent idea and recent work at IBM (Brown et al. 1991) has produced striking non-seeded clusters of corpus usages, many of them displaying a similarity close to an intuitive notion of sense (or you can now explore Google's own version of the very same methodology at labs.google.com/sets).

But there are serious problems in moving any kind of lexicography, traditional or computational, onto any such basis. Hanks (p.c.) has claimed that a dictionary could be written that consisted entirely of usages, and has investigated how those might be clustered for purely lexicographic purposes, yet it remains unclear what kind of volume could result from such a project or who would buy it and how they could use it. One way to think of such a product would be the reduction of monolingual dictionaries to thesauri, so that to look up a word becomes to look up which row or rows of context-bound semi-synonyms it appears in. Thesauri have a real function both for native and non-native speakers of a language, but they rely on the reader knowing what some or all of the words in a row or class mean because they give no explanations. To reduce word sense separation to synonym classes, without explanations attached would limit a dictionary's use in a striking way.

If we then think not of dictionaries for human use but NLP lexicons, the situation might seem more welcoming for Kilgarriff's suggestion, since he could be seen as suggesting, say, a new version of WordNet (Miller 1985) with its synsets established not *a priori* but by statistical corpus clustering. This is indeed a notion that has been kicked around in NLP for a while and is probably worth a try. There are still difficulties: firstly, that any such clustering process produces not only the clean, neat, classes like IBM's (Hindu/Jew/Christian/Buddhist) example but inevitable monsters, produced by some quirk of a particular corpus. Those could, of course, be hand weeded but that is not an automatic process.

Secondly, as is also well known, what classes you get, or rather, the generality of the classes you get, depends on parameter settings in the clustering algorithm: those obtained at different settings may or may not correspond nicely to, say, different levels of a standard lexical hierarchy. They probably will not, since hierarchies are discrete in terms of levels and the parameters used are continuous but, even when they do, there will be none of the hierarchical terms attached, of the sort available in WordNet (e.g. ANIMAL or DOMESTIC ANIMAL). And this is only a special case of the general problem of clustering algorithms, well known in information retrieval, that the clusters so found do not come with names or features attached.

Thirdly, and this may be the most significant point for Kilgarriff's proposal, there will always be some match of such empirical clusters to any new text occurrence of a word and, to that degree, sense-tagging in text is bound to succeed by such a methodology, given the origin of the clusters and the fact that a closest match to one of a set of clusters can always be found. The problem is how you interpret that result because, in this methodology, no hand-tagged text will be available as a control since it is not clear what task the human controls could be asked to carry out. Subjects may find traditional sense-tagging (against e.g. *LDOCE* senses) hard but it is a comprehensible task, because of the role dictionaries and their associated senses have in our cultural world. But the new task (attach one and only one of the classes in which the word appears to its use at this point) is rather less well defined. But again, a range of original and ingenious suggestions may make this task much more tractable, and senses so tagged (against WordNet style classes, though empirically derived) could certainly assist real tasks like MT even if they did not turn out wholly original dictionaries for the book-buying public.

There is, of course, no contradiction between, on the one hand, my suggestion for a compaction of lexicons towards core or homograph senses, done to optimize the sense-tagging process and, on the other, Kilgarriff's suggestion for an empirical basis for the establishment of synsets, or clusters that constitute senses. Given that there are problems with wholly empirically-based sense clusters of the sort mentioned above, the natural move would be to suggest some form of hybrid derivation from corpus statistics, taken together with some machine-readable source of synsets: WordNet itself, standard thesauri, and even bilingual dictionaries which are also convenient reductions of a language to word sets grouped by sense (normally by reference to a word in another language, of course). As many have now realized, both the pure corpus methods and the large-scale hand-crafted sources have their virtues, and their own particular systematic errors, and the hope has to be that clever procedures can cause those to cancel, rather than reinforce, each other. But all that is future work, and beyond the scope of a critical note.

In conclusion, it may be worth noting that the BM, in some form, is probably inescapable, at least in the form of what Pustejovsky (1995) calls a "sense enumerative lexicon", and against which he inveighs for some 20 pages before going on to use one for his illustrations, as we all do, including all lexicographers. This is not hypocrisy but a confusion close to that between (i) and (ii) above: we, as language users and computational modellers, must be able, now or later, to capture a usage that differs from some established sense (problem [ii] above), but that is only loosely connected to problem (i), where senses, if they are real, seem always to come in lists and it is with them we must sense-tag if the task is to be possible at all.

3.   Recent experiments in sense-tagging

We now turn to the claims (Gale et al. 1992; see also Yarowsky 1992, 1993, 1995) that:

(i)   Word tokens in a single text tend to occur with a smaller number of senses than often supposed; and, most specifically,

(ii)   In a single discourse a word will appear in one and only one sense, even if several are listed for it in a lexicon, at a level of about 94% likelihood for non-monosemous words (a figure that naturally becomes higher if the monosemous text words are added in).

These are most important claims if true for they would, at a stroke, remove a major excuse for the bad progress of MT, make redundant a whole sub-industry of NLP, namely sense resolution, and greatly simplify the currently fashionable NLP task of sense-tagging texts by any method whatever (e.g. Cowie, Guthrie and Guthrie 1992; Bruce and Wiebe 1994).

Gale et al.'s claim would not make sense-tagging of text irrelevant, of course, but it would allow one to assume that resolving any single token of a word (by any method at all) in a text would then serve for all occurrences in the text, at a high level of probability.

Gale et al.'s claims are not directly related to those of Kilgarriff, who aimed to show only that it was difficult to assign text tokens to any lexical sense at all. Indeed, Kilgarriff and Gale et al. use quite different procedures: Kilgarriff's is one of assigning a word token in context to one of a set of lexical sense descriptions, while Gale et al.'s is one of assessing whether or not two tokens in context are the same sense or not. The procedures are incommensurable and no outcome on one would be predictive for the other: Gale et al.'s procedures do not use standard lexicons and are in terms of closeness-of-fit, which means that, unlike Kilgarriff's, they can never fail to match a text token to a sense, defined in the way they do (see below).

However, Gale et al.'s claims are incompatible with Kilgarriff's in spirit in that Kilgarriff assumes there is a lot of polysemy about and that resolving it is tricky, whereas Gale et al. assume the opposite.

Both Kilgarriff and Gale et al. have given rise to potent myths about word-sense-tagging in text that I believe are wrong, or at best unproven. Kilgarriff's paper, as we saw earlier, has some subtle analysis but one crucial statistical flaw. Gale et al.'s is quite different: it is a mush of hard-to-interpret claims and procedures, but ones that may still, nonetheless, be basically true.

Gale et al.'s methodology is essentially impressionistic: the texts they chose are, of course, those available, which turn out to be Grolier's *Encyclopedia*. There is no dispute about one-sense-per-discourse (their name for claim [ii] above) for certain classes of texts: the more technical a text the more anyone, whatever their other prejudices about language, would expect the claim to be true. Announcing that the claim had been shown true for mathematical or chemical texts would surprise no-one; encyclopaedias are also technical texts.

Their key fact in support of claim (i) above, based on a sense-tagging of 97 selected word types in the whole *Encyclopedia*, and sense-tagged by the statistical method described below, was that 7,569 of the tokens associated with those types are monosemous in the corpus, while 6,725 are of words with more than two senses. Curiously, they claim this shows "most words (both by token and by type) have only one sense" (Gale et al. 1992: 63). I have no idea whether to be surprised by this figure or not but it certainly does nothing to show that "Perhaps word sense disambiguation is not as difficult as we might have thought" (p. 67). It shows me that, even in fairly technical prose like that of an encyclopaedia, nearly half the words occur in more than one sense.

And that fact, of course, has no relation at all to mono- or polysemousness in whatever base lexicon we happen to be using in an NLP system. Given a large lexicon, based on say the *Oxford English Dictionary* (*OED*), one could safely assume that virtually all words are polysemous. As will be often the case, Gale et al.'s claim at this point is true of exactly the domain they are dealing with, and their (non-stated) assumption is that any lexicon is created for the domain text they are dealing with and with no relation to any other lexicon for any other text. One claim per discourse, one might say.

This last point is fundamental because we know that distinctions of sense are lexicon- or procedure-dependent. Kilgarriff faced this explicitly, and took *LDOCE* as an admittedly arbitrary starting point. Gale et al. never discuss the issue, which makes all their claims about numbers of senses totally, but inexplicitly, dependent on the procedures they have adopted in their experiments to give a canonical sense-tagging against which to test their claims.

This is a real problem for them. They admit right away that few or no extensive hand-tagged sense-resolved corpora exist for control purposes, So, they must adopt a sense-discrimination procedure to provide their data that is unsupervised. This is where the ingenuity of the paper comes in, but also its fragility. They have two methods for providing sense-tagged data against which to test their one-sense-per-discourse claim (ii).

The first rests on a criterion of sense distinction provided by correspondence to differing non-English words in a parallel corpus, in their case the French-English Canadian Hansard because, as always, it is there. So, the correspondence of *duty* to an aligned sentence containing either *devoir* or *impot* (i.e. 'obligation' or 'tax') is taken as an effective method of distinguishing the obligation/tax senses of the English word, which was indeed the criterion for sense argued for in Dagan and Itai (1994). It has well-known drawbacks: most obviously that whatever we mean by sense distinction in English, it is unlikely to be criterially revealed by what the French happen to do in their language.

More relevantly to the particular case, Gale et al. found it very hard to find plausible pairs for test, which must not of course share ambiguities across the French/English boundaries (as *interest/interet* do). In the end they were reduced to a test based on the six (!) pairs they found in the Hansard corpus that met their criteria for sense separation and occurrence more than 150 times in two or more senses. In Gale et al.'s defence one could argue that, since they do not expect much polysemy in texts, examples of this sort would, of course, be hard to find. Taking this bilingual method of sense-tagging for the six-word set as criterial they then run their basic word sense discrimination method over the English Hansard data. This consists, very roughly, of a training method over 100-word surrounding contexts for 60 instances of each member of a pair of senses (hand selected), i.e. for each pair $2 \times 60 \times 100 = 12,000$ words. Notice that this eyeballing method is not inconsistent with anything in Kilgarriff's argument: Gale et al. selected 120 contexts in Hansard for each word that *did* correspond intuitively to one of the (French) selected senses. It says nothing about any tokens that may have been hard to classify in this way. The figures claimed for the discrimination method against the criterial data vary between 82% and 100% (for different word pairs) of the data for that sense correctly discriminated.

They then move on to a monolingual method that provides sense-tagged data in an unsupervised way. It rests on previous work by Yarowsky (1992) and uses the assignment of a single Roget category (from the 1,042) as a sense-discrimination. Yarowsky sense-tagged some of the Grolier corpus in the following way: 100-word contexts for words like *crane* (ambiguous between 'bird' and 'machinery') are taken and those words are scored by (very roughly, and given interpolation for local context) which of the 1,042 Roget categories they appear under as tokens. The sense of a given token of *crane* is determined by which Roget category wins out: e.g. category 348 (TOOLS/MACHINERY) for the machinery contexts, and category 414 (ANIMALS/INSECTS) for the bird contexts. Yarowsky (1992) claimed 93% correctness for this procedure over a sample of 12 selected words, presumably checked against earlier hand-tagged data.

The interpolation for local effects is in fact very sophisticated and involves training with the 100-word contexts in Grolier of all the words that appear under a given candidate Roget head, a method that they acknowledge introduces some noise, since it adds into the training material Grolier contexts that involve senses of a category 348 word, say, that is not its MACHINERY sense (e.g. *crane* as a bird). However, this method, they note, does not have the problems that come with the Hansard training method, in particular the notion, unacceptable to many, that sense distinctions in a source langue are defined by those in the target language (advocated in e.g. Dagon and Itai 1994), in that, for any word pair where two French and English words had identical senses, there could be no sense distinction at all.

In a broad sense, this is an old method, perhaps the oldest in lexical computation, and was used by Masterman (reported in Wilks 1972) in what was probably the first clear algorithm ever implemented for usage discrimination against Roget categories as sense-criterial. In the very limited computations of those days the hypothesis was deemed conclusively falsified; i.e. the hypothesis that any method overlapping the Roget categories for a word with the Roget categories of neighbouring words would determine an appropriate Roget category for that word in context.

This remains, I suspect, an open question: it may well be that Yarowsky's local interpolation statistics have made the general method viable, and that the 100-word window of context used is far more effective than a sentence. It may be the 12 words that confirm the disambiguation hypothesis at 93% would not be confirmed by 12 more words chosen at random (the early Cambridge work did at least try to resolve by means of Roget all the words in a sentence). But we can pass over that for now, and head on, to discuss Gale et al.'s main claim (ii) given the two types of data gathered.

Two very strange things happen at this point as the Gale et al. paper approaches its conclusion: namely, the proof of claim (ii) or one-sense-per-discourse. Firstly, the two types of sense-tagged data just gathered, especially the Roget-tagged data, should now be sufficient to test the claim, if a 93% level is deemed adequate for a preliminary test. Strangely, the data derived in the first part of the paper are never used or cited and the reader is not told whether Yarowsky's Roget data confirm or disconfirm (ii).

Secondly, the testing of (ii) is done purely by human judgement: a "blind" team of the three authors and two colleagues who are confronted by the *Oxford Advanced Learner's Dictionary* (*OALD*) main senses for one of nine test words, and who then make judgements of pairs of contexts for one of the nine words drawn from a single Grolier article. The subjects are shown to have pretty consistent judgements and, of 54 pairs of contexts from the same article, 51 shared the same sense and three did not.

Notice here that the display of the *OALD* senses is pointless, since the subjects are not asked to decide which if any *OALD* sense the words appear in, and so no Kilgarriff-style problems can arise. The test is simply to assign SAME or NOTSAME, and there are some control pairs added to force discrimination in some cases.

What can one say of this ingenious mini-experiment? Lexicographers traditionally distinguish "lumpers" and "splitters" among colleagues: those who tend to break up senses further and those who go for large, homonymic, senses, of which Antal would be the extreme case. Five Gale et al. colleagues (one had to be dropped to get consistency among the team) from a "lumper" team decided that 51 out of 54 contexts for a word in a single encyclopaedia article (repeated for eight other words) are in the same sense. Is this significant? I suspect not very, and nothing at all follows to support the myth of discovery that has grown round the paper: the team and data are tiny and not disinterested. The Grolier articles are mini-texts where the hypothesis would, if true, surprise one least. Much more testing is needed before a universal hypothesis about text polysemy enters our beliefs. Of course, they may in the end be right, and all the dogma of the field so far be wrong.

More recently, Yarowsky (1993, 1995) has extended this methodology in two ways: firstly, he has established a separate claim he calls "one sense per collocation", which is quite independent of local discourse context (which was the separate "one-sense-per-discourse" claim) and could be expressed crudely by saying that it is highly unlikely that the following two sentences (with the "same" collocations for *plants*) can both be attested in a corpus:

(1)   *Plastic plants can fool you if really well made* [= organic]
(2)   *Plastic plants can contaminate whole regions* [= factory]

One's first reaction may be to counter-cite examples like *Un golpe bajo* which can mean either a low blow in boxing, or a score one below par, in golf, although *golpe* could plausibly be said to have the same collocates in both cases. One can dismiss such examples (due to Jim Cowie in this case) by claiming both readings are idioms, but that should only focus our mind more on what Yarowsky does mean by collocation.

That work, although statistically impressive, gives no procedure for large-scale sense-tagging taken alone, since one has no immediate access to what cue words would, in general, constitute a collocation sufficient for disambiguation independent of discourse context. An interesting aspect of Yarowsky's paper is that he sought to show that on many definitions of sense and on many definitions of collocation (e.g. noun to the right, next verb to the left etc.) the hypothesis was still true at an interesting level, although better for some definitions of collocation than for others.

In his most recent work, Yarowsky (1995) has combined this approach with an assumption that the earlier claim ([ii]: one-sense-per-discourse) is true, so as to set up an iterative bootstrapping algorithm that both extends disambiguating collocational keys (Yarowsky 1993) and retrains against a corpus, while at the same time filtering the result iteratively by assuming (ii): i.e. that tokens from the same discourse will have the same sense. The result, on selected pairs (as always) of bisemous words is between 93% and 97% (for different word pairs again) correct against hand-coded samples, which is somewhat better than he obtained with his Roget method (93% in 1991) and better than figures from Schütze and Pederson (1995) who produce unsupervised clusterings from a corpus that have to be related by hand to intelligible, established, senses.

However, although this work has shown increasing sophistication, and has the great advantage, as he puts it, of not requiring costly hand-tagged training sets but instead "thrives on raw, unannotated, monolingual corpora – the more the merrier" (Yarowsky 1995: 173), it has the defect at present that it requires an extensive iterative computation for each identified bisemous word, so as to cluster its text tokens into two exclusive classes that cover almost all the identified tokens. In that sense it is still some way from a general sense-tagging procedure for full text corpora, especially one that tags with respect to some generally acceptable taxonomy of senses for a word. Paradoxically, Yarowsky was much closer to that last criterion with his (1991) work using Roget that did produce a sense-tagging for selected word pairs that had some "objectivity" predating the experiment.

Although Yarowsky compares his work favourably with that of Schütze and Pederson in terms of percentages (96.7 to 92.2) of tokens correctly tagged, it is not clear that their lack of grounding for the classes in an established lexicon is that different from Yarowsky's, since his sense distinctions in his experiments (e.g. *plant* as organic or factory) are intuitively fine but pretty *ad hoc* to the experiment in question and have no real grounding in dictionaries.

4. Conclusion

It will probably be clear to the reader by now that a crucial problem in assessing this area of work is the fluctuation of the notion of word sense in it, and that is a real problem outside the scope of this paper. For example, sense as between binary oppositions of words is probably not the same as what the Roget categories discriminate, or words in French and English in aligned Hansard sentences have in common.

Another question arises here about the future development of large-scale sense-tagging: Yarowsky contrasts his work with that of efforts like Cowie, Guthrie and Guthrie (1992) that were dictionary-based, as opposed to (unannotated) corpus-based like his own. But a difference he does not bring out is that the Cowie, Guthrie and Guthrie work, when optimized with simulated annealing, did go through substantial sentences, mini-texts if you will, and sense-tag all the words in them against *LDOCE* at about the 80% level. It is not clear that doing that is less useful than procedures like Yarowsky's that achieve higher levels of sense-tagging but only for carefully selected pairs of words, whose sense-distinctions are not clearly dictionary-based, and which would require enormous prior computations to set up *ad hoc* sense oppositions for a useful number of words.

These are still early days, and the techniques now in play have probably not yet been combined or otherwise optimized to give the best results. It may not be necessary yet to oppose, as one now standardly does in MT, large-scale, less accurate, methods, though useful, with other higher-performance methods that cannot be used for practical applications. That the field of sense-tagging is still open to further development follows if one accepts the aim of this paper which is to attack two claims, both of which are widely believed, though not at once: that sense-tagging of corpora cannot be done, and that it has been solved. As many will remember, MT lived with both these, ultimately misleading, claims for many years.

Acknowledgements

Work referred to was supported by the NSF under grant #IRI 9101232 and the ECRAN project (LE-2110) funded by the European Commission's Language Engineering Division. The paper is also indebted to comments and criticisms from Adam Kilgarriff, David Yarowsky, Karen Sparck Jones, Rebecca Bruce and members of the CRL-New Mexico and University of Sheffield NLP groups. The mistakes are all my own, as always.

References

Antal, Laszlo
    1963   *Questions of Meaning.* The Hague: Mouton.
Brown, Peter F., Stephen A. Della Pietra, Vincent J. Della Pietra and Robert L. Mercer
    1991   Word sense disambiguation using statistical methods. In: *Proceedings,*
                ACL 91, 142–146.
Bruce, Rebecca and Janyce Wiebe
    1994   Word-sense disambiguation using decomposable models. In: *Pro-*
                ceedings, ACL 94, 251–256.
Copestake, Ann and Ted Briscoe
    1991   Lexical operations in a unification-based framework. In: *Proceedings,*
                ACL Siglex Workshop, 61–68, Berkeley, CA.
Cowie, Jim, Joe Guthrie and Louise Guthrie
    1992   Lexical disambiguation using simulated annealing. In: *Proceedings,*
                COLING 92, 903–909.
Dagan, Ido and Alon Itai
    1994   Word sense disambiguation using a second language monolingual
                corpus. *Computational Linguistics* 20(4): 563–596.
Gale, William A., K. Church, Kenneth Ward and David Yarowsky
    1992   One sense per discourse. In: *Proceedings, Fourth DARPA Speech*
                and Natural Language Workshop, 61–69, Monterey, CA.
Givón, Talmy
    1967   *Transformations of Ellipsis, Sense Development and Rules of Lexical*
                Derivation. SP-2896, Systems Development Corp., Santa Monica,
                CA.
Green, Georgia M.
    1989   *Pragmatics and Natural Language Understanding.* Hillsdale, NJ:
                Erlbaum.
Ide, Nancy and Jean Véronis
    1994   Have we wasted our time? In: *Proceedings, International Workshop*
                on the Future of the Dictionary, 103–107, Grenoble.
Jorgensen, Julia C.
    1990   The psychological reality of word senses. *Journal of Psycholinguistic*
                Research 19(3): 167–190.
Kilgarriff, Adam
    1993   Dictionary word-sense distinctions: an enquiry into their nature.
                Computers and the Humanities 26(1–2): 365–387.

Miller, George
 1985   WordNet: a dictionary browser, In: *Proc. First Internat. Conf. on Information in Data*. Waterloo OED Centre, Canada.
Pustejovsky, James
 1995   *The Generative Lexicon*. Cambridge, MA: MIT Press.
Schütze, Hinrich and Jan O. Pederson
 1995   Information retrieval based on word sense. In: *Proceedings, Fourth Annual Symposium on Document Analysis and Information Retrieval*, 86–94, Las Vegas, NV.
Small, Steven I., Garrison W. Cottrell and Michael K. Tanenhaus
 1988   *Lexical Ambiguity Resolution: Perspectives from Psycholinguistics, Neuropsychology, and Artificial Intelligence*. San Mateo, CA: Morgan Kaufmann.
Stevenson, Mark and Yorick Wilks
 2001   The interaction of knowledge sources for all-word word-sense disambiguation. *Computational Linguistics* 27(3): 44–62.
Wierzbicka, Anna
 1989   *Semantics, Culture and Cognition*. Oxford: Oxford University Press.
Wilks, Yorick
 1972   *Grammar, Meaning and the Machine Analysis of Language*. London: Routledge.
 1978   Making preferences more active. *Artificial Intelligence* 11: 55–75.
Wilks, Yorick, Dan C. Fass, Cheng Ming Guo, James E. McDonald, Tony Plate and Brian M. Slator
 1990   Providing machine-tractable dictionary tools. *Journal of Machine Translation* 5: 183–199.
Wilks, Yorick, Brian M. Slator and Louise M. Guthrie
 1996   *Electric Words*. Cambridge, MA: MIT Press.
Yarowsky, David
 1992   Word-sense disambiguation using statistical models of Roget's categories, trained on very large corpora. In: *Proceedings, COLING 92*, 801–809.
 1993   One sense per collocation. In: *Proceedings, ARPA Human Language Technology Workshop*, 112–117, Princeton, NJ.
 1995   Unsupervised word-sense disambiguation rivalling supervised methods. In: *Proceedings, ACL 95*, 189–196, MIT.

Index